THE HISTORY OF ICELAND

GUNNAR KARLSSON

The History of Iceland

University of Minnesota Press
Minneapolis

Maps and diagrams by Jean-Pierre Biard

First published by C. Hurst & Co. (Publishers) Ltd, London, 2000

Published simultaneously in the United States, 2000
by the University of Minnesota Press
111 Third Avenue South, Suite 290
Minneapolis, MN 55401-2520
http://www.upress.umm.edu

Second impression 2003

Printed in Malaysia

The University of Minnesota is an equal-opportunity educator and employer.

Library of Congress Cataloging-in-Publication Data
Gunnar Karlsson.
    The history of Iceland / Gunnar Karlsson.
    p. cm.
    Includes bibliographical references.
    ISBN 0-8166-3588-9 – ISBN 0-8166-3589-7 (pbk.)
    1. Iceland–History. I. Title
  DL338 H849 2000

  949 .12–dc21   99-054536

11 10 09 08 07 06 05 04 03   10 9 8 7 6 5 4 3 2

Contents

Part III

A PRIMITIVE SOCIETY BUILDS A STATE, 1809-1918

Part IV

THE GREAT 20TH-CENTURY TRANSFORMATION

Illustrations

Maps

Figures

Tables

Foreword

Writing a substantial one-volume history of my home country for publication in English has been on my agenda ever since I taught Nordic history at the Department of Scandinavian Studies, University College London, in 1974-6. However, other tasks appeared more urgent, until in 1995 when Christopher Hurst, directed by our common friend Sigurður A. Magnússon, approached me about the subject and even managed to convince me that I would be able to write the text in English. This was more than dubious, but anyway that was how the work started and proceeded, with a great amount of help from many people, to whom I am sincerely thankful.

My wife Silja Aðalsteinsdóttir read my first draft chapter by chapter as I wrote it, corrected my worst linguistic errors and encouraged me to go on with the work. A fellow historian and dear friend Helgi Skúli Kjartansson read the whole manuscript and helped me immensely in erasing factual errors and in finding appropriate terms in English for concepts of Icelandic history. Five of my colleagues at the Institute of History, University of Iceland – Helgi Þorláksson, Loftur Guttormsson, Anna Agnarsdóttir, Guðmundur Hálfdanarson and Guðmundur Jónsson – were allocated the part of the manuscript that came closest to his or her field of study, and each of them read it carefully and suggested important improvements. Two more Icelandic historians were of great help to me: Orri Vésteinsson and Valur Ingimundarson borrowed my text at the manuscript stage to use it in a course in Icelandic history in English at the University of Iceland, and both returned it with a number of valuable remarks. Christopher Hurst and Munizha Ahmad have done their best to transform my text into proper English. Anna Yates also read a proof of the text and made valuable corrections and suggestions for improvements.

Furthermore, I have had a pleasant collaboration with Jean-Pierre Biard, who drew most of the maps and diagrams. Hörður Ágústsson allowed me to use his drawing of the suggested timber construction of a medieval farmhouse (fig. 1.7-1). Róbert Guillemette lent me his diagram of a pattern of a saga feud (fig. 1.9-1). Illustrations have also been provided by the National Museum of Iceland, the National Library and the photographer Mats Wibe Lund. A fund for promoting progress of education at the University of Iceland (Kennslumálasjóður) has helped me to cover expenses, for instance for Jean-Pierre Biard's work. Translations of Jónas

Hallgrímsson's poems are printed in Chs 2.19 and 3.2 by kind permission of the translator, Richard N. Ringler.

The manuscript was mostly written in 1996-8. Since then I have tried to incorporate new subjectmatter up to this year, in regard both to historical occurrences and historical research. However, in many cases statistical information in the book goes only to the early 1990s, and it is more than likely that some of the newest research results have escaped my attention. And from today the editing process is closed; not even the founding of a new political party, which will almost certainly take place in early May (see Ch. 4.8), will be related in this edition of the book.

Reykjavík, 11 April 2000   GUNNAR KARLSSON

Note on Icelandic Names

Most Icelanders use patronymics and not family names. It follows from this that it sounds natural to mention a person, even a complete stranger, by his or her first name alone. Thus it is not a sign of a over-familiarity when the author speaks of Jón Sigurðsson, Iceland's national leader in the 19th century, as Jón. Thus Icelanders are placed in the order of their first names in the Bibliography and Index.

The names of Viking Age and medieval Icelandic people are written in the same way as in publications of medieval Icelandic texts with a normalized orthography. Thus the name of the discoverer of America is written Leifr Eiríksson, but not in the form of modern Icelandic: Leifur Eiríksson, or in an anglicized form: Leif Erikson. The same applies to Scandinavians until the 14 th century, when their names take on modern forms, which are English rather than Scandinavian. Most Icelandic placenames, on the other hand, are still today attached to the same places as in early times and are therefore written from the beginning in the modern Icelandic form: Flugumýri, not Flugumýrr; Haukadalur, not Haukadalr; Skálholt, not Skálaholt.

Note on Orthography

Old Norse as well as modern Icelandic is written with some letters that are unfamiliar to most English readers. The letters *á, é, ó* and *æ* denoted long vowels in the medieval language, but now stand for diphtongs (see Ch. 2.3). The difference between *i* and *í, u* and *ú,* was also one of length in the old language, but now they have different values: *i* is like *i* in "pin", *í* like *ee* in "see"; *ú* is similar to English *u* in "loom" and "womb", while *u* has no close equivalents in English. In modern Icelandic *y* and *ý* have the same values as *i* and *í. Ö* sounds similar to *u* in "but". *Ð/ð* and *Þ/þ* denote a fricative: *ð* is the voiced variant, like *th* in "brother" and "weather", *and þ* the unvoiced one, like *th* in "thin".

The alphabetical order which is followed in the bibliography and index of the book is:

a/á, b, c, d, ð, e/é, f, g, h, i/í, j, k, l, m, n, o/ó, p, q, r, s, t, u/ú, v, w, x, y/ý, z, þ, æ, ö

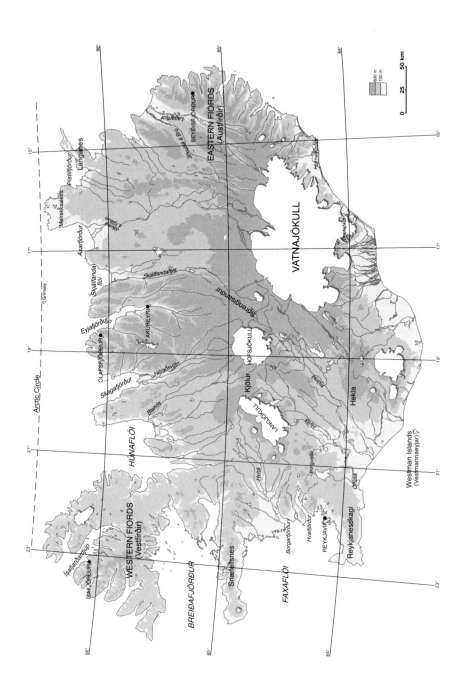

WESTERN FIORDS (Vestfirðir)

ÍSAFJÖRÐUR

Ísafjarðardjúp

HÚNAFLÓI

Langanes

Þistilfjörður

Melrakkaslétta

Axarfjörður

Grímsey

Arctic Circle

BREIÐAFJÖRÐUR

Snæfellsnes

ÓLAFSFJÖRÐUR

Eyjafjörður

AKUREYRI

Skjálfanda flói

Skjálfandafljöt

Skagafjörður

Héraðsvötn

Blanda

EASTERN FIORDS (Austfirðir)

SEYÐISFJÖRÐUR

Lagarfljöt

Jökulsá á Brú

Breiðamerkurjökull

VATNAJÖKULL

Sprengisandur

HOFSJÖKULL

Kjölur

LANGJÖKULL

Hvítá

Hvítá

Hekla

Þjórsá

Tungnaá

FAXAFLÓI

Borgarfjörður

Hvalfjörður

Þingvellir

REYKJAVÍK

Ölfusá

Reykjanesskagi

Westman Islands (Vestmannaeyjar)

600 m
100 m

0   25   50 km

Introduction

In the national anthem of Iceland, written when the millennium of settlement in the country was celebrated in 1874, the poet and clergyman Matthías Jochumsson alluded to King David's words in Psalm 90: "For a thousand years in thy sight are but as yesterday when it is past and as a watch in the night." Pastor Matthías wrote:

> *With Thee is each day as a thousand years,*
> *Each thousand of years, but a day.*
> *Eternity's flow'r, with its homage of tears,*
> *That reverently passes away.*[1]

In the poem Pastor Matthías contrasts the tearful "Iceland's thousand years" of the past with the hopefully prosperous "Iceland's thousand years" to come. In this book a historian considers Iceland's 1100 years, not in the romantic and optimistic way of a 19th-century poet at a millennium, but in the critical way of a late 20th-century scholar which is more appropriate for the anniversary of eleven centuries.

Talking about Iceland's 1100 years in 2000 would be regarded as inaccurate in Iceland, since there are good reasons to believe that the colonization of the country started some three decades before AD 900. On the other hand, an organized polity does not seem to have been established there until around three decades later. So we can say that counting 1100 years back from 2000 takes us to the middle of the settlement period, halfway between the beginning of settlement and the beginning of formal social organization in the country. It is a compromise date for the origin of Iceland.

To the historian of any other European society this discussion must seem absurd. Nowhere else would one dream of determining the origin of a society in terms of exact decades. Iceland is unique among European societies in being populated as late as the Viking Age and in being provided with copious sources about its origin, written as well as archaeological. It is also unique in existing without any central power for centuries after Christianity had brought to the country the art of writing on parchment in the Latin alphabet. Therefore Iceland produced an abundant literature

---

[1] Beck (ed.) (1930), 101. Translated by Jakobina Johnson.

about a society that had to do without a monarch or anyone with the force and authority to determine who was right and who was wrong. The Icelandic sagas are not only excellent literature but also a rare treasure of sources about a stateless society.

Strangely, the history of Iceland, as it has been interpreted since the 17th century at least, seems to form a miniature of the traditional European world history as it has been related since the Renaissance. Corresponding to the splendid antiquity of world history, we have our golden age in the society that the sagas portray. Also, corresponding to the dark Middle Ages of Europe, Iceland has its dreary period, starting with its loss of political independence in the late 13th century and proceeding with an epoch of poverty and humility, especially during the early modern age.

The marginality indicated in the subtitle of the book applies particularly to this period and is meant to refer to the concept in a double way. First, Iceland is on the very margin of Europe. It is the most westerly settlement of people of European origin from before the 16th century which has survived. Two attempts that were made by Viking Age Norsemen to colonize more westerly lands both failed – that on the continent of North America and Newfoundland as early as the 11th century, and that in Greenland some four centuries later. Secondly, it has often been maintained that Icelandic society was marginal in the sense that it verged on extinction when it was in its poorest stage. This is probably an exaggeration but, as we shall see later, there was a proposal in the late 18th century to move the whole population away from the country and leave it desolate.

Instead, Iceland had its renaissance, consisting in a successful struggle for independence in the 19th and early 20th centuries, and in industrial and technical modernization in the first half of the 20th century. For Iceland adopted nationalism quickly and thoroughly. Around the mid-19th century, the *c.* 60,000 inhabitants of Iceland, mostly poor peasants, set out to achieve practical independence from Denmark. This goal was approached gradually and finally attained in 1944, with the foundation of a republic. In the 20th century, Iceland also caught up with its neighbours in economic terms, mainly through the mechanization of fishing, which gave rise to a second battle for sovereignty, this time over its offshore fishing grounds.

It is a challenging question whether the deterioration of Iceland was due to foreign rule since the 13th century, a colder climate, or an unfortunate internal power structure – or was the early golden age maybe just the invention of 19th-century nationalists? Is it a coincidence that the history of Iceland seems to duplicate world history, though on such an extremely small scale? Or is this just the form that stories tend to take, whether fictional or historical: the romantic form of initial happiness, times of trouble and regained happiness?

In this book the traditional romantic view of the history of Iceland will certainly be given its due weight, governing the basic structure of the book.

Part I is devoted to the settlement and Commonwealth period, up till around 1262, when Iceland was an independent polity without a central power. Part II is devoted to the period from the late 13th to the early 19th century, the period of growing dominance of foreign kingdoms ruling over Iceland, first the Norwegian and later the Danish. Part III deals with a long 19th century. It starts with an event which took place in 1809, when the waves of liberal and democratic ideas shook the rock of traditional Iceland for the first time, and it ends with the establishment of a separate Icelandic state in a personal union with Denmark in 1918. In Part IV, the modernization process is traced from the beginning of the 20th century and the history of the country told until the late 1990s.

The story of Iceland has been written many times in the vernacular. The first work of that kind was the slim *Íslendingabók* (Book of the Icelanders) by Ari Þorgilsson the Learned, written in the early 12th century. The concept of this book seems to be remarkably similar to that of a modern national history, where the author records the most important milestones in the development of the country. Of course, we now look upon Ari's book as an original source rather than a scholarly work, but it nevertheless serves as an invaluable guide through our first chapters.

Since the origin of history as an academic discipline, a number of single-volume histories of Iceland have been written in Icelandic, the last, *Íslandssaga til okkar daga* (The History of Iceland until Our Days) by Björn Þorsteinsson and Bergsteinn Jónsson, being published in 1991. On the other hand, no multi-volume history has yet been published from the beginning to its intended end. A number of ambitious projects have been started, but all of them have either failed or are still in progress.

In the early 1940s a planned ten-volume history of the country, *Saga Íslendinga* (History of the Icelanders), was launched by the Cultural Council of Iceland (Menntamálaráð). Only seven volumes came out, in 1942-58, covering a period which was supposed to have been covered by five and a half volumes. Volumes IV-VII deal with the period from the early 16th century until around 1830. Volume VIII:1 covers some aspects of the period from 1830 to 1874, and Volumes IX:1 and IX:2 cover 1874-1904. No volumes appeared about the Viking Age or the Middle Ages, or about the 20th century. The first lacuna was mostly filled by Jón Jóhannesson's *Íslendinga saga* (History of the Icelanders) in two volumes (1956-8). The first deals with the settlement and Commonwealth period and is a very important book. The second was published posthumously, partly from the manuscripts of university lectures, and covers the late Middle Ages in a rather unsatisfactory way. A new major plan was *Saga Íslands* (History of Iceland), launched in 1974, but only the first five volumes of this work, which carry the story up to the early 16th century, have so far been published. Thus it can be said that these three works together cover Iceland's history until 1904, but the older parts of them are now dated.

A more recent but less comprehensive work that goes through the whole history is *Íslenskur söguatlas* (Atlas of Icelandic History) in three volumes (1989-93), with a substantial written text. Einar Laxness has written a lexicon of the history of Iceland, called *Íslandssaga,* also in three volumes – a–h, i–r, s–ö (1995). Mention should also be made of three textbooks for upper secondary school level, which together form a short survey of Iceland's history.[2] Considerable use is made of these books here because I wrote them myself, alone or in collaboration with others, and put into them what I see as most important in Iceland's 1100 years.

All these general works have been consulted frequently in this book, normally without citation. Only occasionally, when I suspect that a reader may wonder about the authority of a definite statement, do I include a reference to them. Works in English, which could serve as further reading, are frequently referred to in the footnotes. I have referred to texts in English on the subjects treated in the book whenever I know of them. Two very useful introductions to Icelandic history and contemporary society are Guðmundur Hálfdanarson's *Historical Dictionary of Iceland* (1997) and *Iceland: The Republic,* a handbook published by the Central Bank of Iceland (1996).[3]

Within the last two decades, a number of books in English have presented relatively static descriptions of the old Icelandic society. Most of them are listed in my footnotes and Bibliography, and at least one, *Medieval Iceland* by Jesse L. Byock (1988), has influenced my views more than the number of references to it would suggest.

On the other hand, most general surveys of Icelandic history in English are unfortunately either old and dated or written for tourists in a way that will inevitably seem superficial to anyone who has ploughed through my book. As an exception I must mention *A History of the Old Icelandic Commonwealth* (1974), an English translation of the first volume of Jón Jóhannesson's *Íslendinga saga.* Although the original is more than four decades old, this work still contains much useful information, besides many references to original sources.

Being able to read foreign languages other than English does not help much for further reading, although it should be mentioned that a history of Iceland by Björn Þorsteinsson and Bergsteinn Jónsson is available in Danish, with the title *Island* (1985), largely with the same text as their above-mentioned book in Icelandic.

Our knowledge of Icelandic history is mostly conserved in monographs and articles in Icelandic. Here this fact is indicated frequently by references

---

[2] Gunnar Karlsson *et al.* (1989); Gunnar Karlsson (1990); Bragi Guðmundsson and Gunnar Karlsson (1988).

[3] A thorough bibliography of works on Iceland in English is provided by McBride (1996).

to the most basic works on the subject of each chapter and to interpretations and opinions which are clearly attributable to definite authors. English-speaking readers who are not able to make use of texts in Icelandic may be uninterested in all this information, but they will sometimes be compensated by a summary in English at the end of these works. However, the history of Iceland is for the most part a secret kept for those who can read the language which has developed in the country through eleven centuries.

PART I

Colonization and Commonwealth

c. 870-1262

1.1 Colonization

For centuries after humans had colonized almost all dry and habitable parts of the globe, a large island in the North Atlantic, not far from the western coast of Greenland, remained uninhabited. Its area was some 103,000 km.^{2} (40,000 sq. m.), larger than Scotland by a quarter and almost the size of Cuba. Most of it was a high plateau with negligible vegetation and huge glaciers on the highest mountains. But along the coastline, in valleys stretching from the bottom of the fiords, and in large lowland plains, particularly in the central south, the soil was covered with low, close-growing and succulent grass, which in many places was sheltered by birchwood. Birds were numerous, on cliffs along the coast and on moor-lands, heaths and shrubbery inland. No mammals lived there, except foxes, which must have come drifting on ice floes from Greenland, seals resting on sandy beaches and whales tumbling about in the sea.

This country was sheltered from humans by the Atlantic Ocean on one side and the glacier of Greenland on the other. The odd traveller may have landed there, among them perhaps the Greek explorer Pytheas of Marseille, who sailed north on the Atlantic Ocean around 400 BC. He told of how he had discovered the country Thule six days' sailing north of Britain, but learned authors in the Mediterranean area disbelieved him and ridiculed him for centuries because he had maintained that the sun could be seen throughout the night around the summer solstice in this country.

In the 8th century AD Irish monks, who used to drift along on the ocean in search of solitary islands, came upon a country which seemed to fit Pytheas' description. This is first mentioned by the English historian Bede around 730, although the Thule that he describes could equally be the western coast of Norway. On the other hand the Irish author Dicuil, writing around 825, can hardly be referring to any other country than Iceland when he says that some priests had told him, thirty years previously, that they had come to the uninhabited Thule, where it was so bright at midnight in the summer that "a man could do whatever he wished as though the sun were there, even remove lice from his shirt".[1]

---

[1] Dicuil (1967), 75 (VII.11). A more sceptical attitude towards Dicuil's account, too sceptical in my view, is expressed by Helgi Guðmundsson (1997), 92-8.

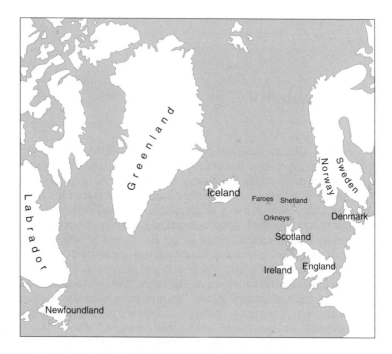

Map 1.1-1 Iceland's situation in the North Atlantic, sheltered on one side by the Atlantic and on the other by the Greenland ice-cap.

Icelandic sources confirm that Irish monks came to Iceland before the Norse settlers. Ari Þorgilsson the Learned, our first historian, mentioned in the Introduction, says in his *Book of the Icelanders* that they went away because they did not wish to live with heathens.

Just about the time when Dicuil was learning of Thule from the Irish priests, an enormous change was taking place among the pagan inhabitants of Scandinavia. They began to build ocean-going vessels and communicate with the external world: the British Isles, France, Russia. In 793 Norsemen made the first documented Viking raid, on the monastery on the island of Lindisfarne, off the Northumbrian coast of eastern England. This event traditionally marks the beginning of the Viking Age, which stresses the aggressive aspect of the expeditions, though, they could just as well have been relatively peaceful process of trade and colonization. Yet these activities were bound to combine in various ways, and colonization could not be carried out in a peaceful way until the Vikings had discovered uninhabited lands.

Technically the Viking ship was a big step forward, but it was only a primitive beginning of what Europe was to produce in the ensuing centuries.

It had only one sail and could not tack directly against the wind. The Vikings had no compass to sail by and, in cloudy weather, which is fairly common in the North Atlantic, they had little way of knowing in which direction they were sailing. After regular journeys started between Norway and the British Isles, it could not be long before someone chanced upon the Faroe Islands, which indeed were colonized by people from Norway during the first half of the 9th century. And after people began to sail from Norway to the Faroe Islands, someone had to miss the Islands and encounter the large country in the west. According to one version of the *Book of Settlements (Landnámabók)*, an Icelandic chronicle of the colonization, the country was actually discovered in this way by a Norwegian Viking named Naddoddr. According to another version of the same book, the country was first discovered by a Swede named Garðarr Svavarsson who lost his way in a storm when he intended to sail to the Hebrides to claim his wife's inheritance. Both versions agree, however, that the name Iceland (Ísland in the vernacular) was given to the country by Flóki, a disappointed Norwegian who had made the first attempt to inhabit the country but lost all his livestock during a hard winter. Both versions also agree on the essential point that the discovery of Iceland by Norsemen was a consequence of the insatiable lust for travel among the Scandinavians during the Viking Age.

I have already mentioned the two principal written sources for the settlement. The *Book of the Icelanders (Íslendingabók)* is a short chronicle of Iceland's early history, of only some twenty printed pages, written by the priest Ari Þorgilsson the Learned in the period 1122-33. Ari has enjoyed an almost unanimous reputation as an authority on Iceland's early history throughout the period from the Middle Ages to the 20th century. He has aroused some scepticism owing to the vogue of strict source criticism in the 20th century, but no one can deny his keen sense of chronology and almost scientific preoccupation with what we call natural as opposed to supernatural events. The *Book of Settlements* is basically a report of the settlement and first settlers practically all over the habitable parts of the country. Its preserved versions, composed in the late 13th century and later, amount to between 100 and 200 printed pages each, but the material has accumulated gradually. References to lost versions and their authors clearly indicate that the collecting and writing of the material started in the days of Ari, and there are some indications that point to him as at least a participant in that work.

Ari leaves out all stories of the first discoveries of Iceland and starts his *Book of the Icelanders* thus:

Iceland was first settled from Norway in the days of Harald Fairhair, son of Halfdan the Black, at the time ... when Ivar Ragnar Lodbrok's son had the English king Saint Edmund put to death; and that was 870 years after the birth of Christ, according to what is written in his, Edmund's, saga.

A Norwegian named Ingolf is the man of whom it is reliably reported that he was the first to leave there for Iceland, when Harald Fairhair was sixteen years old, and a second time a few years later. He settled south in Reykjavik.[2]

Later Ari completes and supports his chronology of the settlement period by stating that the whole country became colonized in sixty years, and that the settlement period ended sixty years after the killing of King Edmund, one or two years before the death of King Haraldr Fairhair of

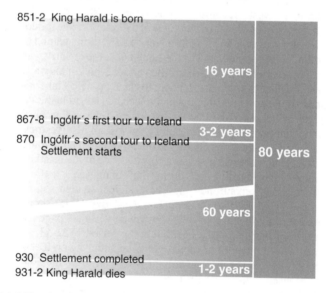

Fig. 1.1-1 The chronology of the settlement period according to Ari the Learned in his *Book of the Icelanders.*

Norway, whom Ari has already said reached the age of eighty. The conclusion is clear and precise, as illustrated in a graphic form in Fig. 1.1-1.

The *Book of Settlements* has a long story to tell about Ingólfr Arnarson and his act of settlement. His wife was Hallveig Fróðadóttir, the sister of a settler in Iceland, but the story does not say whether she accompanied Ingólfr to Iceland or was married to him there. What is most astonishing in Ingólfr's story is that his gods directed him to build his farm at Reykjavík, a place which was to become Iceland's capital but was nothing more than an ordinary farm when the story was written down and for almost half a millennium after that. This source also claims to know that Ingólfr came to Iceland in 874 to stay there permanently, which gave the Icelanders occasion to celebrate the 1000 years' anniversary of their settlement in 1874

[2] Jones (1986), 143-4 (Ch. 1).

and receive a written constitution from their king on that occasion, as we shall see later (Chapter 3.6). Historians no longer believe that the author of the *Book of Settlements* could know the date better than Ari – which however did not prevent the Icelanders from celebrating the 1100 years' anniversary in 1974. Anyway, a much more important question has vexed scholars in recent decades: is Ari's chronology anything more than pure guesswork?

In 1956 the Australian-English prehistorian Gordon Childe visited Iceland. On a trip in the open country, the car stopped on the edge of a high hill with a view over the southern lowland, which stretches out, flat and grassy, for scores of miles in each direction. It is said that Childe stepped out of the car and shouted: "I don't believe it!" Asked what it was that he did not believe, he said he refused to believe that mankind had not colonized such a land centuries before the Viking Age. Being told that the archaeological evidence supported that of the chronicles, he said: "Dig deeper."

There has been no lack of attempts by archaeologists to dig for something that could overturn the evidence of the written sources. Their most important result is based on an auxiliary science called 'tephrochronology', developed by the Icelandic geologist Sigurður Þórarinsson in the 1940s.[3] As Iceland has always had strong volcanic activity, a number of tephra layers can be found in the soil, and we can be sure that anything beneath a definite layer is older than the eruption which produced it and anything above it is younger. It has been discovered that the remnants of human habitation in many places start just above a double layer of two different colours which covers most of the country. In many cases, the layer can be found in the turf of which the oldest houses are built, suggesting that the turf was cut a few decades after the eruption. Pollen analyses also reveal a sudden change in vegetation, decrease of birch, increase of grass and beginning of grain, close to the layer and sometimes, it seems, just beneath it.[4] For these reasons this double tephra layer has been referred to as the settlement layer (*landnámslag*).

This means that all depends on the age of the settlement layer. ^{14}C-datings have been tried with deviating results, from the 7th to the 9th century, which has aroused much disagreement among scholars. But now the riddle seems to have been solved with assistance from the Greenland ice-cap. Scientists have drilled down into the glacier and determined its age at each point by counting the annual waves of snowfall like annual rings in a tree. Recently glass shards which characterize the settlement layer have been identified in ice which is supposed to have fallen as snow within a couple of years of AD 871.[5] This result may make it unlikely that Ari's

[3] Sigurður Þórarinsson (1944), 3-6.
[4] Þorleifur Einarsson (1960-3), 449-63; Margrét Hallsdóttir (1987), 33-4.
[5] Karl Grönvold *et al.* (1995), 149-53.

chronology is exactly right. If humans began to influence the vegetation at more than one place before 873, at the latest, Ari seems to have put the start of the settlement period a few years too late. That, however, is only a negative result about Ari's detailed chronology, not about Iceland's history. For all relevant historical purposes Ari proves to be right.

This conclusion must give us increased confidence in the chronicles of Iceland's colonization, although of course they are not to be taken as reliable documents. The *Book of Settlements* tells the story of over 400 original settlers, persons who came with their followers and established farms at definite, named places, most of which are still known by the same names.[6] Most of these settlers were men, but the group also includes a few women, the best known of whom is Auðr or Unnr the Deep-Minded, who is reported to have fled to Iceland from Scotland, where her son had ruled as a Viking king and been killed by the Scots. Most of the settlers came from the western coast of Norway, either directly or, like Auðr, via Viking settlements in the British Isles. A few settlers are said to have been of Irish or other Celtic origin, and a considerable number of Celts may have accompanied the settlers as slaves, servants and perhaps wives. However, the Icelandic language shows clearly that the culture was predominantly of Norse origin. For centuries, the language used in Iceland was not distinguishable from other West Norwegian dialects. Objects found in Icelandic graves are predominantly characteristic of the Norse Viking Age.[7] The oldest houses are typical Viking Age turf houses, often 15-20 metre-long halls, with no significant houses adjacent to them.

The typical Viking ship, the so-called longship, was, at least later on, not considered able to cross the ocean to Iceland. For that purpose another kind of ship was used, the *knörr*, which was deeper and took a greater load. Indications are that a *knörr* could be 16-25 m. (50-80 ft) long and carry up to 50 tons. That capacity had to suffice not only to carry people with provisions and water for some weeks of drifting on the ocean, but it also had to carry livestock: cattle, horses, sheep, goats, pigs, dogs and cats, even geese, all of both sexes, as in Noah's ark. Some implements were indispensable, at least for cutting turf for houses and mowing grass. Weapons would hardly have been forgotten, at least an axe, which could be used on either men or wood, must have been contained in the luggage. Some settlers took fishing-nets or line and tackle and grain to sow the following spring. Fire was kept in a tub. Probably minimal timber for housing was considered necessary, as it soon became known that the country had no proper forests, and one could not rely on landing on a beach covered with driftwood, which many beaches were.

---

[6] A systematic survey of the settlement, perhaps based on somewhat excessive reliance on the *Book of Settlements*, is provided by Haraldur Matthíasson (1982).
[7] See Kristján Eldjárn (1956).

Once on dry land houses had to be built for people and livestock before winter. Some hay had to be made, at least for the cows if they were to yield milk in the winter. But where did the people get food to live on through the first winter? We would hardly believe this to have been possible if we did not know for sure that Iceland became inhabited by people.

According to the *Book of Settlements*, some of the original settlers laid hold of large areas of land. In the north Helgi the Lean claimed for himself the whole of Eyjafjörður, which was later to form one of the twenty districts into which Iceland was divided (see Map 2.12-1). Helgi gave parts of this land to his followers and relatives, so that 20-30 settlers built their farms within its limits in the colonization period. There was plenty of space for them, because in the 18th century there were some 450 farms in the area.

The population that colonized Iceland must have amounted to thousands; if we assume that it was around 50,000 in 1100 (see Ch. 1.7), mostly descended from the pioneers of the settlement period, it is unlikely that such a number could have grown from less than 10,000 in the early 10th century.

What made people embark on such an undertaking? In the *Book of Settlements* the most common cause of the emigration of individual settlers is the aggression of the king of Norway, Haraldr Fairhair. According to the tradition, preserved in several sagas, he inherited a kingdom in eastern Norway but decided to unify the whole country under his rule – the idea of doing so is attributed to a young woman whom the king desired as a concubine. Haraldr succeeded in conquering what was then called the whole of Norway, thereby creating the Norwegian kingdom, and many of the minor rulers fled the country, some to Iceland. Others fled to the British Isles, but there too political upheaval raged. Norse Vikings had conquered Dublin and the surrounding area, but the Irish managed to seize the town shortly after the year 900, which may have led to a considerable flight to Iceland.

But the emigration to Iceland must be seen as, above all, a part of the remarkable expansion among Nordic people during the Viking Age, which I shall not attempt to explain here. Nor did the expansion stop in Iceland; it went on to Greenland and North America. We shall come to that later (Ch. 1.4), but first let us look at three characteristics of the early Icelanders: their religion, poetry and political system.

1.2 Paganism and Poetry

"According to well-informed people", says the *Book of Settlements*, "some of the settlers of Iceland were baptized, mostly those who came from the British Isles. [. . .] Some of them kept up their faith till they died, but in most families this didn't last, for the sons of some built temples and made sacrifices, and Iceland was completely pagan for about 120 years."[1]

It is not easy to say with any certainty what this paganism consisted of.[2] Unlike the Greeks and Romans, the Germanic peoples of Europe did not become literate, apart from the minor use of runic inscriptions on stones and sticks, until they had adopted Christianity. Practically all written descriptions of pre-Christian religion among Germanic people are written by Christians and may therefore be either coloured by blind antagonism or influenced by Christian rituals.

In Iceland, no runic inscriptions from pagan times have been discovered. On the other hand, the Christian Iceland of the high Middle Ages preserved for posterity more information about the pagan world of Germanic Europe than any other country. By far the most important of these sources are two works which – because of a misconception – both have the name Edda. One of these, *Sæmundar-Edda* (the *Poetic Edda*, often referred to as the "Elder Edda"), is a collection of poems, partly about human heroes, some of whom are historical characters from the times of the great migrations in Europe, and partly about heathen deities. Among these is the "Prophecy of the Seeress" (*Völuspá*), a lay that tells a world history from the creation, through a golden age and then moral degeneration, towards the end of the world and a resurrection. Another one, "The Sayings of Hár" (*Hávamál*), is a collection of moral wisdom and good advice. A few lays are purely didactic and in a dialogue form typical of that kind of text. Others are epics telling of episodes among the gods.[3] There are strong indications that some of these poems were intended for some kind of dramatic performance.[4]

Strictly, it cannot be asserted that the Eddic poetry was composed before the 13th century, when the oldest manuscripts containing it were

---

[1] *Book of Settlements* (1972), 147 (Ch. 399).
[2] The principal work on paganism in Iceland is Ólafur Briem (1985).
[3] *Poetic Edda* (1986).
[4] Gunnell (1995), 182-329.

written. It is likely, though, that most or all of it was composed by heathen people. The language is West Nordic, which shows that the poems attained their present form in Norway or countries colonized from there, and all are preserved in Icelandic manuscripts.

The other *Edda* is *Snorra-Edda* (Prose Edda), a textbook of poetics written by the 13th-century Icelandic author Snorri Sturluson. The poetry that most interested Snorri was not of the Eddic kind, but so-called skaldic poetry, which first and foremost consisted of eulogies about kings or other notables. Its form was extremely complex, with regular alliteration and internal rhyme. The following translation of a stanza by the Icelandic poet Sighvatr Þórðarson gives a rough idea of the metre, although it does not follow its rules completely. The poet is describing the beginning of a battle between King Óláfr Haraldsson and Earl Sweyn:

> *Olaf in spring from eastward*
> *Out of the gulf sailed stoutly;*
> *Sweyn from the north came sweeping,*
> *Swift black oars were lifting.*
> *My tongue can tell their story,*
> *Treat their bloody meeting;*
> *Answer, too, for Olaf;*
> *I was there beside him.*[5]

To make this poetry still more difficult, poetic language based on heathen mythology was used extensively. Thus gold was not referred to simply as gold but as "Freyja's tears" because, according to the legend, the goddess Freyja wept golden tears.

It seems to have become almost a prerogative of Icelanders to compose poems of this kind about the kings of Norway and receive precious gifts as recompense. However, the art degenerated and Snorri probably wished to revive it by writing down the heathen myths that he knew. This he did in his elegant and humorous style and thus made his textbook a literary masterpiece.

Snorri portrays an extended family of deities called Æsir (sing. Áss), which has partly absorbed the smaller family of Vanir (sing. Vanr), also sometimes referred to as Æsir. In all, he enumerates twelve male gods and twelve goddesses. At least some, perhaps all, of them are of common Germanic ancestry. Around the year AD 100, when the Roman author Tacitus described the manners of the Germans, they worshipped the goddess Nerthus, whose name is obviously identical with that of the male Vanr god Njörðr, whom Snorri knew well eleven centuries later. The German priest Adam of Bremen described the temple of Uppsala in Sweden in the late 11th century where, he said, Thor, Odin and Freyr were worshipped – the

---

[5] Kirkconnell (1930), 73.

three gods who occur most often in Icelandic sources. According to Snorri, "Odin is highest and most ancient of the Æsir. He rules all things, and mighty though the other gods are, yet they all submit to him like children to their father."[6] But Óðinn is rarely mentioned in Icelandic sagas, and the only known Óðinn worshippers in Iceland are a few poets, of whom the warrior Egill Skallagrímsson is best known.

Þórr, the powerful defender of the divine world against giants, seems to have been more popular among the Icelanders. There are over forty personal names composed with *Þór-*, carried by almost 1,000 persons, in the *Book of Settlements* alone. Three names carried by four persons are composed with *Frey-*, and none with the names of other gods. A score or more place names seem to refer to Þórr and only some seven to all other Æsir. This is worth noting, although one must no doubt be particularly careful not to misinterpret the etymology of place names.

Further evidence for the popularity of Þórr is provided by the sagas. The battle between paganism and Christianity is described as a battle between Þórr and Christ: "Have you heard . . . that Thor challenged Christ to a duel and that Christ didn't dare to fight with him?" the poetess Steinunn in *Njal's Saga* asks the Christian missionary Þangbrandr.[7]

In mythological tales Þórr frequently appears in rather comic roles, which may indicate his and his earthly followers' lower social status than Óðinn's. The same is hinted at in the didactic poem "The Lay of Hárbarth", when Óðinn, disguised as a ferryman, says to Þórr:

> *Gets Óthin all earls*
> *slain by edge of swords,*
> *but Thór, the breed of thralls.*[8]

Perhaps Óðinn was primarily the god of aristocrats and their hangers-on, the poets, while the hard-working peasantry relied more on the physically strong and not too smart Þórr. If so, Freyr probably appealed to people of a similar kind to those worshipping Þórr. Snorri refers to Freyr as the "ruler of rain and sunshine and thus of the produce of the earth", stating that "it is good to pray to him for prosperity and peace".[9] In the sagas, three men are called *Freysgoði*, "Freyr's Priest", which indicates that traditions of the worship of Freyr were known by Christian Icelanders of the 13th century.

The worship of goddesses has left little evidence in the sources. In Snorri's mythology, Freyja, the goddess of love, plays the largest role, and she is the only goddess who is mentioned in sagas: in the time of Christianization, one Christian convert was outlawed for declaring that he valued

---

[6] Snorri Sturluson (1987), 21.
[7] *Complete Sagas of Icelanders* III (1997), 125 (Ch. 102).
[8] *Poetic Edda* (1986), 78.
[9] Snorri Sturluson (1987), 24.

Freyja no more than a bitch. Snorri attempts to give each of the twelve goddesses he mentions some role and characteristics, but these mostly mirror the limited position of women in society. No fewer than four goddesses are mainly occupied with love, according to Snorri – has this something to do with the interests of the male author?

Whatever we make of Snorri's mythology, it is obviously not exhaustive about religious ideas among pagan Icelanders. The sagas frequently reveal traditions of animistic belief in trees, rocks, hills, mountains and waterfalls. The *Book of Settlements,* for instance, tells the story of Þorsteinn Red-Nose, who used to make sacrifices to a waterfall and had thousands of sheep because he could see in the autumn which of the sheep were doomed to die and had them slaughtered. Then, one autumn, he said: "Now you can slaughter any of the sheep you like. Either I'm doomed to die or the sheep are doomed, or all of us are." The following night he died and a gale swept all the sheep into the waterfall.[10]

However, this is not the most common picture that the sagas give of pagan religion. Usually it is described as highly organized and, in the opinion of some scholars, suspiciously reminiscent of the Christian Church. A congregation is said to have paid tolls to a temple, which was called *hof.* In the temple a person with special status, a *hofgoði,* performed rituals which consisted of sprinkling the blood of animals.[11] In Iceland a number of farms have the name Hof or Hofstaðir, and in many of them people are able to point out the ruins of pagan temples. In most cases archaeological excavations show that the ruins are something else. Others are disputed, and it has also been suggested, and supported by evidence from sagas, that the *hof* was not intended for rituals only, but it was also a large dwelling where the neighbourhood came together for religious feasts.[12]

This is a riddle that will probably never be solved. What we do know and will discuss thoroughly in the next chapter, is that persons called *goðar* (sing. *goði*) played a central role in the governing system of Iceland also in Christian times. The word is obviously related to *guð/goð,* which means "god", and seems to indicate that their office originated in a religious role. Some scholars would object that there is no proof of any such role for the *goðar* in Iceland, whatever the origin of their occupational name. But in my opinion, the simplest, and therefore preferable, interpretation of the sources is to assume that the governing system of Iceland grew up around persons who simultaneously had religious and secular tasks and were referred to as *goðar.*

[10] *Book of Settlements* (1972), 134 (Ch. 355).
[11] See the *Complete Sagas of Icelanders* V (1997), 133-4 (The Saga of the People of Eyri, Ch. 4).
[12] Arnheiður Sigurðardóttir (1966), 24-6.

1.3 Constitution

Wherever Norsemen settled they established a regular assembly, which was commonly called *al-þing* (Althing), the assembly of all free males, perhaps of some minimal social status. In Iceland, according to Ari's *Book of the Icelanders*, this happened near the end of the settlement period, and, when the thousand-year anniversary approached, it was decided to make 930 the founding year of the Icelandic Althing and celebrate in 1930.[1] Ari also relates:

> And when Iceland had become settled far and wide, a Norwegian named Ulfljot first brought law out here from Norway . . . this was called Ulfljot's Law. [. . .] For the most part these laws were modelled upon the then Gulathing Law [in Western Norway] . . . Ulfljot lived east in Lon. It is said that Grim Geitskor was his foster-brother, he who at Ulfljot's direction explored the whole of Iceland before the Althing was established.

Then the story proceeds: "The Althing was established where it now is at the instance of Ulfljot and all the people of Iceland."[2] With Úlfljótr, Ari provided the Icelanders with the author of the law, who is a common figure in origin myths,[3] which of course does not preclude Úlfljótr's historical existence. Someone must have instigated the formation of the unified law district which Iceland was from before the time of contemporary sources, with an annual assembly, which met at a place called Þingvellir in the southwestern part of the country, for two weeks around the summer solstice.

National histories are usually crowded with dubious world records; one of them is the establishment of the Icelandic Althing. It has often been suggested that this was a unique event and a great novelty, because nowhere else had an assembly been established for whole nations, but only for parts of them. No other Nordic nation, it is said, had one law or one assembly in the high Middle Ages.[4] The dubious aspect of this argument is that we do not have sufficiently good reason to call the population of

---

[1] The best survey of the development and formal aspects of the Icelandic constitution, either in Icelandic or English, is in Jón Jóhannesson (1956), 53-113, and (1974), 35-93.

[2] Jones (1986), 144-5 (Ch. 2-3).

[3] Sigurður Líndal (1969), 21-4.

[4] See, for example, Jón Jóhannesson (1974), 36-7.

Iceland a nation as early as 930. Therefore, the Althing was hardly founded by or for a nation; it is more likely that it served the unintended purpose of creating an ethnic community with a strong resemblance to a nation (cf. Ch. 1.10).

It is nevertheless true that Iceland was, by Nordic standards of the time, a large law district. It cannot have been a simple task to persuade the whole population to attend one and the same assembly, where only a limited number of chieftains could acquire a leading role. Nor was it a straightforward thing for settlers from different law districts in Norway, mixed with people from various parts of the British Isles, to accept one set of laws. To explain how this could be done it has been suggested that one family, the descendants of a Norwegian chieftain called Björn Buna, played a leading role in the process.[5] The *Book of Settlements* states: "Almost all the prominent Icelanders are descended from Bjorn Buna,"[6] – no great wonder if it was Björn's descendants who decided to become the prominent Icelanders.

There is no reason to assume that the constitution of Iceland was in the beginning very different from any other Norse – or Germanic – governing system in the centuries preceding the Viking Age. But, in all other countries which were to leave behind a considerable amount of written sources, Christianization, accompanied by literacy, and the consolidation of royal power went hand in hand. Therefore in most countries, we are left with few and unreliable sources about their political systems before the advent of royal power. Iceland alone housed for centuries a Christian, literate society which had no prince of any kind and no unified executive power. Iceland thus offers a rare example of a society that tried to preserve law and order without a ruler, whether it was a remnant of a world that was lost elsewhere or a new development.

The political system of Iceland is of course at work in all of saga literature. However, its exact constitution and development is rather obscure in most of the sagas; they were written for people who knew the system. Therefore the history of the Icelandic government system has mainly been based on two sources. One is the frequently-mentioned *Book of the Icelanders* by Ari the Learned. The other is the written law code of the Icelandic Commonwealth, called (for unknown reasons) Greylag (*Grágás*). According to Ari, the codification of the law began in the winter of 1117-18, a few years before he wrote his book, and at the same time a radical revision of the law took place.[7] Greylag is now preserved in two manuscripts, which are both more than a century younger than the first codification. Their texts are only partly identical and may both have

---

[5] Sigurður Nordal (1990), 66-73.

[6] *Book of Settlements* (1972), 22 (Ch. 10).

[7] Jones (1986), 154 (Ch. 10).

changed considerably after the first codification. The result is that the extant text of the law bears only slight marks of its oral ancestry and is in many ways radically different from its assumed relative, the Gulathing law. Greylag is much longer than any other Nordic medieval law; the whole text, a compilation of both versions, has been printed on 480 pages.[8] Alliteration and other mnemonic techniques are only found in a few formulas. However, in spite of this obvious revision of the law, there is no doubt that considerable parts of it – for instance, the extensive regulations on slavery – were obsolete when the extant manuscripts were written.

Both in Norway and in Iceland, the law council (*lögrétta*, which means literally "law rectifier") formed the central institution of each assembly. In Norway, the law councils seem to have served both as a courts of justice and as legislative bodies, as long and as far as the latter role was not considered to be the prerogative of the king. In the beginning, this may have been similar in Iceland. We have little evidence about the constitution until the 960s, when a major amendment was made to it, according to Ari:

The land was then divided into Quarters, so that there were three Things [district assemblies] in each Quarter . . . save that in the Northerners' Quarter there were four, because they could not reach any other agreement . . . Still, the nomination of judges and the constitution of the Logretta [law council] should be the same from this Quarter as from any other.[9]

Here we have a system with a central Althing and thirteen district assemblies. Although Ari does not say so, it is generally assumed that the Quarter Courts at the Althing were established when the country was divided into Quarters, whereby a distinction was made between the legislative power of the Law Council and the judicial power of the Quarter Courts. Anyway, it cannot have happened much later because sometime between 1004 and 1030 the Fifth Court (*Fimmtardómr*) was established at the Althing.

As might be expected, it seems in the main to be this stage of the constitution which is described in the law code Greylag.[10] It sets out rules of an Althing which consisted of four Quarter Courts, each dealing with cases from one Quarter of the country; the Fifth Court, which handled cases that had been left undecided at the Quarter Courts; and the Law Council, which made new law (*nýmæli*), decided what was law and gave exemptions from laws. In addition, the Law Rock (*Lögberg*) formed a central institution within the Althing. Each assembly started with a procession to this place and it was there that public announcements were made. The president of

[8] *Grágás* (1992).

[9] Jones (1986), 147 (Ch. 5).

[10] *Laws of Early Iceland* I (1980), 53-138, 187-93, 205-8.

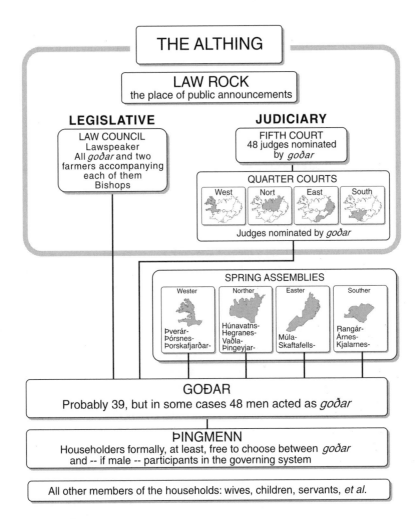

Fig. 1.3-1 Constitutional structure of the Icelandic Commonwealth after *c.* 1030. In the Eastern Quarter, only two assemblies can be identified with any certainty (see Map 1.3-1).

the Althing was the lawspeaker (*lögsögumaðr*), who was elected by the Law Council for a period of three years. Among his roles was that of reciting the law at the Law Rock or in the Law Council, the assembly procedures and one third of the entire law each year. Thus the laws seem to have been kept in memory before they were written down.

The local chieftains (*goðar*), mentioned in the last chapter as – presumably – leaders of religious rites in pagan times played a central role in this system. They nominated the men who sat in the courts, both at the Althing and in the district assemblies, and they themselves sat in the Law Council, each with two advisers from their retinue. Thus, in modern terminology, they had a direct hold on legislative power and an indirect hold on the judicial power. The exact number of *goðar* in the country is disputed, and the problem cannot be explained thoroughly without going into rather complicated detail. Here only a sample of the evidence will be presented: Ari states that the number of district assemblies became thirteen when the country was divided into Quarters in the 960s. According to Greylag, three *goðar* were to hold a district assembly together, which means that there were thirty-nine *goðar* in all. This number is confirmed by Greylag's regulations of the Law Council, where thirty-nine *goðar*, twelve from the Northern Quarter and nine from each other Quarter, should sit on the middle bench, accompanied by three men from each of the three less represented Quarters, thus making the legislators of the Law Council forty-eight in all. Together with their advisers, one on the bench in front of each *goði* and one behind him, the lawspeaker and, in Christian times, the two bishops of the country, the Law Council consisted of an assembly of 147 men.

The constitution was in many ways characterized by the absence of a centralized executive power. Thus, there were no official prosecutors and no official executioners. A wronged party was supposed to pursue the case and enforce the penalty himself. Penalties normally consisted of compensation (*bætr*) or outlawry, either full (*skóggangr*) or limited to three years (*fjörbaugsgarðr*). In all cases, it was left to the individual, with some support from his *goði*, to claim the compensation or try to kill the outlaw. Those who did not have the power to do this had to ask for the support of some more powerful person, and, according to the sagas, this sometimes had the consequence of benefiting the powerful person alone. Thus a farmer who was wrongfully deprived of a piece of woodland by an aggressive neighbour might have little choice but to hand the ownership of the land over to his *goði*, hoping to get some reward if the chieftain managed to reclaim it.[11] Judging by the sagas, most cases were not settled by formal courts but by arbitration, and it is the nature of arbitration to try and obtain peace rather than secure justice. As a weak party has more to gain

[11] Byock (1988), 168-73.

Map 1.3-1 Administrative division in the Commonwealth period. The *þing* districts were not demarcated by law; any *goði* was entitled to have a *þingmaðr*, a person belonging to his *goðorð* (chieftaincy), living anywhere within the Quarter. However, in most cases, the *þing* districts probably assumed fairly definite boundaries, which are echoed in the division into *sýslur* (districts) later (see Ch. 2.1 and Map 2.12-1). There is some doubt about the organization of *þing*s in the Eastern Quarter (see Fig. 1.3-1 and Ch. 1.12); the solution presented here is only one among the more probable ones.

from peace than a strong one, the arbitrations must have tended to favour the latter.[12]

Furthermore, the absence of central power made most common people heavily dependent on their chieftains for protection. However, the dependency worked both ways. The chieftains had no police force or standing army to carry out their protection, except the group of common people they were supposed to protect. In a way, therefore, the *goðar* were no more than heads and unifiers in the self-protection of the local community. This reciprocity is mirrored in the law, where it is stipulated that a farmer can leave the chieftaincy (*goðorð*) of his *goði*, with his household, and enter another one, and in the same way a chieftain is free to repudiate any of his

---

[12] Gunnar Karlsson (1977b), 362-5.

followers (*þingmenn*). Thus a chieftaincy was not a geographically defined unit but consisted of a group of households. The followers of two or more chieftains could live intermixed with each other.

This apparently free choice of chieftains by farmers has led some scholars to equate the Icelandic Commonwealth with a modern democracy. It is true that the chieftaincies were normally acquired by inheritance and could also be bought or received as a gift. However, an unpopular chieftain, it has been maintained, would have been abandoned by so many of his followers that he would even have been unable to nominate his men to the courts, and then he was finished, like a parliamentarian who does not get reelected.[13]

It cannot be expected in a society without any central power that the choice of a chieftain by farmers always worked in a democratic way, but there is evidence that the stipulations about it were not a dead letter. One of the so-called contemporary sagas, *Sturlu saga*, which takes place in the second half of the 12th century (see Ch. 1.11), contains examples of both more and less democratic relationships between chieftains and householders. The farmer Álfr Örnólfsson at Fagradalur did not get the support which he thought he was entitled to from his chieftain, Einarr Þorgilsson at Staðarhóll, so he went to the hero of the tale, Sturla Þórðarson at Hvammur, obtained his support and entered his chieftaincy. This sounds rather democratic, but in another instance a group of men who were on their way to summon Sturla to a court stayed overnight with his neighbour, Bjarni Steinsson, at Ásgarður. A little later, Sturla rode to Ásgarður and told Bjarni that one of them would have to move to another place. Bjarni, of course, took the hint and sold his farm.[14]

One may assume that the author of *Sturlu saga* gave a realistic picture of how the system worked between chieftains and farmers. The theme of the saga is the growing authority of Sturla, which among other things appears from the fact that Álfr can leave another chieftain and go to Sturla without moving from his farm, but Bjarni cannot with impunity partake in a hostile act towards Sturla. Thus the system had an inbuilt trend towards imbalance; a strong chieftain was on average likely to become still stronger. This trend may have been a major cause of the collapse of the system, as we see in Chapter 1.12.

However great or limited the political freedom of farmers was, the democracy did not reach further down the social ladder. The entire household belonged to the chieftaincy of the householder, and women were completely excluded from the ruling system, whatever their social status in other respects. Thus a woman could own and run a farm, she could even own a chieftaincy, but she had to commission a man to act as chieftain on her

[13] See, for example, Sigurður Nordal (1990), 84.
[14] *Sturlunga Saga* I (1970), 92-3, 99-100 (Chs 23 and 27).

behalf. Women were not allowed to sit in the courts either, not even to bear witness.

The Icelandic Commonwealth has attracted the interest of libertarians as the society of ultimate individual freedom, where even seats in parliament were a marketable commodity and the enforcement of law was privatized.[15] Those who hold equality and social justice in higher esteem may be less impressed. Still, it could be asked whether the Icelandic system offered the individual less opportunity to seek justice than a system of royal officials would have done in those times. At any rate, this was a society that gave many people good reasons to think – and write – about problems of peace and justice, as is discussed further in Chapter 1.11.

---

[15] Friedman (1979).

1.4 The Exploration of the West

Once seafaring people had colonized Iceland, it could not be long before someone caught sight of the much larger island to the west that we call Greenland, or – for that matter – the very continent of North America. According to the *Book of Settlements,* Icelandic people had a vague knowledge of Greenland already in the colonization period, although little interest was shown in exploring the country at that time.[1] Iceland must have had enough to offer this generation, and the eastern coast of Greenland, with its extremely high mountains and glaciers cascading into the sea, looks anything but hospitable.

However, the 10th century had not yet come to an end when a man ventured to settle in the country that he had heard of in the west. His name was Eiríkr Þorvaldsson the Red. He was born in Norway, but had left the country after committing manslaughter and moved to Iceland. There he married Þjóðhildr Jörundardóttir with whom he had a son, Leifr. In Iceland too, Eiríkr got into fatal feuds and was outlawed from the country. The story illustrates how there was no way back to Norway for Eiríkr, which is probably why he took the course further to the west.

This account is based on a saga called *Eirik the Red's Saga,* which is one of the two most comprehensive sources on the exploration and colonization by Norsemen in Greenland and North America. The other is the *Saga of the Greenlanders,* which to a large extent relates the same events but often in a very different way. Scholars have differed over the relative age and reliability of the *Vinland Sagas,* as they are sometimes called, but the most recent conclusion is that we have no reason to prefer one of them to the other as a source. They were probably both written in the 13th century, and it is impossible to know which is older. The texts are most probably connected through oral tradition only.[2] If this is true, as I believe, these two sagas offer a rare insight into the impact of oral tradition on the sagas.

Fortunately, we are not entirely dependent on these sagas for our knowledge about the colonization of Greenland or America. Ari the Learned in his *Book of the Icelanders* includes a short chapter on the colonization of Greenland, and, although he does not describe any expeditions further

---

[1] *Book of Settlements* (1972), 41, 49, 71, 73 (Chs 76, 89, 150, 152).
[2] Ólafur Halldórsson (1978), 393-4, 398-400.

west, he reveals that he knew about them by mentioning "Vinland", the Norsemen's name for the southernmost region which they gave a name to in America.[3] Ari says:

> The land which is called Greenland was discovered and settled from Iceland. Eirik the Red was the name of a Breidafjord man who went out there from here and took land in settlement at the place which has ever since been called Eiriksfjord. He gave the land a name, and called it Greenland, arguing that men would be drawn to go there if the land had a good name. Both east and west in the country they found the habitations of men, fragments of boats, and stone artefacts, from which it may be seen that the same kind of people had passed that way as those that inhabited Vinland, whom the Greenlanders call Skrælings. When he began to settle the land, that was fourteen or fifteen years before Christianity came to Iceland [i.e. between 984 and 986], according to what a man who had himself gone out with Eirik the Red told Thorkel Gellisson in Greenland.[4]

Þorkell Gellisson, whom Ari mentions as his authority on this, was his uncle, so Ari's evidence must be considered fairly reliable. The later existence of Norse settlement in Greenland is well attested, as it lasted more than four centuries, and the Greenlanders stayed in contact with Iceland and Norway most of the time. They inhabited two settlements, called the Eastern Settlement (Eystribyggð) and the Western Settlement (Vestribyggð), although they were both on the west coast, but separated by hundreds of miles. A medieval description of Greenland states that there were 190 farms in the Eastern Settlement and ninety in the Western Settlement, which amounts to an estimated population of around 3,000. Archaeologists have discovered the ruins of some 330 Norse farms in Greenland. All things considered, that fits rather well.

Adam of Bremen, writing in the 1070s, is the first author who mentions the discovery of continental North America by Norsemen. Among the most remote islands in the ocean, he counts one which "is called Wineland, because vines grow wild there, which yield the most excellent wine". As his source for this, Adam gives King Svein Estridsson of Denmark.[5] Still, we might dismiss it as a fairy tale if we had not heard of the name Vinland through Ari, and – more importantly – the narratives of the Vinland sagas.

Among contemporary Americans, Leifr Eiríksson, the son of Eiríkr the Red, has received all the honour that has been attributed to Norsemen for discovering the continent. This he owes to *Eirik the Red's Saga* and Snorri Sturluson's *Heimskringla* (The Earth's Round), according to which Leifr left Norway in the year 1000 heading for Greenland, having been assigned

---

[3] It is usually assumed that the original form is "Vínland", derived from *vín*, which means "wine". But the form "Vinland" has also been suggested, which would derive from *vin*, "meadow" – (Magnús Stefánsson, 1997b).

[4] Jones (1986), 148 (Ch. 6).

[5] Ingstad, H. (1985), 299-300.

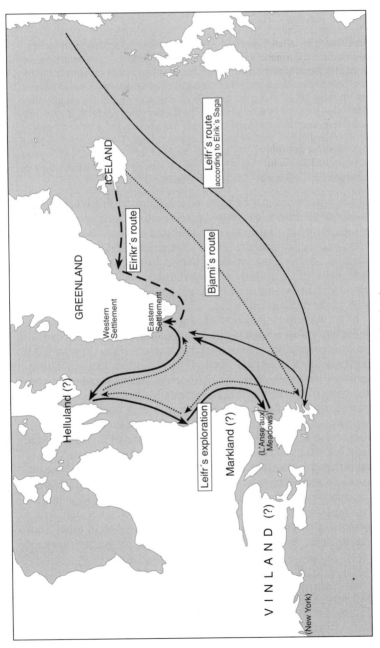

Map 1.4-1 Norse settlement and exploration of the lands west of Iceland.

by the Norwegian King Óláfr Tryggvason to preach Christianity to the Greenlanders:

Once he had made ready, Leif set sail. After being tossed about at sea for a long time he chanced upon land where he had not expected any to be found. Fields of self-sown wheat and vines were growing there; also, there were trees known as maple, and they took specimens of all of them.

Leif also chanced upon men clinging to a ship's wreck, whom he brought home and found shelter for over the winter. In so doing he showed his strong character and kindness. He converted the country [i.e. Greenland] to Christianity. Afterwards he became known as Leif the Lucky.[6]

If we consider it desirable to be counted as the discoverer of America, we might say that Leifr's luck also depends on the doubtful assumption that *Eirik the Red's Saga* is a more reliable source than the *Saga of the Greenlanders*, together with the fame of *Heimskringla* as a literary masterpiece. According to the *Saga of the Greenlanders,* it was not Leifr who was the first Norseman to catch sight of the American continent, but an Icelander named Bjarni Herjólfsson. He intended to sail from Iceland to Greenland one summer but lost his way in northerly winds and fog. Bjarni lighted on three lands, without landing on any of them, before he finally came to the country that fitted his image of, and indeed proved to be, Greenland.[7]

Nevertheless the Vinland sagas agree on the point that Leifr – or someone from his crew – was the first one to set foot on the continent. According to the *Saga of the Greenlanders*, Leifr bought Bjarni's ship in Greenland and made the first expedition to the newly-discovered lands. They came to the three lands which Bjarni had seen in reverse order and named them according to their nature: "Helluland" (Flatstone Land), "Markland" (Wood Land) and "Vínland" (Wine Land).

The Vinland sagas further agree that the most serious attempt to settle permanently in Vinland was made by Þorfinnr Þórðarson, whose cognomen was Karlsefni, and his wife Guðríðr Þorbjarnardóttir. They went there with scores of people and settled in a country where no snow fell and the entire stock could graze in the open throughout the winter. In Vinland, Þorfinnr and Guðríðr had their son Snorri, who would be the first person of European origin to be born on the continent of America. The sagas tell many stories of the relations between the settlers and native people, who, like the natives of Greenland, are called Skrælings in the sagas, but were probably Indians rather than Inuits. Sometimes they are said to have traded peacefully, but sometimes they fought. These tales seem to transmit a genuine idea of the culture of Stone Age hunters. The Skrælings became extremely scared when they heard a bull bellow, and their encounter with an iron axe is most interesting. After a battle, *Eirik the Red's Saga* says:

[6] *Complete Sagas of Icelanders* I (1997), 8 (Eirik the Red's Saga, Ch. 5).
[7] *Complete Sagas of Icelanders* I (1997), 20-1 (Ch. 1).

The natives also found one of the dead men, whose axe lay beside him. One of them picked up the axe and chopped at a tree, and then each took his turn at it. They thought this thing which cut so well a real treasure. One of them struck a stone, and the axe broke. He thought a thing which could not withstand stone to be of little worth, and tossed it away.[8]

In Iceland there is a story, which I have not managed to confirm, that Oscar Wilde said something about the Icelanders being the most ingenious people he knew of since they found America but had the good sense to let it go again. Most of us would be rather surprised that the aggressive and land-hungry Viking Age Norsemen gave up their attempts to utilize the endless source of wealth which they had discovered in America. Whatever the reason, no settlement west of Greenland is mentioned in contemporary sources from the Middle Ages. Vinland became only a saga. The strict source criticism of the late 19th and 20th centuries could not even take it for granted that Norsemen had ever reached America; legends of fabulous islands in the ocean are widely known. Since the 1960s, however, no one can doubt that Viking Age Norsemen sailed to the coasts of North America. It was then that the Norwegian couple Anne Stine Ingstad and Helge Ingstad discovered and excavated ruins of eight turf houses on the northern coast of Newfoundland, close to a small village called L'Anse aux Meadows. That the ruins are of Norse Viking Age origin was proved conclusively by the type of the houses, the artefacts found in them and the remains of iron-working.[9]

However, vines have hardly ever grown in Newfoundland, and L'Anse aux Meadows also provided evidence of sailings further south. In Norse wood debris there, two butter-nuts were found, of a kind that does not grow further north than St Lawrence and New Brunswick, around the border of Canada and the United States, and not far from the northern limit of wild grapes. The nuts are too big to be carried by birds and too heavy to float; people must have brought them north to L'Anse aux Meadows, which was perhaps no more than a base camp on the way to the bountiful Vinland.[10]

---

[8] *Complete Sagas of Icelanders* I (1997), 16 (Ch. 11).

[9] Ingstad, A.S. (1977); Ingstad, H. (1985).

[10] Wallace (1986), 299-302.

1.5 Christianization

In the years 995-1000 a Christian convert, Óláfr Tryggvason, ruled as king of Norway and made a serious attempt to introduce Christianity in his realm and in the Norse Viking Age settlements in the North Atlantic. It is considered unlikely that Óláfr ever reached the inland regions of Norway with his mission, and tradition maintains that his successor and namesake Óláfr Haraldsson, later St Óláfr, had to repeat the process after he came to power in 1015. On the other hand, medieval Icelandic historiography is unanimous in claiming that the Christianization of Iceland took place in the years of Óláfr Tryggvason, and there is no mention of any backlash after his death.[1] The authority for this is Ari Þorgilsson's *Book of the Icelanders*, which contains a relatively detailed and at the same time realistic and remarkably dispassionate story of how Iceland was Christianized by public consent at the Althing in the summer of 999 or 1000.

Ari starts his story "Of how Christianity came to Iceland" with a foreign missionary named Þangbrandr, whom King Óláfr Tryggvason sent to Iceland. He baptized a number of chieftains, Ari states, of whom three are mentioned: Hallr Þorsteinsson of Síða, Hjalti Skeggjason from Þjórsárdalur and Hjalti's father-in-law, Gizurr Teitsson the White, who according to another source lived at Skálholt in Árnesþing. After a year or two, Þangbrandr was forced to leave the country because he had killed two or three men. In the same summer two of the leaders of the Christian party in Iceland, Hjalti and Gizurr, came to Norway and took on the task of converting Iceland to Christianity. The next year they returned to Iceland with a priest in their company and arrived there just in time to get to the Althing. There they communicated their message at the Law Rock, after which the two parties declared that they would not continue living together under the same laws. The lawspeaker, Þorgeirr Þorkelsson from Ljósavatn, was heathen, so the Christians asked Hallr of Síða to proclaim their law. But Hallr struck a bargain with Þorgeirr that the latter should proclaim the law for both of them. It is disputed whether the text implies that payment was included or not.[2] Then Ari proceeds:

---

[1] For a survey of the Christianization of Iceland in English, see Strömbäck (1975) and Jón Hnefill Aðalsteinsson (1978).

[2] The original text, *hann keypti at Þorgeiri lögsögumanni, at hann skyldi upp segja*, is ambiguous on that point (*Íslenzk fornrit* I (1968), 16 (Ch. 7)).

And later when men had returned to their booths, Thorgeir lay down and spread his cloak over him, and lay quiet all that day and the night following, and spoke never a word. But the next morning he sat up and announced that men should proceed to the Law Rock. And once men had made their way there he began his speech. The affairs of the people, he said, would be in sorry plight if men were not to have one law, all of them, in this land; and he put this to men in many ways, how they must never let such a state of affairs come about, maintaining that strife would be the result, so that it could be taken as certain that such contention would arise among men that the land would be laid waste by reason of it. He related how the kings of Norway and Denmark had carried on war and battles between them for a long time till the people of those countries made peace between them, even though they themselves did not want it. And that policy answered so well that in no time at all they were sending each other precious gifts, and peace was maintained for the rest of their lives. "And now," he added, "I think it policy that we do not let those prevail who are most anxious to be at each other's throats, but reach such a compromise in these matters that each shall win part of his case, and let all have one law and one faith. It will prove true, if we break the law in pieces, that we break the peace in pieces too." And he so concluded his speech that both sides agreed that all should have that one law which he would proclaim.

Then it was made law that all men should be Christians, and be baptized, those who so far were unbaptized here in Iceland. But as for the exposure of infants the old laws should stand, and for the eating of horse-flesh too. Men might sacrifice in secret if they so wished, but it would be a case for lesser outlawry should witnesses come forward. But a few years later this heathendom was abolished like the rest. This was the way, Teit told us, that Christianity came to Iceland.

And this summer, according to what Sæmund the priest relates, King Olaf Tryggvason fell . . . That was 130 years after the slaughter of Edmund [see Ch. 1.1], and 1,000 after the birth of Christ, according to the general count.[3]

It may seem obvious from the last sentence that Ari meant that the Christianization had taken place in the year 1000, and until comparatively recent times this was one of the very first dates in Icelandic history that schoolchildren learned. However, it has now been convincingly argued that Ari reckoned with a year which started on 1 September, after the Althing but before the death of King Óláfr, which would move the Christianization to the year 999.[4]

Other narratives of these events, written around 1200 and later, are all based on Ari but add in many ways to his tale, and consist partly of hagiographic material, which is so conspicuously absent from Ari's account, but also deal partly with details that may well have been stored in memory until they were written down. The story of the earliest Christian mission in Iceland is one of those that are not found in Ari's chronicle, but only in later narratives. It says that an Icelander, Þorvaldr Koðránsson, called the "Far-Traveller", returned home from abroad with a bishop named Friðrekr,

[3] Jones (1986), 149-51 (Ch. 7).
[4] Ólafía Einarsdóttir (1964), 72-82, 103-4.

who had baptized Þorvaldr in Saxony. They stayed in Húnavatnsþing in northern Iceland for five years in the 980s and converted a number of chieftains in the Northern Quarter. One of them even built a church, which was still standing in the mid-13th century.[5]

One might suspect that this was pure hagiography, perhaps written in order to improve the role of the northerners in the conversion and thereby increase the prestige of their bishopric at Hólar. But although Ari starts his narrative of the Christianization with the acts of King Óláfr Tryggvason, he writes in a later chapter, "Of Foreign Bishops", the sentence "Fridrek came here in heathen times".[6] Was it perhaps Ari who left out the story of Þorvaldr's mission? He might have had good reason to do so, since he had been fostered by Teitr Ísleifsson at Haukadalur and refers to him as his authority on the Christianization. Teitr was the grandson of Gizurr Teitsson the White, one of the leaders of the Christian party in 999/1000. Gizurr's son and Teitr's father, Ísleifr, was the first native bishop in Iceland and lived on his farm, Skálholt, which his son and successor, Gizurr Ísleifsson, was to turn into a formal episcopal see. The family descended from Ketilbjörn the Old, the settler at Mosfell in Árnesþing and was originally called Mosfellingar, but after Teitr had moved to Haukadalur the family was referred to as Haukdælir.

There is no doubt that Ari was strongly attached to the Mosfellingar/ Haukdælir family; Bishop Gizurr is the only person whom he praises in as strong words as one would expect from a medieval chronicler. It is indeed possible that Ari overestimated the importance of Óláfr Tryggvason and Gizurr the White in the introduction of Christianity, even more so as King Óláfr and Gizurr were second cousins.[7] Such uncertainty may not only apply to what happened before the reign of Óláfr Tryggvason, but also after that; it is worth noting that Ari refers repeatedly to St Óláfr Haraldsson with his seemingly derogative agnomen "the Stout" (*enn digri*) and never hints at his sainthood.[8]

Nevertheless there are reasons to believe that Ari is right in indicating that the Icelanders adopted some kind of Christianity, relatively peacefully, around the turn of the 11th century. Adam of Bremen, writing in the 1070s, admittedly maintains that the Icelanders were Christianized in the time of Archbishop Adalbert, 1043-72. On the other hand, he confirms the evidence of the Icelandic sources that Bishop Ísleifr was consecrated by Adalbert.[9] Archaeological evidence seems to support Ari. Pagan burials are in many cases recognizable, as they contain artefacts that are not found

---

[5] *Kristnisaga* (1905), 1-13 (Ch. 1-4).

[6] Jones (1986), 151 (Ch. 8).

[7] *Kristnisaga* (1905), 35 (Ch. 11).

[8] Halldór Kiljan Laxness (1979), 15.

[9] Adam of Bremen (1959), 183, 218 (book III, Ch. 77; book IV, Ch. 36).

Fig. 1.5-1 Family tree of the Mosfellingar/Haukdælir, initiators of Christianization and an organized Church, and dominant chieftains in the area around Þingvellir and Skálholt.

in Christian graveyards. In Iceland, only one brooch with an 11th-century dating has been found in a grave, which indicates that pagan burial practices were abandoned around the year 1000.[10] Narrative sources in Iceland contain no stories of serious rifts over religion in the 11th century or later. In the written law, prohibitions against heathen practices are brief and seem rather unimportant.[11]

So one is led to question, as a number of scholars have done, why the Icelanders adopted the Christian faith so easily, sometimes in a way that implies undue reliance on Ari's evidence. People have asked why Þorgeirr the lawspeaker suddenly and secretly changed sides. The answers range widely, from Dag Strömbäck's mundane conclusion that he was simply bribed with money from the king,[12] to Jón Hnefill Aðalsteinsson's assumption that Þorgeirr clandestinely carried out an ancient soothsaying ritual and received the oracular prophecy that he should adopt Christianity.[13]

---

[10] Orri Vésteinsson (1996), Ch. II 4.2.

[11] *Laws of Early Iceland* I (1980), 38-9 (Konungsbók, Ch. 7).

[12] Strömbäck (1975), 30-1.

[13] Jón Hnefill Aðalsteinsson (1978), 103-23.

With no less enthusiasm, it has been asked why the assembly accepted Þorgeirr's proposal. This is a more fruitful question because the answers are equally valid whether or not we believe that the crucial decision was made as a reaction to the lawspeaker's speech at the Althing in 999/1000. Thus, some scholars have maintained that the pagan religion had already given way to individualistic, godless self-reliance and fatalism in the Viking Age. In support of this, people have referred to saga characters who are said to have believed in their own "might and main".[14] Then, of course, the impact of the king has been central to the attempts of scholars to see beneath the surface of these events. It has been pointed out, in reference to sources, that King Óláfr kept the sons of four Icelandic pagan chieftains as hostages in Norway when he sent Gizurr and Hjalti to Iceland.[15] Did the Icelanders perhaps adopt Christianity because they were afraid of a king on the other side of the Atlantic? Furthermore, historians of the nationalistic trend have suggested that the conversion was accepted in order to escape interference in their domestic affairs by the Crown of Norway and thus to preserve the independence of the country.[16] Others have seen the acceptance of Christianity as an acknowledgement of the king's power in Iceland. By substituting Christ for Þórr, it is maintained, the Icelanders were not evading the king but pleasing him and in some way subjecting themselves to him.[17] This may appear to be a reasonable interpretation, considering that the introduction of Christianity and the consolidation of royal power tended to go hand in hand in Northern Europe during the Viking Age. However, these two processes were kept separate in Iceland. Christ was let in but the king was not. This distinction may have had important consequences for the development of Icelandic culture and society.

[14] Sigurður Nordal (1990), 115-37.
[15] *Kristnisaga* (1905), 35 (Ch 11).
[16] Jón Jóhannesson (1974), 138.
[17] Sigurður Líndal (1974), 244-5.

1.6 The Church

What kept the Icelanders Christian through the 11th century remains an enigma, although there are indications that the kings of Norway did not keep their hands entirely off them after the death of Ólafr Tryggvason.[1] Two Norwegian kings in the 11th century, St Óláfr Haraldsson (1015-30) and Haraldr Sigurðarson (1046-66), are said to have sent timber and a bell for a church at Þingvellir. Chronicles mention a number of foreign bishops in Iceland in this period; it is most likely that they were sent by Norwegian kings as a part of their Christian mission among Norse people. Furthermore, the very first contact of Icelanders with the Christian education we have evidence of seems to have been mediated by St Óláfr. Gizurr the White had his son Ísleifr educated at a convent school in Herford in Westphalia, where the Abbess was the aunt of King Óláfr's son-in-law. Later Ísleifr "was chosen bishop by the general public of Iceland",[2] whatever that may mean. Then he set out for Saxony, supplied with a polar bear from Greenland to give to the Emperor, and was consecrated by Archbishop Adalbert in Bremen on Whit Sunday in 1056.

Traditionally, this date has been taken as the founding year of the bishopric at Skálholt, but in fact Ísleifr was hardly more than a missionary bishop, who resided at his patrimony, Skálholt. After his death, however, his son Gizurr succeeded him as bishop, and he – in the words of Ari the Learned – "had it laid down as law that the see of the bishop that was in Iceland should be at Skalholt, whereas before it had been nowhere; and he endowed the see with the land at Skalholt and further riches of many kinds, both in land and chattels."[3] The years of Bishop Gizurr, 1082-1118, seem to be the real founding years of the Icelandic Church. He had the tithe introduced in 1096, thereby making Iceland the first Nordic country where tithe was paid to the Church. Not only did he establish a see in Skálholt, he also allowed the northerners to found their own bishopric at Hólar, which included the Northern Quarter, while the three other quarters were subject to the bishop at Skálholt. A cathedral school was established at Hólar already by the first bishop, Jón Ögmundarson (1106-21), while in the south

---

[1] A survey of the history of the Church in Iceland until the 19th century, although perhaps somewhat dated, can be found in Hood (1946).

[2] *Byskupa sögur* I (1938), 76 (Hungrvaka, Ch. 2). My translation.

[3] Jones (1986), 153 (Book of the Icelanders, Ch. 10).

a few churchmen are said to have been educated by Bishop Gizurr's brother, Teitr Ísleifsson, at Haukadalur.

The successor of Gizurr at Skálholt, Þorlákr Runólfsson (1118-33), and his colleague at Hólar, Ketill Þorsteinsson (1122-45), continued the good work and composed a Code of Church Law, which forms the first section of the lawbook Greylag.[4] They also assigned Ari Þorgilsson to write his *Book of the Icelanders* and thereby provide the population of Iceland with an official history. In addition, the codification of the *Book of Settlements* is considered to have started around this time, and it is tempting to see both undertakings as a part of the formation of a civilized Christian society, the representatives of which could cite their ancestry with complete self-respect within the community of Europe at the time, the Catholic Church.

The consolidation of the Church went on throughout the 12th century. In 1133, the first monastery was established at Þingeyrar in Húnavatnsþing and in 1186 the first nunnery at Kirkjubær in Skaftafellsþing. By the beginning of the 13th century, two Icelandic bishops, Þorlákr Þórhallsson at Skálholt (1178-93) and Jón Ögmundarson at Hólar, had been canonized as saints, not by the Pope but, in a peculiarly Icelandic fashion, by an announcement made by the bishop at the Althing. (St Þorlákr was canonized by Pope John Paul II in 1984.) Around 1200, the bishop at Skálholt had the parish churches in his diocese counted and found that they numbered 220 and needed 290 priests to serve them. No comparable count is available from the north until more than two centuries later, when the diocese had 108 parish churches, which employed 136 priests. The sees at Skálholt and Hólar were by far the largest ecclesiastical institutions in Iceland. In the 1190s, there were some seventy or eighty people living at Skálholt.[5] Archaeological excavation has revealed that the cathedral there, built of wood, was almost 50 m. (160 ft) long.

The Icelandic Church was under the aegis of Nordic archbishoprics from the early 12th century, Lund (then in Denmark) from 1104 to 1152 and Trondheim in Norway after that. Nevertheless, it developed some characteristics of its own. While in Scandinavia parish churches were mostly built and run by a community of farmers, Iceland developed an old German *Eigenkirchenwesen,* where individuals built churches and endowed them with profitable property to meet their expenses.[6] These men, who were normally the occupants of the farm where the church stood, were rarely called owners of the church – more often its keepers – but for most practical purposes they acted as owners. The tithe, which in Iceland was in fact 1% property tax, was divided into four equal parts, one for the bishop,

---

[4] *Laws of Early Iceland* I (1980), 23-50. (Konungsbók, Chs 1-17).

[5] *Byskupa sögur* II (1978), 415 (Páls saga, Ch. 4).

[6] Magnús Stefánsson (1997a).

one for the parish church, one for the priest and one for paupers. However, the keeper of the church received two parts – those for the church and the the priest – and hired a priest, if he was not a priest himself. If the enterprise was run at a profit, there can scarcely be any doubt that he was free to make it his own. Some churches owned only an unspecified part of the farm – for instance, it owned a quarter Haukadalur. Other churches owned the whole farm or such a large part of it that it could be run as a separate entity. In the latter case, the farm was called *staðr*. Whether a *staðr* or not, most often the keeping of a church was inherited like personal property.

Another characteristic of the Icelandic church was the chieftain-priests. According to the so-called *Kristnisaga*, (Chronicle of Christianity) in the days of Bishop Gizurr "most respectable men were educated and ordained as priests, even those who were chieftains". As examples, the chronicle mentions Hallr Teitsson at Haukadalur, Sæmundr Sigfússon the Learned at Oddi, Ari Þorgilsson the Learned and others.[7] It is not known when Icelandic chieftains started to seek Christian learning and ordination. However, knowing that other scholars are of different opinions,[8] in my view it is most likely that the custom was a direct continuation of the dual role of the pagan *goðar* (chieftains). To put it simply, at the time of Christianization they just changed gods but went on with their social roles as far as they possibly could.[9]

The close relationship between the Church and the lay aristocracy in Iceland has been considered one of the most important prerequisites of the extraordinary literary achievement of medieval Iceland. The literary historian Sigurður Nordal wrote in the 1940s:

Nowhere but in Iceland . . . was there a class like the ordained goðar, who combined secular aristocratic status and the cultivation of national traditions with clerical learning. They preserved the old culture and their traditional freedom, pride, and solicitude for family and society, and practiced a moderate and lenient form of Christianity.[10]

Now most scholars would tend to take Sigurður Nordal's somewhat romantic views with a pinch of salt. However, I see no reason to doubt that literate education in the minds of people who were responsible for keeping law and order in lay society played an important role in creating a flourishing literature in the vernacular.

"As later events show, however", Sigurður Nordal continues, "the Church authorities were bound eventually to feel that it was not in the best interests of the Church to have such independent servants. They

---

[7] *Kristnisaga* (1905), 50-1 (Ch. 17). My translation.

[8] See Orri Vésteinsson (1996), Ch. III 5.2, Ch. IV 1.

[9] A similar opinion is expressed by Jón Viðar Sigurðsson (1999), 185-8.

[10] Sigurður Nordal (1990), 253.

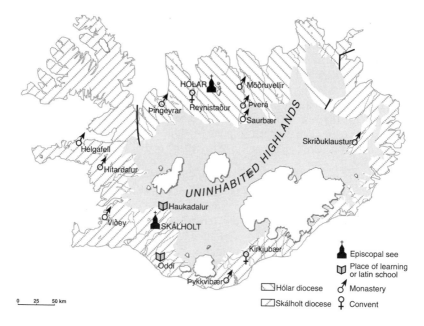

Map 1.6-1 Ecclesiastical institutions in Catholic Iceland.

would naturally prefer a clergy who had no power or wealth other than that which they had received from the Church." The first Icelandic church-man who is reported to have represented this view and raised demand in Iceland for what was called the liberty of the Church was Bishop Þorlákr Þórhallsson at Skálholt, later St Þorlákr. He was of poor parentage, but was brought up at Oddi by one of the most influential chieftain families in Iceland. He was elected bishop at Skálholt in 1174, four years after the murder of Archbishop Thomas à Becket in Canterbury Cathedral, and Þorlákr's dealings with Jón Loftsson at Oddi may be reminiscent of those of Becket with King Henry II.

It is not altogether easy to say what Bishop Þorlákr actually did. An account of his life *(Þorláks saga* in Icelandic; we call all kinds of stories *sagas)* is preserved in two versions that are relevant here. His quarrels with laymen are only reported in the later one, which may have been writ-ten under the auspices of churchmen who needed the saint as a model for their demands. On the other hand, the earlier version may have had no less reason to omit Þorlákr's and Jón Loftsson's disagreements, as it was prob-ably written under the auspices of Þorlákr's successor, Bishop Páll Jónsson, who was the fruit of an illegitimate relationship between Jón and Bishop Þorlákr's sister Ragnheiðr Þórhallsdóttir. Anyway the later version of the saga reports that he, supported by the archbishop, demanded that all churches and their properties be handed over to the bishop. At most church farms in the Eastern Quarter, he managed to have his demands met, but afterwards he invested the former 'wardens' with the patronage of the churches, apparently content to have the formal authority of his episcopacy acknowledged. Then Þorlákr met Jón Loftsson, who, in an eloquent speech, refused to respect the archbishop's message. After that, other keepers of churches followed Jón's lead, and the bishop's offensive was halted for the rest of his days. The demand for domination over the churches seems to have been dormant for three-quarters of a century after that, and was taken up again shortly after the end of the Commonwealth (see Ch. 2.2).

Also in the days of St Þorlákr, Church authorities attacked the other most important tie between the lay aristocracy and the Church, the ordination of chieftains. In a letter in or around 1190, the archbishop forbade the Icelandic bishops to ordain *goðar*.[11] It may well be that the chieftains were already losing interest in the priesthood at this time.[12] Therefore, we do not know to what degree the prohibition of the archbishops caused chieftain-priests to disappear during the first half of the 13th century, although some of the major chieftains of that period took minor orders.

After the death of Bishop Þorlákr in 1193, the chieftains in Skálholt diocese took care not to choose as his successor someone strongly attached to the Church. The bishop-elect, Páll Jónsson, was a chieftain and had not even been ordained as a priest. The northerners, on the other hand, chose a Becket-type bishop in 1201. Guðmundr Arason was his name, popularly called the Good. It is explicitly stated in a contemporary saga that the chieftain of the district of Hólar, Kolbeinn Tumason, thought that he could rule over the bishopric alone if he arranged to have chosen as bishop this relative of his wife, who was an illegitimate son from a minor chieftain family and was already well known for his miracles but not at all for his abilities to administer a large institution. However, Guðmundr disappointed Kolbeinn bitterly.

Two issues were at the centre of the struggle between Bishop Guðmundr and Kolbeinn Tumason. One was the running of the see at Hólar, where Guðmundr wanted to be more generous to paupers than Kolbeinn considered wise. The other was juridical power in cases against clergymen. For a number of years the dispute accelerated, and sentences passed by each party were ignored by the other. Priests that Kolbeinn had had sentenced to outlawry found abode at the see at Hólar. Kolbeinn and his men entered churches after being excommunicated by the bishop. Finally, in 1208, a battle broke out between their groups, and Kolbeinn was killed by a stone that was thrown at his head.

[11] *Diplomatarium Islandicum* I (1857-76), 291 (no. 72).
[12] Orri Vésteinsson (1996), 238-43. Ch. III 5.2.

After the death of Kolbeinn Tumason, the chieftains of Iceland saw Bishop Guðmundr as a major threat to their authority, although it is not easy to see exactly what they feared. What we know, however, is that Guðmundr was repeatedly expelled from his see. Sometimes he wandered about with a large following. When, for instance, he sought refuge in Grímsey, a small island north of Iceland, he had in his company seventy able-bodied fighters and thirty women and beggars. Twice the bishop fled to Norway and stayed there for four years at a time. Finally, in 1234, when he had become infirm and almost blind, he was left in peace at Hólar, where he died three years later.

After the death of Guðmundr Arason, the archbishopric, perhaps urged by the king, adopted a new policy and consecrated Norwegian bishops to both of the sees in Iceland for the rest of the Commonwealth period. None of them seems to have laid any stress on the increased independence or power of the Church in Iceland.

Thus, the Icelandic Church remained closely connected to the lay society throughout the Commonwealth period. Although the chieftains no longer served as priests, many of them still lived on property belonging to the Church, the *staðir*. It was to a large extent the Church which provided the lay aristocracy with its economic base. We shall return to the development of that aristocracy later (Ch. 1.12). Let us now look at the economic base of Commonwealth Iceland.

1.7 Population and Sustenance

If we try to estimate the size of the population of early Iceland, we must once again turn to Ari's *Book of the Icelanders* for information. There it says that Bishop Gizurr had a count made of farmers in the country around the beginning of the 12th century – that is, all those who were liable to pay the tax that was paid by all self-supporting farmers, the assembly attendance dues. The farmers proved to be 38 "hundreds" in number, which means that there were 4,560 of them – if we assume that Ari used the more common custom of the time, to count in long hundreds (120). It is always hazardous to rely on one source for important facts, not least numbers. Therefore it is a great comfort to be able to compare this number with the result of a count of tax-paying farmers in Iceland in 1311, where the result was 3,812. The two numbers ought to be comparable, as the minimum which farmers had to own to be liable to pay assembly attendance due in the Commonwealth period and tax to the king in 1311 was exactly the same (see Ch. 1.14). I see no reason to worry much about the decrease in the number from *c.* 1100 to 1311, because all calculations based on the farmers' counts are bound to be fairly inaccurate anyway, and in this period a fall in the number of taxpayers is likely; relatively fewer farmers reached the minimum as time went on, because tenancy and cattle hire became more common. What we can safely conclude from the counts is that there were somewhere around 4,000 farmers, able to sustain themselves and their families, in Iceland in the high Middle Ages. This is an important piece of information and must be considered exact by the standards of medieval history.

There were no towns in Iceland in the Middle Ages, and practically the whole population lived on farms. Therefore we can calculate a population number from the farmers' counts, if we estimate the number of farmers who did not pay taxes and the number of people per household. Here most scholars have chosen one of two possible approaches.

One of them, which was common in the 19th and early 20th centuries, is based on the assumption that the same proportion of the population were tax-paying farmers in the Middle Ages as at some definite point of time in the 18th or 19th century, when this proportion was known. This tended to lead to very high estimates, because in the 18th and 19th centuries only a minority of farmers reached the minimum to pay tax to the king.

Thus scholars came to the conclusion that the population of Iceland had reached 70,000-100,00 around the year 1100, which is 40-100% more than in the first census at the beginning of the 18th century (see Ch. 2.14).

The other appproach is based on the fact that most estimates give higher results than one would expect. Therefore, it has been said, it is wiser to keep to the safe side and estimate a minimum number. We can do that by assuming that most farmers paid tax and putting the number of households at 5,000. If we take the large households that are sometimes described in sagas to be either fictional or restricted to a small top layer of society, the average household may not have numbered more than eight people: a couple, three children, one elder and two farm-hands, male and female. This results in a population figure of 40,000.[1] Even according to such a low estimate, Iceland's population seems to have been around one-seventh of Norway's, whereas it is now only about one-seventeenth.

Still, when one enters the ruins of a medieval farm in Iceland, one is bound to suspect that the houses were built for more than eight people. In Þjórsárdalur in the central south, where a group of farms appears to have been abandoned after an eruption of Mount Hekla in 1104, one finds a main hall (*skáli*) of 50 m.[2] (540 sq. ft) or more, and a living-room (*stofa*) of about half that size, not only on one farm, which might have belonged to the local chieftain, but on a number of farms.[2] One attempt has actually been made to calculate the population at the time of Bishop Gizurr's count from the area of medieval dwellings. The conclusion, inevitably based on a number of bold assumptions, was 70,000 inhabitants.[3]

Other scholars have rejected the idea of calculating the population number from the farmers' counts. Instead, it has been argued that the country would never have been able to sustain a much larger population than the 18th-century maximum – around 50,000.[4] Let us therefore take a brief look at the country and how people lived in it.

The colonization period was relatively warm in the North Atlantic; in Iceland, the average temperature was at least as high as in the warmest documented period – from the 1920s to the 1960s. Until recently, the general opinion was that the deterioration of the climate began in the 13th or 14th century, but evidence from the Greenland icecap shows that there it started as early as in first half of the 11th century.[5] During this warm period grain may have been grown in all parts of Iceland, but in the times of written records – from the 12th century onwards – grain-growing only

[1] Gunnar Karlsson (1975), 5-7.
[2] Stenberger, ed. (1943), 62, 65, 82, 85; Kristján Eldjárn (1961), 20, 25; Sveinbjörn Rafnsson (1977), 61-2, 70.
[3] Jón Steffensen (1963), 143-6.
[4] Ólafur Lárusson (1936), 134-5.
[5] Dansgaard et al. (1975).

Reconstruction of a medieval Icelandic farm, based on the farm excavated at Stöng in Þjórsárdalur. Photo: Mats Wibe Lund.

occurs in the southern and western parts, where it decreased gradually, to disappear completely in the 15th or early 16th century.

Animal husbandry has no doubt always been more important than grain-growing in all parts of the country. Hay for winter fodder was probably the only crop of any real importance. Icelandic farmers were in fact sedentary pastoralists, whose households lived on milk products from cows and ewes and the meat of cattle, sheep and pigs. They dressed in homespun wool and used skin for shoes, oilskins and parchment. Goats were also kept; geese and hens are mentioned occasionally. Horses were of vital importance for transport – after the Church had forbidden the consumption of horsemeat – although no carriages were used. Packhorses were indispensable for carrying hay home from the hayfields, milk products from summer dairy farms and fish from the seashore to inland farms. Furthermore, without the sure-footed ponies, now known as Icelandic ponies, it would have been difficult to use the interior of the country for summer grazing for sheep and to attend the Althing at Þingvellir. Good horses were also a great source of joy and pride.

It seems perfectly possible that Icelandic pastoralism could sustain more people in the 11th and 12th centuries than in the 18th century, as a considerably larger part of the country was grass-covered in the earlier centuries. Erosion has probably always been at work in Iceland; the volcanic activity has produced a large quantity of loess, which through erosion makes extremely thick soil that is ever more susceptible to the effects of wind and running water. While there were no grazing animals in the country except swans and geese, the eroded land could regain vegetation relatively quickly, but after colonization the livestock prevented the recovery of the land in many places. At the same time, people burnt and cut down for fuel the birchwood which, according to Ari, covered the country "between mountain and seashore" at the time of colonization.[6] This again exposed the grass cover to wind and water and accelerated the erosion. It is not known how large a part of the country was covered with vegetation when Ingólfr arrived there. However, a rough estimate, which has the merit of being easy to remember, says that the vegetational cover has diminished from 40,000 to 20,000 km.^{2}, and the birch cover from 20,000 to 1,000 km.^{2}, during the eleven centuries of human habitation in Iceland.[7]

If the land yielded more in the high Middle Ages than later, it may be that the fishing grounds yielded less. Saga authors were definitely of the opinion that fish had been caught in Iceland from the very beginning. The *Book of Settlements*, for instance, reports that the female settler Þuríðr in Bolungarvík was called Sound-Filler because, before coming to Iceland, "during a famine in Halogaland she filled every sound with fish by means of witchcraft. She also marked out the Kviar fishing ground in Isafjord Bay [in Iceland], and took a hornless ewe in return from every farmer in Isafjord."[8]

Once people had been taught to observe fast days, fish was of vital importance, and internal trade between rural and fishing districts developed. A number of fishing ports are mentioned in sources from the Commonwealth period. The strange thing is that only a few of them are situated in that part of the country where the most prosperous fishing districts later were – on the south-western coast from Grindavík to Snæfellsnes.[9] This indicates that the very best fishing season – in late winter off the southern and western coast (see Ch. 2.4) – had not been discovered in this period. If that is the case, it is possible, in our comparison

---

[6] Jones (1986), 144 (Book of the Icelanders, Ch. 1).

[7] Much has been written about the structure of settlement in early Iceland. A recent study in English is Guðrún Sveinbjarnardóttir (1992).

[8] *Book of Settlements* (1972), 70 (Ch. 145).

[9] Lúðvík Kristjánsson II (1982), 31-84. In the *Book of Settlements* (1972), 133 (ch. 351), it is said that, in Vestmannaeyjar, before the settlement of Ormr the Unfree, "there used to be a fishing station, with hardly anyone living there permanently".

of the living conditions of 11th- and 18th-century Iceland, that better land in the 11th century was more or less evened up by less use of the sea.

Apart from fishing, which was mainly cod fishing, seals were hunted on the shores, and the Greylag law code contains more extensive regulations on whaling than on fishing or any other type of hunting. In sagas, however, whales most often drift to the coast, where they are divided among the inhabitants of the neighbourhood. This may be due to the different nature of these sources. Whaling demanded extensive regulation because the hunter, or so it seems, killed the whale with some kind of a harpoon, but did not catch it. When the whale drifted ashore, he could demand a part of its value if his harpoon was recognized in it. In sagas, on the other hand, the dividing of stranded whales is often the origin of disputes and killings.[10]

Another immensely valuable commodity provided by the beaches was driftwood. Medieval documents reveal that ecclesiastical institutions were keen to get hold of plenteous beaches, and driftwood is commonly mentioned in sagas too.[11] One might almost conclude that Iceland had been self-sufficient in timber if we did not know from laws and sagas that it was in fact also imported from Norway.

Besides wood, building material consisted of turf and stones which came straight from nature. The fuel used was wood, charcoal made from wood, dung and peat. Geothermal water, where available, was used for washing and bathing. Salt was produced on a small scale, perhaps by burning seaweed and salting food with the ash. Iron was extracted from bog-iron ore, melted by charcoal.[12] Some iron artefacts, such as weapons, were, of course, imported, but import of iron for items like horseshoes, scythes and spade edges does not occur in sources from this period.

From a strictly physical point of view, it seems as if it would have been possible for iron-age pastoralists, such as the early Icelanders, to survive in the country without any trade with the external world. Nevertheless, the Icelanders kept contact with their neighbours, especially Norway. Evidence of this is a contract which the Icelanders, led by their bishop, made with the Norwegian Crown. Normally it is called, with dubious authority, Iceland's treaty with King Óláfr the Saint.[13] Most of the contract is about the rights and duties of Icelanders in Norway. Thus they were to enjoy the status of Norwegian freeholders and were obliged to defend the country alongside the king, if it was attacked while they were there. Icelandic sagas contain a number of episodes where Icelandic ships landed in Ireland, Scotland or Denmark, and ship, cargo and crew were treated like any

[10] Lúðvík Kristjánsson V (1986), 27-41.
[11] Lúðvík Kristjánsson I (1980), 199-239, 291.
[12] Þorbjörn Á. Friðriksson and Margrét Hermanns-Auðardóttir (1991).
[13] *Diplomatarium Islandicum* I (1857-76), 54, 64-70 (nos 16, 21); *Grágás* (1992), 478-80.

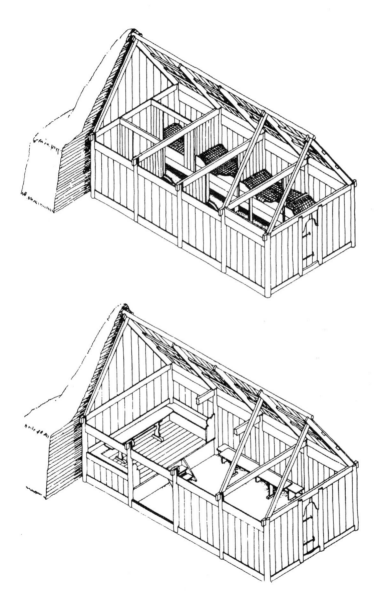

Fig. 1.7-1 The Icelanders seem to have built their houses in a fashion that required ample use of timber. This is Hörður Ágústsson's (1972) suggestion of how the two main rooms, the hall (*skáli*) and living-room (*stofa*), were built.

other wreck. By the treaty, Icelanders tried to secure for themselves some minimal human rights in one country on the other side of the ocean. How did they use this contact with the external world? In the period under discussion here they usually brought with them wool products, either homespun in rolls or woollen overcoats with the look of sheepskins (*vararfeldir*). When the silver booty of the Viking raids had been spent or lost, a traveller had to take with him spending money in woollen goods; a 3-km. (2-mile)-long runner of homespun, weighing some two tons, seems to have been a normal amount for a trip abroad.[14] Imports were naturally of a more varied kind, but the goods which occur most often are timber and grain. With regard to timber, it is possible that the supply of driftwood was insufficient. However, Icelandic housing of the Commonwealth period does not give the impression of a limited supply of wood. On the contrary, both dwellings and churches were built in a way that used a great quantity of timber. Perhaps import of timber served principally cultural purposes and was intended to exhibit the social status of the person or institution that built from the wood. This purpose of external trade is even more likely with regard to grain, which was hardly ever imported on a scale for it to have made up a considerable part of the population's diet.

We can estimate roughly the quantity of external trade in Iceland with the help of the treaty which was made in 1262, when the Icelanders succumbed to the power of the Norwegian king (see Ch. 1.14). Among the conditions was that the king should ensure the sailing of six ships to Iceland annually. At that time, an ocean-going ship may have carried 180 tons, and not much more than half of it would have been cargo. If 600 tons of foreign goods was considered to be a sufficient supply annually, half of it being grain, and the population of Iceland was 50,000, then each person got only 6 kilos a year on average. If that consumption was restricted to a top layer of society, some 5,000, each of them got 60 kilos, which would create a welcome diversity in the diet, perhaps including a vat or two of beer.

Other foreign necessities were even more culturally conditioned. Thus Christianity could not be observed in a proper way without imported wine, wheat, incense and candle wax. It could even be maintained that cultural contact as such was a more important aim of sailing to other countries than transport of goods. Prestige, education, absolution for sins, all these were available at home, but certainly not in the assortment that an educated medieval society required. Distance from others was probably the most distinctive characteristic of Iceland within medieval Christianity. It was indeed a cultural achievement to overcome this distance and remain for centuries a part of European medieval culture.

Even so, medieval Icelanders were not in the long run the seafarers one would expect, being the descendants of those who crossed the North

[14] Helgi Þorláksson (1988), 48.

Atlantic for the first time in history. Throughout the Commonwealth period, ever fewer ships owned by Icelanders and more Norwegian ships are mentioned in Icelandic sources. In the 13th century, before 1262, we know of only two Icelanders who owned an ocean-going ship or a share in such a ship. In the same period some thirty Norwegian skippers are reported in Iceland.[15] From the viewpoint of the competitive position this was a natural development: because of the availability of wood, shipbuilding was easier in Norway than in Iceland. In the beginning, the trade in both countries was an auxiliary occupation of prosperous farmers, but in the 11th century towns began to develop in Norway, and they offered new opportunities for professional merchants. Later on, the Archbishop and the Crown ran foreign trade on a large scale, which could be difficult to compete with. Thus the Icelanders lagged behind in the development of trade and lost their own foreign trade to others.

It is a long-held opinion in Iceland that the so-called Saga Age – the first century after the end of the colonization period – was a prosperous time, a real golden age.[16] Most present-day scholars would probably discard this view as obsolete romanticism, created by the 19th-century nationalist movement. Indeed, it has been argued convincingly that all ethnic groups find a golden age in their past if they need it in the present.[17] However, there seems to be no reason to doubt that Iceland was a prosperous country in the first part of the Commonwealth period – even when they support the myths, historians are obliged to take good sources seriously! As time went on deteriorating climate and decreasing vegetation were bound to impose limits on a growing population, at the same time as the external world was developing. It cannot, of course, be determined exactly when these limits began to be felt by people, but there are reasons to suppose it was already happening in the Commonwealth period.

[15] Bogi Th. Melsteð (1907-15), 844-7, 877.
[16] See Jón Jónsson Aðils (1906).
[17] Smith (1986), 191-200.

1.8. Social Stratification

Iceland may have been a good country for the first generations of Icelanders, but it was not equally good to all its children. Although Icelandic law stipulates that *réttr*, the right to compensation for offences, is the same for all free persons,[1] the society was divided into different social groups, like any other medieval society.

In pagan and early Christian times, the most striking dividing line was that between free people and slaves. It is not known whether Norse people kept slaves before the Viking Age, but in Icelandic sagas and laws slaves of both sexes appear frequently. In sagas they are usually Viking booty, often from Ireland and sometimes bought by Icelanders abroad from professional slave-dealers. More rarely, they are Icelanders enslaved by their creditors. According to the law, debt slavery was intended to be temporary, until the slave had paid the debt by his or her work. One was also entitled to sell one's children into slavery if one was unable to cover the expenses of their upbringing. Slavery was never forbidden in Iceland, as far as we know, but it was abandoned in the 11th or 12th century. No slave is mentioned in narrative sources later than a certain Gilli (a Celtic name) around 1055, who was castrated by his owner, killed him in return and was himself killed by having a red hot bucket put on his stomach.[2] On the other hand extensive regulations on slavery were codified when the law was revised and written down for the first time in 1117 and the following years (see Ch. 1.3). Even in the Church Law, which was not enacted until between 1122 and 1133 (see Ch. 1.6), slavery is taken to be a reality. It stipulates, for instance: "If household men have taken part in the work [after 3 o'clock on Saturday afternoon] and bounden debtors or slaves, then it is the free men who are to be first prosecuted."[3] This has normally been taken as evidence of the existence of slavery at that time, which is then thought to have been abandoned before the middle of the century, when more extensive evidence is provided by contemporary sagas. But it has also been pointed out that these regulations could have been made as a precaution by men who anticipated that a slave could be brought to Iceland at any time, because slavery was still in existence in Scandinavia.[4]

[1] Vilhjálmur Finsen (1883), 661.

[2] *Complete Sagas of Icelanders* IV (1997), 463-4 (Thorstein Sidu-Hallsson's Dream).

[3] *Laws of Early Iceland* I (1980), 42 (Konungsbók, Ch. 9).

[4] Foote (1977), 63.

Why did Iceland abandon slavery even earlier than its neighbours? A number of explanations have been suggested, most of them of an economic nature. It has been suggested that slavery never paid off very well on small farms in a sparsely populated country, where supervision would be too cumbersome. It has also been argued that it stopped paying off as the population grew and a larger free work force became available when farming land became scarcer and gave fewer people the opportunity to found their own farms.[5]

At roughly the same time as the dividing line between free men and slaves disappeared, a new one slowly emerged between laymen and clergy. At first, it seems that clergymen could be situated almost at the extreme ends of the male social scale; while among them were some of the most dignified chieftains, others had a status close to that of debt slaves, obliged to serve at the church kept by the man who had paid for their education. In the late 12th century, however, the archbishopric began its efforts to secure a special status for all clergymen, mainly by setting them apart from the feuds of laymen. Clergymen were forbidden to carry weapons, and for laymen the penalty of excommunication was imposed for the slaying of clergymen. Gradually, these efforts bore fruit. According to one narrative, in the first half of the 13th century, two Icelandic chieftains went on a pilgrimage to Rome. The reason is not mentioned, but the readers are probably intended to understand that they went there to seek absolution for the slaying of a father and son, one of whom was a deacon and the other an acolyte.[6] In the service of 13th-century chieftains, clerics appear repeatedly as mediators, who are obviously regarded as being more trustworthy than laymen because they stood outside the fights.[7]

As regards another dividing line, that between males and females, there has been thorough discussion, without a unanimous conclusion, as to whether it became stronger or weaker with Christianity.[8] It seems to me most likely that the differentiation between the sexes was so deep that it remained much the same before and after the conversion. Even if this is not the case, our description is inevitably based mainly on evidence from Christian times.

As already mentioned (Ch. 1.3), politics and jurisdiction were entirely the prerogative of men. The same applies to physical force; women were explicitly forbidden to carry weapons, and when they tried they were, according to the sagas, unsuccessful. The female sphere was the personal, familial one. Women's political influence was activated through their husbands, sons or other male relatives.[9] Because of this family ties, kin

---

[5] Anna Agnarsdóttir and Ragnar Árnason (1983).

[6] Helgi Þorláksson (1982), 55-62; *Sturlunga Saga* I (1970). 272.

[7] Orri Vésteinsson (1996), Ch. III 5.5.2; Sverrir Jakobsson (1998).

[8] For a comprehensive and sober survey of the status of women in Old Norse society, see Jochens (1995).

[9] Agnes S. Arnórsdóttir (1995), 173-97.

groups and marriages were the most important social relations for women, so it is natural to discuss these ties in connection with the status of the female half of society.

The kinship system of early Iceland consisted of a mixture of different principles, but predominantly it was that of cognatic kindred; the kin group (*ætt*) was defined in relation to oneself, both in the father's and the mother's line.[10] Thus every individual formed a kin group of his/her own and was related to a number of persons who were not related to each other. This also meant that women went on belonging to their parents' families after marriage, at the same time as they formed a family with their husbands. This could give some freedom; a woman who could hope for the support of her father or brothers was not as dependent on her husband as she would otherwise have been. On the other hand, the system could easily lead to a conflict of allegiance if there was any tension between the father's and husband's families. In an Eddic lay which was written down in Iceland in the 13th century, Guðrún Gjúkadóttir kills her two sons and serves their hearts as a meal for her husband, Attila, king of the Huns, in revenge for the killing of her brothers. After that, she kills her husband and tries to drown herself. There is no story of Icelandic women acting as violently as the Germanic Guðrún, but the nature of the conflict was certainly familiar to them.

Icelandic women could inherit property, but in the order of inheritance they were always secondary to a male who was equally close to the bequeather. Thus legitimate daughters were the heirs of their father if he had no legitimate sons. Apart from inheritance, daughters acquired property from their parents in the form of a dowry, which could be as large as the inheritance of each of the sons, even larger with their permission. The dowry and the bride-price (*mundr*) were the wife's property. However, the husband was the sole guardian of all the property while the marriage lasted. It was only when it ended, through death or divorce, that the division of the property between the couple made any difference.

According to law, women had little say in whom they were to marry. Only those who wanted to enter a convent had the legal right to refuse, and women whose fathers were no longer living were given some chance of negotiating with their relatives on the choice of a husband. However, sagas seem to reveal a general opinion that it was not advisable to force a woman into a marriage against her will. Such marriages usually proved to be a mistake, and not for the wife alone. In saga episodes that are set in pagan times, divorce is presented as something that was simple for both parties. But in the extant law the right to divorce depended almost entirely on the bishop's permission. Only in exceptional cases, as when the husband had been impotent for three years, could his wife leave him, taking her property with her.

[10] Hastrup (1985), 70-82.

Among saga characters, there are a number of strong, resolute women who goad their male relatives into revenge or women who take outlaws under their protection against their husband's will. This has led many scholars to assume that women enjoyed an exceptionally high status in early Icelandic – or Old Norse – society. There may be something in this opinion; nevertheless there are two reasons for caution here. Firstly, the sagas deal with personal and familial affairs more than medieval texts normally do. Therefore they may reveal a female role which women also played elsewhere but which has been forgotten in other countries due to lack of sources. Secondly, many of the sagas have a certain romantic flavour in their character-building. Thus, if we took them perfectly seriously as sources, we would also argue that women were more beautiful then than later, and that men were also greater in Saga Age Iceland than in other times or places. The laws certainly reveal great interest in the status of women, their marriages and property, but a sceptical reader suspects that this was not exclusively grounded in concern for the women themselves but for their role as carriers of possessions between families.[11]

Within the population of free laymen of the same sex there were two main distinctions. One was between farmers and their servants and the other between self-supporting and non-self-supporting people. All people were obliged to have a domicile at a farm. Normally, they were supposed to work as farm-hands at the farm most or all of the year. There were certain exceptions to that rule. For instance carpenters who worked with "eastern", that is Norwegian, timber were free to work wherever they were hired to work, even in the haymaking season. There was also a legal way of founding a home without farming, but only with the permission of the farmers of the commune (*hreppr*), who would be responsible for the maintenance of the family if it became destitute. Thus already in the Commonwealth period, a policy had been adopted which was to characterize Icelandic history through the centuries (see Ch. 2.4), to restrict the workforce to the farms and prohibit fishing from developing into an independent occupation.

Farmers (*bœndr*) formed a social group of their own and had mostly the same legal rights whether they were landowners or tenants. Even chieftains (*goðar*) did not enjoy any considerable privileges codified in the law. None the less, farmers must have enjoyed a very different social status according to their finances. It is a matter of dispute whether tenancy of land was practised from the beginning in Iceland. However that may have been, in the Christian era a considerable proportion of the farmers were tenants. Churches and other ecclesiastical institutions owned many farms, besides the farms where the churches stood, and they must have been farmed by tenants. Some of these properties were donated by wealthy individuals who owned a number of farms; the first one we know of from

[11] Gunnar Karlsson (1986).

reliable sources was Bishop Gizurr Ísleifsson, who, as noted earlier (Ch. 1.6), "endowed the see with the land at Skalholt and further riches of many kinds, both in land and chattels".[12] There is no reason to assume that all rich landowners were equally generous towards the Church, so that we have here another long-lasting characteristic of Icelandic society – large possessions of separated farms owned by rich individuals and farmed by tenants (see Ch. 2.14).

People who needed social help to support themselves formed two different categories. Farmers who could not sustain their families received the paupers' part of the tithe (see Ch. 1.6). Individuals who were unable to work and had no relatives to sustain them were allowed to rove within a certain area, normally the commune and receive one meal or one night's lodging at each farm. But persons capable of work who wandered about were to receive the most severe punishments – unemployment was a major crime in this society.

Finally, it should be mentioned that the life of the individual was divided into three periods, each of a different status. As to youth, the most noticeable feature is how short it seems to have been. At twelve, boys were considered able to prosecute at courts or sit in courts as judges. Sons of chieftains could even take over their own chieftaincies at that age, with their followers' permission. At sixteen boys were to receive their inheritance and choose their domicile. Girls did not get that right until they were twenty, but there are examples of their being married at the age of thirteen. Old age was supposed to start around seventy or eighty. At eighty, one lost the right to marry or sell one's property without the permission of one's heirs. The saga literature reveals little of the respect for the wisdom of old age that one might expect in a traditional society.[13] The Icelandic Commonwealth was a society that exalted the able-bodied, able-minded, self-sustaining male individual. The man who was able to earn his own living and defend his own honour was the norm by which all were judged.

---

[12] Jones (1986), 153 (Book of the Icelanders, Ch. 10).
[13] Jón Viðar Sigurðsson (1991).

1.9 Honour, Revenge, and Feud

Cattle die and kinsmen die,
thyself eke soon wilt die;
but fair fame will fade never,
I ween, for him who wins it.[1]

This is the attitude towards life and death presented by the Eddic lay "The Sayings of Hár". Similar emphasis on reputation above other values pervades the family sagas, which are set in the 10th and early 11th centuries.[2] Good reputation was acquired by preserving and increasing one's honour, and honour consisted above all in bravery and honesty, in appearing fearless and keeping one's word. Physical strength alone was not sufficient to produce honour, although it was an admired quality, and excessive use of force to increase one's share could easily turn into *ójöfnuðr* (inequality) and become intolerable. Moderation *(hóf)* was a highly esteemed quality.[3] Wealth in itself did not produce honour either, but to accept the deprivation of property could indicate a lack of courage and thus spoil one's reputation.

In the Icelandic Commonwealth violence was the legitimate tool of anyone to restore justice, and the moral demand for courage turned that right into a duty. Thus, if a close relative of yours was killed, the most shameful result was that the killer – and his family – got away with it with impunity. In most cases it was regarded as satisfactory to claim compensation – the higher the amount paid the better. But a man could be so ambitious in his search for honour – or feel so badly hurt – that he refused to "carry" his relatives "in his purse".[4] Then two options were open: full outlawry through a court, which often in fact amounted to a death sentence, or blood-revenge. However, since respect for moderation counterbalanced excessive demands for blood, the situation could emerge where it was most admirable to have the courage to act in an opposite way to the heroic ideal. This was what Hallr of Síða did, according to Njal's Saga, after a fight at the Althing, when he offered to renounce compensation for his own son.[5]

[1] *Poetic Edda* (1986), 25.
[2] Vilhjálmur Árnason (1991).
[3] Byock (1982), 27-30.
[4] *Complete Sagas of Icelanders* II (1997),88 (The Saga of Grettir the Strong, Ch. 24).
[5] *Complete Sagas of Icelanders* III (1997), 195 (Njal's Saga, Ch. 145).

Because Hallr was one of the protagonists of Christianity (see Ch. 1.5), it could be argued that his offer was meant by the saga author to contrast new, Christian values of peace and forgiveness to the old, pagan ones of blood-revenge. However, Hallr does not mention God in his speech, but only the need for peace and settlement.

Of course, if we try to estimate the value of the sagas as sources of real social attitudes prevailing through the Commonwealth period, we face difficult problems. First, the family sagas are certainly heroic literature of a kind; the almost Homeric values which we find there may be literary devices, intended to present a lost world. Secondly, the sagas usually abstain strictly from passing judgements on persons and their actions. Therefore the modern reader, who inevitably will often find the rules of honour somewhat vain, is sometimes left in great doubt about the attitude of the saga author. In Hallr's case, we are helped unusually well, as the saga adds that "everybody praised his goodwill"; it is therefore interesting to look at other sources for comparison.

In the Icelandic law code, Greylag, the use of violence was attributed to anyone who wanted to execute a judicial decision. A sentence of full outlawry amounted to a general hunting licence on the outlaw. Apart from this, a right to revenge, to kill a person without the warrant of any formal judgement, was granted to men in certain circumstances. Thus, one was allowed to kill for a sexual assault against women in any one of six relationships to oneself: one's wife, daughter, mother, sister, foster-daughter and foster-mother. If intercourse had taken place, the right to kill lasted until the next Althing; if not, that right was restricted to the place of action.[6] This was not a remnant of outdated law, as so many clauses in Greylag apparently are; the clause was kept in the law code that succeeded Greylag in the 1270s (see Ch. 2.1), the number of relationships even being raised to seven as stepmother, daughter-in-law and sister-in-law replaced foster-daughter and foster-mother.[7]

If we turn to the so-called contemporary sagas, which take place in the 12th and 13th centuries, we may not find the same gallant heroism as in many of the family sagas. Nevertheless, these sagas are permeated with reverence for bravery and sympathy with the urge for revenge. When the see at Hólar was ransacked by the enemies of Bishop Guðmundr Arason the Good (see Ch. 1.6), one of his followers, whom the attackers were pursuing for an unknown reason, managed to flee into the cathedral. He then offered to leave the church on the condition that they cut off his hands and feet before they beheaded him. This offer was of course accepted. He sang the *Ave Maria* while he was being mutilated and stretched out his head under the axe, and everyone praised him – not for his piety, the saga

---

[6] *Laws of Early Iceland* I (1980), 154 (Konungsbók, Ch. 90); *Grágás* (1992), 233-4 (Staðarhólsbók).

[7] *Járnsíða* (1847), 27-8 (Mannhelge, ch. 10).

says, but for his courage. In the early 13th century the śame saga also relates the story of two young men, one aged eighteen and the other a few years older, who were advised not to ride through a district where their enemy would be likely to ambush them. The older one answered that they would get a bad reputation if they did not ride by the way they had intended. When attacked, they refused to surrender because there would then be little to relate from the meeting. Both were killed, probably convinced that they were about to earn the fair fame that would never fade – as has actually proved to be the case.[8] The tough values of honour and revenge were still a living part of the moral code of 13th-century Icelanders.

A number of scholars, especially Americans from the 1970s onwards have interpreted the conflicts of Icelandic sagas as feuds, which indeed tend to pervade societies where honour is held in high esteem and the systems of government are decentralized.[9] It has been pointed out, often with supporting evidence acquired by anthropologists about remote societies, that Iceland developed (or preserved) a complicated system of social norms and customs, which served the purpose of settling disputes and keeping conflicts to a minimum without the help of a prince, army or police. Through mutual acts of violence conflicts tended to accelerate. The offences might increase in severity from minor blows or seizure of property to killing. At the same time the hostilities often moved up the social ladder as more powerful people, normally chieftains, took over the cases, sometimes for financial gain and sometimes to demonstrate their strength and thereby increase their honour. Sooner or later the conflict assumed a dimension that threatened the order of society, and then it was solved, usually with the interference of benevolent men or people who had links with both sides. The outcome was some kind of arbitration. Formal courts of justice could certainly play a role in this process, but usually they did this as tools of the conflicting parties, either in the acceleration of the conflict or in the search for a settlement, rather than assuming the capacity of ultimate authorities.

This may seem rather different from the ideas that we normally associate with the feud – namely, endless mutual killings between two clans. However, it has been pointed out that a feud takes on different forms according to the system of kin groupings that a society employs. In a society with bilateral kin groups, like the Icelandic one (see Ch. 1.8), it emerges between *ad hoc* groups, which may or may not coincide with kin groups, and the urge to settle the conflict is relatively strong and effective.[10]

[8] *Sturlunga Saga* I (1970), 144, 249-58 (The Saga of the Icelanders, Ch. 24, 84-5). These examples and more are related by Gunnar Karlsson (1988), 213-17.
[9] Byock (1982); Byock (1988), 103-36; Miller (1990), 179-299.
[10] Helgi Þorláksson (1994), 399-406.

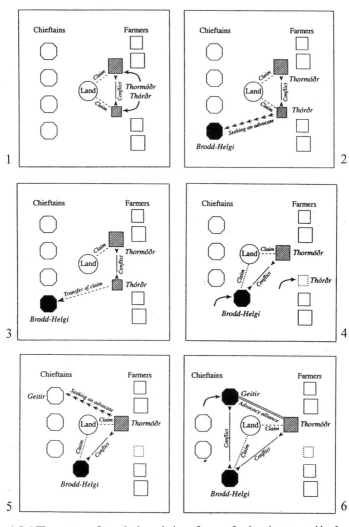

Fig. 1.9-1 The pattern of a typical escalation of a saga feud, as interpreted by Jesse Byock with the help of an example from the *Saga of the People of Vopnafjord*. Diagram by Róbert Guillemette.

1. Conflict: farmer with farmer.
2. Seeking an advocate: farmer to chieftain.
3. Transferring a claim: farmer to chieftain.
4. Conflict: farmer with chieftain.
5. Seeking an advocate: farmer to chieftain.
6. Conflict: chieftain with chieftain.

The American anthropological school has made a valuable contribution to the study of early Icelandic society.[11] However, there may have been some tendency within this school of thought to show the society in too kind a light. Therefore I feel obliged to end this chapter on two rather negative comments.

First, the heroic ideal was beneficial to those who conformed to it, but it was not as favourable to those who could not. Thus, one of the words for the qualities which produced honour – bravery and honesty – was *karlmennska*, "masculinity". It seems obvious that women stood little chance in the competition for honour in this society. Although they of course had their own pride, they were doomed from the outset to be the second sex.

Secondly, in spite of all efforts to restrict conflict, it cannot be denied that the ideology of early Iceland exalted aggression, and I think that it did so because it served, or appeared to serve, the interests of the ruling social group, the chieftains.[12] The ties between chieftains and their followers were personal and not geographically determined (see Ch. 1.3). In order for farmers to feel the need to stick firmly to the following of a chieftain, it was necessary that they considered themselves in need of his protection. A feeling of imminent conflict was a social necessity. On the other hand, in order to carry out this very protection the chieftain had to rely on his farm-hands and neighbours. He needed men who felt that it was honourable to be courageous and shameful to be too concerned with one's own security. Ideologically the Icelandic Commonwealth was based on a delicate balance between moderation and aggression, and in the end that balance was upset drastically, probably with fatal consequences for the social order (see Ch. 1.13). But, before we come to that, we still have some things to consider. First, how did this society define itself in relation to the external world?

[11] See Helgi Þorláksson (1987); Gunnar Karlsson (1993), 20-4.
[12] Gunnar Karlsson (1985).

1.10 Identity

Iceland was settled mainly from Norway and was to become a part of the Norwegian kingdom in the 13th century. The sagas reveal that the Icelanders were well aware of their origin in Norway and preserved the tradition of their Christianization by a Norwegian king. They also shared a language with the Norwegians throughout the Commonwealth period; Icelandic texts are scarcely distinguishable from Norwegian ones until the 14th century. Subjectively, in the minds of medieval Icelanders, the scope of the common language was even wider. They used alternatively the terms Norse (*norræna*) and Danish (*dönsk tunga*) about the language which was spoken by the Germanic inhabitants of the whole Nordic area. The name Icelandic (*íslenska*) was not adopted until the 16th century (see Ch. 2.3). Icelanders not only occupied the posts of court poets to the Norwegian king (see Ch. 1.2), but they were also, with few exceptions, their historiographers (see Ch. 1.11).

So it would be a plausible theory that the medieval population of Iceland looked upon itself as a group of Norwegians living away from their mother country. This also used to be the general opinion of Norwegian scholars, but by the turn of the 20th century Iceland had acquired its first professional historians, who, of course, felt a strong need to root in history the national identification of the emerging Icelandic state. This was a period of ardent nationalism, not only in Norway and Iceland but in Europe in general, and nowhere did people distinguish clearly between being a people, an ethnic community, and a nation – a people that forms, or at least wishes to form, a political entity. In other words, it was assumed that all (at any rate, all white and educated) peoples wished to rule themselves. Additionally, in Icelandic the same term, *þjóð*, covers the concepts of a people and a nation, so it is a far-fetched idea, when writing in that language, to distinguish between the two. It was therefore natural for early 20th-century historians to see the origin of an Icelandic *þjóð* in the establishment of the Althing in *c*. 930. At that moment, it was said, an Icelandic *þjóð* and an Icelandic state were born. However, taking into account that Norse *þing* districts rarely if ever coincided with the boundaries of ethnic communities or kingdoms, the establishment of the Althing in Iceland does not reveal much about the self-identification of those who attended it (see Ch. 1.3).

The protagonists of Iceland's national and nationalistic history did not stop at the Althing. They also managed to point out examples from Icelandic sagas which undeniably seem to indicate a clear idea of a separate Icelandic identity, distinct from that of Norwegians as a whole. Thus a family saga written in the 13th century about 10th-century characters tells of a Norwegian who used to sail to Iceland to trade. His brother was particularly inimical to Icelanders and said to him: "I don't know why you like visiting that worst of peoples."[1] In *Heimskringla*, Snorri Sturluson relates a dispute between the kings of Norway and Sweden in the early 11th century. At the Norwegian court there was talk of making the Swedish king a peace proposal, but people feared that the Swedes might harm the messengers who brought it. Then the Icelander Hjalti Skeggjason offered to undertake the mission because, as Snorri makes him say, "I am not a Norwegian, so the Swedes will not have anything against me."[2]

In a Norwegian chronicle, written in Latin in the second half of the 12th century, the Icelanders are referred to as a *populus*, which probably indicates the idea of a separate ethnicity. In the same sentence, a special characteristic is attributed to them, as the author refers to them as authorities about a historical fact, adding that they are the most skilful and inquisitive of northern *populis* in such things.[3] Characterization does not necessarily indicate an idea of ethnicity; we might well say that the inhabitants of one village are more skilful than those of another. Still, it is worth noting that sagas preserve some references to peculiarities attributed to the Icelanders by others. They were named *mörlandar*, "sheep-suet-landers" (or even *mörfjandar*, "sheep-suet devils"), which probably refers to the use of sheep fat in their diet, while also forming an opposite impression to their chilly collective name, Icelanders. Furthermore, they were said to be *tómlátir* and *fálátir*, both words that would translate as "phlegmatic" or "introverted", and even *seinlátir*, "sluggish". One episode appears to contain a reply to Norwegians on behalf of the Icelanders. An Icelandic 13th-century chieftain is reported to have refused to disclose his plans to a Norwegian merchant who was in his following, saying: "The men of the east are often indiscreet."[4] If Norwegians find that Icelanders talk too little, Icelanders find that Norwegians talk too much.

If this sounds trivial, the Danish ethnologist Kirsten Hastrup leads us towards a deeper study of the ethnic identification of early Icelanders.[5] In

[1] *Complete Sagas of Icelanders* II (1997), 270 (Killer-Glum's Saga, Ch. 3).

[2] Snorri Sturluson (1964), 302 (Saint Óláf's Saga, Ch. 70). The original uses the term *norrænn*, which could mean either "Norwegian", "Norse" or "Nordic". *Íslenzk fornrit* XXVII (1945), 91.

[3] *Monumenta historica Norvegiæ* (1880), 6.

[4] *Sturlunga Saga* II (1974), 277 (The Saga of Þórð Kakali, Ch. 22). In the original: "Austmenn eru oft skjótorðir". *Sturlunga saga* II (1946), 44.

[5] Hastrup (1984), 237-40.

the law code Greylag she discovered an identification in three successive stages. In the most inclusive stage, a distinction was made between "us", who speak the Danish or Nordic language, and "the others", who speak all other languages. Nordic people had, for instance, the right to claim inheritance in Iceland after a fourth cousin, but only a father, son or brother if they were not Danish-speaking. In the middle stage, a distinction was made between "us of Norway", Norwegians and Icelanders, and those in the other Nordic kingdoms, Denmark and Sweden. Thus Norwegians alone were exempt from paying harbour tax. Finally, the least inclusive dividing line came between Icelanders and Norwegians. All Icelanders were thus obliged to pay tithe annually while foreigners (*útlendir menn*) did not have to until they had established a farm or stayed in the country for three years.

In the course of the 12th century, Hastrup proceeds, the last-mentioned distinction was consciously made stronger and extended to the cultural sphere. First, Ari the Learned gave the Icelanders a history in the *Book of the Icelanders*. Around the middle of the century an unknown author, in the so-called *Fyrsta málfræðiritgerðin* (First Grammatical Treatise), adapted the Latin alphabet to the West Nordic language with the explicit intention of designing an alphabet for "us the Icelanders". Thus, in a way, the treatise was an attempt to give the young Icelandic people a language of its own.

There can thus hardly be any question that the Icelanders considered themselves to be a separate ethnic entity (*þjóð*) from the 12th century onwards. There is no evidence of an Icelander ever pronouncing him- or herself to be a Norwegian, and perhaps the idea of a Norwegian identity was never exported to Iceland. As far as we know the idea of a Norwegian ethnicity first emerged during the 9th century, and it is far from certain that the people who moved from the western coast of Norway to Iceland around the beginning of the 10th century knew that they were Norwegians. Even though it may be true that King Haraldr Fairhair had adopted the idea that the west coast was a part of a country named Norway, it is not particularly likely that the idea had won general adherence among the inhabitants there. Very probably, the people there called themselves by the names of their districts, Sygnir from Sogn, Hörðar from Hörðaland, Mærir from Mæri, Þrændir from Þrándheimr, and so on. When these people mixed in Iceland, between themselves and with other people, the first or second generation already had no name available to use about themselves collectively other than Icelanders.[6] We do not know, of course, how much ethnic content, if any, was attached to the name at the beginning. Maybe that emerged and grew slowly up to the 12th century.

Simultaneously, the idea of a special relationship with Norway remained alive. The so-called treaty with King Óláfr Haraldsson (see Ch. 1.7) seems

---

[6] Gunnar Karlsson (1994b), 113-14.

to offer a clear picture of the attitude towards Norwegianness. On the one hand, it presents an idea of special ties with Norway and its king, but at the same time the independent status of Iceland allows the Icelanders to arrange their affairs in a treaty with the king. From a Norwegian point of view, it may have seemed that Iceland's proper political status was within the realm. At any rate, it is counted among the "tributary islands" of Norway in the 12th-century Norwegian chronicle, *Historia Norwegiæ*.[7] According to the political ideology of the time, a separate ethnicity did not necessarily exclude the idea of a political affiliation with another people. However, there was definitely in the minds of some Icelanders at least some scepticism towards the Crown. This led to a tension which is expressed clearly in the *Book of Settlements*. There the Norwegian origin is stressed, but at the same time a number of settlers are said to have moved to Iceland to get away from the tyranny of the Norwegian king.

---

[7] *Monumenta historica Norvegiæ* (1880), 92-6.

1.11 Sagas

As the reader of this book will already have noticed, it is impossible to write a critical history of early Iceland without referring to sagas in every chapter and even sometimes discussing their source value. However, it may be appropriate now, before we come to the political development of the late Commonwealth period, to give a brief account of the saga literature as a whole. In Old Norse, as in modern Icelandic, *saga* (pl. *sögur*) means simply a narrative, oral or written, true or fictitious. What we mean by "sagas" (*fornsögur*), however, is a corpus of prose narratives, written down in West Norse, almost all of them in Iceland, in the 12th, 13th and 14th centuries. The saga literature can be divided into a number of subclasses according to subject and style. Here a rather traditional classification will be used and the classes described, as far as possible, in the order of appearance.[1]

It seems that the craft started as part of the formation of an Icelandic identity, described in the previous chapter. According to Snorri Sturluson, "Priest Ari the Learned, the son of Thorgils, the son of Gellir, was the first man in this country to write in the Norse tongue about lore both ancient and recent."[2] This evidence is supported by the first grammarian (see Ch. 1.10), who enumerates what had been written in Iceland in his time, including "that sagacious (historical) lore that Ari Þorgilsson has recorded in books with such reasonable understanding".[3]

The *Book of the Icelanders* is the only extant work which is explicitly attributed to Ari. But, as already mentioned (see Ch. 1.1), there are good reasons to believe that he participated in the original codification of the work which we now know as the *Book of Settlements*. These two works form a category of their own, which can be called *historical sagas*, as their main concern is to relate events and developments which we still consider important in the history of the society. As literature, these works compare with the later family sagas no better than academic history does with fiction in our times.

---

[1] For a recent and comprehensive survey in English of Old Icelandic literature, see Jónas Kristjánsson (1988).

[2] Snorri Sturluson (1964), 4 (Foreword).

[3] *First Grammatical Treatise* (1972), 209.

Ari may be the originator of *kings' sagas* too. In his prologue to the *Book of the Icelanders,* he mentions an earlier version of the work, which had included lives of kings, omitted in the extant version. Ari's slightly older contemporary, Sæmundr Sigfússon the Learned at Oddi, is also reported to have written about the kings of Norway. But, as Sæmundr is nowhere mentioned among the pioneers of writing in the vernacular, it is generally assumed that he wrote his work in Latin. Later in the 12th century, however, Icelanders began to write chronicles of the kings of Norway in the Norse language. The oldest extant work of this kind is *King Sverrir's Saga*, the incredible story of the Faroese priest who came to Norway in 1176 claiming to be the heir to the crown, took over the leadership of a guerrilla group and conquered the country. The writing of the saga was begun in the days of Sverrir himself, after his own account of it, by an Icelandic abbot, Karl Jónsson. At about the same time, three Norwegian authors wrote synoptic works which cover centuries of the history of the Norwegian dynasty, two of them in Latin and one in Norse. But in Iceland the genre developed through a number of sagas in the vernacular, some covering long periods, others individual kings' lives, most of them about Norwegian kings but a few about Danish ones. The kings' sagas reached their absolute peak in Snorri Sturluson's huge work *Heimskringla* (The Earth's Round) in the first half of the 13th century.

Later we meet Snorri Sturluson as one of the most ambitious chieftains of his time (see Chs 1.12 and 1.13). For our present purpose it is more important to mention that he was brought up at Oddi by Jón Loftsson, the grandson of Sæmundr the Learned. It is assumed that Oddi was one of the most important centres of learning in the country at that time. Two works are attributed to Snorri in medieval and early modern sources – his mythological and poetic textbook *Snorra-Edda* (see Ch. 1.2) and *Heimskringla*. The name of the latter work is not given by Snorri but derived from the remarkably cosmopolitan opening words of its first saga: "The earth's round, on which mankind lives, is much indented."[4] *Heimskringla* tells the story of the Norwegian dynasty from the time of Óðinn, who is said to be its ancestor, until 1177, when *Sverrir's Saga* takes over. In print it covers some 800 pages. The majority of it is based on older, still extant sagas, which gives us an excellent opportunity to see how Snorri improves the presentation, sets scenes with appropriate weather and surroundings, composes direct speeches and improves the logic and strength of the story. From the viewpoint of modern source criticism, he would not be counted as a good historian. But in the prologue to his work he presents a discussion of source value, which is rare in medieval works. There Snorri declares his intention to rely mainly on poems

---

[4] Snorri Sturluson (1964), 6 (The Saga of the Ynglings, Ch. 1).

which were recited before the chieftains [i.e.rulers] themselves or their sons. We regard all that to be true which is found in those poems about their expeditions and battles. It is [to be sure] the habit of poets to give highest praise to those princes in whose presence they are; but no one would have dared to tell them to their faces about deeds which all who listened, as well as the prince himself, knew were only falsehoods and fabrications. That would have been mockery, still not praise.[5]

In the course of his work, however, Snorri seems to have forgotten his strict demands regarding the reliability of sources, and when I read his excellent prose I must admit that I am glad he did.

If the lives of secular rulers were interesting material for medieval Icelanders, the lives of saints were an absolute necessity. In order to be able to observe the day of the patron saint of your church properly, you had to have a *legenda*, something to read about him or her. The text could be read in Latin, but nevertheless a large amount of hagiography was translated from Latin into the vernacular languages of medieval Europe. In Old Norse, saints' lives were, of course, called sagas – *heilagra manna sögur* (holy people's sagas) – and we have extant a good collection of sagas of foreign saints: the Virgin Mary, the Apostles, St Nicholas, Thomas à Becket and many others.

It is possible that the translation of these stories antedates some or even all of the genres of sagas which have been discussed so far, and the importance of these works as models for indigenous sagas is not easy to evaluate. At least it is certain that the Icelandic *bishops' sagas* were modelled on them. As already mentioned (see Ch. 1.6), Iceland acquired its own saints around the turn of the 13th century, Bishop Þorlákr Þórhallsson at Skálholt and Bishop Jón Ögmundarson at Hólar. Their lives and miracles had to be written down in Latin, but these works were soon translated into, or written simultaneously in, Norse. And in typical Icelandic fashion – whether we attribute it to the vitality of the indigenous high culture or to provincialism – scarcely a snippet has been preserved of the Latin texts while the Norse ones are extant in two or three versions of each saga.

At the see of Skálholt, two bishops' sagas were probably written soon after Þorlákr's Saga. *Hungrvaka* (The Appetizer) seems to have been intended as a kind of a preamble to the latter, as it covers the lives of all the five Icelandic bishops who preceded Þorlákr at the see. *Páll's Saga* is the biography of Þorlákr's successor and nephew Páll Jónsson (1195-1211), and thus forms a kind of continuation of Þorlákr's Saga. After Páll, only one bishop of Skálholt was honoured with a saga. That was Árni Þorláksson (1269-98), the great champion of the rights of the Church (see Ch. 2.2). Likewise, in the see of Hólar sagas are extant about two bishops other than

[5] Snorri Sturluson (1964), 4.

the saint. They are Guðmundr Arason the Good (1203-37) and Laurentius Kálfsson (1324-31).

The bishops' sagas certainly contain chapters in an excellent saga style, particularly *Laurentius' Saga*, which is written with a vivid sense of humour. However, they are enumerated here mainly for their historical value. Although they contain much praise of their heroes, which must be taken with a pinch of salt, they are great sources of valuable information. And the miracles give a rare insight into the daily problems of common people, who seek the help of the saints when a cow gets stuck in a morass, mice spoil a field of grain, a fishbone sticks in a child's throat or a raven flies off with a shoe.

Some scholars would count the bishops' sagas as part of the *contemporary sagas*, but here that name will be reserved for a group of sagas that tell of lay chieftains and their disputes of the period from around 1120 until the end of the Commonwealth. Most of these sagas are preserved only in a compilation from the early 14th century, which is traditionally named after one of the chieftain families and called *Sturlunga saga*, or *Sturlunga* for short. Scholars have claimed to be able to discern individual sagas within *Sturlunga*, and in most editions the original sagas are reconstructed and printed separately. Apart from a few minor stories and genealogical tables, some ten contemporary sagas are preserved, most written in the 13th century, hardly any earlier and probably only one later.

The largest and most important of the contemporary sagas, from a historical, as perhaps from an artistic point of view, is *Íslendinga saga* (Saga of the Icelanders), which is attributed on good grounds to Sturla Þórðarson (1214-84). It makes up a considerable part of the entire corpus (300 pages out of 800 in one edition) and recounts political intrigues, disputes and fights during the last eight decades of the Commonwealth. It does not make for easy reading, with its large number of characters and minute descriptions of events. However, to a tenacious reader it transmits a strong feeling of the immense richness and variety of human life.

According to current opinion, the generation which began writing contemporary sagas also started to write sagas of Icelanders living in the early Commonwealth period, mostly the century *c*. 930-1030. These sagas were to reach what is now considered the peak of the saga literature.[6] They are called *Íslendingasögur* in modern Icelandic, the Sagas of Icelanders, but in English *family sagas*. Both terms are misleading: many other sagas also have Icelanders as their heroes, as we have seen, and these so-called family sagas have families as their subject no more often than, for instance, modern novels. Nevertheless, in this book I shall conform to custom and use the term family sagas.

---

[6] The most recent scholarly discussion about the family sagas in English is by Vésteinn Ólason (1998).

There are about forty of them, apart from a similar number of shorter works, which are usually not called *sögur* but *þættir* (sing. *þáttur*) in Icelandic. In all, their text makes up about 2,000 pages in printed editions. To the modern reader, the most striking characteristic of these sagas is their resemblance to the 19th- and 20th-century novel. They deal with personal rather than political affairs: love, jealousy, vengefulness, greed, pride and crimes. They are relatively realistic compared with most medieval literature, although some magic realism is allowed. Many of them have one central hero, although the course of events may stretch over two or three generations, and some have an obvious central plot. Most of the heroes are common people rather than chieftains. The narrator usually stands well aside and describes the actions of people without passing his or her own judgements on them. The best sagas present complicated characters, who are often caught in moral dilemmas, where they have to choose between two undesirable alternatives.

Of course, a general description never does justice to individual sagas. Nor does a description of individual sagas in one sentence, although it will be attempted here. *Egil's Saga* is the biography of a poet, warrior and a great character. The *Saga of Grettir the Strong* and *Gisli Sursson's Saga* are the biographies of honourable men whom fortune deceives and who live as outlaws for years. In the *Saga of the People of Laxardal* and the *Saga of Gunnlaug Serpent-Tongue* love is the prime motive force of actions. In the *Saga of Hrafnkel Frey's Godi*, it is pride, honour and power. The *Saga of the Confederates* is a sarcastic, anti-aristocratic comedy. *Njal's Saga*, the longest and richest of all the family sagas, deals primarily with humanity's hopeless struggle against fate.[7]

No family saga is preserved with an author's name attached to it, and the dating of the sagas is by no means certain.[8] Still, the general opinion now is that the majority of them were written in the 13th century and the rest mainly in the 14th century. The creation and nature, and thereby source value, of these sagas are an even more controversial issue. For a long time, two schools of thought dominated the discussion. According to the free-prose theory, which was popular in the 19th and early 20th century, the sagas were basically true accounts of the events they described and had been preserved orally until they were written down in a basically unaltered form. The book-prose theory, on the other hand, maintained that the sagas were first and foremost works of art, composed by individual authors at the time of writing. It was rarely questioned that the sagas might be based more or less on an oral tradition, but it was denied that this tradition could be an object of study since it did not exist any more. This theory was mainly presented by Icelandic scholars during the first half of the 20th century.

---

[7] The whole corpus of family sagas is published in English in *Complete Sagas of Icelanders* I-V (1997).

[8] Einar Ól. Sveinsson (1958).

From about 1940 until the 1960s it enjoyed a practically unanimous consensus among academics – although some Icelandic farmers living on farms famous from sagas were certainly of a different opinion. But now scholars have again ventured into a study of the oral stage of the sagas, with help not least from anthropological information (see Ch. 1.9). A new free-prose theory is sometimes mentioned, although it is of course a very distant relative of the old one.

Two groups of sagas still remain to be mentioned. One consists of *heroic sagas*, in Icelandic *fornaldarsögur Norðurlanda*. Their subject-matter is a remote past, usually within Scandinavia. Their heroes are normally of royal ancestry, and are allowed to be stronger and bigger and live longer than the heroes of family sagas. Doubtless there is some traditional material in these sagas; a few Eddic poems are even preserved in them. Still, most scholars believe that these sagas were not written down until the second half of the 13th century. The other group consists of *sagas of chivalry*, in Icelandic *riddarasögur*. Originally they were prose translations of French epic poems, *chansons de geste*, and other foreign works; the first reported one, *Tristrams saga*, was created at the Norwegian court in 1226. Later the Icelanders began to imitate these stories and compose their own sagas of southern heroes and their loves.

As works of art the heroic sagas and sagas of chivalry have long been overshadowed by the family sagas. Still, they have their own literary merits if they are assessed on their own terms. In the end, they in fact proved to appeal more lastingly to the taste of the Icelanders. An amalgamation of heroic sagas and sagas of chivalry kept on being written and recomposed in verse form (*rímur*, sing. *ríma*) for centuries after the writing of family sagas had been abandoned (see Ch. 2.9).

Why did the art of narrative composition reach such a height in medieval Iceland? It has been suggested that the Celtic impact on the population brought with it the tradition of story-telling, which is well known in Ireland but unknown in the Nordic world.[9] Others see the challenge of settling in a new country and creating a new community as a more satisfactory explanation.[10] Did the peculiar emergence of a Christian church in the hands of secular chieftains (see Ch. 1.6) create such a novel application of written language? Did the art of keeping thedelicate balance between aggressive heroism and pacific behaviour, on which the Commonwealth was based (see Ch. 1.9), lead to this remarkable development of story-telling? Are the sagas principally studies in the art of keeping order in a society without executive power? If so, the political changes in this society and the crisis it met in the 13th century (Ch. 1.13) offer a further explanation for the flourishing of saga literature in that period.

---

[9] Gísli Sigurðsson (1988).
[10] Schier (1975).

1.12 Concentration of Power

Let us recall what can be concluded from the words of Ari the Learned, together with the stipulations of Greylag: the ruling system of the Commonwealth, from the 960s onwards, consisted of thirty-nine chieftains (*goðar*) who held a district assembly (*várþing*) in groups of three and thus formed thirteen assembly districts (see Ch. 1.3). It is far from certain, though, that this was at any time the exact number of chieftains, and there are certain indications that they may have been more numerous in the earlier centuries. It is possible, and can be concluded from family sagas if we rely on them, that men could serve as *goðar* at home, without being allocated a seat in the Law Council at the Althing, and women are also mentioned as temple-keepers, although they had no role to play in the political system.[1] These people could, of course, perform their pagan observances with a group of followers, but after Christianization the significance of such a *goðorð* (chieftaincy) would have waned. It is also known, from both laws and sagas, that chieftaincies could be owned by two or more persons in common or divided between them.

Also, the organization of the district assemblies was definitely less stable than the above-mentioned sources indicate. There are stories of chieftains who held their assemblies alone or abolished them altogether. The northern part of the Eastern Quarter, an area which ought to have formed two assembly districts according to the system, had only one after the arrival of written sources, with the name Múlaþing.

What is more important here, however, is the concentration of two or more chieftaincies in the hands of one man. Early sources mention chieftaincies being given away. It could also have happened that the same man inherited more than one or acquired a chieftaincy as the inheritance of his wife. Thus some limited concentration of power can be expected at any time, and there are indications of it, even from the late 10th century.[2]

Still, it was not until the 12th and 13th centuries that the unification of chieftaincies changed the governing system of the country. Before the mid-13th century, almost all the country had been divided into some eight dominions – with unstable boundaries, however. In contemporary sources these dominions were often called *ríki*, which originally meant "power"

[1] Helgi Skúli Kjartansson (1989a); Jón Hnefill Aðalsteinsson (1988).
[2] Björn Sigfússon (1934).

and hence "sphere of influence". The rulers of these dominions were practically all closely related to each other, as the small aristocracy of Iceland had to use most possibilities for intermarriage. However, if we count the male line only, which is justifiable in this case as that was how chieftaincies were usually inherited, we can accept a statement, which has almost become a tradition in Icelandic historiography, that they all belonged to five or six families.[3]

With regard to the dating of this process, scholars disagree considerably. One extreme is the assumption that it was almost halfway through before 1120,[4] while the other assumes that it had started in only a few districts before 1200.[5] My description here will be closer to the second opinion, as it is based on a more thorough investigation, although in most cases it cannot be determined with any certainty which one is closer to reality. Anyway, the end result is much the same, and what is important here is to give the reader a rough survey of the ruling families and their dominions in order to set the scene and introduce the main actors of the fights of the mid-13th century, which is the subject of the next chapter.

The Svínfellingar family

The chieftain family that lived at Svínafell, by the southern edge of the Vatnajökull glacier, seems to have been among the first to expand beyond one or two chieftaincies, and in the early 13th century its members got hold of the whole Eastern Quarter, where they formed two distinct dominions:
(1) the Svínfellingar dominion in Skaftafellsþing, which was ruled over by Ormr Jónsson and two of his sons in succession, Sæmundr and Ormr, from 1212 and throughout the Commonwealth period; and
(2) the Svínfellingar dominion in Múlaþing which was, from the 1220s, under the command of Þórarinn Jónsson, the brother of Ormr Jónsson at Svínafell. After his death in 1239, his son, Þorvarðr, succeeded him.

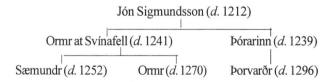

Jón Sigmundsson (*d.* 1212)

Ormr at Svínafell (*d.* 1241)   Þórarinn (*d.* 1239)

Sæmundr (*d.* 1252)   Ormr (*d.* 1270)   Þorvarðr (*d.* 1296)

Fig. 1.12-1 The Svínfellingar family.

[3] Gunnar Karlsson (1994a).
[4] Jón Viðar Sigurðsson (1989), 55-65.
[5] Lúðvík Ingvarsson I (1986), 257-61.

The Ásbirningar family and their dominion in the western half of the Northern Quarter

This family is named after a certain Ásbjörn Arnórsson who lived around 1100. It was not until the 1180s, however, that his descendant, Kolbeinn Tumason, appeared as a ruler over the Skagafjörður (Hegranesþing) district in the Northern Quarter. Later, he gained some power in the western-most district of the Quarter, Húnavatnsþing, and before the mid-13th century the dominion of Ásbirningar had reached the western boundaries of the Quarter. The best-known chieftain of the family was Kolbeinn Tumason's nephew Kolbeinn Arnórsson, called "the Young".

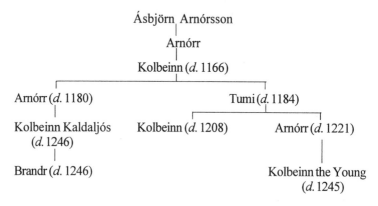

Fig. 1.12-2 The Ásbirningar family.

The Oddaverjar family and their dominion in Rangárþing

In the second half of the 12th century Jón Loftsson at Oddi was held in exceptionally high esteem as an arbitrator in disputes between chieftains in any part of the country. There is no doubt that Jón and two of his sons, Ormr and Páll (later Bishop Páll) ruled over all chieftaincies in the district. From then on, the Oddaverjar obviously looked upon Rangárþing as their area of influence, but they seem to have ruled the district as a group. We never hear of a sole district chieftain there, until perhaps the very last years of the Commonwealth.

The Haukdælir family and their dominion in Árnesþing

The Haukdælir have already been introduced to the readers of this book in connection with the Christianization process (see Ch. 1.5). They were for a long time counted among the most prominent chieftains of the country. Still, it is not until the days of Gizurr Þorvaldsson in the 1230s that we have direct evidence of their possession of all three chieftaincies in the district.

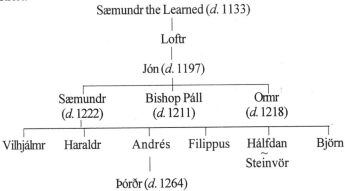

Fig. 1.12-3 The Oddaverjar family.

The Sturlungar family

The Sturlungar family descended from Sturla Þórðarson at Hvammur in Dalir in the Western Quarter, a 12th-century chieftain. He never seems to have had command over more than one chieftaincy, but with his second wife, Guðný Böðvarsdóttir, he had three sons, who were among the most powerful and ambitious chieftains of the 13th century. They and their descendants provided the name *Sturlungaöld* (the Sturlungar period), for the turbulent last decades of the Commonwealth. The sons of Hvamm-Sturla founded three distinct dominions.

(1) Þórðr Sturluson's dominion in Snæfellsnes and Dalir. Þórðr lived at different places in the central west. Most of the time he seems to have had to content himself with one chieftaincy, and for almost two decades he had to share the district with his ambitious nephew, Sturla Sighvatsson. Nevertheless Þórðr can be counted among the major chieftains until his death in 1237. His only legitimate son and successor to the chieftaincy was Böðvarr, whose son was the ambitious Þorgils Skarði. Among Þórðr's illegitimate sons was Sturla, the author of the Saga of the Icelanders (see Ch. 1.11).

(2) Snorri Sturluson's dominion in Borgarfjörður. As already mentioned, Snorri Sturluson was brought up at Oddi (see Ch. 1.11). In 1202 he moved to Borgarfjörður (Þverárþing), where his wife had inherited immense wealth and probably a chieftaincy. In a few years Snorri collected chieftaincies and expanded for a while even into Húnavatnsþing in the Northern

Quarter. In the long run, however, his dominion was Borgarfjörður on both sides of the old borders between the Western and Southern Quarters at the river Hvítá.

(3) Sighvatr Sturluson's dominion in the eastern half of the Northern Quarter. The third son of Sturla and Guðný, Sighvatr, started off at his patrimony in Dalir, but in 1215 he moved north to Eyjafjörður to take over chieftaincies (how many we do not know) that had been presented to his son. Somehow Sighvatr seems to have turned the whole eastern part of the Northern Quarter, the districts called Vaðlaþing and Þingeyjarþing, into a dominion, which he was to control until his death in 1238. His best-known children were his sons Sturla and Þórðr, who had the cognomen Kakali, and a daughter Steinvör, who was married to Hálfdan of the Odda-verjar family.

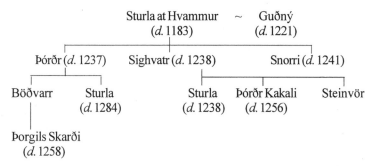

Fig. 1.12-4 The Sturlungar family.

There were minor areas outside these eight dominions, as they have been described here. The largest of them is the Vestfirðir peninsula, which was most often controlled by some member of the Sturlungar. It cannot be assumed either that the major chieftains owned all chieftaincies within the boundaries of their dominions. Sometimes, they just "borrowed" chief-taincies. Sometimes, minor chieftains may have become the followers of a more powerful chieftain and held the control of their chieftaincies under his protection. The power system that emerged in the late 12th and early 13th centuries was a strange mixture of old and new. Sometimes the sources mention the dominions (*ríki*) as if the old chieftaincies had disappeared altogether. For instance, in a dispute over the inheritance of Snorri Sturluson's dominion, no source mentions his chieftaincies, only his *ríki*. Similarly, when new chieftains took over the control of dominions in the 13th cen-tury, or wished to do so, it is repeatedly reported that they summoned the farmers to a meeting and asked for their consent. This was not a formality: the farmers sometimes refused and the chieftain gave up his claim. Such a

Map 1.12-1 Dominions of the principal chieftains, early 1230s.

practice had no support in the laws or in the old system. Either you had the legal right to control a chieftaincy or not. If you had, you did not need consent; if you did not have the legal right, no public consent could substitute it.[6] On the other hand, the concept of *goðorð* crops up often enough to convince the scholar that formal authority in Iceland consisted in the control of chieftaincies until the end of the Commonwealth. The power structure of the 13th century was new from a socio-political point of view, but from a legal point of view it was old.

Why did the governing system change so radically? In most cases, when the contemporary sagas speak of the capacity in which a chieftain assumed an additional chieftaincy, he received it as a gift. In two instances, the sagas explain the generosity of the donors – both of them were finding it difficult to protect their followers against the aggression of other chieftains. It seems that chieftains who did not manage to carry out their duties towards their followers, rather than suffer humiliation, preferred to give their chieftaincies away. Of course, they hoped for a reward in the form of a privileged status within the group of followers of the recipient.

The system seems always to have been rather defenceless against this

---

[6] Gunnar Karlsson (1977b), 366-7; Gunnar Karlsson (1972b), 37-9.

tendency of power to accumulate. Nevertheless, if the *goðar* were originally pagan priests, it might have been unthinkable that one man could
collect a number of *goðorðs*. And if Christian religious duties succeeded
the pagan ones, they may have preserved some ties between chieftain and
neighbourhood which were lost when the Church developed as a separate
institution with its own servants (see Ch. 1.6). This is all rather speculative; nevertheless, the concentration of the chieftaincies seems to coincide
with the disappearance of the priest-chieftains.

1.13 *Sturlungaöld*: an Internal Crisis

Sturlungaöld (the Age of the Sturlungar) has long been a rather vague concept in Icelandic history, although in all cases it refers to the last period of the Commonwealth and ends simultaneously with it. In the times when personal history was more fashionable than now, the word simply referred to the period when members of the Sturlungar family were active and influential; therefore it was considered to have started either in the middle of the 12th century, when Sturla came to power in his chieftaincy at Hvammur, or around 1200, when his sons started their unique expansion (see Ch. 1.12). Later, however, the term began to refer specifically to the period of exceptional warfare in the last decades of the Commonwealth. At the same time the king of Norway began his attempts to add Iceland to his realm with the help of Icelandic chieftains, and it seems likely that the escalation of warfare had some connection with these attempts. Chieftains who had been content to get hold of one assembly district or so may have had new ambitions kindled by the prospect of becoming the king's representative over the whole country.[1] Therefore it seems appropriate to start the story in 1220, when the Norwegian Crown made its first move to annex Iceland. The narrative inevitably relies heavily on the evidence of Sturla Þórðarson as the author of two of the most important sources, the *Saga of the Icelanders* (see Ch. 1.11) and the *Saga of King Hákon Hákonarson*.[2]

From its early days in the Viking Age, the Norwegian Crown had never restricted its ambitions to the mainland of Norway. When good fortune was with it, it had ruled over Orkney, Shetland, the Hebrides, the Isle of Man and even parts of the Scottish mainland. Faroe became a tributary in the 11th century. From about 1130, however, the Crown had been politically weakened by endless warfare between the supporters of different contenders to the throne. Norwegian historians talk of a century of civil wars. In the early 13th century, during the rule of King Hákon Hákonarson (called "the Elder"), stable peace was established. The Crown then seems to have adopted the policy of gaining hold of all lands in the North Atlantic that were inhabited by Norse people.

---

[1] See Einar Ól. Sveinsson (1953), 11.

[2] For a detailed survey in English covering the course of events in Icelandic politics of the period, see Jón Jóhannesson (1974), 239-82.

With Iceland the opportunity appeared to arise in 1220 when Snorri Sturluson was at the court, trying to settle a dispute between Norwegian merchants and the Oddaverjar family in Iceland. Earl Skúli Bárðarson, the father-in-law of the teenage king and the real ruler of the country at the time, threatened to send a navy to Iceland, but Snorri advised against such a drastic measure and offered instead to persuade the Icelandic chieftains to accept the authority of the Norwegian Crown. In the following years Snorri was an active and prosperous chieftain in Iceland, but did little to propagate the Crown's cause. We do not know whether his inactivity was due to lack of will or his conviction that the case was hopeless. What we can ascertain is that if he was not directly opposed to the introduction of royal power in Iceland, he could at least see both sides of the argument. In *Heimskringla* (see Ch. 1.11) he describes the attempts of King Óláfr Haraldsson to annex Iceland in the 1020s and he puts into the mouth of an opponent of the idea one of the most eloquent speeches of his entire work.

It was not until 1235 that a new opportunity seemed to present itself to the Crown, when another ambitious chieftain of the Sturlungar family, Sturla Sighvatsson, came to Norway on his way home from Rome. He promised the king that he would carry out his mission in Iceland by capturing the chieftains, one after the other, and sending them abroad, where the king would deal with them. The idea was obviously that the chieftains should give up their chieftaincies to the king, until he had all political power in the country in his hands. On his return to Iceland, Sturla proved willing to take his promise more seriously than his uncle Snorri had done. He made an alliance with his father Sighvatr, the ruler of the eastern half of the Northern Quarter, and they started their campaign in March the following year, from Sighvatr's residence in Eyjafjörður. First they turned on Snorri Sturluson with a thousand men. He avoided the fight against his brother and fled to the south and later to Norway, while Sturla and Sighvatr conquered his dominion in Borgarfjörður. That was about all they managed that year, and in the next one, 1237, they achieved little except the strengthening of their grip on the Western Quarter.

In the spring of 1238 Sturla decided to turn on the Southern Quarter. He summoned the chieftain of Árnesþing, Gizurr Þorvaldsson, to a meeting, turned up there with a large following, captured Gizurr and forced him to swear to sail abroad. While Gizurr was kept in a rather unreliable captivity, his men established contact with Kolbeinn Arnórsson the Young, the leader of the Ásbirningar family in the western half of the Northern Quarter. Maybe fearing the same fate as Gizurr, Kolbeinn was quick to ally with him. Gizurr was soon released, and both sides collected all the following that they could muster. On 21 August, their armies met at a place called Örlygsstaðir in Skagafjörður. Gizurr and Kolbeinn had almost 1,700 men; Sighvatr had almost 500, while no evidence is available about the number of Sturla's following. This time, the Sturlungar were caught badly prepared, and the fight was short. Sighvatr and Sturla were both killed, together with around fifty of their men. Gizurr lost only seven men and Kolbeinn none, if the report of the Saga of the Icelanders is to be believed.

While this was happening in Iceland, Snorri Sturluson remained in Norway with his old friend Skúli Bárðarson and undoubtedly learned of his plans to overthrow his son-in-law, King Hákon. In 1239 Snorri returned to Iceland, in spite of the king's prohibition to leave the country, with the title of earl secretly bestowed by Skúli. Sturla's narrative is obscure here, but the most straightforward interpretation seems to be that Snorri would become Skúli's earl of Iceland when Skúli had become the king of Norway – which did not happen, because in the following year he was killed in an attempted coup. This put Snorri in a difficult situation; he was the king's courtier, and his disobedience, not to mention the inevitable suspicion of his complicity with Skúli, made him a traitor. So King Hákon wrote to another Icelandic courtier of his, Gizurr Þorvaldsson, and asked him to capture Snorri and send him abroad, or kill him if he refused to go. One night in September 1241 Gizurr came to Snorri's farm, Reykholt in Borgarfjörður, with seventy followers. They found Snorri defenceless, trying to hide in a basement, and killed him without offering him any alternative. Thus the staunchest supporter of the Norwegian dynasty, whose sagas had made it immortal, lost his life as a traitor to a Norwegian king.

Between 1242 and 1250 Þórðr Kakali, Sighvatr Sturluson's son, dominated the scene. In 1242 he came from Norway and set out to reconquer his patrimony from the Ásbirningar, who had added it to their dominion after the battle at Örlygsstaðir. Suffering from a mortal illness, Kolbeinn the Young gave up the eastern part of the Quarter to him in 1245. By then, however, Þórðr was not content with that conclusion, and in the next year he killed Kolbeinn's successor, Brandr Kolbeinsson, in the most lethal battle of the period, where about 100 men were killed. Thus Þórðr had managed to subdue the Ásbirningar. They ran out of able leaders, and so their ally from the south, Gizurr Þorvaldsson, accepted their dominion, in the new way described in the previous chapter, by securing the general consent of the farmers.

Now one would have expected Þórðr Kakali and Gizurr to fight to the bitter end, but they proved too shrewd politically to do that. Instead they both agreed to sail to Norway and ask King Hákon to arbitrate between them. The king seems to have turned the issue into a question of which of the two would get the next opportunity to lay Iceland at his feet. He sent Þórðr on the mission and kept Gizurr in Norway. Þórðr had almost total authority in Iceland for three years, 1247-50. However he forgot his mission as the king's man and was therefore forced by a Norwegian bishop at Hólar to sail back to Norway. There he went into the king's service and died six years later.

When Þórðr Kakali failed, the king decided to try Gizurr Þorvaldsson. In 1252 he came to Iceland, together with two other Icelandic courtiers, one of whom was Sturlungr Þorgils Skarði Böðvarsson. A complicated course of events now ensued, where the agents of Þórðr Kakali fought against Gizurr. Þorgils Skarði changed sides, and for a while the fighting seemed to take on the form of a family war between the Sturlungar and the Haukdælir. Neither party managed to destroy the other, but Þórðr's men damaged Gizurr in such a way that for a while the king seemed to lose confidence in him. They attacked his farm at Flugumýri in Skagafjörður and, unable to conquer it with weapons, set fire to the houses. Gizurr's wife and three sons lost their lives, but Gizurr escaped in the unheroic way of hiding in a barrel full of sour whey. The next year, 1254, he was summoned to Norway by the king.

In the following years King Hákon put his confidence in Þorgils Skarði and, together with a Norwegian emissary of the king, Þorgils managed to make most farmers in the Northern Quarter accept tax obligations to the Crown. The dispute then took a new course after the death of Þórðr Kakali in 1256. His lawful heir was his sister Steinvör, one of those exceptional women who managed partly to overcome the suppression of her sex. (Once she acted as an arbitrator together with the bishop of Skálholt, even on the condition that she would decide alone if they did not agree.) However, Steinvör could not claim Þórðr's dominion for herself, so she handed the claim over to her son-in-law, Þorvarðr Þórarinsson, chieftain of the Svínfellingar family in Múlaþing. Þorvarðr caught Þorgils Skarði unawares and had him killed in 1258.

It had long been the custom for the young sons of Icelandic chieftains to go to Norway and enter the king's court. After the killing of Snorri Sturluson, however, it seems as if they realized that it was not as easy as it had seemed to be good servants of the king when in Norway and autonomous chieftains when in Iceland. We do not know of any Icelander entering the king's service after Snorri's death until the end of the Commonwealth. Therefore King Hákon had in fact only one Icelandic courtier left at his disposition, and that was Gizurr Þorvaldsson. In 1258 the king sent him to Iceland as his earl, with the commission to bring about submission to the throne. However, the issue dragged on year after year. In 1261 the king sent a Norwegian emissary, Hallvarðr Gullskór, to Iceland to press Gizurr. This he did during the winter and the following summer. And finally in 1262 chieftains and representatives from the farmers in the Northern Quarter and the two westernmost districts of the Southern Quarter swore allegiance to King Hákon and his son Magnúss at the Althing. Subsequently the representatives of the Western Quarter did the same at a special district assembly within the Quarter. Over the next two years the rest of the country followed suit. In 1264 the Icelandic Commonwealth had come to an end. Why and how this happened remains to be discussed.

1.14 The End of an Era

In the 1260s the North Atlantic empire, which was called the Kingdom of Norway, was to reach its largest extent ever and to attain the boundaries which it had for the rest of its days. Norwegian rule over Faroe, Shetland and Orkney was relatively secure in these years. In 1261 news arrived from Greenland that the Norse inhabitants of the country had sworn allegiance to the king. Two years later, King Hákon went on a campaign to the Hebrides, which the Scottish king had coveted, but he had no great success and died at Kirkwall in Orkney the following winter. His son and successor, Magnúss, to whom the last Icelandic chieftain swore allegience in 1264, abandoned the Hebrides and the Isle of Man to the Scottish Crown in 1266, but secured Scottish recognition of Norwegian rule over Shetland and Orkney instead.

The status of Iceland within the realm was set out in a treaty made at the Althing in 1262. This treaty was to enjoy a long-lasting political significance, as we shall see later (Ch. 3.4). For lack of a specific name, it was frequently referred to as the old or oldest treaty made between the king and his Icelandic subjects, and it thus acquired the name Old Covenant (*Gamli sáttmáli*). It is in form a unilateral declaration of representatives of the farmers who were present at the Althing and runs as follows in an English translation:[1]

This was the agreement of farmers in both the northern and the southern parts of the country:

(1) That under oath they agree to pay in perpetuity a tribute amounting to twenty ells for each payer of the thing-tax to His Majesty King Hákon and to King Magnús, and at the same time they yield to them their country and agree to become their subjects. This tribute is to be collected by chief administrators of the local districts [*hreppstjórar*] and then brought by them aboard a ship and placed in the hands of the king's deputy, at which point they shall have no further responsibility with regard to these payments.

(2) In consideration hereof the king will let us enjoy peace and the Icelandic laws.

(3) Six ships are to sail from Norway to Iceland during each of the next two summers; from that time forth their number shall be decided according to what the king and the most judicious farmers in Iceland believe to be in the best interests of the country.

[1] Jón Jóhannesson (1974), 282-3.

(4) Any inheritance which falls to Icelanders in Norway is to be given to them, however long it may remain due, as soon as the rightful heirs, or their legal representatives, present themselves to claim it.

(5) The land-dues are to be abolished.

(6) In Norway Icelanders are to have rights as advantageous as they have ever enjoyed there and which you [King Hákon] have yourself determined in your letters; you are to maintain peace for us in so far as God gives you the strength to do so.

(7) We accept the earl as our overlord so long as he keeps faith with you and peace with us.

(8) We and our descendants shall keep faith with you so long as you and your descendants keep this covenant, but be free of all obligations if, in the opinion of the best of men, it is broken.

It can hardly be said that this document gives a clear prescription of the intended constitutional status of Iceland. Three major things, however, are clear. First, the Icelanders were to become subjects of the Norwegian Crown, whereby the preservation of peace was to become the king's obligation. Second, Iceland was to remain a separate legal district, although no rules were set out about legislative power in the country.[2] Third, the rule of taxation is clear; the stipulation refers to ells of homespun, which was originally a strip of marketable homespun *c.* 50 cm. (1.6 ft) long, two ells (*c.* 1 yard) broad. At this time, the ell had long since become an abstract unit of value, and 20 ells amounted to one ewe with a lamb and a fleece, or one-sixth of a cow. This would not be called heavy taxation nowadays, but by medieval standards it may have been considered quite severe.

Why the Icelanders succumbed to the Norwegian Crown has been a much debated question in Icelandic historiography, and a number of explanations have been suggested: people were tired of the endless fights and hoped that the king would bring about peace; they feared that the king might put an embargo on Iceland: hence the clause on shipping in the Old Covenant; the Church, with Norwegian bishops as heads since 1237 (see Ch. 1.6), supported the king's cause and was suspected of having formed a fifth column within the Commonwealth; the Icelandic chieftains betrayed the Commonwealth by entering the king's service as courtiers. In fact, the king claimed to own the chieftaincies left by Snorri Sturluson, apparently because he had died as a traitor to the Crown. Some chieftains gave their chieftaincies to the king, probably to get them back as fiefs. Thus, King Hákon was actually the largest *goði* in Iceland well before 1262.

In spite of all these explanations, the surrender of the Icelanders was bound to be an enigma to the generations of scholars who were moulded

---

[2] Gunnar Karlsson (1991).

by the struggle for indepencence and never doubted that the will to national freedom is inherent in all "awakened" peoples (see Ch. 1.10). Thus it was pointed out that nothing had compelled the inhabitants of Iceland to give up their independence. The country was never invaded by a foreign army, which would have been a hazardous undertaking. Even if we count the loss in the internal fights as a sacrifice for the cause of freedom, only some 350 men are reported to have been killed in the years 1208-60. Many peoples have suffered greater losses, it was said, and not surrendered.

In 1964, however, an Icelandic scholar, Sigurður Líndal, pointed out that history had judged the Icelanders of the Sturlunga Age on mistaken premisses. The idea of sovereignty of states was just emerging in Europe in the 13th century out of the dominating systems of Church rule and feudalism, he maintained, and it cannot be expected that the Icelanders who negotiated with the king and his deputies were familiar with it.[3] Since the breakthrough of the modernist interpretation of nationalism (the opinion that it is a modern idea to want the polity and the ethnic community to coincide) it appears even less surprising that 13th-century Iceland entered the Norwegian realm. It may in fact seem more strange that it did not happen earlier. Why did it take the Crown more than four decades to persuade the Icelanders that it was in their best interest to become its subjects?

Within Iceland, there was unmistakably considerable resistance to the annexation, whether it was against the king as a political figure, as can be deduced from the speech which Snorri Sturluson attributed to his 11th-century hero (see Ch. 1.13), or against the financial burden and humiliation of taxation, as Sigurður Líndal has suggested. The resistance is most evident in the narrative of Sturla Þórðarson in the Saga of King Hákon Hákonarson about the events of 1261-2. In the autumn of 1261, the Norwegian emissary Hallvarðr Gullskór and Earl Gizurr Þorvaldsson managed to persuade some farmers to swear allegiance to the king, "among them some who had stood firmly against it". In the Northern Quarter during the winter, "the truth was exposed about what he [Earl Gizurr] had promised the King. Then it was planned that the farmers promised the Earl a huge amount of money in order to relieve them of the payment that was demanded." Finally, at the Althing in 1262, "the Earl spoke for the King's cause both to the Northerners and Southerners, begged them with kind words and called it a plot against his own life if they did not accept".[4] No less was needed to make the farmers agree.

Since we have such strong evidence concerning the reluctance of the Icelanders to enter the union with Norway, we may again ask why they ultimately did so. All the explanations given above may have some value.

---

[3] Sigurður Líndal (1964), 16-35.
[4] *Hákonar saga Hákonarsonar* (1977), 189-90 (Ch. 311). My translation.

More generally, it can be said that the royal power was a much stronger political force than the Icelandic Commonwealth. In the high Middle Ages, the Commonwealth must have looked to many people like an outdated remnant of bygone times. This is expressed in the story of an Italian cardinal who was staying at the Norwegian court when Þórðr Kakali was sent to Iceland to annex the country for the king in 1247. The cardinal "called it improper that this country did not serve under some king as all other countries in the world".[5] Paradoxically, from his experience at home, this particular cardinal must have been well acquainted and satisfied with an arrangement where countries did not serve under some king, but were directly subject to the Pope.[6] Nevertheless, whatever the cardinal may have said or thought, the narrative probably reveals what many Icelanders felt that civilized Europeans would think about their system of government.

So the Commonwealth was abolished, and European culture lost one of its small varieties. It is of course safest not to make too many assertions about the social consequences of this change. In the modern context, however, it sounds as if Iceland was silenced by it. We hear of no major warfare in the country after this, and no contemporary sagas describe the acts of its secular aristocracy. Two bishops' sagas and a few brief annals are the only narrative sources about the following centuries. Family sagas which are thought to have been written in the 14th century are much less to our taste and are less informative about social norms and attitudes than those attributed to the 13th century. One must be careful about causes and effects here: periods that leave poor narrative sources inevitably appear peaceful to posterity. On the other hand, in a community where the traditional subject matter of narratives is feud and warfare, peaceful periods leave behind few colourful stories. And of course, no cultural peak lasts for ever, because then it would not be a peak. Yet, while it is safest not to make too many assertions, it ought to be permissible to think that Icelandic culture lost something valuable when the Norwegian Crown relieved it of the challenge of maintaining law and order in the country without a pyramidal system of government.

---

[5] *Hákonar saga Hákonarsonar* (1977), 144 (Ch. 257). My translation.
[6] Ólafía Einarsdóttir (1994), 647-9.

PART II

Under Foreign Rule
1262-*c*.1800

2.1   A Dependency of the Norwegian King

The annexation of Iceland by King Hákon Hákonarson was part of a deliberate policy that aimed at collecting under the throne of Norway all lands which were predominantly inhabited by the descendants of Norse Viking Age settlers. As mentioned in the last chapter (1.14), Hákon's son and successor, Magnúss, abandoned the policy of expansion and concentrated instead on the internal consolidation of his realm, particularly within the boundaries of Norway proper.

At this time Norway was still divided into four *þing* districts, each with its separate legal code. King Magnúss set out to coordinate the legislation of his kingdom and gained for his work the agnomen Law-Reformer (*lagabœtir*). His revision of Norwegian law was carried out in two successive stages and ended in the 1270s in a practically unified legislation for the whole country, although formally each *þing* district still had its own code.

At the same time Icelandic law underwent a revision in two stages.[1] In 1271 the king sent to Iceland a new legal code, which is named *Járnsíða* (Ironbound) in Icelandic annals.[2] The book, which was largely based on the newly-enacted Norwegian law,[3] had a rather cool reception in Iceland; it took three years, from 1271 to 1273, for it all to gain acceptance. However, interestingly enough, the parts that were already accepted in 1271 included its two most important constitutional changes.

One of them was the assembly procedures section, whereby the *goði* institution was abolished and the members of the Law Council were to be farmers, appointed by the king's representative. In accordance with a Norwegian custom, the Law Council became predominantly an appeal court, which judged cases that were taken there from local courts. At the same time, the Quarter Courts and the Fifth Court of the old Althing were abolished. Thus the distinction which seems to have existed between

---

[1] On the constitution of Iceland from 1271 onwards, see Einar Arnórsson (1945), 114-380.

[2] *Járnsíða* (1847). The text is in the Old Norse original, with a Latin translation.

[3] Ólafur Lárusson (1923), 7-24.

legislative and judicial power in the Commonwealth (see Ch. 1.3) disappeared, and the term *dómr* (verdict), which had only referred to judgements in individual cases, came to mean either such a judgement or a general ruling of a legislative nature.

The other most important constitutional change was the introduction of royal wergild (*þegngildi*), which meant that manslaughter became an offence against the king as well as the family of the person who had been killed. Although blood revenge was still allowed in certain cases in Ironbound, the royal wergild was a large step towards the introduction of an institution with a monopoly on the execution of force, which is, according to Max Weber's definition, the state.

Thus, although we know next to nothing about the rule of Iceland beetween the Old Covenant of 1262 and Ironbound, we can assert that the Icelandic Commonwealth was abolished by law with the passing of the first part of Ironbound in 1271.

In the wake of Magnúss the Law-Reformer's second round of legal revision, in 1280, the Crown sent a new code of law to Iceland. The book was called *Jónsbók* (Jón's Book), after one of the royal emissaries who brought it to Iceland and probably its main author, the Icelander Jón Einarsson.[4] *Jónsbók* did not bring Icelandic legislation closer to its Norwegian counterpart. On the contrary, although the book is mainly based on Magnúss's new law, it includes considerably more of the old Icelandic Greylag material than *Járnsíða* had done.[5] With regard to the constitution, however, few considerable changes were made from *Járnsíða*.

No one knows why the king had a new legal code drawn up, since it did not aim at a closer affinity with Norwegian law; the most likely explanation seems to be that *Járnsíða* was rather sketchy and very incomplete. In that respect *Jónsbók* marks a big step forward.[6]

Even so, *Jónsbók* was not received with much enthusiasm in Iceland. According to the Saga of Bishop Árni Þorláksson or *Árna saga*, three groups at the Althing session of 1281 put into writing their criticism of the book. One group was formed by the bishop and his friends, another by the king's officers and the third by farmers.

At this the Norwegian emissary, Loðinn Leppr,

became all worked up, when peasants made themselves so pompous that they intended to decide about the law of the land, which [he maintained] was the prerogative of the king alone. Then he demanded of the assembly that it accept the book indiscriminately. But each group answered that it would not do so and thus forfeit the freedom of the country.[7]

[4] *Jónsbók* (1904).

[5] Ólafur Lárusson (1923), 25, 65-6.

[6] Ólafur Lárusson (1923), 82-7.

[7] *Árna saga biskups* (1972), 79 (Ch. 63). My translation.

However, most of the book was accepted at the Àlthing, although nine of the bishop's friends left the session without reaching any agreement with Loðinn. This must have been seen as too large an opposition group to leave behind in Iceland, as before Loðinn departed, a meeting was arranged between him and Bishop Árni and a compromise reached.

In spite of its cool reception in Iceland, *Jónsbók* was destined to obtain great popularity and form the core of Icelandic legislation for more than four centuries. It is preserved in about 200 manuscripts, more than any other medieval Icelandic work.

From a constitutional point of view, the enactment of *Jónsbók* is also an extremely important event in Icelandic history, since it placed Iceland firmly outside the unified law district of Norway. It is true that there was much confusion about legislation in Iceland in the following centuries, partly because the concept of law was not clearly circumscribed. Predominantly, law was what was written in the law-book, but the king could issue amendments (*réttarbœtr*) to it. Sometimes he did this at the request of the Althing, sometimes with its acceptance afterwards, but in many cases we do not know whether the Althing dealt with the matter. The Althing could also pass decrees (*dómar*) containing general rules, which the king either confirmed or rejected – and perhaps sometimes accepted by his silence. Neither the Crown nor the Althing kept any regular minutes in the Middle Ages, so we are often left in doubt as to whether lacunae in the source material stem from inactivity or loss of documents.

The matter is not made any simpler by the fact that Iceland's demand for an independent legislative body in the 19th century was based on the theory that the Althing had been vested with legislative power, together with the king, after the end of the Commonwealth (see Ch. 3.4). According to this theory, the Old Covenant of 1262 secured Iceland's participation in legislation by the clause "In consideration hereof the king will let us enjoy peace and the Icelandic laws" (see Ch. 1.14). The 19th-century nationalists maintained that from then on until the introduction of absolutism in 1662 Iceland enjoyed a status similar to a 19th-century constitutional monarchy where either party – the Crown and the parliament – could initiate law and either party could veto it.

This appears to be more than doubtful. The Old Covenant was probably never intended to set out any rule about legislative power. And in spite of their reluctance to accept the legal codes in the late 13th century, medieval Icelanders evidently had no clear opinion as to what was needed for a stipulation to become valid in the country.[8] The main rule, however, was the important one that law which was enacted for Norway did not automatically become valid in Iceland. This was sufficient to keep Iceland a separate law district through the centuries.

[8] Gunnar Karlsson (1991).

Another, and perhaps more important, indicator of the status of a society in relation to other societies in these times is the organization of the official ruling system and the participation of indigenous people in it. Starting at the top, the king himself was, of course, external to Iceland, and the Icelanders hardly ever doubted the right of the king of Norway to be the king of Iceland. When Iceland entered the realm, Norway had become a hereditary state without any election except in extreme cases, and the Norwegian law of succession is written in *Jón's Book.*[9]

Nevertheless, the Icelanders swore allegiance to a new king – at least to some of them – and that occasion could be used to renew the Old Covenant and even add to it new stipulations. Thus in 1302 allegiance was sworn to King Hákon Magnússon at the Althing on the conditions of the Old Covenant, with an apparently important addition. The Icelanders demanded that only Icelanders – from the families that had surrendered the *goðorð* to the king – should occupy the official posts of law-men and local sheriffs in Iceland. A few more resolutions are preserved from the late Middle Ages, passed on different occasions, where this demand for indigenous officials is repeated, sometimes with the requirement of their origin in the old *goði* families, sometimes without it.

This recurring demand for indigenous officials has been seen as a clear sign of nationalistic sentiment in Iceland at the time. The modernist view on nationalism, referred to in Chapter 1.14, has cast some doubt on that interpretation. It can be said, of course, that the demand only reflects the self-interest of the Icelandic aristocracy, who wanted to get something from the king in return for their *goðorð*. However, one of these resolutions was passed at a meeting of farmers of the district of Árnesþing. They met at a place called Áshildarmýri in 1496 to protest against repeated violations of the Old Covenant and diverse lawlessness. Hence they agreed to have no feudatory (sheriff or his bailiff) over the district, except an Icelandic one. Undeniably, this indicates that Icelandic farmers were generally of the opinion that it was better to live under Icelandic officials than foreigners, which is an embryonic stage of political nationalism.[10] Whether it was because of this policy among the Icelanders or the reluctance of Norwegian – and later Danish – officials to go to Iceland, the country was at all times mostly administered by Icelandic officials.

In observing the administration of Iceland in the late Middle Ages, it should be kept in mind that a stable system of officials developed very slowly during this period. At the start, it appears to have been for the king himself to decide which titles and which tasks were allocated to the men who stayed as his commissaries in Iceland or were sent there to present the king's wishes at the Althing and collect his taxes. The offices did not

[9] *Jónsbók* (1904), 20-5.
[10] Gunnar Karlsson (1996b).

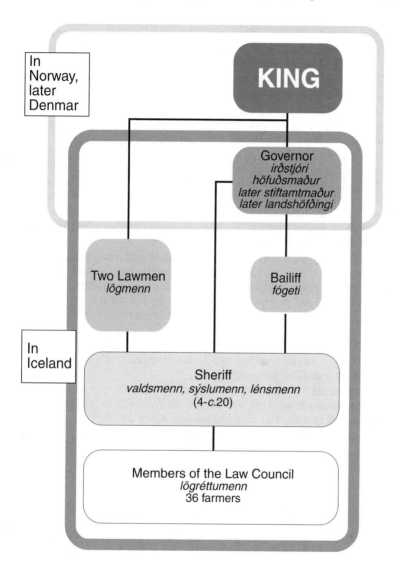

Fig. 2.1-1 The system of rule in Iceland after submission to the Norwegian Crown.

exist in advance, like boxes to put persons into. What existed were tasks, and the king decided to whom they should be entrusted in what size of district and for how long a period. No one succeeded Gizurr Þorvaldsson as an earl at his death in 1268. In the following years Icelandic annals occasionally mention whom the king sent to Iceland to rule over the country, usually two men, most of them Icelanders of well-known aristocratic families. It would hardly be right to look upon these emissaries as officials in a definite post, but in the 14th century the head of the royal servants in Iceland acquired the title *hirðstjóri*, which literally means "court-ruler". Later on, when the Danish Crown had taken over in Iceland, it became more common for a sea captain to be sent to Iceland, and hence the title of captain (*höfuðsmaðr*) became more common. Here the title of governor will be used to denote this post, as well as that of his successors – *stiftamtmaður* from the late 17th century and *landshöfðingi* in the period 1873-1904. Sometimes, when the governor did not have his residence in Iceland, he had a bailiff (*fógeti*) stationed there.

Unlike the post of governor, that of law-man (*lögmaðr*) had its support in law. According to *Jón's Book*, the law-man presided over the Law Council at the Althing and decided on its sentences if the nominated members of the council did not agree. Although the number of law-men was not fixed in the law-book, it soon became a custom that there were two at a time, one for the Southern and Eastern Quarters of the country, the other for the Western and Northern Quarters. In ordinary proceedings, then, the Law Council was divided into two departments, each of which dealt with cases from its half of the country.

Local administration was in the hands of officers, who were alternatively called *valdsmenn, sýslumenn*, or even *lénsmenn*, and whom we shall designate as sheriffs. The word *sýslumaður*, which became the most widely used as time went on, is symptomatic of the nature of the post. *Sýsla* originally meant "work" or "task", and, before the annexation of Iceland, in Norway the word referred to a person who carried out any task that the king needed to have done in the various parts of his kingdom. Thus the Icelandic sheriffs became, at one and the same time, tax-collectors, police officers and judges within their districts. This arrangement was not abolished completely in Iceland until the 1990s when the European Court of Human Rights judged it incompatible with basic human rights to let the same officer inquire, charge, judge and execute a penalty in the same case.

At first there were sometimes only four sheriffs in Iceland, but as time went on their number increased and their districts became more permanent. Finally the country was divided into some twenty *sýslur*, which in many cases coincided more or less exactly with the thirteen *þing* districts that had come into existence in the Commonwealth period (see Ch. 1.3 and Map 1.3-1).

The governors were rarely included in the above-mentioned demands for indigenous officials. However, a number of Icelanders served as governors, although more of them were probably foreigners, while almost all the law-men and sheriffs were Icelanders. Most of them were members of the Icelandic aristocracy, the group of people who in the early 18th century owned at least a quarter of all land in the country (see Ch. 2.12). These people naturally used Icelandic as an administrative language, as far as they could, and must have given preference to Icelandic law over foreign law. Thus, for better or worse, it was largely this group that secured Iceland as a separate unit within the realm.

This group of Icelandic officials naturally tended to recruit itself. There is even evidence that the Althing, in 1501, demanded the right to confirm the appointment of governors, but we do not know if this was ever recognized by the Crown. In the appointment of law-men, the Althing is likely to have played a somewhat greater part. At times, before the introduction of absolutism, the main rule appears to have been that both parties, the king and the Law Council, sanctioned the appointment of a new law-man; either of them made the choice and the other confirmed it. The sheriffs were appointed by the king or his governor, and they, in turn, appointed the farmers who rode to the Althing and sat in the Law Council. Thus, as in Norway and probably most of Europe at the time, the ruling system of Iceland formed a closed circle around the prince: those who were appointed to guard the royal power were selected by some part of that power itself.

The Icelanders who occupied official posts resided at their farms, wherever they were, even outside their districts. But the foreign governors, or their bailiffs, began as early as the 14th century to have a permanent residence at the king's farm, Bessastaðir, near the trading port of Hafnarfjörður, close to the present-day capital Reykjavík. Thus Bessastaðir formed the first administrative centre within the country.

This was the status of Iceland within the kingdom of Norway and later Denmark. It definitely had its autonomy and could not properly be designated as a part of the mother state. On the other hand, it cannot be considered to have been a state of its own in a personal union with Norway or Denmark. Nor was it a colony; that term belongs to a later period and different parts of the world. In the period in question, it was usually defined as a *skattland*, a "tax-land" or tributary to Norway or the Norwegian king, together with the other North Atlantic islands and sometimes the northernmost part of present-day Norway, the Finnmark. Later, under Danish rule, Iceland was often referred to in Danish as a *biland*, a dependency, of Denmark.

2.2 The Victory of the Church

Readers may remember that, in the late 12th century, Bishop Þorlákr Þórhallsson of Skálholt had to give up his demands for episcopal rule over individual parish churches in Iceland (see Ch. 1.6). Most of the churches remained under the secular rule of the person who farmed the church farm, and thus they contributed to the economic basis of the chieftain group throughout the Commonwealth period.

In 1269 a new Icelandic bishop, Árni Þorláksson, returned home from his ordination to take over the bishopric of Skálholt. He brought with him orders from his superior, the archbishop of Niðaróss in Norway, which strictly prescribed that "all *staðir* and tithes should be relinquished to the control of the bishop".[1] This was the beginning of the second round of *staðamál*, the struggle over Church property.[2]

During his first autumn in office and the following summer, Bishop Árni visited the Southern and Eastern Quarters of his diocese and demanded individual church farms in accordance with the archbishop's order. The reaction varied, according to the bishop's saga; most of the minor church keepers gave in, together with those in the Eastern Quarter, who had to admit that their forefathers had received their property as a fief from Bishop Þorlákr. But those who had a secure hold over more prosperous churches were not so compliant. For instance, it is reported that the keepers of Oddi, the great-grandsons of Jón Loftsson, the principal opponent of Bishop Þorlákr, now maintained that Oddi had been bought by their mother, Steinvör Sighvatsdóttir, a prominent member of the Sturlungar family (see Ch. 1.13). This, however, did not help much, since in the summer of 1270 a ruling was passed at the Althing that Oddi was Church property, probably because it was generally considered unlawful to dispose of real property owned by the Church.

This judgement did not solve the dispute, since it was not a question of what belonged to the Church but of who was the rightful agent of the patron saint, to whom the local church in question was dedicated. (In the case of Oddi this patron saint happened to be Saint Nicholas,[3] who later

---

[1] *Árna saga biskups* (1972), 13-14 (Ch. 9). My translation.

[2] The most extensive survey of this round of *staðamál* is Magnús Stefánsson (1978), 123-226.

[3] *Diplomatarium Islandicum* II (1893), 86-8 (no. 34).

became known as Santa Claus and has had a greater supply of worldly agents than any other Christian saint.) Since no agreement could be reached on this issue, the parties decided to refer the case to higher authorities. In 1272 a large commission set off for Norway, including Bishop Árni, one of Steinvör's sons from Oddi, named Sighvatr, Einarr Þorvaldsson, church-keeper of Vatnsfjörður, who was the grandson of Snorri Sturluson, and Hrafn Oddsson, who had recently been appointed royal commissary over half the country and was about to become a staunch leader of the lay church-keepers.

This time the bishop was the lucky one. In the spring of 1273 King Magnúss and Archbishop Jón reached an agreement on the limits of secular and episcopal power in Norway, whereby the Crown made important concessions to the Church. When in July the king, the archbishop and the group of Icelanders all met in Bergen, King Magnúss was still in the same mood and even declined to be present when the archbishop passed his sentence on the case. As expected, he judged that both the *staðr* of Oddi and the church farm of Vatnsfjörður, of which only one half belonged to the local church, should be handed over to the bishop's rule. These two farms seem to have been chosen as test cases, representing the two main groups of church property (see Ch. 1.6), and the result reveals that the bishop had his way with both of them. On his return home, Bishop Árni claimed a number of church farms. Among others, Steinvör's sons of Oddi had to leave their patrimony, which the bishop placed under a priest.

In the wake of his victory in the property issue, Bishop Árni went on to introduce further reforms in his diocese. His saga relates that he divorced a couple named Egill Sölmundarson and Þórunn Einarsdóttir at Reykholt, because Egill was a subdeacon. The episode is probably included in the saga to show how far the Icelandic Church had managed to advance the case of celibacy of its clergy, not least because Egill was descended from the once powerful Sturlungar family. Furthermore, in 1275 the bishop had a new Christian Law section passed at the Althing, whereby most of the major demands that constituted the so-called liberty of the Church were adopted. There are many obscurities about the formal validity of Árni's Christian Law: it was repealed by the Crown at least once; it was not formally enacted for the northern diocese of Hólar until eight decades later; and we do not know whether King Magnúss ever ratified it. Nevertheless, it remained in force for centuries, and two short clauses from it, dealing with the duties of church farmers, are still considered to be valid, thus making it the oldest valid law in Iceland.[4]

However, the bishop's victory did not prove final. When King Magnúss the Law-Reformer died in 1280, his son and successor was only twelve

[4] *Lagasafn* (1999), xxiii, 552.

years old, and a decidedly anticlerical government took over in Norway, led by the queen mother and the Council of State. The regency declared invalid all church legislation that had been enacted in the realm during the rule of King Magnúss. Bishop Árni had no doubt heard this news before the Althing of 1281, and his hostile reaction towards Jón's Book there (see Ch. 2.1) seems to indicate that he did not even try to avoid further clashes. He did not have to wait long. In 1282 Archbishop Jón was outlawed from Norway, at a meeting where Hrafn Oddsson was present. In the following year, Hrafn returned to Iceland armed with a royal decree which re-enacted the old Christian Law section from the early 12th century and prescribed that all church farms should be handed over to laymen, who had been wrongfully deprived of them. The bishop had no choice but to accept this. At a meeting in 1284 he made a statement which is a masterpiece of diplomacy: he promised to tolerate the message of the royal decree until a new archbishop had been appointed – the outlawed archbishop was dead by then – insofar as this did not go against his dutiful obedience to almighty God. After this laymen got hold of seventeen church farms in the Skálholt diocese, including Oddi, where Steinvör's sons again succeeded Bishop Árni's vassal. Since Árni's Saga is the basic source for these events, we know less about the process in the Hólar diocese, but odd comments in the saga indicate that a parallel development took place there throughout this process.

When King Eiríkr came to power himself, he attempted to re-establish a *modus vivendi* with the Church, and that policy was soon echoed in Iceland. In 1288, the disputants agreed, urged by the king, to sail to Norway and have the case judged again by the king and a new archbishop. As it turned out, Bishop Árni and Hrafn Oddsson were to stay in Norway for years after this, without any final decision being made. Eventually they were personally reconciled and went together with King Eiríkr on a campaign to Denmark. According to *Árna saga*, Hrafn used to receive Árni's blessing every morning before he went out to fight. One morning he forgot to do this, and on the very same day his little finger was struck by an arrow. The wound caused blood poisoning which led to his death. Shortly after that *Árna saga* ends suddenly; either the end is lost or it was never written.

For the continuation we must rely on rather laconic Icelandic annals, which nevertheless inform us that in 1291 Bishop Árni returned to Iceland and began once more to hand over church farms to his clergy. This action still met resistance, but in 1295 a royal decree on the issue arrived in Iceland. Nothing is said about its content, but it seems that it led to the compromise that was made in Iceland the same year. It was probably this agreement that was confirmed by Bishop Árni and King Eiríkr at Ögvaldsnes in Norway in 1296 or 1297. Their treaty is preserved and prescribes that those church farms which the Church owned entirely should be ruled by the bishop, but those farms where the Church owned only a half or less should be kept by laymen.[5] (Strangely enough, nothing is prescribed for cases where the Church owned more than half but not the entire farm.) Roughly, this meant that the bishop got control of the *staðir* but laymen retained the other church farms.

Compared with Árni's original aim and the prescription of his Christian Law section, this result was a concession. But in relation to the situation he came home to in 1269, he had won a great victory. It is a fair estimate that the bishops of both dioceses obtained just over 100 church farms to rule over, while the laymen kept over 200.[6]

When this result is evaluated, two things must be noted. First, the dispute probably never applied to more than half the value of each of the laymen's farms at most. For that reason alone the *c.* 100 bishops' farms included at least as much Church property as the *c.* 200 laymen's farms and probably more. Secondly, the dispute did not only concern those *c.* 330 farms; many local churches owned a group of other farms, which in a way belonged to the farm where the church stood. Those farms were also included in the dispute, together with the income from tithes and other church taxes from the whole parish. There is every reason to believe that those properties and incomes were larger on the bishops' farms than on the laymen's farms, so that the Church collected a considerably larger share.

It would be wrong to assume that the arrangement of the Icelandic Church was fixed for centuries at Ögvaldsnes. The bishops did not always invest priests with the church farms, as Bishop Árni did. On the other hand, at some time in the 14th or 15th century the bishops seem to have obtained the right to appoint priests to the laymen's vicarages also. Nevertheless, laymen kept on running these vicarages. Thus a considerable part of the Icelandic *Eigenkirchenwesen* was preserved, and some remnants of it are still at work in Iceland today.

The result of *staðamál* used to be considered one of the most decisive steps towards the ruin of the old Icelandic aristocracy and thereby the gradual loss of Iceland's autonomy.[7] This interpretation has lost some of its support among scholars, since it is now taken into account, more than previously, that the country was to be largely ruled by an Icelandic aristocracy for centuries (see Ch. 2.1). Nevertheless it can be assumed that losing control of most of the richest local churches meant a great change in the status of the internal aristocracy and made it more important than before for its members to enter the service of the king as his sheriffs.

---

[5] *Diplomatarium Islandicum* II (1893), 324-5 (no. 167).

[6] See Magnús Stefánsson (1978), 224-5.

[7] See, for example, Jón Jóhannesson II (1958), 108-9.

2.3 Collapse of the North Atlantic Empire

In the 1260s, when Greenland and Iceland had entered it, the realm of the king of Norway covered an impressive area stretching from the Western Settlement of Greenland to the Barents Sea, including the islands of Faroe, Shetland, Orkney, the Hebrides and the Isle of Man, and reaching down to Gothenburg in Sweden.

In terms of distance it is no great exaggeration to say that Iceland lay at the centre of this empire. From the viewpoint of population numbers, it was of course on the periphery – in spite of its large population compared with later times (see Ch. 1.7). Still, with Bergen as the main residence of the king and Trondheim of the archbishop, Iceland was not remote at all. With a favourable wind, the trip from these centres to any place on Iceland's coast could take less time than riding from the Eastern Quarter of Iceland to the Althing.

The first drastic change in Iceland's position within the realm took place in the days of King Hákon V Magnússon (1299-1319), who moved his main residence from Bergen to Oslo. This move was also consonant with King Hákon's view of his kingdom, which he saw predominantly as a Nordic and not a North Atlantic monarchy, with potential for expansion to the south and south-east. He was so eager to mix the blood of his dynasty with Swedish royalty that he arranged the betrothal of his daughter Ingeborg to Erik, the brother of the Swedish king, when she was in her second year. A decade later they were married, and four years after that they had a son, Magnus. It so happened that this child inherited the crowns of both Norway and Sweden in 1319 when he was three years old.[1]

In Scandinavia a politically unstable period set in at this time. Frequent wars were fought, sometimes kindled by the Hanseatic League, a confederation of powerful trading towns in northern Germany, or by individual German towns and German princes. The Danish state went into complete dissolution during the 1330s. The Norwegians, who felt that King Magnus favoured Sweden, repeatedly revolted against him and finally had his

---

[1] The political development of Scandinavia which is related in this chapter is discussed in all surveys of Scandinavian history. For works in English see Derry (1968), 63-88; Oakley (1969), 44-69; Oakley (1972), 73-92; Popperwell (1972), 93-100; Derry (1979), 64-85.

younger son Hakon installed on the Norwegian throne. A contender to the Swedish throne, Duke Albrecht of Mecklenburg, overthrew Magnus and kept him in captivity for six years. At times, the union of Norway and Iceland was dissolved, since Magnus kept Iceland, and probably some other tributaries, for himself, while his son Hakon ruled in Norway. However, when in 1374 Magnus's ship foundered and he drowned, Hakon succeeded him as the king of Norway and all its tributaries, while Albrecht occupied the throne of Sweden.

As if this turbulence were not enough, the plague epidemic, later known as the Black Death, ravaged Scandinavia just before the middle of the century. It was particularly lethal in Norway, where it has been estimated that the population was decreased by some two-thirds in three successive epidemics during the 14th century, with no considerable growth starting again until the 16th or 17th century.[2]

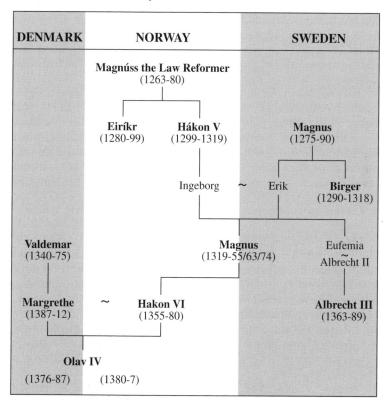

Fig. 2.3-1 Mixing of the Scandinavian dynasties, 14th century.

[2] Walløe (1995), 9-11, 27-35, 41-8.

In his attempts to fight Albrecht, King Hakon VI made an alliance with the Danish king, Valdemar Atterdag, who had managed to restore the Danish monarchy. In 1363 Hakon married the twelve-year-old daughter of King Valdemar, Margrethe. In 1376 their five- or six-year-old son, Olav, succeeded his grandfather on the Danish throne. Four years later King Olav also inherited the Norwegian throne, at the death of his father. That event introduced a personal union of Denmark and Norway, which was to last for more than four centuries, until 1814, and the subjection of Iceland to the Danish Crown, which was not abolished completely and formally until 1944.

Not only did King Olav claim kingship in Denmark and Norway. He was also the sole descendant of the Swedish dynasty in the direct male line and, of course, a contender for the Swedish throne – which also ruled Finland – against Albrecht. His mother, Queen Margrethe, was his guardian, and entered the political scene of Scandinavia in full force and with a flair that has become legendary. It seems likely that the vision of a unified Northern kingdom was born in the mind of an ambitious mother of the noblest child who had ever been born in Scandinavia. If so, her dreams must have come to a tragic end in 1387, when Olav died, suddenly and unexpectedly, when he was only seventeen years old.

However, Margrethe did not give in. She had herself elected as a regent in both Norway and Denmark, with a title that indicates that she was looked on as a sovereign in her own right.[3] She made an alliance with an opposition party in Sweden and was also elected regent there, when Albrecht had been deposed in 1389. Simultaneously she had the six-year old son of her niece brought to her from Pomerania in Germany, adopted him, renamed him Erik and offered him as future king to her Scandinavian subjects. In the following years her offer was accepted and in 1397 King Erik of Pomerania was crowned king of the three Nordic kingdoms at Kalmar in Sweden.

The so-called Kalmar Union proved to be dominated by Denmark, with a virtually unbroken line of kings resident there. In 1448 a new dynasty, the Oldenburgh line, came to power, and was to rule Denmark for more than four centuries. (Conveniently for history students, the kings have, with the sole exception of Hans in 1481-1513, borne alternately the names Christian and Frederik.) Norway remained perfectly loyal to the union, but Sweden did so for only half the time before it finally broke away and elected its own king in the early 1520s. Thus Scandinavia narrowly missed – or escaped – developing into one state in the late Middle Ages, like Spain, which found itself in a similar situation in this period.[4]

Norway still existed as a state with its own council until the council was dissolved because of its resistance to the Reformation in the 1530s.

[3] Bøgh (1997), 2-5.
[4] See Gustafsson (1997), 77.

However, for all practical purposes Norway became in the late Middle Ages a dependency of Denmark, largely ruled by Danish officials. This degeneration of the prosperous Norwegian state is no doubt closely connected with a serious crisis in Norwegian society, entailing the depopulation and desertion of the land, which has been the subject of much scholarly discussion.[5] The explanations have varied, as is the case with the late medieval agrarian crisis of Europe in general, with climatic deterioration and the plague being among the most convincing explanatory factors.

For Iceland the important result of this development was that the country became a dependency of a Danish dependency, with a capital in Copenhagen on far-away Zealand. Iceland's position became even more remote in the next century, when the Danish Crown virtually lost and forgot its dependency in Greenland.[6] The Norse settlement in Greenland had already shrunk considerably, as the Western Settlement was abandoned, reportedly after being attacked by Inuits, in the 14th century. The last ship known to have sailed from the Eastern Settlement to the Nordic countries arrived in Norway in 1410. But strangely, corpses that have been exhumed from a cemetery there were dressed according to late 15th-century European fashion, indicating communication that is completely unrecorded in written sources. Still later, probably around the mid-16th century, a certain Jón, apparently an Icelander, is said to have been a crew member of a German ship that drifted to Greenland. They came ashore on a small island and found one dead man lying face down, demonstrating cultural traits of both Norsemen and Inuits: "He had a hood on his head, well sewn, and clothes from both homespun and sealskin. At his side lay a carving knive bent and worn down by whetting. This knife they took with them for display."[7]

It was not until 1605 that a Danish expedition landed in Greenland and met only Inuits where the Norsemen had lived. And it was more than a century later, in 1721, that a Norwegian clergyman Hans Egede managed to persuade the Danish government to help him found a mission centre in Greenland, mainly to convert the descendants of Norsemen to the proper Lutheran religion. He found none there, but his initiative marked the beginning of actual Danish rule in Greenland. This 300-year-long neglect of Greenland by the Danish Crown shows better than anything else how little interest it had in its North Atlantic dependencies. The idea of a North Atlantic empire had vanished completely.

King Christian I (1448-81) ran his foreign policy in complete accordance with this orientation of the Crown. First, he spent huge sums buying out his rivals from the Duchy of Holstein, with the more northerly Duchy of

---

[5] See *Desertion and Land Colonization in the Nordic Countries* c. *1300-1600* (1981).

[6] See Gad I (1970), 141-318; Gad II (1973), 1-119.

[7] Ólafur Halldórsson (1978), 51 (see also xx and 271-2). My translation.

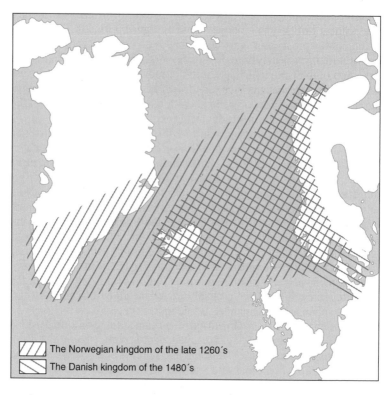

Map 2.3-1 The transfer of Iceland from the North Atlantic empire of the king of Norway, late 13th century (after 1266), to the Nordic, land-based realm of the Danish crown of the late 14th century. The extent of the kingdoms is marked roughly by their outposts, which does not indicate that they controlled or claimed control over the areas of sea seemingly within their boundaries.

Slesvig as a satellite. Then, in order to lessen his debts, he pawned Orkney and Shetland for the dowry of his daughter when he married her to King James III of Scotland. The pledge was never redeemed. From then until Greenland was recolonized, nothing was left of the North Atlantic side of King Hákon Hákonarson's monarchy except for Norway's west coast, Faroe and Iceland. The monarchy of which Iceland became a part in 1380 had minimal interest in the riches of the ocean; it was preoccupied with narrow straits and fertile grain fields on their banks. Denmark's control of both sides of the Sound (which it enjoyed until the 17th century) allowed it to impose a toll on foreign ships passing between the Baltic Sea and the Atlantic. After the incorporation of Holstein into the monarchy, its fertile fields reached all the way south to Hamburg. To this monarchy

Iceland was of little interest, and – for better or worse – this was in many ways characteristic of its history for centuries.

To mention only one consequence of the political development in the late Middle Ages, it was in this period that Icelandic emerged as a separate language (see Ch. 1.10). In Norway the language, especially that of the central government and higher social classes, was heavily influenced by the language of Denmark, which again was strongly influenced by German and particularly Low German. In Iceland the language of course underwent some changes too, but they were mostly of a phonetic kind, which did not affect the grammatical system or demand considerable changes in the written language. For instance, the long vowels [a:], [e:] and [o:] were substituted by the dipthongs [au], [je] and [ou] (either long or short). But they could be written with the same letters, *á*, *é* and *ó*, as before, and no change was apparent in written texts.

In the 16th century the Icelanders found it impossible to call their language Norse any more, even less Danish, and coined the term Icelandic (*íslenska*). Thus in the culturally important field of language the distance between Iceland and its partners in the union was also increasing. Instead of being predominantly connected through a common language, as in the Viking Age and high Middle Ages, Icelandic society was now, together with its geographical remoteness, distinguished mainly by its language.

2.4 Iceland the Fishing Camp

The *Saga of the People of Laxardal* contains the story of a Norwegian family who discuss fleeing King Haraldr Fairhair's tyranny in the late 9th century (see Ch. 1.1). The sons want to settle in Iceland, but their father, Ketill Flat-Nose, remarks: "I do not intend to spend my old age in that fishing camp."[1] If Ketill's words are quoted correctly (which I would not bet on), he showed great foresight. Although fishing was no doubt an important occupation in Iceland in the Commonwealth period (see Ch. 1.7), it was not until the late Middle Ages that the term fishing camp could begin to apply to the country.

In the entire saga literature there is only one rather unreliable piece of evidence for the export of fish from Iceland. One of the two versions of the *Saga of the Confederates*, which takes place in the 11th century but was not written until the late 13th century, describes how a young upstart became wealthy by buying stockfish and going abroad.[2] On the other hand, the export of fish is nowhere mentioned in *Sturlunga saga* or in documents from the Commonwealth period, so it is scarcely possible that it took place on any considerable scale in the 12th and early 13th centuries.

The first concrete evidence of fish exporting from Iceland is an amendment to the Icelandic law code, issued by King Eiríkr Magnússon in 1294, evidently following a request from Iceland. There the king rules: "We do not want much stockfish to be exported from here while there is dearth in the country."[3] If we look for evidence of shortages in Icelandic annals, they tell of unusually heavy snow and the death of livestock in 1291,[4] which may well be the occasion for the king's order three years later. Unfortunately the word "much" is one of the most difficult to interpret in texts from remote times, so that we cannot say anything definite about the amount of fish exported at this time. On the other hand, it seems obvious that it would not have been mentioned had it not been known to take place.

We next hear about Icelandic fish in Lynn in England in 1307. There a Norwegian merchant brought a cargo with, among other goods, "*piscibus*

---

[1] *Complete Sagas of Icelanders* V (1997), 2 (Ch. 2).

[2] *Íslenzk fornrit* VII (1936), 296-7 (Ch. 1). See also *Complete Sagas of Icelanders* V (1997), 284 (Ch. 1).

[3] *Diplomatarium Islandicum* II (1893), 287 (no. 155). My translation.

[4] *Islandske Annaler* (1888), 30, 51, 71, 143, 197, 338, 384.

de Islonde".[5] Two decades later, in 1319, the Icelandic representatives at the Althing passed a resolution on the conditions for swearing allegiance to King Magnus Erikson. There they repeated and expanded the clause of the 1294 amendment: "We do not want more stockfish and meal to be exported, while there is dearth in the country, than merchants need for their maintenance."[6] The mention of meal does indeed cast some doubt on the economic importance of this export, since it seems unlikely that grain has ever been exported from Iceland on any considerable scale.

We have to wait until two decades later for unambiguous evidence that fish export from Iceland has become considerable. In 1340 a sentence was passed in Bergen, Norway, in a case against merchants who had sailed to Iceland and refused to pay a tithe on stockfish, fish oil and sulphur in their cargoes. They claimed their right to pay it only on homespun, "as all other merchants coming from Iceland had done before them, according to ancient custom". However, they got the answer that

. . . until recently little stockfish was exported from Iceland, and was called consumption fish, but in homespun large quantities. But now is brought from Iceland a lot of excellent goods in stockfish and fish oil.[7]

"Recently" (*fyrir skömmu*) is also a difficult word in history. However, it is reasonably safe to assume that large-scale export of fish products from Iceland started in the period between the time covered by *Sturlunga saga*, which ends in the 1260s, and the sentence of 1340.

Further support for the dating of this important innovation lies in the gradual change of the location of centres of power and culture in Iceland. The episcopal sees of Skálholt and Hólar had been placed far from the coast; Haukadalur, the residence of the important Haukdælir family, lies almost as far from the coast as one can settle in Iceland. Most of the monasteries and convents had been located in farming rather than fishing districts, with the interesting exceptions of Helgafell in Snæfellsnes (1184) and Viðey (1225). Most chieftains of the Sturlungar age (see Ch. 1.13) seemed to rely on farming in their choice of residence; Snorri Sturluson moved from Borg, by the sea, up to Reykholt. Gizurr Þorvaldsson lived at some seven different farms during his adventurous career, only three of them being reasonably close to fishing stations.

On the other hand, from the 14th century onwards the most prosperous families tended to settle and to obtain farms in the coastal areas of the western part of the country, in Vatnsfjörður in Ísafjörður, Reykhólar, and Skarð in Skarðsströnd. At the same time, the Crown chose Bessastaðir in Álftanes as its centre in the country (see Ch. 2.1).

---

[5] *Diplomatarium Norvegicum* XIX (1914), 515 (no. 436). See also Nedkvitne (1983), 502.

[6] *Diplomatarium Islandicum* II (1893), 498 (no. 343). My translation.

[7] *Diplomatarium Islandicum* II (1893), 729 (no. 469). My translation.

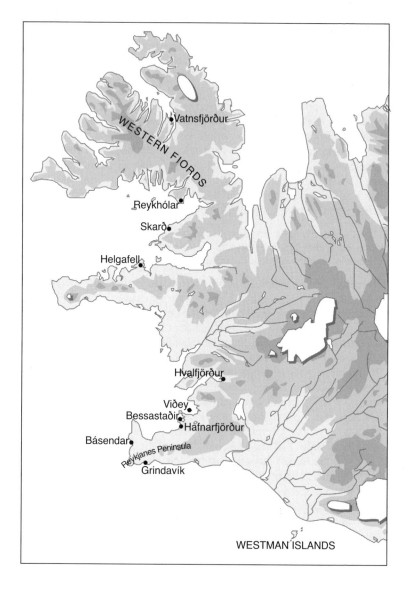

Map 2.4-1 Some important fishing stations, trading harbours and centres of power and administration in western Iceland, late Middle Ages.

This was probably the development period of the system of mixed farming and fishing that was to characterize Iceland for centuries. Farming was seen as the basic occupation and, in most cases, it determined people's main residence. In other words, it was at the farming residences that the women lived and the children were raised. Fishing was predominantly carried out in late winter, from January or February until May. This was the time of the year when a small workforce was needed in farming, and also when the cod comes to the southern and western coast of Iceland for spawning. Those who lived at or close to fishing stations, of course, just set out in their boats from their own landing places. But most of the fishermen lived in primitive camps during the fishing season. They were farmers and farm-hands and came, on horseback or on foot, from the southern lowland and the Northern Quarter to the fishing camps on the western and south-western coast – roughly from Snæfellsnes in the west to the Westman Islands in the south.

Fishing was almost exclusively carried out in open rowing-boats with two to twelve oars, often with a mast that could hold up a sail if the wind was favourable. Complicated skills were developed to recognize fishing banks by landmarks (the Icelandic word for fishing bank is *fiskimið*, or simply *mið*, which originally meant "landmark") and also to land boats, even on sandy beaches facing the open ocean, to forecast weather and so on. The fishing gear was mostly hand-line and hook.[8]

The fishing stations consisted of what can be described as seasonal villages. But hardly anywhere until the 19th century did fishing develop into a year-round occupation with its own fishing towns. It is open to discussion whether this was due to the practicality of the symbiosis of farming and fishing or to political dictates. What we do know is that the indigenous rulers of the country, the group of landowners who held most of the royal offices (see Chs 2.1 and 2.12), kept almost constantly to the policy, already adopted in the Commonwealth period (see Ch. 1.8), that those who did not acquire the status of farmers – of either sex – should be in year-round service as farm-hands.[9] This policy served a double purpose. First, it restricted the number of households who relied on fishing for their maintenance and were, rightly or not, more likely to become a burden to the community in years of hardship than farming people. Secondly, it secured a workforce for the farmers, and often a profitable one, since it was customary for the farmers to send their farm-hands fishing, take all their share of the catch and pay them only low annual wages. It may well have been the practice for centuries, although I do not find it recorded until the early 20th century, that it was thought to be a poor fishing season if a

---

[8] The basic work on the ethnography of Icelandic fishing is Lúðvík Kristjánsson I-V (1980-6).

[9] Guðbrandur Jónsson (1932-4), 130-1; Gísli Gunnarsson (1983a), 21-2.

farm-hand who went to the fishing station did not earn his master the equivalent of what the latter paid him in money as annual wages.[10]

The origin of the large-scale export of stockfish from Iceland in the 14th century is normally attributed to improved trading routes and a growing demand for fish in Central Europe. By this time the German Hanseatic League had gained control of fish export from Norway and had its Norwegian headquarters in Bergen. As far as we know, the Germans did not sail to Iceland for fish in the 14th century. They left that to the Norwegians, and occasionally Icelanders also owned ocean-going ships in this period; for instance, ships were owned by the sees. But the Germans were ready to buy fish in Bergen and sell it on the Continent, where the spread of Christianity eastwards meant an increased demand for fish as lenten fare, and the growth of towns increased the demand for fish oil for street lighting.

This development was extremely important for Iceland, although may be not so much because of the import of necessities that were bought in exchange for the fish. It seems likely that more nourishment was exported as fish than imported as grain, and most other peasant necessities were available in the country (see Ch. 1.7). More important was the contact with European culture which relied on ships that ploughed through the North Atlantic in search of precious stockfish. It may be fanciful to imagine the Icelanders passing into oblivion as the Greenlanders, who were ten or twenty times less numerous, had done (see Ch. 2.3). However, remaining within the sphere of European culture demanded constant communication, which could only be secured by profitable trade.

Since it was as lenten fare that Icelandic stockfish became popular in Europe, it can be maintained that the most important decision ever made about Iceland's fate was the one that allowed the eating of fish in lent. Originally Christian fasting consisted in abstaining from all eating, in vegetarianism, or at least in consuming no meat and wine. It would seem logical to count fish as a kind of meat, but from the 7th and 8th centuries onwards it gradually became customary to accept that eating fish was sufficiently ascetic to be allowed in Lent and at other fasts.[11] This theory became more important for the future inhabitants of Iceland than any other.

[10] Haraldur Ólafsson (1987), 73.

[11] *Dictionary of the Middle Ages* V (1985), 18 (Daniel Callam).

2.5 Plague Without Rats

It was maintained at the end of last chapter that communication was important for Iceland's fate, not that it was necessarily beneficial or that isolation was always an evil. As a reminder of this point, we should note that isolation saved Iceland from the Black Death of the mid-14th century, which affected the Norwegians so badly (see Ch. 2.3). On the other hand, it was because of communication that the country was not spared for more than half a century. In 1402 a plague epidemic arrived in Iceland and raged until 1404, but it does not seem to have become endemic, and nothing is heard of plague epidemics there again until 1494-5 when another one swept through the whole country except for the peninsula of the Western Fiords, which was spared entirely this time.[1] No plague epidemics are recorded in Iceland after this – at least, no major ones – so in Iceland we talk about the first and second plagues which framed the 15th century.

Unfortunately for plague studies, the 15th century is the only period in Iceland's history that has left no extensive written narratives. Most of the Icelandic annals, which guide the historian through the third part of the 13th century after the end of *Sturlunga saga*, and the 14th century, come to an end before 1400. Only one contemporary annal, the so-called *New Annal* (*Nýi annáll*), is preserved from the 15th century, and that only goes up to 1430. From then on, one annal from the late 16th century, *Gottskálk's Annal* (*Gottskálks annáll*), and a few 17th-century annals relate the events of the period from year to year – Icelanders kept the medieval custom of writing annals until well into the 19th century. The 16th- and 17th-century annals are evidently based to a certain extent on lost sources from the 15th century, but most are extremely short, and often it cannot be determined at all what is old and what new in them.

New Annal describes the advent of the plague with the ship of a certain Einarr Herjólfsson in 1402, and later sources add that it landed at the harbour of Hvalfjörður in western Iceland. *New Annal* names the pastor, Áli Svarthöfðason, who died first, "in the autumn", and from other sources we know that the date of death of a man with the same name is 26 August.[2] So we can assume that the epidemic started its course in Iceland just after the middle of August. By Christmas it had reached the bishop's see at

---

[1] The most extensive study of plague in Iceland is Gunnar Karlsson and Helgi Skúli Kjartansson (1994). For a briefer study in English, see Gunnar Karlsson (1996a).

[2] Jón Steffensen (1974), 45-6.

Skálholt, according to the *New Annal*, and the district of Skagafjörður in the central north, according to documentary evidence. *New Annal* refers to 1403 as the year of great mortality and names people who died, both in the central Western Fiords and in the central Eastern Quarter. The autumn of 1403 is referred to in a document as the second autumn of pestilence, which confirms that it lasted for more than a year. According to an annal, it receded shortly after Easter 1404, thus persisting in the country for more than 19 months.

The course of the second epidemic is more obscure. However, it can be deduced from annals and documents that it arrived somewhere in the south-western part of the country in 1494, raging through the winter and probably until the autumn of 1495. A foothold in documentary evidence is provided by the will of the lady Solveig Björnsdóttir, made at Skarð in the Dalir District in the central west on 17 January 1495, and an attestation of her death from plague, which took place in Húnavatnsþing in the north-west, before 28 March. This clearly indicates that Solveig fled the plague to the north (January was not the month for voluntary travels in Iceland), but the calamity followed her and caught up with her in Húnavatnsþing.

The annalists are preoccupied with the scarcity of priests after the epidemics. According to one annal, only six priests survived in the diocese of Hólar and scarcely fifty in that of Skálholt after the first epidemic. After the second one twenty priests are said to have survived in the diocese of Hólar, but no information is preserved from Skálholt. If we take these numbers literally, they give death rates of 80-95% among priests, which is a bit too much to believe. Nevertheless, even if we allow for some exaggeration and uncertainty in the confusion after the epidemics, the low numbers of surviving priests indicate that not many localities were altogether spared by the plague (apart from the Western Fiords in the second epidemic). Although the priest may have been more exposed than other people, since he administered the sacrament to the sick and met, at church services and funerals, more infected individuals than the average person, his death indicates that the plague visited his parish.

The annals contain much miscellaneous information about death rates. Some give numbers that are far too high to be taken literally, while others seem more reasonable. Thus *New Annal* tells that at the convent of Kirkjubær the abbess and seven sisters died, but six sisters survived, which gives a death rate of 57%. Of the monastery of Þykkvibær the annalist tells two stories (one of which may be intended to refer to another monastery). The first gives a death rate of 54%, the other still higher. The bishop's residence of Skálholt was almost emptied of people in 1402; only the bishop and two laymen survived, which would give a death rate of at least 97%, if we do not suppose that some of the servants fled the see. In 1404, the plague visited Skálholt again and deprived the see of servants "three times". This time, three priests died and two survived.

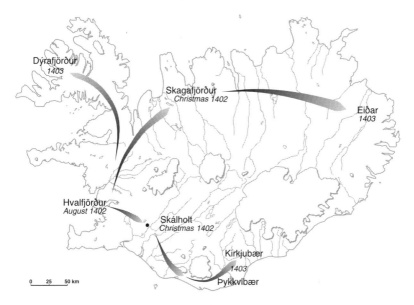

Map. 2.5-1 The spread of the plague epidemic of 1402-4: its major steps that can be deduced from written sources. It is not known whether the epidemic spread to the east from the north, as indicated here, or from the south, but the former seems more likely considering transport routes. Apart from the spread shown on the map, the high death-rate among priests, which is accounted for in the sources, makes it likely that the epidemic visited most parishes in the country.

A poignant portrayal of the second epidemic is given in the *Bishops' Annals* (Biskupaannálar), by the clergyman Jón Egilsson. He wrote his annals in 1605, and based the description of the epidemic partly on accounts by eyewitnesses. He says:

In this plague the mortality was so great, that no-one remembered or had heard of anything like it, because at many farms all people were exterminated, and on most farms only three or two survived, sometimes children, usually two or mostly three, and some of them yearlings, and some of them sucking from their dead mothers. Of these I saw one, who was called Tungufells-Manga. [. . .] Where there had been nine children, two or three were left alive.[3]

It would be reasonable to guess that eight people had been living at each farm, with crofters and two-family households on some of them (see Ch. 2.14). If none, or two or three survived on each farm, and of nine children two or three lived, as Jón maintains, a direct conclusion from his evidence would be a mortality rate of 70-80% on farms that were visited by the

[3] *Safn til sögu Íslands* I (1856), 43. My translation.

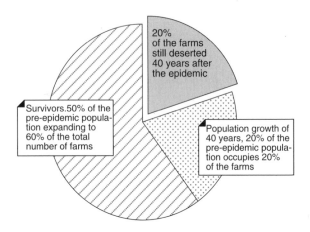

Fig. 2.5-1 Model of the desertion of farms after the first plague epidemic, if the death rate was 50%, and 20% of the farms were still deserted forty years after the epidemic.

plague. But how many farms were spared altogether? From the evidence of Jón Egilsson, it may be concluded that people in the area spoke about it as an exception if a farm escaped. If 10% of the farms did so, and the remaining 90% suffered a 70% death rate, that would lead to an overall death rate of 63% in localities that were affected. If we assume that 5% of all localities escaped (apart from the Western Fiords), we come down to a 60% death rate, which is not far from the conclusion one would draw from New Annal's description of the first plague.

This, of course, is highly speculative, but there are other sources independent of the annals that can be used for comparison and control. From around four decades after the first epidemic, from the years 1431-49 to be exact, we have a number of lists of farms from northern and western Iceland, where one can find which farms were deserted. The overall result is that almost 20% of them were. It would be so complicated to deduce a death rate from that number that we must go the other way round and draw up a simple model. Let us suppose that out of every 100 people living in 1402, fifty died in the epidemic. In the very first years, this may not have led to an immense desertion of farms, while the survivors clung to their homesteads, but fairly soon households reached sizes that were practical in the circumstances: orphans were adopted by relatives or taken in as servants, widows and widowers remarried, and so on. Still, we may assume that ten of the fifty survivors used the opportunity to settle on farms that were available after the epidemic, so that fifty people inhabited 60% of the farms that had been occupied by our population of 100. The availability of land meant availability of early marriages and hence rapid procreation, so we get a 1% average population growth during the forty-year period between the epidemic and the writing of the preserved lists of farms. To keep the model simple, I leave out the growth rate of the additional population born after 1404. Thus, a 1% population growth among fifty persons in forty years provides an addition of twenty persons, who inhabit 20% of the farms. By 1444, 20% of the farms were still deserted, as the lists of farms indicate. Thus the rate of deserted farms around 1444 fits the assumption of a 50% mortality rate.

If we proceed from 1444 with a slowly decreasing rate of population growth, the pre-1402 number may well have been reached by the arrival of the second epidemic in 1494. There is also considerable evidence of desertion of farms after this epidemic, though this appears to have had a slightly lower death rate than the first.

All in all, it can be assumed from these data that the first epidemic in Iceland killed some 50-60% of the population, but the second one maybe 30-50%. If these estimates seem too high or too daring, it can be pointed out that even if decreased by 10%, they would verify that the plague epidemics in Iceland were no less lethal than the Black Death in Europe in the mid-14th century.

I have dwelt on the issue of mortality because I wanted to prove that we had real, devastating plague epidemics in Iceland. This is necessary because it concerns the question of dissemination of the medieval plague pandemic in general. When, early in the 20th century, it was discovered how the present pandemic spread in China and India, it was generally assumed that plague could only form major epidemics when it was spread by fleas, which carried the bacteria between rats and people. In truth, it has been known most of the time that plague can also spread in at least two other ways: by fleas that live predominantly on humans, without rats, and as pneumonia from person to person. Still, some scholars stick to rat-flea dissemination as the only possible explanation of the Black Death.[4]

These general considerations concern us here, because it can be safely ruled out that rats played any role in the dissemination of plague in medieval Iceland. Firstly, there is no evidence of rats in Iceland, either in written sources or in archaeological excavations, until the late 17th or even 18th century. In a description of the nature of Iceland written by an Icelandic bishop in the 1660s, it is stated explicitly that there are no rats in the country. The extremely accurate and scholarly study of Iceland by Eggert Ólafsson in the mid-18th century (see Ch. 2.16) mentions rats in only one place, Snæfellsnes, where they are said to have recently arrived by ship.

---

[4] See, for example, Benedictow (1992).

Secondly, it is difficult to see how the rat or rat flea could spread the disease around a country like Iceland as quickly as it did spread, with no carriages of any kind, with mountain passages between districts, and with unbridged rivers, so deep and rapid that they could only be forded on horses at chosen places. Thirdly, the plague spread in temperatures that were far below the level of 10-18°C, which is known to form the lower limit for the rat flea to be active. As related above, it is incontrovertible that the epidemics raged through the middle of winter in Iceland, even in the coolest regions of the inhabitable parts of the country, with an average winter temperature very probably well below zero in the open air.

It is beyond the scope of this work to discuss whether the plague in Iceland spread by species of fleas that did not depend on rats, or in its pneumonic form, or even in yet another, unknown way. However, two arguments for the pneumonic plague can be mentioned. Firstly, there is no mention in Icelandic sources of the carbuncles that normally characterize flea-borne plague. Secondly, no one is reported to have recovered from the plague in Iceland, which fits the fact that pneumonic plague kills practically all who catch it.

Although the plague epidemics were extremely lethal in Iceland, it is difficult to point out any drastic long-term economic or social consequences of them. Many people who lived directly on livestock probably lived in better conditions than before, since they had more and better land on which to make hay and graze their livestock. Those who lived on the labour of others, the landowning aristocracy and the Church, must have suffered severe losses. However, there are no signs of a general collapse or disintegration of society. Documents testify that the Althing was held in 1404 and in 1407 (and probably in the years between, about which no evidence is preserved). In 1405, the governor of Iceland, the Icelander Vigfúss Ívarsson, held a great wedding feast at Viðey for a couple who must have been relatives of his. In the same year, a well-known Icelandic couple, Björn Einarsson and Solveig Þorsteinsdóttir, started their pilgrimage to Rome and Jerusalem. From the year after the second plague, a number of sentences are preserved, which proves that the judiciary systems, both secular and ecclesiastical, were workable. The resolution of Áshildarmýri (see Ch. 2.1) was passed in the same year.

As elsewhere in European history, practically all changes in the late Middle Ages, especially changes for the worse, have been attributed to the plague. However, closer study seems to reveal that these were mostly long-term developments, which the epidemics may sometimes have accelerated, but, then again, the scarcity of people after the epidemics could just as well have slowed down the developments instead. For instance, it is likely that the epidemics increased the landed property of the Church, since many dying people gave it land for the sake of their souls. All in all, however, fewer people died in Iceland in the Middle Ages than would have been the case if the plague had not reached the country, but of course those who died in the decades following the epidemic were on average richer in landed property and perhaps correspondingly more generous towards the Church.

In fact, it seems just as likely that the epidemics postponed changes and thus acted as a conservative force. If the country had been overfilled with people in the 15th and early 16th centuries, it seems unlikely that the Icelandic authorities could have hindered the emergence of permanent fishing villages, perhaps more or less under the protection and rule of English and later German merchants (see Chs 2.6 and 2.7). The epidemics may have relieved the country of a population pressure that would have led to inevitable economic and social transformation. Later on, other epidemics, especially smallpox, were repeatedly going to solve the same problem in their merciless way.

2.6 The English Century

In the 14th century, if not earlier, English merchants became acquainted with Icelandic stockfish in Bergen in Norway, where they competed constantly and sometimes violently with their German counterparts over the fish supply. However, we do not know if it was this acquaintance that gave English fishermen the idea, shortly after the turn of the 15th century, to sail to Iceland for fishing. What we do know is that in 1415 emissaries from the Danish-Norwegian monarchy had already asked the king of England to prohibit the sailing of English ships to Iceland; the Lower House of the English Parliament protested and maintained that English fishermen had fished off Iceland for six or seven years, after some unspecified fishing grounds, probably off England, where fish had been caught for salt-processing, had been depleted.[1]

In Icelandic sources, English fishermen are first mentioned in 1412. In that year *New Annal* records that an English fishing boat arrived to the east of Dyrhólmaey, the southernmost point of Iceland. The following winter, the *Annal* continues, five Englishmen stayed in Iceland because, according to their story, they were sent ashore to buy food and were left behind. In the next year, an English trading ship arrived in Iceland, provided with a licence from the king of Denmark-Norway. This year also, at least thirty English fishing boats sailed to Iceland. On Maundy Thursday 1419, the New Annal claims, at least twenty-five English ships went down around Iceland in bad weather.[2] Later in the 15th century, there are reasons to believe that some 100 English fishing boats went to Iceland annually, most of them from the ports of East Anglia. Customs accounts from England indicate that, on average, some ten trading ships sailed to Iceland annually in the period 1430-1550, most of them large ships, which could carry 100-400 tons and had up to ninety men in their crew. Inevitably such a large number of foreign sailors, some of them armed, would usually get what they wanted in the practically defenceless Iceland. At times the country may have been ruled by the English almost as much as by the Danes in the 15th century, which accordingly has assumed the name "the English century" in Icelandic historiography.[3]

[1] *Diplomatarium Islandicum* XVI (1952-72), 227-8 (no. 80).

[2] *Annálar 1400-1800* I (1922-7), 18-22.

[3] The term was coined by the Icelandic historian Björn Þorsteinsson, whose dissertation on this period (1970) is the basic work about it. English documents about Iceland

118

After Iceland entered the Norwegian kingdom, the Crown seems to have assumed extensive rights to prohibit sailing to the country, and in the 14th century these rights were applied to serve the official policy of making Bergen a staple of stockfish trade in the realm and prohibiting the traffic of foreigners to its more remote parts. Therefore, a prohibition of English sailing to Iceland was only to be expected. Attempts on behalf of the English to ignore the prohibition were equally predictable, making clashes inevitable.

In 1425 the English went so far as to capture the Danish governor in Iceland, Hannes Paulsson, and take him with them to England. There he wrote a long report of complaints, where he listed the crimes which the English had committed in Iceland. They had settled in the Westman Islands, which were a royal property, and built fortifications around their camps there. They had devastated a valley in the north, Ólafsfjörður (a locality with some twenty farms around 1700), and burnt down a number of churches. They kidnapped children or enticed their parents to give them away for small gifts. On the whole, the governor does not have much respect for his Icelandic subjects: "Those who are considered to be chiefs in this country can be tempted in a foolishly easy way with requests, drinks or bribes. Nevertheless the poor common people believe them and get tricked."[4]

There are, of course, good reasons to be sceptical of the governor's evidence, and he may well have blamed the English for devastation that was due to the plague (see Ch. 2.5). *New Annal* does not report any harassment by the English except for a few minor robberies of livestock and stockfish. In 1425, the *Annal* relates that the governor's pages shot a man dead in the churchyard of Helgafell monastery. After this, it adds that Hannes was captured in the Westman Islands and brought to England, "which was regretted by few".[5] Then again the author of *New Annal* may well be biased in favour of the English; they had naturally acquired contacts among the Icelandic population.

At least it is known to be true, as Governor Hannes maintained, that the English stole Icelandic children; a Danish bishop of Skálholt, Jón Gerreksson,[6] went to England in 1429 on his way to his see and managed to expose the kidnapping of some thirteen Icelandic children. This was the origin of a

---

in the 15th and early 16th century are published in the original languages in *Diplomatarium Islandicum* XVI (1952-72). For a report on these sources, see Björn Þorsteinsson (1969).

[4] *Diplomatarium Islandicum* IV (1897), 324-34 (no. 381). See also Björn Þorsteinsson (1953), 148-58.

[5] *Annálar 1400-1800* I (1922-7), 19-24.

[6] The Icelandic form of the bishop's name is used here, since Icelanders are the only people who keep up his memory. The Latinized form is Johannes Gerechini Lodehat. See Björn Þorsteinsson (1976a).

long-held belief about Iceland in the geographical literature of Europe, that the inhabitants used to give away their children but sold their dogs dear.[7]

Even more mysterious than the case of Hannes Paulsson is the fate of Bishop Jón Gerreksson of Skálholt. When he met his death, New Annal had come to an end, and no contemporary annals are preserved after its ending in 1430 until the second half of the 16th century. From strictly contemporary sources we know only that the bishop was killed in the spring of 1433. The Curia obviously assumed that the killers could be found in Iceland, because two successors of Bishop Jón, in 1448 and 1474, were commissioned to absolve them and set them suitable penances. After the revival of annal-writing in Iceland, the annalists claimed to know a lot about the event and blamed it mainly on the foreign pages of the bishop. In addition to other crimes, they are said to have captured two young upper-class Icelanders and held them in prison at Skálholt. When they escaped, they attacked the see in revenge, seized the bishop in the church, put him into a sack and drowned him in a nearby river. The attackers were well-known Icelanders and were obviously held in high respect in the country after the outrage.

During the heyday of nationalist historiography in Iceland, this was seen as a perfectly comprehensible story; it was just one among many testimonies of the undesirability of having foreign rulers in the country. But in the second half of the 20th century, when the nationalist interpretation of history had come into disrepute, scholars began to look for other explanations. It has been suggested that Bishop Jón, who had been the king's man, had committed some major crime against the Crown, perhaps through some kind of alliance with the English, and was assassinated on the command of the king.[8] Another suggestion is that the bishop was killed by Icelandic allies of the English, perhaps at the behest of the Bishop of Hólar, the Englishman John Williamson Craxton. In that case the immunity of the killers would be a sign of an absolute lack of control in Iceland on the part of the Crown.[9] However, no such conclusion can be drawn, because, after all, no one has been able to disprove that it was the misdeeds of the bishop's escort that prompted his death. In fact the author of *New Annal*, who was probably alive when the bishop was murdered, may be hinting at this explanation when he describes the arrival of Bishop Jón in 1430: "He was accompanied by many pages, who pretended to be Danish. Most of them were of little use to the country, therefore I do not bother to write down their names."[10]

In contrast to Bishop Jón, it seems perfectly clear who killed the king's governor, the native Icelander Björn Þorleifsson, in 1467. At this time the

[7] Helgi Þorláksson (1983).

[8] Skarphéðinn Pétursson (1959), 77-8.

[9] Björn Þorsteinsson (1976a).

[10] *Annálar 1400-1800* I (1922-7), 27. My translation.

kings of England and Denmark had failed to reach an agreement on the Sound fee which the Danish king had imposed on foreign ships (see Ch. 2.3). Perhaps for this reason the Danish king withdrew all licences that he had issued to English ships to sail to Iceland. Then some English merchants went to Iceland without a licence, killed the governor (probably because he tried to expel them), threw his body into the sea, stole gold, silver and clothing from his wife and children, burnt down houses and seized the taxes collected for the king. This is the version of the king himself, and it is largely supported by other documentary evidence.

In Icelandic tradition, on the other hand, the episode has developed into a heroic tale of the widow, Ólöf Loftsdóttir, who is reported to have said when she heard the news: "Let us not cry for Björn, but gather troops." In another version she is said to have had all the Englishmen she could find in Iceland executed; twelve of them she had tied to a single piece of rope and beheaded. However, there is no documentary evidence of any revenge for Björn Þorleifsson in Iceland which, if it had taken place, would surely have been mentioned in some of the endless complaints and charges that were exchanged between the kings of Denmark and England in these years. Perhaps the image of the Icelandic hero as a woman may be seen as expressing a feeling of the utter defencelessness of the country.

Although Björn Þorleifsson was probably not avenged by his wife, it can be maintained that he was honoured with a greater revenge than any other Icelander. In 1468-73 Denmark and the Hanseatic League fought a war against England which we in Iceland like to see as triggered by the killing of Björn,[11] although undeniably there had been no lack of controversies between the states before that. However, in the wake of the war German merchants obtained a stronger hold on Icelandic trade than before, so the English century was approaching its end.

English fishing off Iceland was the beginning of the foreign exploitation of fishing grounds around the country, which was to last uninterrupted until the late 1970s (see Ch. 4.11). In the 15th century the English connection no doubt brought many a novelty into the life of Icelanders. Never before had such a variety of shoes and boots, linen and cloths, tools, weapons and wine been available in the country. However, it is not easy to point to any lasting influence of the English presence. The Icelanders did not imitate the English way of fishing, on decked vessels for salting. Nor did the English fishing camps develop into permanent villages with inhabitants living predominantly on fishing, perhaps because the plague epidemics reduced the population pressure on the countryside (see Ch. 2.5). Furthermore the English influence on the Icelandic language seems negligible until the 20th century.

It may be that the English Iceland traffic had a more profound and lasting effect in England than in Iceland. It was the first regular long-distance

[11] See Björn Þorsteinsson (1970), 213-20.

ocean sailing that was undertaken by the English. Thus it served as a rehearsal for sailing to North America in the 16th century and the subsequent conquest of the world. The contradictory fact is that Iceland never became a part of the British Empire, for which it had served as a training ground. According to Björn Þorsteinsson's suggestion, this did not happen because Denmark had the means of putting pressure on England if it did not behave properly in Iceland. At any time, the Sound could be closed to English ships. As Björn Þorsteinsson himself puts it,[12] "The cannons at Krogen [a Danish castle by the Sound] have been more effective than anything else for Iceland's defence."

[12] Björn Þorsteinsson (1976a), 506. My translation.

2.7 Enter the Germans

Before the establishment of the Hanseatic League in the 14th century (see Ch. 2.3), German merchants were already resident in Bergen in Norway, and around the mid-14th century a Hansa centre (*Kontor*) was founded there. Normally, the German merchants in Bergen were not allowed to sail to the tributaries for trading, although they may occasionally have bought licences to do so, as Hannes Paulsson hints in his report of 1425 (see Ch. 2.6), when he complains that the English have "violated . . . the trade of foreign merchants of the [Norwegian] state, who have got licences to trade" in Iceland. In the same year the king also complains about foreign merchants who sail to the tributaries – Halogaland, Finnmark, Iceland and others.[1] These merchants were most probably Germans living in Bergen. But the first ship that is reported to have sailed from a German town without calling in at Norway made its journey in 1431 or 1432. According to a contemporary testimony it came from Danzig and was loaded with goods in England, which were sold in Iceland. The testimony was given because a crew member was killed in Iceland on 20 March 1432.[2]

However, it was not until around 1470, during or after the war against England (see Ch. 2.6), that German merchants not resident in Bergen began to frequent Iceland. In 1481 their activity was seen as such a threat to the interests of Bergen that the Germans there, dominated by Lübeck merchants, complained to other Hansa towns and demanded that the Hanseatic League forbid its members to sail to Iceland except through Bergen. This the Hanseatic Diet did repeatedly in the following years, but to no avail. The German Iceland trade was mainly run from Hamburg, against the official policy of the Hanseatic League, and no doubt contributed to its dissolution.

At first most of the stockfish, which the Germans were after in Iceland, was brought to England and sold there. The Germans were thus penetrating the trade route between Iceland and England, rather than stealing the fish for their home country. But around the turn of the 16th century they seem to have sold most of it in German towns. A report from 1514 informs us that at that time six to ten ships sailed from Hamburg to Iceland annually and brought the fish directly home to Hamburg. The goods that were

---

[1] *Diplomatarium Islandicum* IV (1897), 321 (no. 380).
[2] *Diplomatarium Islandicum* V (1899-1902), 8-9 (nos 10-11).

exported to Iceland were, at least partially, of German origin. At any rate German annals tell of a riot in Hamburg in 1483 raised by townspeople who maintained that they starved because all grain was taken to Iceland.[3]

The arrival of the German traders soon led to clashes with the English over the Iceland trade. The Danish Crown tended to collaborate with the Germans and even made a German sea captain, Didrich Pining, a governor in Iceland. After that it happened that Englishmen, whose fellow-countrymen had run fortified fishing camps in the Westman Islands earlier in the century (see Ch. 2.6), had to resign themselves to pillage in the Islands, after Pining had claimed duties from them and robbed them of all their goods. The English Crown replied by offering naval protection to ships going to Iceland from England.[4] In trade at all major centres where large ships could operate, the Germans were undoubtedly gaining ground in these years. In fishing, on the other hand, and probably in the considerable amount of small-scale trade run in connection with fishing, the English probably kept their share largely intact.

Around 1490 King Hans of Denmark adopted a completely new foreign policy which aimed at collecting powerful allies in preparation for regaining Sweden for the Crown (see Ch. 2.3). In 1489 he confirmed the old privileges of the Hanseatic League in his realm. In January 1490 he concluded a treaty with the English Crown, whereby all subjects of the English king were allowed to sail freely to Iceland for all future trading and fishing, provided they paid ordinary duties and taxes and bought licences from the Danish king every seventh year. In March, King Hans gave Dutch towns the equally free or even freer right to trade in Iceland. The attempt to keep Iceland as an annexe of Bergen was abandoned completely.

This news was brought to Iceland by Didrich Pining and made known at the Althing. The Althing reacted by passing a new law, called Pining's Verdict, the gist of which is as follows:

(1) German and English merchants shall keep peace between them, while they are in Icelandic harbours. No one is to trade with anybody who violates the peace.

(2) No foreigners are allowed to stay in Iceland through the winter, except in urgent need, if they are wounded or sick or their ships are damaged. If they do, they may not sell their goods more dearly than in summer, have Icelandic people in their service or run boats for fishing. Whoever houses foreigners staying illegally in the country shall be punished as if he had housed an outlaw.

---

[3] Björn Þorsteinsson (1970) is the basic work on the origin of German trade in Iceland.

[4] The conflicts over the fishing grounds around Iceland from the 15th century to 1976, which the English press referred to as cod wars, have been described by Björn Þorsteinsson (1976b).

(3) No cottars shall be in the country – those who do not have livestock for their maintenance, even those who own no less than the equivalent of three hundreds ells homespun, men as well as women. All who own less are obliged to work for farmers, men as well as women.[5]

It is not known who initiated Pining's Verdict – Pining himself or the Icelandic officials and better-off farmers at the Althing. In any case the Verdict clearly illustrates the continuing policy of the Icelandic élite, already mentioned in Chapters 1.8 and 2.4, that all those who could not afford to run a farm of their own were supposed to work as farm-hands. No occupation independent of farming was to be tolerated in the country. Therefore, trade could not be accepted as a year-long occupation; hence no foreigners were allowed to stay in the country permanently or to run fishing on their own.

The royal administration in Iceland had no means of enforcing the regulations of Pining's Verdict against foreign merchants – either to make them keep peace between themselves or to abstain from staying in the country throughout the winter. Icelandic, English and German sources also relate a number of incidents when ships belonging to one of the competitors were captured by the other, cargoes seized and men killed. The conflict of 1532 is particularly well documented.[6]

The skirmishes began in the natural harbour of Básendar on the southwestern Reykjanes peninsula. At the beginning of April, the crews of two English ships, 140 men in all, fought a bloody battle with cannons, crossbows and spears, against a German crew of thirty, supported by an additional eighty German and Icelandic men. The Germans won, beheaded two of the English for old offences and tortured two others until they were close to death. Then the English had to hand over 40 tons of stockfish before they were allowed to sail away on one of their ships, while the other one lay stranded in the harbour.

The Englishmen fled to Grindavík, which had been among the most important English harbours in Iceland for a long time. In June they were attacked there by a German or German-Icelandic force, either 180 or 280 men strong, headed by the royal bailiff at Bessastaðir. Again the English lost – fifteen of them fell in the battle, and the crew of one ship drowned when the ship was stranded in its flight from the scene of the battle. All Englishmen were either killed or expelled from Grindavík, whether they had been involved in the conflicts or not.

This conflict reached such a scale that the English and Danish kings themselves, together with the Council of Hamburg, concluded a peace treaty on it in 1533. According to the treaty, sailing to Iceland was to remain free

---

[5] *Diplomatarium Islandicum* VI (1900-4), 703-5 (no. 617). This is not an exact translation of the clauses, nor are they numbered in the original.

[6] This is dealt with thoroughly, with references to original sources, by Björn Þorsteinsson (1976b), 56-89.

for Englishmen and Hamburgers. However, the Althing seems to have restricted this freedom considerably in the summer, when it confirmed the
treaty and added that the sailing of fishing vessels (*duggarar*) was to be
prohibited, "because they rob both property and people from this poor
country and thus reduce the tax of our gracious Lord the King and the
tithe of our God".[7] In the same year this verdict was confirmed by the Norwegian Council of State (which executed royal power in Norway after the
death of Frederik I).[8] Thus foreign fishing off Iceland seems to have been
already legally prohibited in 1533, although of course there was no satisfactory force to back that decision.

The ban was predominantly aimed against the English, who alone are
known to have fished off Iceland on decked fishing vessels, which the
word *dugga* must refer to. In the coming years, the offensive against the
English was continued. In 1539 one of the two Icelandic law-men had three
Englishmen sentenced for exorbitant prices, pillage and attacks on people.
The Icelandic chronicler Jón Egilsson, writing in 1605, describes these events
more like a military action than a legal procedure. The result was that the
English were finally expelled from Grindavík, which was then their last
stronghold on the mainland of Iceland. In the Westman Islands, they had
a permanent camp, whence they ran both trade and fishing, until in 1558
the Crown confiscated all their property there. Nevertheless, the English
went on sailing to Iceland on some sixty fishing vessels annually, to trade
illegally with the inhabitants and sometimes to pillage.[9]

It seems as if German merchants, mainly Hamburgers, the royal administration and the Icelandic élite all joined forces in expelling the English
from the country. The Hamburgers remained in Iceland, with their main base
in Hafnarfjörður, where they built permanent timber houses no later than
the 1530s, perhaps earlier.[10] However, they did not enjoy the grace of the
Crown for long. King Christian III (1534-59) started a new Iceland policy,
according to which the Danish state was to reap the benefits of the country. In 1542 he once again renewed the prohibition against the winter dwelling
of foreigners in Iceland. A year or two later the governor confiscated a
number of fishing boats which the Germans owned in the Reykjanes area.
According to the chronicler Jón Egilsson, there were sixty-five boats in
total, "small and large", probably open rowing-boats, used for one-day
fishing expeditions from the coast (see Ch. 2.4). At this time, the royal administration at Bessastaðir had, justified by the Reformation, confiscated
all the property of Viðey monastery (see Ch. 2.8). Included in this property
were a number of farms, and Jón gives a clear hint that the boats were

---

[7] *Diplomatarium Islandicum* IX (1909-13), 670 (no. 550). My translation.
[8] *Diplomatarium Islandicum* IX (1909-13), 685-6 (no. 564).
[9] Helgi Þorláksson (1999).
[10] Sigurður Skúlason (1933), 128.

confiscated in order to provide the new tenants of the Crown with vessels to fish on.[11]

This was the beginning of a slow retreat by the Germans from Iceland trade giving way to the Danes, who enjoyed the support of the Crown. Thus for Iceland the end of the Middle Ages marked a change of the opposite kind to that which characterized most European countries. In Europe generally, modern times meant the beginning of greatly increased trade and communication in terms of both quantity and distance. Late medieval Iceland had been the battlefield of great powers, competing for its country's products. In the modern age the country remained outside the mainstreams of trade and became for centuries a remote satellite of a minor trading power. The organization of trade in Iceland in that period is discussed in Chapter 2.10.

[11] *Safn til sögu Íslands* I (1856), 68, 82.

2.8 Reformation

Influential though the German merchants were in Iceland in the 16th century, it was a religious and political movement originating in Germany which was to have the most profound and lasting effect there. Traditionally it is said that Martin Luther started the Reformation in Wittenberg in 1517 with his criticism of the sale of indulgences. More generally, his thesis consisted in strict monotheism and individualism. His monotheism forbade the worship of saints and reverence for holy relics. His individualism stressed the personal contact of every individual with God and relied heavily on the revelation of the Bible, transcending theological scholarship or ecclesiastical commands. Hence the distinction between clergy and laity was partly abandoned; convents, monasteries and clerical celibacy were abolished. This theology proved sufficiently challenging to sever the Lutheran Church completely from the Roman Catholic Church, and therefore it was to bring the supreme Church rule of large parts of Germany and the whole of Scandinavia into the hands of national and regional princes. Politically the Lutheran Reformation was a coup in which the state appropriated the Church.

To some extent at least, Lutheranism spread to Scandinavia as a popular religious movement. Still it was no doubt predominantly the strong appeal of Church property and its sources of income for the Crown which secured its rapid victory in these countries. In 1527 the Swedish Crown severed all ties with Rome, and nine years later King Christian III did the same in Denmark; he was badly in need of cash after the years of civil war that had brought him to the throne. A revolt in Norway, led by the archbishop of Trondheim, was crushed and only led to the abolition of the Norwegian Council of State, and thus virtually of the Norwegian state, in 1537.

In Iceland observance in the Lutheran style was probably first performed in German in a church which the Hamburg merchants had built in Hafnarfjörður not later than 1537. Among Icelanders no popular Protestant movement is known to have existed at all. The only known adherents of Lutheranism in these years were some four young men at the bishop's see of Skálholt, some of them educated in Germany.[1]

---

[1] There are three major works on the Reformation in Iceland, all with references to original sources: Páll Eggert Ólason I-II (1919-22); Tryggvi Þórhallsson (1989), written in 1917 but not published until 1989; Vilborg Auður Ísleifsdóttir (1997).

In his *Bishops' Annals* Jón Egilsson tells a few stories of how these young men narrowly escaped being exposed by the bishop, Ögmundur Pálsson. One of them, Oddur Gottskálksson, began to translate the Gospel of St Matthew into Icelandic – or Norse (*norræna*) as the language was still called – in the byre at Skálholt, pretending to be copying old bishops' statutes and Church law. The story does not sound credible, since it seems to assume that translating the Holy Scripture into the vernacular was prohibited by the Catholic Church, which is absurd. Nevertheless it is a fact that the New Testament was published in Norse in Oddur's translation in Denmark in 1540 and is the oldest printed book in that language which has been preserved.

The Skálholt group could do little for their cause but wait for the initiative of the Crown, and they did not have to wait long. In Iceland the Reformation was almost exclusively brought about by command and military force. It was a revolution from above, as an Icelandic author has recently described it.[2] In 1537 King Christian III had a new Church Ordinance, the constitution of a Protestant Church, promulgated in Denmark and sent it to Iceland either that year or the next. No direct reply by the Icelanders is preserved, but another document states that such a reply was given by a court of twelve priests, nominated by Bishop Ögmundur of Skálholt, which in essence must have been negative. In a circular that was to be distributed in his diocese, Bishop Ögmundur warned against "a certain grey friar [who has] preached new heresy and infidelity".[3] Nothing is known about the response of the Bishop of Hólar, Jón Arason, until 1540, when he wrote to the king and rejected the Ordinance, though in rather vague terms.

The Crown was in no hurry to impose Lutheranism on its Icelandic subjects. Instead someone decided to use the new theology to improve the facilities of the royal administration in Iceland. Resident in Bessastaðir, the governor or his bailiff only had access to two small farms in the neighbourhood, which were said to be insufficient for his livestock, probably referring in particular to horses needed for his travels. Therefore on Whit Sunday 1539, with or without a warrant from the king, the bailiff Didrich von Minden took thirteen men and stormed the neighbouring monastery of Viðey, causing serious damage, according to sworn witnesses, and stealing food and livestock. After this the monastery was run as a fief of the royal servants at Bessastaðir.

In August that year Didrich von Minden rode away from Bessastaðir with an escort of ten, supposedly intending to lay hold of the convent of Kirkjubær and the monastery of Þykkvibær in the south-east of the country. On his way he seems to have had the idea of making a detour to Skálholt,

---

[2] Vilborg Auður Ísleifsdóttir (1997). This is in fact the subtitle of her book: *Byltingin að ofan.*

[3] *Diplomatarium Islandicum* X (1911-21), 414 (no. 167). Of course, it was inaccurate to call Luther a grey friar, since he was not a Franciscan but an Augustinian.

with no particular errand except to annoy the bishop. In Skálholt the visitors were received with food and beer before they lay down to sleep. The next day they stayed on, in spite of the warnings of the bishop. On the following morning a group of neighbouring farmers, summoned by the steward of Skálholt, attacked and killed them all, except for one twelve-year-old boy. Shortly after this Viðey monastery was recaptured by Icelanders and four more foreigners were killed – the king's men are alternately called Danes or Germans in Icelandic sources. With this the entire royal administration in Iceland was destroyed. If there were any able-bodied men in royal service left alive, they chose not to advertise their presence.

When this happened, Bishop Ögmundur was almost blind and had already begun to prepare his resignation. As his successor he had chosen a prominent member of the Lutheran Skálholt group, Gissur Einarsson, and sent him to Denmark for ordination before the killings at Skálholt. It is not exactly clear whether Gissur had managed to conceal his Protestant tendencies from the blind bishop, or whether Ögmundur had been tempted for a moment to give in to the superior strength of the royal power. Anyway Gissur returned home in 1540, not ordained as a Protestant bishop ("superintendent" was their official title) but nominated by the king. He took over Skálholt see in the summer of 1540, and Ögmundur moved away to the neighbouring farm Haukadalur.

During the winter of 1540-1 Ögmundur seems to have begun to regret his decision. The reason may not have been exclusively religious since he was also in trouble for not returning the property of the see intact, which was a bishop's duty. So he wrote to Bishop Jón Arason at Hólar, complained about the running of Skálholt by Gissur, and suggested that Jón nominate a court of priests to pass a sentence on Gissur's behaviour. He probably intended to have him sentenced to leave his office. This letter got into the hands of Gissur, and its text is preserved only in his copybook.

This was the situation in Iceland in May 1541 when a Danish naval captain finally arrived in his ship and restored royal authority in the country. Gissur made contact with him immediately, and a few days later the captain's men captured Ögmundur. They took him back to Denmark with them, but sources differ over whether he died on the way there or lived for a few years in Denmark. His considerable private property – forty-seven farms and hundreds of ells in silver – was confiscated by the Crown.

After this, all resistance against the Reformation disappeared in the diocese of Skálholt. Gissur Einarsson obviously did what he could to maintain the status of the Church and its independence *vis-à-vis* the Crown. In this way, he behaved more like a Catholic bishop than a Protestant superintendent. On the other hand, he attempted to introduce the Lutheran faith and observances, albeit with great caution. Even priests who had refused officially at a synod to accept the Church Ordinance were able to continue in their offices, if they chose to do so. The relics of St Þorlákr Þórhallsson were kept intact at Skálholt, and remained there even until the early 18th century. On the other hand in 1547 Gissur took down a renowned crucifix at Kaldaðarnes in Árnessýsla and had it placed in the choir of the church, probably where it could not be seen by the congregation. Ironically it was while he was travelling home after this act that he first became aware of the disease that resulted in his death early the next year, when he was about thirty-six years old.

Bishop Jón Arason set off for the Althing in the summer of 1541, but returned home when he heard of Ögmundur's capture. The Danish captain also made no attempt to enforce Protestantism in the northern diocese. It was left intact for the entire period of Gissur Einarsson at Skálholt. Letters between the two bishops mention an agreement they reached and most scholars agree that it must have been about not intervening in each other's affairs.

It fits well with this interpretation that after the death of Gissur in 1548 Jón Arason started a counter-offensive in the diocese of Skálholt. In June he attended a synod in Skálholt and there had an abbot, a solid Catholic, elected as bishop by twenty-four priests, and himself chosen as provisional administrator of the see with a bishop's power. At the same time Jón's opponents chose their own candidate, Marteinn Einarsson. He was of course appointed by the Crown and came home ordained as a "superintendent and bishop" the following year.

Jón Arason probably did not get a hold on Skálholt this time. Instead he had a fortress built at Hólar and intended to provide it with cannons and guns. In the autumn of 1549 two of his sons (Bishop Jón had six children by a concubine) managed to capture Bishop Marteinn and bring him to Hólar. He was kept in captivity in the north through the winter.

By this time the Crown decided that it was about time to get rid of this stubborn rebel, who had been the only Catholic bishop in the Nordic countries for almost a decade. Sometime in 1549 King Christian wrote to Marteinn's brother-in-law, Sheriff Daði Guðmundsson, and asked him to capture Bishop Jón and his sons so that sending an armed force to the country could be avoided. However, Daði did not venture to carry out the royal request. In the summer of 1550 Bishop Jón went to Skálholt and took Bishop Marteinn with him. By threatening to carry the bishop before his escort to be shot, Bishop Jón had the see given up to him. He reconsecrated the cathedral and dug up Bishop Gissur's body which he had thrown into a pit. He then went to the Althing and once more had himself declared the proper overlord of Christianity in Skálholt diocese. From there he went to Viðey and to Helgafell and restored the monasteries. After this Jón is said to have announced: "Now the whole of Iceland submits to me, except for one and a half cottar's sons." Scholars have been in some doubt about whom these words refer to; all agree, though, that the half was Daði Guðmundsson.

It is true that Bishop Jón was practically the sole ruler within Iceland. The royal administration at Bessastaðir was probably even weaker than before, and the Icelander to whom the king had entrusted the role of removing the bishop did not risk his life in trying. On the other hand, it is difficult to see how Bishop Jón intended to play his strong cards in the future. Did he simply do what he saw as his duty for a good cause, without planning a sensible political solution? Or did he have a political plan? There are contemporary sources which indicate that he attempted to contact the Emperor in Germany, who was the nearest major supporter of the Catholic faith in Europe. After Jón's death it was maintained that he had intended to commit high treason against the Danish Crown and hand the country over to the Emperor. It must be remembered that no one knew the outcome of the religious battle in Germany at this moment. When Jón Arason started his counter-attack, the Catholics were gaining ground there and Luther himself was recently dead. Bishop Jón may have had good reason to hope that the whole Reformation business was just a passing phase.

Another question is what the predominant content of Bishop Jón's good cause was. The old nationalist historians tended to see him first and foremost as a protector of Iceland's autonomy against an intrusive foreign power. As might be expected, this view has lost ground during the second half of the 20th century. But what do the sources say? Jón Arason was a good poet and left behind a number of somewhat boastful verses, often comic ones, about his struggle against his enemies. Religion, God, the Pope or Luther never occur there, while heresy occurs only once. On the other hand, the bishop boasts of being useful to Iceland and brave against the Danes. He complains about the prospect of being sentenced by Danes and dying as a victim of the king's power. It seems as if he saw the Reformation predominantly as a political event, where the Danish Crown was seizing power that belonged to the Icelandic élite.[4]

Whatever the long-term plans of Bishop Jón, they were never put to the test because one of his short-term plans failed so badly. In the autumn of 1550 he went with two of his sons, Ari and Björn, and perhaps about thirty men, to the farm Sauðafell in Dalasýsla in the west, in the neighbourhood of Daði Guðmundsson's home. The purpose was to summon Daði before a court for a number of charges (there were usually no lack of charges in disputes within the Icelandic élite). Daði arrived at Sauðafell with a superior force and attacked the northerners. They soon fled into the church, where the bishop and his sons were captured. They were brought to Skálholt, where Daði, Bishop Marteinn who had now been released, and the royal bailiff Christian Skriver discussed how the captives could be kept secure during the winter until they could be taken to Denmark. The obvious threat was that the northerners, who used to flock to the south in

[4] Gunnar Karlsson (1999) 141-2, 150-5.

the late winter fishing season, would free them and everything would remain the same. Then someone is said to have suggested – sources disagree as to who it was – that "the axe and the earth will keep them best". This advice was followed: Bishop Jón and his two sons were beheaded at Skálholt on 7 November 1550, without the passing of any death sentence.

In the winter it appeared that the fear of the northerners had not been without cause. In January some sixty men came south seeking revenge; later it was said that the campaign was initiated by Þórunn, the daughter of Bishop Jón. They found Bailiff Christian and killed him immediately, with his seven or nine men. Then they searched for all Danes in the area and killed those they found, whether they were supposed to have had anything to do with the execution or not; according to a 17th-century annalist, fourteen men were killed.[5] For the second time in the struggle over the Reformation, the Danish administration in Iceland was wiped out. On the other hand, no attempt seems to have been made to take revenge on Daði or any other Icelander; the northerners apparently shared the view of their dead bishop that the Reformation was a battle between Icelanders and Danes. In the spring of 1551 also, a surviving son of the bishop, Sigurður Jónsson, sent to Skálholt for the bodies of his father and brothers and had them brought home to Hólar and buried there.

No news had reached Copenhagen about the capture of Bishop Jón when in the spring of 1551 the king finally decided to use Danish force to do away with the rebels. He sent to the Northern Quarter two warships, with a 300-strong force, which landed at Oddeyri in Eyjafjörður, where the town of Akureyri now is. There a court was nominated, which sentenced the bishop and his sons as traitors who had been rightfully executed, and declared their property to be confiscated by the Crown. As a coup the Reformation had finally won full victory in Iceland. As a religious reform it still had a long way to go.

---

[5] *Annálar 1400-1800* I (1922-7), 124 (Skarðsárannáll).

2.9 Lutheran Society

The Icelandic bishoprics of the late medieval period had been by far the largest institutions in the country, dividing between them a quarter of the tithe (0.25% general property tax annually, see Ch. 1.6), owning hundreds of farms each, which were rented out to tenants, partly together with livestock, and receiving a considerable part of the fines for offences against the Church or Christian law. Skálholt and Hólar were probably the homes of 100-200 people. According to the reformative Church Ordinance of Christian III, these institutions were to be abolished and bishops to be succeeded by superintendents, who would be allowed to hold two maids, a scribe, a messenger, a coachman and a boy,[1] a household no larger than a well-to-do farmer in Iceland might have. Unlike Denmark and Norway, this abolition of the bishoprics as institutions did not take place in Iceland until the late 18th century (see Ch. 2.18).

Certainly, in 1556 the Crown decided to appropriate the bishops' share of the tithe, which led to the resignation of Bishop Marteinn Einarsson at Skálholt. However, approximately half of the tithe was soon re-introduced, since it proved impossible to run the bishoprics and their schools without it. From then on, in around half of the districts, people paid the king's tithe and in the other half they paid the bishop's tithe. All income from fines was taken over by the Crown, but the bishoprics kept the landed property almost intact.

On this financial basis the bishoprics ran seminaries, called Latin schools, for future clergymen and university students, the only formal educational institutions in the country for centuries. The sees also formed the only permanent centres of scholarship in the country; they were the places where manuscripts were kept and copied, books were translated and published, and so on. In the exclusively rural Iceland, without a university or educated bourgeoisie, the cultural role of the bishoprics was invaluable. All bishops in Protestant Iceland were Icelanders. Until the period of absolutism (see Ch. 2.12) they were chosen by the clergy of the bishopric and their choice was ratified by the king. In all cases the king accepted their choice, except when the clergy of Hólar bishopric chose Sigurður, the son of Jón Arason, which they actually did twice with an interval of twenty

---

[1] *Diplomatarium Islandicum* X (1911-21), 229, 292 (no. 95).

years.[2] The northerners do not appear to have felt tyrannized by the military action of 1551.

The parish churches also kept through the Reformation their status as independent institutions, received as fiefs by the pastors. This remnant of feudalism was not abolished completely until the 20th century. In formal terms, the bishops lost to the royal administration their right to appoint vicars to the benefices, but they seem to have made the real decisions on appointments well into the 17th century.

The religious houses were the only ecclesiastical institutions that were abolished as such. Bishop Gissur Einarsson obtained royal permission to establish schools in most of those in his diocese, but he seems to have failed to realize it, perhaps because in his day they were still occupied by monks and nuns. In the 1550s this opportunity to establish public schools in the country was lost, and the cloisters were all turned into royal fiefs, mostly run by Icelandic commissaries. Nothing was left of them but a group of farms, often with livestock, which were rented out to tenants. All in all, the Reformation handed some 17% of the landed property of Iceland over to the Crown, thereby making it the second largest landowner in the country after the Church, which still owned almost one-third of Iceland's farming land (see Ch. 2.14).

Not only did the Church lose its income from fines after the Reformation, but it also lost most of its judicial power. Most important, on so-called moral issues – that is, on offences against accepted rules of sexual behaviour – a new law was passed at the Althing in 1564 and ratified by the king the following year.[3] According to this law, which was called the Great Verdict (*Stóridómur*), these offences became an exclusively secular matter. Being somewhat stricter and much more exhaustive than the corresponding law in Denmark, the Great Verdict clearly reveals the intolerance which was to become the concomitant of Lutheranism. In general, the Catholic Church had not seen any offence as so serious that it could not be compensated for. Now, the Lutheran secular rulers introduced the death penalty for a number of offences, such as incest (which even included relations between brother- and sister-in-law), and adultery committed three times. Men were beheaded but women were drowned. For less serious offences the penalties were fines, whipping and outlawry. It has been assumed that up to 100 men and women were executed on the authority of the Great Verdict during the two centuries that it remained in full force.

The Lutheran Church abandoned its judicial function, taking on instead a new task – namely, the literary education of the common people. In its individualistic spirit Lutheranism emphasized the familiarity of every person with the Holy Scripture and the correct interpretations of it in religious

[2] Hjalti Hugason (1989), 90-1.

[3] Inga Huld Hákonardóttir (1992), 61ff.; Már Jónsson (1993), 90-127; *Diplomatarium Islandicum* XIV (1944-9), 271-6 (no. 188).

literature. For the purpose of this programme, the newly-invented technique of printing opened up immense possibilities. Ironically, though, the art of printing had been introduced in Iceland in the days of Bishop Jón Arason and probably by him.[4] What we know for sure is that a Swedish priest and typographer, Jon Mattheusson, came to Iceland in the 1530s with a printing press and received the church at Breiðabólstaður in Húnavatnsþing as a benefice. No book printed on his press has been preserved, but it is generally assumed that two leaves from a handbook for priests, *Breviarium*, which are preserved in Stockholm are the remnant of a copy printed there.

Pastor Jon Mattheusson accepted the Reformation and went on serving as a vicar and printing books under the first Protestant bishop in Hólar. Apart from that, the first generation of reformers had books printed in Denmark and Germany, the first being the New Testament in Oddur Gottskálksson's translation in 1540, as already mentioned (Ch. 2.8).[5]

Among these books were the first collections of hymns in the vernacular, all translated from German and Danish. They are mentioned here because they presented a considerable threat to the Icelandic language and the distinctive mode of composing poetry in it. Regular alliteration, which is so characteristic of Icelandic poetry, was abandoned completely, and often regular rhyme was also dropped. Words were borrowed from Danish on a previously unknown scale; declensions of Icelandic words were violated if the melody demanded it. The only aspect of the text that was respected was its religious message.

A strong counter-offensive on behalf of Icelandic traditions within the literary culture was started by Bishop Guðbrandur Þorláksson of Hólar, an exceptionally active and effective man. He was appointed to the see in 1571 and a little later bought the printing-press from Breiðabólstaður and hired a typographer, Pastor Jón Jónsson, the son of Jon Mattheusson. He probably procured a bindery from abroad and hired a foreign bookbinder. It has been assumed that almost 110 books were published at Hólar under Guðbrandur's auspices.[6] This included the entire Bible in Icelandic, in 1584. This was partly an improved republication of Oddur Gottskálksson's New Testament translation, and partly a new translation, some of it by the bishop himself. Guðbrandur's Bible is an elegant book with illustrations, ornamented initials and vignettes. Five hundred copies were printed and each was sold for the value of two or three cows, according to the means of the buyer.

[4] Steingrímur Jónsson (1989) has written the most recent survey of book-publishing in Iceland up to the 19th century.

[5] The literature and literary activity of the period, until *c.* 1630, is discussed, from a highly nationalistic viewpoint, in Páll Eggert Ólason II (1922), 528-643; III (1924), 707-21; IV (1926), 1-786. For a more recent and moderate view, see *Íslensk bókmenntasaga* II (1993), 379-521.

[6] Haraldur Sigurðsson (1976), 52.

Guðbrandur also published a large hymn-book and a prayer-book, which were a big step forward from earlier books and laid the foundation for Icelandic church-singing until the early 19th century.

However, Guðbrandur's most original and challenging enterprise was his *Verse Book* (*Vísnabók*) in 1612, which was intended to put an end to the two major kinds of secular poetry produced in the country. One of these was ballads, which Guðbrandur, in his introduction to the book, refers to as lustful verses and amorous poetry. The other was *rímur*, extremely long epic poems composed in a strict verse form, which had been composed in immense quantity in Iceland since the 14th century. Their commonest subjects came from medieval sagas of chivalry or heroic sagas (see Ch. 1.11), where bodily strength and aggression prevailed, and all kinds of monstrous creatures appeared. In order to oust such ungodly trivia, Guðbrandur hired poets to write religious *rímur* on scriptural subjects.

Guðbrandur was not successful in this last enterprise; the descendants of the saga authors went on composing *rímur* in their thousands for more than the next three centuries, in a surprisingly similar way, and chanting them in a half-spoken, half-sung mode to extremely monotonous melodies. Thus although the Lutheran Church was practically the only cultural institution in Iceland for centuries, it did not succeed in its goal of monopolizing literary culture. On the other hand, Bishop Guðbrandur Þorláksson contributed more than anyone else to the more successful task of ensuring that when the Lutheran Church changed over to the vernacular as required, its language in Iceland would be Icelandic and not Danish, as it was mostly in Norway and even more so in Faroe. In Iceland we believe that this is one of the reasons why Icelandic is now much closer to medieval Norse than any other modern language.

2.10 Trade Monopoly

In Chapter 2.7 we left the trade policy of the Crown in the 1540s when it had been relieved of its need to use German merchants to oust the English from Iceland. The Crown then proceeded to make arrangements to get rid of the Germans. These attempts to obtain Iceland as a trading region continued into the following decades. In 1547 Christian III leased the top administration of Iceland to the city council of Copenhagen for ten years for a fixed sum of money.[1] There is hardly any doubt that this was meant to lead the merchants of Copenhagen into the Iceland trade, but the attempt proved painfully unsuccessful. The council sent a governor to Iceland but failed to support him with the necessary military force. The Hamburgers even carried out a short-lived coup in 1550. While the governor himself was abroad, they captured his bailiff Christian Skriver, forced him to run in front of their horses between the fishing camps in the Reykjanes area and point out where the Crown or Danish merchants kept their stockfish. The case was settled the next year in a treaty of an already familiar kind, which allowed anyone to trade but forbade foreigners to have winter-dwelling in Iceland and engage in fishing activity from its coasts. In 1552 the king gave up the attempt to hand the Iceland trade over to his Copenhagen citizens and cancelled the lease of the Council, leaving only the Westman Islands to them for the rest of the period.

In the reign of Frederik II (1559-88) the Crown, being unable to expel the Germans, developed a new way of exploiting them. It began to lease individual trading harbours to individual merchants for a specific period. A large majority of the merchants were German; among them the Hamburg merchants held the lion's share, though they were by no means alone. Thus in 1585 Hamburg merchants leased fifteen harbours in Iceland and sailed there on fourteen ships, but other German cities leased eight harbours and sent eight ships. It is not known how many harbours Danish merchants leased at this time, but from about 1564 on they were active participants in the Iceland trade, sometimes in collaboration with their more experienced German colleagues. A few Icelanders bought trading licences in this

---

[1] The patent is printed in Danish in *Diplomatarium Islandicum* XI (1915-25), 529-31 (no. 477). This story is told by Jón Jónsson Aðils (1919), who covers the whole period of trade monopoly in what is still the most extensive survey of its development. For a Danish translation, see Jón Jónsson Aðils (1926-7).

period, usually in collaboration with foreigners, but none of them made trade his main permanent occupation.

The beneficial consequence of this system for the Icelanders was a lively trade, where every usable natural harbour was utilized. On the other hand, the cost of foreign goods was said to rise, while the prices of Icelandic export goods remained constant, perhaps because of lack of competition in the area of each trading centre. In Iceland traditional prices were supposed to be observed, both in internal and external trade, but that could not prevent changes in pricing in the long run.

The policy adopted by the successor of Frederik II, Christian IV (1588-1648), was different again. From the beginning of his reign he was a strong adherent of mercantilism, the fashionable policy at the time, which aimed at improving the wealth of the state by promoting the foreign trade of its citizens, especially through monopolies and privileges. Under King Christian's rule the naval strength of Denmark greatly increased while the German towns lagged behind. At the turn of the 17th century the king felt able to capture Iceland. On 20 April 1602 he issued a decree whereby the citizens of three Danish towns – Copenhagen, Elsinore and Malmø (now in Sweden) – were given the monopoly of all trade with Iceland for twelve years.[2] There is no mention of this decree in the minutes of the Althing, although its text is preserved in an Icelandic translation from that time.[3] The arrangement of foreign trade was obviously considered not to come within the Althing's remit in legislation.

This was the beginning of a 186-year-long unrestricted monopoly of all foreign trade in Iceland. It was based on two principles: that managing the trade was restricted to Danish citizens, mostly Copenhageners; and that competition between merchants was excluded as far as possibile. Both of these aims were realised by combating illegal trade by foreigners, mainly English, Dutch and later also French fishermen, although never with complete success. Apart from this, the arrangement of the monopoly varied from time to time.[4]

At each of the approximately twenty harbours that formed permanent trading centres in the period, there was only one shop. Originally Copenhagen was to cater for trade in six harbours, Elsinore in seven and Malmø also in seven, but in each harbour a number of merchants ran the shop together, because most Danish merchants still had a very limited capacity. They were even forced to deal with Germans to sail to Iceland, so that the German trade did not come to an end until after 1620. Then the arrangement of the trade was altered in order to make it easier to avoid the Germans. This time thirty-six merchants, all but three resident in Copenhagen, founded a

---

[2] *Lovsamling for Island* I (1853), 138-43.

[3] *Alþingisbækur Íslands* III (1917-18), 250-5.

[4] A thorough study of the economic and social history of the monopoly trade is provided by Gísli Gunnarsson in English (1983a) and in Icelandic (1987).

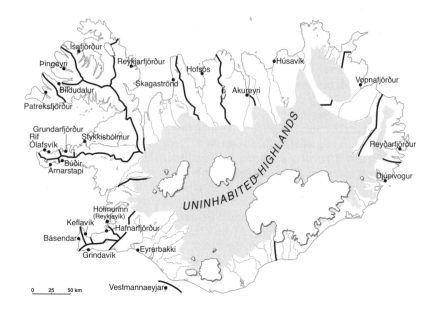

Map 2.10-1 Licensed trading harbours and their districts from 1684 onwards. The density of harbours in the west mirrors the importance of fishing there and of fish exports. The scarcity of trading centres on the south coast is due to a lack of natural harbours.

company to run the trade with Iceland, Faroe and northern Norway. This was called the Icelandic, Faroese and Nordic Trade Company. It was quite successful for decades, but during the Danish–Swedish war of 1657-60 (which introduced absolutism in Denmark, see Ch. 2.12), the Company proved to be unable to secure regular commerce with Iceland, which led to its dissolution in 1662.

After this the lease of individual harbours was taken up again. Usually two harbours were leased together in auction, one for the export of the profitable stockfish, and another where little except mutton and woollens, which did not sell well, were available. Now the whole country was divided into trading districts around the harbours so that no Icelander could possibly use the services of one merchant rather than another in order to obtain a better deal. Strict punishments – appropriation of property, detention in Denmark or whipping – were the penalties for breaking these rules. Hólmfastur Guðmundsson, a poor tenant in the Reykjanes area, got his name into the history books during the heyday of nationalism because he was flogged for selling the Keflavík merchant ten haddock, three ling and a few swim-bladders which the merchant in Hafnarfjörður had refused to buy. Merchants, for their part, were never punished for trading outside their districts.

Furthermore, according to the merchants' interpretation of the regulation, the owners of exportable goods were not even free to carry them between trading districts. Thus the merchants pressed charges against the Bishop of Hólar for taking home to the see the rents from its landed property in other districts. Peasants who went to remote parts of the country for the fishing season were obliged to sell their catch within the district where it was brought ashore. However, it is unclear how widely these rules were enforced, and there are certainly also cases, not often mentioned in Icelandic history books, when the division into districts was taken less seriously.

After almost half a century of district trade, the policy was changed to company trade again. In 1732 a new company was licensed to trade in the whole of Iceland for ten years for 8,000 rigsdalers (rdl.) annual rent. This proved profitable, and at the end of the period the Crown refused to lease the monopoly again for less than 16,000 rdl. a year. When the company declined, the monopoly was auctioned to another company, the so-called Flaxmongers' Company, for 16,000 rdl. The period of this company's activity happened to coincide with years of serious famine in Iceland in the late 1750s (see Ch. 2.17). The company failed to supply the country with sufficient unspoilt grain, which it was obliged to do, and finally abandoned the licence to escape prosecution.

In this situation no one made a bid for the Iceland trade, so the Crown managed it on its own for five years, from 1759 to 1763. Then a new company was founded, only to lose the licence a decade later, partly for importing spoilt grain to Iceland. The Crown ran the trade again for fourteen years, 1774-87, and this time made serious attempts to improve Icelandic fishing and agriculture. These attempts, which may have been hopeless anyway, came to nothing in the terrible famine of the 1780s, which led to the sudden abolition of the monopoly trade in 1787 (see Ch. 2.17).

In the decree of 1602 the merchants were obliged to carry sufficient and unspoilt necessities to Iceland and price them in accordance with old customs within the country. In 1619 an official price list was issued by the king, stating the price of every item that was supposed to be imported into Iceland and exported from it. The prices were still mostly in accordance with old Icelandic customs, and the value unit was a standard fish, which amounted to half an ell (of homespun) in the price system. This list was kept unchanged for sixty-five years, irrespective of fluctuations on the European market. Then in 1684 a new one was issued, somewhat less favourable to the Icelanders, only to have the old one reissued with minor changes in 1702. It was not until 1776 that a basically new system was introduced, calculated in money and roughly in accordance with European market prices.

By being obliged regularly to supply every trading harbour, even the least profitable, with sufficient necessities at a fixed price, the monopoly system attempted to place a safety net under the rural society of Iceland. This, of course, failed in times of severe hardship; a welfare state was not possible in a pre-industrial society. However, there is hardly any doubt that the trade monopoly secured trade to harbours that would have been without it under free trade. On the whole, it worked as a levelling force; it equalled out price fluctuations, it helped small and poor districts to get some minimal trade, and it tended to favour farming over the more profitable fishing.

The monopoly system was also a conservative force, and not only in terms of pricing. It retained the earlier policy of forbidding foreign merchants or their servants to winter in Iceland; they were also usually excluded from participating in farming or fishing. Thus the system supported the rural set-up, which is said to be common in pre-industrial societies, keeping external trade apart and preventing it from challenging the social dominance of farming and rural life (see Chs 2.4 and 2.7).

How could it happen that a trading system, introduced by Danish mercantilists in order to serve the Danish bourgeoisie and the Danish state, actually served the leading stratum of Icelandic peasant society so perfectly? Far too little is known about how and by whom decisions about the governing of Iceland were in fact made in the period when the monopoly system was taking shape, but it is possible that the system developed as an alliance between the Crown, the Copenhagen merchants and the Icelandic aristocracy, in other words the better-off farmers.

Of course the Icelanders complained about the trade. They were like any other people in wanting to get more and better goods in exchange for their products. A 17th-century sheriff said sarcastically that he refused to pay for mites in the grain or sea water in the schnapps, because there was no lack of either in Iceland.[5] However, as time went on both parties were more or less content with the arrangement, and few expressed any desire to have the trade monopoly abolished before it actually happened. The conservatism of the Icelandic aristocracy was combined with the general aversion to risk of the poorer strata of society, which constantly faced the danger of starvation.

The merchants complained in turn about rotten stockfish, sand in the wool and badly knitted socks or mittens. But in general they had good reason to be content. Normally the trade was run at a profit, and the results of recent research indicate that Icelandic historians of the older, nationalistic generation were right in assuming that the Iceland trade played a considerable part in making Denmark a commercial power able to participate in the European grab for colonies. And when all went well the Danish treasury received a handsome sum for the trading licences.

---

[5] Þórður Hinriksson (1912), 124-5.

2.11 The Gloomy 17th Century

The 17th century has had a bad image in Icelandic historiography. Between the heroic struggle of Ögmundur Pálsson and Jón Arason against the Reformation, on the one hand, and the first signs of enlightened, progressive thinking in the 18th century, on the other, it is seen as the nadir of Iceland's history. The trade monopoly described in the last chapter and the introduction of absolutism (see Ch. 2.12) apparently mark the culmination of foreign rule in the country. In addition to this, two deplorable occurrences have been seen as characterizing the century, the so-called Turkish Raid of 1627, and the witch-hunt. Although it may appear as outdated in modern historiography to characterize periods as dark or bright ages, the present chapter will mainly be devoted to these two sad occurrences, though with some counterweight at the end.

There has been repeated evidence of how utterly defenceless Iceland was in the centuries we have covered so far. In the monopoly period the Crown usually sent a warship to protect the trading ships on their way to Iceland, and sometimes these warships stayed in the waters around the country during the summer, trying to keep foreign fishing vessels away from the coast, until the trading ships were ready to return to Denmark. Sometimes the same ship was commanded to protect both Iceland and the Faroe Islands, countries separated by hundreds of nautical miles. Once the naval management in Copenhagen even revealed its ignorance by proposing that one ship should be sent to Iceland and another one to the Faroe Islands and the Westman Islands.[1]

Normally, this lack of defence had no harmful consequences in Iceland. On the contrary, being absolutely free from the presence of a military force was certainly a blessing for most people. However, around this time, pirates resident in North Africa, a mixture of native Muslims and European outlaws, were roaming about the North Atlantic, and once, in 1627, four pirate ships from Algeria and Morocco reached Iceland. Since these countries belonged to the Ottoman Empire, which in Icelandic was referred to as the Turkish Empire, the pirates have always been called Turks in Iceland.[2]

---

[1] Kristinn Jóhannesson (1968), 125.

[2] The basic work on the Turkish Raid is *Tyrkjaránið á Íslandi 1627* (1906-9), mainly a collection of original sources.

One of the pirate ships came to the harbour of Grindavík in the south, where fifteen Icelanders and a few Danes were captured. On the way from there, the ship met a Danish cargo ship, which was captured with its crew. Then both the ships sailed towards the royal residence at Bessastaðir. When the Danish governor, Holger Rosenkrantz, heard the news from Grindavík, he had a small fortress built close to his residence and cannons brought into it. The defence force included an experienced cannoneer, the Icelander Jón Ólafsson, who had served in the Danish navy, sailed with it to India and – in Icelandic fashion – written a book about it.[3] Just outside Bessastaðir one of the ships became stranded, and the pirates spent two days moving cargo and captives in order to lighten it. To Jón Ólafsson's indignation, the governor dared not open fire. When the ship was afloat again, the pirates sailed home with their booty. This was the kind of protection Denmark gave Iceland at that time.

Two of the pirate ships landed in the Eastern Fiords and spent around a week there, capturing some 110 people and killing at least nine. They then met a third ship, and all three headed for the Westman Islands, where the pirates did not have to worry about losing their prey in the mountainous interior of the country. Within two days they managed to capture 242 people. Between thirty and forty were killed and the church and the warehouses were burnt down.

Not much defence was offered by the descendants of the Vikings in Iceland. However, the descendants of the saga authors remained true to their tradition of writing down the story of a memorable event, and therefore we have minute descriptions of the conduct of the pirates. A farmer from the mainland, Kláus Eyjólfsson, who probably came to the Westman Islands immediately after the attack, described the scene:

Some of the women lay dead, cut to pieces beside their husbands, but lying so disgracefully that their clothes were always pulled up over the head so that they were most naked where they should have been least. One man, named Ásmundur, lay sick in his bed. This man they had repeatedly cut and stabbed, so that the bed and his body were all stained with blood. And this had been their amusement and pleasure, to tear the bodies to pieces as best they could, and stab and cut them. In a word: far and wide in the trading centre and the fields dead bodies lay, shot and stabbed and cut, not only of people but also of the livestock in the same way.[4]

Another self-educated farmer, the well-known annalist Björn Jónsson at Skarðsá, later wrote the *Story of the Turkish Raid*. To mention just one of his observations, he says that all those who most seemed to get enjoyment out of killing and mutilating the people in the Westman Islands

---

[3] Jón Ólafsson I-II (1923-32). For his account of the defence of Bessastaðir, see II (1932), 258-9.

[4] *Tyrkjaránið á Íslandi 1627* (1906-9), 70-1. My translation.

were former Christians who had converted to Islam. They were the worst, just as such renegades usually are, states Björn with a surprisingly universal outlook.[5]

After it became known that most of the captives had been enslaved in Algeria, a collection of money to ransom them was started in Iceland, Denmark and even other European countries. A pastor from the Westman Islands, Ólafur Egilsson, was sent by the kidnappers from Algeria to Denmark to ease the ransoming of captives. He managed to reach Copenhagen and later Iceland, and – faithful to the Icelandic custom – he wrote a travelogue.[6]

While this was going on, the slaves slowly decreased in number. Many had died from disease shortly after their arrival in Algeria; some were lost; some got free on their own; a few converted to Islam and declined to return. However, ten years after the raid, twenty-seven Icelanders came back among whom the most famous in Icelandic history is Guðríður Símonardóttir, a married woman from the Westman Islands. On the way to Iceland the freed people stopped in Copenhagen, where a young Icelandic student, Hallgrímur Pétursson, was hired to help them revive their knowledge of Christianity. He returned to Iceland with the group, and shortly afterwards Guðríður bore him a baby. Luckily for them, Guðríður's husband had recently died, so that their offence was defined as concubinage and not adultery. Therefore they were free to marry, which they soon did. Of course this love story would be long forgotten if the student had not gone on to become one of Iceland's greatest poets. Before coming to this, let us look at the other deplorable occurrence in the 17th century, the persecutions for sorcery.[7]

In Iceland the first victim was burnt to death in 1625. This was a young man in Eyjafjörður who was accused of having conjured up a ghost and sent him to his neighbour where, among other outrages, he killed some horses. The accused never confessed; nevertheless, when sheets with runic inscriptions were found in his possession, he was sentenced to be burned at the stake. This sentence was unique at the time and probably instigated by the sheriff of the district, who had recently returned from his studies in Hamburg. In the following decades there were charges of witchcraft from time to time, but they received a rather cool reception among officials, until shortly after the mid-17th century when a new sheriff, Þorleifur Kortsson, assumed his post in the Western Fiords. He had spent his early years in Hamburg, where he had probably learned to deal with cases of this kind in the newest European fashion. In his very first year as a sheriff in Strandasýsla, three men were burnt to death there. Three years later a

---

[5] *Tyrkjaránið á Íslandi 1627* (1906-9), 263.

[6] Ólafur Egilsson (1852, 1969); *Tyrkjaránið á Íslandi 1627* (1906-9), 91-203.

[7] The basic work on the subject in Iceland is a posthumously published study by Ólafur Davíðsson (1940-3).

clergyman in the neighbouring district of Ísafjarðarsýsla, Jón Magnússon, experienced a peculiar illness, about which he later wrote a highly impressive book.[8] Having been charged by Pastor Jón, two men, a father and a son, both named Jón Jónsson, confessed to having attempted to kill him and were executed. Some years later a strange illness befell the wife of another clergyman in the Western Fiords, Pastor Páll Björnsson, who was one of the best-educated men of his time in Iceland. By then Þorleifur Kortsson had been elevated to the position of law-man and he dealt with the case in that capacity; the affair cost seven men their lives at the stake.

By this time, witch-hunts had receded in most European countries, and from 1661 onwards the absolute monarchy in Denmark (see Ch. 2.12) tried to stop executions for sorcery. However the Icelanders proved to be as reluctant to abandon the idea as they had been to adopt it. The last person was burnt to death in 1685, and seven years later the life of a convict was saved by the Supreme Court in Copenhagen.

In all, some 120 cases of sorcery have become known through the study of Icelandic sources from the period 1554-1719. Scholars familiar with the period tell me that even more cases could yet be found. Some of the accused were acquitted, others got minor sentences, but twenty-five – twenty-three men and two women – were executed for sorcery (sometimes along with other offences).

It is a peculiar feature of the witch-hunt in Iceland that fewer women than men were executed. The most likely explanation is that in Iceland witchcraft was in many cases connected with writing, runes, magical letters and books of magic, and literary activity was much more common among men than among women.[9] So the lack of opportunity for learning to read and write may have saved scores of Icelandic women from becoming the victims of ambitious officials who had learned abroad the newest theory in criminology.

However, we do happen to know the story of one woman who escaped the stake, not because she was thought unable to perform witchcraft, but through strength, endurance and help from important men. Pastor Jón Magnússon did not recover in spite of the burning of the two Jón Jónssons. He then charged Þuríður Jónsdóttir, the daughter of the elder Jón and sister of the younger, with causing his illness. But now almost every official, lay and clerical, seems to have come to her defence; the case dragged on for years, until in the end she was acquitted. After that she was sufficiently undaunted to charge the pastor with a number of offences, including denying her communion and spitting in her face. The final result is unfortunately not known, but Þuríður obviously escaped the fate of her father and brother.

---

[8] Jón Magnússon (1914, 1967).
[9] Hastrup (1990), 227-8.

Compared with the victims of the Thirty Years' War in Germany, not to mention the slave hunt in Africa or the extermination of aboriginal peoples in America and Australia, the sufferings of 17th-century Icelanders may seem rather trivial. However, these calamities hit a society of only 50,000-60,000 individuals (see Ch. 2.14). The (approximately) 410 Icelanders killed and kidnapped in the Turkish Raid amounted to some 0.75% of the whole population. The twenty-five victims of the witch hunt were around 0.05% of the population.

In sharp contrast to the tragic events that characterize the century, as a glimmer of light in the dark, stands the poetry of the once peccant student Hallgrímur Pétursson.[10] In spite of his offence, he was finally ordained and sent as pastor to one of the poorest and least favoured parishes. Later he obtained a fairly profitable benefice, where he wrote his greatest work, *Passíusálmar* (Hymns of the Passion). This consists of fifty hymns describing the passion and death of Christ and interpreting the symbolic meaning of every episode as a personal message of the Atonement and the salvation of sinful humanity. Whatever one may think of the idea of Atonement, Hallgrímur's cordial confidence and his inventiveness in exposing even seemingly minor episodes as joyful tidings has a fascination. One example will suffice here:

> *Jesus was now to Pilate's hall*
> *By Roman soldiers taken.*
> *He stood there bare before them all,*
> *With courage still unshaken.*
> *A scarlet robe they clothed Him in,*
> *And mocked Him, high above the din –*
> *Thus was my Lord forsaken.*
>
> *No robe I had to hide my shame,*
> *My soul stood all denuded.*
> *My sinful state from Adam came,*
> *From heav'n I was excluded.*
> *Sin's scarlet robe I clothed me in,*
> *Shame and reproach I found therein,*
> *My heart and mind deluded.*
>
> *But my dishonour passed away*
> *And my humiliation;*
> *He clothed my soul with bright array,*
> *The garments of salvation.*

[10] The basic work on Hallgrímur's life and work is by Magnús Jónsson I-II (1947). For a literary study in Danish of his poetry, see Møller (1922).

Beneath His robe I refuge find
And, in His righteousness enshrined,
Eternal consolation.[11]

The Hymns have been published every fourth year, on average, since their first publication in 1666. This is due not only to their great popularity for reading and singing, but also to the widespread custom of burying people with a copy of the volume in their coffin. They are still read on Icelandic State Radio each year throughout Lent, one hymn each evening. People used to know them by heart, and everyone knew jokes about how simple people had misunderstood certain items in them. Thus in a way the Hymns of the Passion are, more than any other book, the Holy Scripture of Iceland.

---

[11] Hallgrímur Pétursson (1966), 107.

2.12 Absolutism

Denmark was an elective kingdom, and in early modern times a Council of State, composed of noblemen, had considerable power. Furthermore, a diet of three or four estates, dominated by the nobility, selected the heir to the throne and sanctioned new or irregular taxes. In fact, the estates normally chose as heir the crown prince, who would have inherited the crown anyway, but nevertheless the election enabled the nobility to restrict the power of a new king by a charter. Thus, as a condition for succeeding his father on the throne in 1648, Frederik III was forced to accept a charter which gave practically all political control to the Council.

It so happens that one of the most detrimental events in the history of the Danish state had the consequence of introducing the principle of royal absolutism. In 1657-60 Denmark fought an unsuccessful war against Sweden and was forced to abandon all its lands east of the Sound: Scania and Bohuslen. The Danish state thereby not only lost a considerable part of its population but also its total control of traffic through the Sound. The Danish nobility were blamed for this humiliating defeat, and in 1660 the unprivileged estates, the clergy and burghers forced them to free King Frederik from his charter and make Denmark a hereditary absolute monarchy in the latest European fashion. In the following year the new arrangement was sanctioned by the signatures of all leading members of Danish society. At the same time the top administration in Copenhagen was reorganized in so-called colleges (*kollegier*). For Iceland three of these colleges are of the greatest importance: the Chancery (*Kanselli*), which occupied a central position in the administration, the Treasury (*Rentekammer*) and the Supreme Court (*Højesteret*), which became the highest appeal court in Icelandic cases and so remained until 1920. In 1665 the absolute monarchy acquired its formal constitution in the Royal Law, which granted the King of Denmark the most absolute power that any sovereign in Europe was ever to attain. The estates were never convened after 1660, and no representative political organization operated in Denmark until the 1830s (see Ch. 3.2).

In 1661 the absolute monarchy was accepted in Norway, but Iceland was allowed to wait until 1662. In March that year the king wrote a letter to his subjects "in Iceland together with the Westman Islands", as the Crown then called its dependency, and announced that his governor, Henrik

Olav	1376/80-87
Margrethe	1387-1412
Erik of Pomerania	1396-1439
Christoffer of Bavaria	1440-8
OLDENBURG DYNASTY	
Christian I	1448-81
Hans	1481-1513
Christian II	1513-23
Frederik I	1523-33
Christian III	1534-59
Frederik II	1559-88
Christian IV	1588-1648
Frederik III	1648-70
Christian V	1670-99
Frederik IV	1699-1730
Christian VI	1730-46
Frederik V	1746-66
Christian VII	1766-1808
Frederik VI	1808-39
Christian VIII	1839-48
Frederik VII	1848-63
GLÜCKSBURG DYNASTY	
Christian IX	1863-1906
Frederik VIII	1906-12
Christian X	1912-44/47

Fig. 2.12-1 Sovereigns of Denmark and Iceland.

Bjelke, was to receive from their representatives an oath of allegiance to His Majesty as a hereditary king, at the Althing on 30 June. For that purpose, he asked both the bishops and law-men, eighteen provosts and pastors, all sheriffs, two Law Council members and two other farmers from each district to attend. Absolutism was not mentioned in the letter.[1]

---

[1] Documents concerning the acceptance of absolutism in Iceland are printed in Danish in *Lovsamling for Island* I (1853), 262-77, in Icelandic and Danish in Jón Þorkelsson and Einar Arnórsson (1908), 142-59, and mostly in Icelandic in *Skjöl um hylling Íslendinga 1649 við Friðrik konung þriðja* (1914), 89-103.

However, the governor did not reach Iceland early enough to come to the Althing. The representatives commented on this fact in the minutes and added that their law-book already contained stipulations on the inheritance of the Crown of Norway.[2] This of course was right and appropriate, since the king had mentioned nothing but inheritance in his letter; Norway had been a hereditary kingdom since the Middle Ages, and there had never been any doubt that Iceland belonged to that kingdom. A more difficult question is how much the Icelanders really knew about what was going on.

Shortly after the Althing, Governor Bjelke finally made his way against the westerly winds to Iceland and summoned the representatives to his residence at Bessastaðir on 26 July to take the oath. Nothing that we know of happened that day or the day after, but on 28 July at Kópavogur, a few miles from Bessastaðir, a document was signed by 109 representatives, where not only the hereditary rights of the king but also his absolute sovereignty were acknowledged. On the same day, however, the representatives wrote other letters to their king, laymen and clergy separately, and declared that they accepted his sovereignty in the confidence that the king would

. . . let us keep our old law of the land, peace and freedom, with the rights that the previous praiseworthy kings of Denmark and Norway, Your Majesty's forefathers, have mercifully granted and rendered us, and our forefathers have accepted under oath.[3]

Thus the Icelanders took back in these letters what they had granted in the first one. Although it is unclear what absolutism actually meant for Iceland, it certainly involved abandoning compliance with old laws and rights. In Iceland's case one would suppose that it meant the annulment of the Old Covenant (see Ch. 1.14), which seems to be referred to in these later letters.

Strictly contemporary sources say little about the reception of the royal message by the Icelanders, but Professor Árni Magnússon (whom we shall return to in Chapter 2.13) wrote down on two small scraps of paper what he claimed was the account of a certain clergyman who was actually among the representatives at Kópavogur. Árni himself was not born until 1663. In this account it says that Bishop Brynjólfur Sveinsson at Skálholt told Governor Bjelke that the Icelanders did not want to abandon the privileges of their country, to which the governor gave no answer other than to point to the soldiers around and ask the bishop if he saw them. Furthermore, according to Árni, Law-man Árni Oddsson refused to sign and held out for a day or so, but finally gave in to threats, shedding tears as he signed. On the other hand an Icelandic annalist, the nephew of Law-man

[2] *Alþingisbækur Íslands* VI (1933-40), 687-8.
[3] Jón Þorkelsson and Einar Arnórsson (1908), 155-6. My translation from the laymen's letter in Icelandic.

Árni Oddsson, in his early twenties at the time, relates that after the ceremony Governor Bjelke gave a huge banquet, with music from trumpets, violins and drums and cannon-shots, rockets and fireworks continuing to explode far into the night.[4]

It hardly needs to be mentioned that early 20th-century historiography saw the events at Kópavogur in 1662 as a major catastrophe, an interpretation reinforced almost magically by the matching of the year with 1262 when the Old Covenant had been sworn to the king of Norway for the first time. This view, of course, made the most of the oppression exercised by the governor but found it irrelevant to mention his banquet. In more recent decades new interpretations have been launched. It has been suggested that the reluctance of Bishop Brynjólfur and Law-man Árni, the former in his late fifties and the latter aged seventy, was exclusively due to the innate conservatism of elderly men, who were more aware of what they had than they were of what the new arrangement would bring them.[5] A more radical view is that the enactment at Kópavogur was nothing but a pure formality, and that there was no need to introduce absolutism in Iceland because the Crown had no nobility to fight with there and the king already had all the power he wanted to have. The story of threats and oppression has been rejected, because the official documents from the meeting testify to an agreement between the governor and the Icelandic leaders in which the absolute monarchy was not actually introduced.[6]

The theory of an agreement is supported by the fact that the administrative system of Iceland underwent no changes at all for the following two decades, which is exactly the time when Bjelke served as governor there. But after his resignation, in 1683-8, the top administration was completely reorganized. The new governor was called *stiftamtmand* in Danish, *stiftamtmaður* in Icelandic, a post that was at first nothing but a sinecure and was bestowed on a five-year-old illegitimate son of the king. But from 1770 onwards the *stiftamtmænd* [7] resided in Iceland and could have a decisive influence in the government of the country, until the post was changed into that of a *landshöfðingi* in 1873 (see Ch. 3.6). The substitute and later assistant of the governor, resident in Iceland throughout, was called the *amtmand* in Danish (*amtmaður* in Icelandic); we refer to him here as the regional governor. After the governors were moved to Iceland they also served as regional governors in the Southern and also at times the Western Quarter, while another one served the Northern and Eastern Quarters. Sometimes the Western Quarter had a further one. Finally, the post of treasurer (*landfoged* in Danish, *landfógeti* in Icelandic) was established, mainly to look after the royal property in the country. The posts of regional

---

[4] *Annálar 1400-1800* II (1927-32), 194 (Fitjaannáll).
[5] Bergsteinn Jónsson (1964), 79-81.
[6] Sigurður Ólason (1964), 76-109.
[7] The word 'man' is *mand* in Danish, pl. *mænd* and *maður* in Icelandic, pl. *menn*.

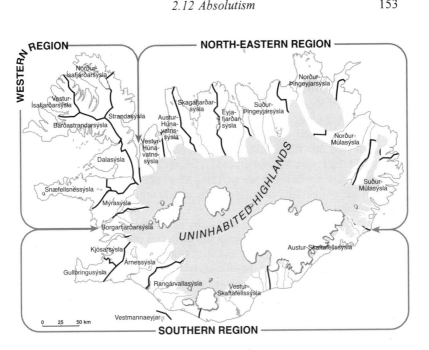

Map 2.12-1 Administrative divisions that emerged in the period of absolutism. Most of the districts (*sýslur*) echo the earlier *þing*s, sometimes with nearly identical names *(Þingeyjarþing* à *Þingeyjarsýsla, Rangárþing* à *Rangárvallasýsla)*. In some places the names are different but the boundaries nearly identical (*Hegranesþing* à *Skagafjarðarsýsla, Vaðlaþing* à *Eyjafjarðarsýsla*). In other cases, the *þing*s have been divided into more *sýslur* (*Þorskafjarðarþing* appears here as four *sýslur*). The regions (*ömt*, pl. of *amt*) were abolished in 1904–7, but for certain purposes the districts (*sýslur*) are still valid administrative units.

governors and treasurer existed until the introduction of home rule in 1904 (see Ch. 3.15).

The Althing was not abolished and underwent no sudden changes in consequence of the absolute monarchy. Thus the Law Council went on passing judgements that were essentially legislation. However, that kind of activity gradually waned; the last judgement of this kind is said to have been made in 1700 concerning the adjustment to the new Gregorian calendar of such important dates as the beginning of summer and winter and of the fishing and haymaking seasons.[8] In 1720 the nomination of farmers to pass sentences at the courts was abolished, and a law imported from Norway whereby sheriffs alone passed sentences in their home districts

[8] *Alþingisbækur Íslands* IX (1957-64), 130-3.

and law-men alone at the Althing. From then on the members of the Law Council only served as witnesses, and the number of farmers that were required to ride to the Althing was gradually reduced from eighty-four from all over the country, according to *Jónsbók*, to ten, all from the three districts closest to Þingvellir.[9]

Thus the Althing shrank considerably during the 18th century in both volume and dignity. Undeniably this assembly of more or less drunken sheriffs, judging and executing thieves and adulterers, is a mockery of the great Althing described in the Sagas.[10] However, it went on providing a forum for the Icelandic aristocracy if it felt inclined to discuss something of interest to the whole of society. This proved of some importance in the second half of the 18th century, when the idea of progress began to emerge in the country (see Ch. 2.16.).

As in Denmark, the absolute monarchy in Iceland became an oligarchy of officials. The important thing for the existence of a separate Icelandic society was that royal decisions that were to apply to Iceland were usually made distinctively for it, and the officials within the country were consulted, normally by letter. It is the conclusion of the most recent research that they usually had their way if they agreed on the issue in question. If the Danish administration in Copenhagen proposed a measure and the Icelandic officials unanimously answered that this could not be done in Iceland (often their view tended to be conservative), it was rare for anyone in the colleges in Copenhagen to have the knowledge or energy to prove or enforce the opposite.[11]

In Copenhagen scarcely more than one Icelander, Jón Eiríksson in the late 18th century, assumed an important post in the part of the administration which dealt with Icelandic affairs. In Iceland, on the other hand, the group of officials was mostly composed of native Icelanders, apart from the very top. Only one Icelander served as a governor with the title of *stift-amtmaður*, except for temporary appointments. The regional governors were more often Icelanders than Danes, and the treasurers more often Danes than Icelanders until the late 19th century. The law-men and sheriffs were almost all Icelanders. During the period 1721-90, which could be called the heyday of absolutism, seventy-eight men served as sheriffs in Iceland. The fathers of only three of them were Danish and those of the remaining seventy-five were Icelandic.[12] These high officials were the truly absolute rulers of Iceland.

At the beginning of the period of absolutism these men were mostly wealthy landowners. Around the turn of the 18th century eighty-one

[9] Einar Arnórsson (1945), 204-5, 310-11.
[10] The procedure of the 18th-century Althing is vividly described in a historical novel by Björn Th. Björnsson (1975), which is available in a Danish translation (1984).
[11] Gustafsson (1985), esp. 161, 168-9, 237-40, 274-82.
[12] Gustafsson (1985), 78-9, 290-3.

individuals owned approximately a quarter of the landed property in Iceland. Among these magnates were twenty-one secular officials (corresponding roughly to the total number of sheriffs), twenty-two clergymen and thirty-eight farmers.[13] It seems that the wealthy officials sometimes held their offices more as sidelines while the running of their property was their main occupation. Thus among the thirty-eight wealthy farmers around 1700, there were eight graduates from Latin school, who supposedly had an opportunity to become pastors or sheriffs if they found it worthwhile. The richest man in the whole country, Brynjólfur Thorlacius, a bishop's son, who owned 1,212 hundreds, was later to abandon his post of sheriff because he did not find it worth the trouble.[14] Formally it was true that there was no nobility in Iceland in the 17th century, but it was a feudal society in the inclusive sense of being largely ruled by men who made their living from exploiting the labour of peasants. Some of these men probably had few qualifications for serving as officials, except the guarantee they could give for the return of royal income.

During the 18th century the Icelandic officials began to rely less on property and more on university education as a basis for their posts. In 1730 almost half the secular officials in Iceland (mostly sheriffs) had no formal education; ten out of twenty-two had not even graduated from Latin school. Of the other half the majority had studied at the University of Copenhagen without graduating (this is not as bad as it may look because a degree in law was not introduced there until 1736). Half a century later, in 1780, almost two-thirds of the occupants of the same posts (seventeen out of twenty-seven) had finished a major university law degree from Copenhagen, and only two had less formal education than graduation from Latin school. Around this time Icelandic sheriffs were considerably better educated than *amtmænd* and *stiftamtmænd* in Denmark and Norway.[15] Thus absolutism in Iceland may have consisted, above all, in a transformation of the ruling class from predominantly landowners to predominantly specialized administrators.

To a certain extent the high standard of education among the Icelandic élite is due to the privileges Icelanders enjoyed at the University of Copenhagen, where they had access to free lodging at a students' hostel for the first years of their study. But it can be assumed that the appreciation of higher learning was also in some way connected with the literary culture within Iceland, to which we return in the next chapter.

---

[13] Bragi Guðmundsson (1985), 40-51.
[14] Bragi Guðmundsson (1985), 40; Gustafsson (1985), 86.
[15] Gustafsson (1985), 84-5, 101.

2.13 Cultural Renaissance

It is not entirely true, as it was taught until recently, that Icelandic saga-writing came to a complete end by the late 14th century or the turn of the 15th. Sagas of chivalry, imitations of the original translations of French romances (see Ch. 1.11), were written every now and then until the 19th century,[1] and in *rímur* this heritage was kept alive in verse form (see Ch. 2.9). Nevertheless the heyday of Icelandic literature came to an end in the late Middle Ages. The period from 1430 until just before the mid-16th century is not even covered by contemporary annals or chronicles relating the most remarkable events within the country (see Ch. 2.5). *Gottskálk's Annal*, written in Skagafjörður in the north in the second half of the 16th century, with very little about most of the 15th century, marks the beginning of a new wave of writing annals.

Around the beginning of the 17th century Bishop Oddur Einarsson at Skálholt began to make arrangements to collect knowledge about the late medieval and Reformation periods. A short account, *On the Bishops of Skálholt before and around the Reformation*, was written down in 1593 from the tale of a farmer named Egill Einarsson, probably by Bishop Oddur himself.[2] A son of Egill, Jón, was a clergyman in the neighbourhood of Skálholt, but after an accident, where he lost three or four fingers, the bishop had him taken home to Skálholt. There he wrote *Bishops' Annals* in 1605, a masterpiece in narrative art which has been quoted repeatedly in this book. Later authors took a course still closer to the medieval sagas. Thus in the early 18th century Pastor Jón Halldórsson, wrote, in addition to other works, bishops' sagas from the first Icelandic bishops in Iceland up to his own day.[3] Jón's son, Bishop Finnur Jónsson at Skálholt, later elaborated on his work in a four-volume history of the Church in Iceland in Latin.[4] At that point indigenous Icelandic scholarship was turned into learned European scholarship, which again merges with modern historiography.

At the Hólar diocese Bishop Þorlákur Skúlason, the successor (and grandson) of Bishop Guðbrandur, hired the farmer Björn Jónsson at Skarðsá to write an annal about the period from about 1400, which he did

---

[1] Driscoll (1997), vii-viii, 1-10.

[2] *Biskupa sögur* II (1878), 235-62; *Safn til sögu Íslands* I (1856), 640-2.

[3] Jón Halldórsson I-II (1903-15).

[4] Finnur Jónsson I-IV (1772-8).

in the late 1630s.[5] With this work Björn set in motion the development of Icelandic annal writing in the 17th and 18th centuries, which culminated in the early 19th century in the twelve volumes (1,982 pages in all) of the history of Iceland in annal form by Sheriff Jón Espólín.[6] This was a revival of the old scholarship, largely an imitation of medieval lore gathering, often excellently written, but devoid of anything comparable with the medieval sagas in literary depth or insight.

Yet another strand of Icelandic scholarship of the early modern period was directed towards the external world. Geographical literature was popular in 16th-century Europe, and Iceland, with its extraordinary natural features, of course became one of its favoured subjects. Bishop Guðbrandur, himself a devoted geographer and the first Icelandic cartographer, found many of the descriptions of the country erroneous and derogatory – for instance, the common contention that the volcano Hekla was the entrance to Hell. So Guðbrandur hired a young Icelandic scholar, Arngrímur Jónsson, to write a reply and reverse some of the worst slanders about Iceland.[7] In 1593 Arngrímur had his first booklet published in Latin in Copenhagen, *Brevis Commentarius de Islandia*.[8] This proved completely unsuccessful because, in common with most people, European authors and their readers preferred the adventurous to the truthful. For a quarter of a century Arngrímur went on correcting falsehoods about Iceland, but they were repeated in the geographical literature of Europe long after his death.

Fortunately, therefore, Arngrímur discovered another way of restoring the reputation of his fatherland when he wrote a history of Iceland, the first since Ari's *Book of the Icelanders* (see Ch. 1.1). But, unlike Ari, Arngrímur wrote his book in Latin and had it published with the Greek title *Crymogæa* (literally "Ice-land") in Hamburg in 1609.[9] It was no simple task to write the history of a society which had never had sovereigns of its own and never fought a war against other countries. But Arngrímur solved the problem by retelling stories of saga heroes, especially how bravely they dealt with foreign princes. *Crymogæa* is the manifesto of Icelandic patriotism. Thus the idea that Iceland has preserved the pure common Nordic language, which therefore should be kept free of foreign words, is expressed here for the first time. Here we also meet a historical interpretation which has pervaded most Icelandic historiography ever since. Arngrímur maintains

---

[5] *Annálar 1400-1800* I (1922-7), 28ff.

[6] Jón Espólín I-XII (1821-55). Jón Espólín's works have been studied thoroughly by Ingi Sigurðsson (1972).

[7] A survey of Arngrímur's life and works is provided by Jakob Benediktsson (1957).

[8] An English translation was published in London in 1598 by Richard Hakluyt in *The Principal Navigations* I, 515-90.

[9] An extract of *Crymogæa* in English was published in London in 1625 in *Purchas' Haklvytus posthumus, or Purchas his pilgrimes* III, 654-68.

that the Icelandic people enjoyed a period of prosperity during the first centuries of habitation (see Ch. 1.7), that this golden age was corrupted by concentration of power (see Ch. 1.12), and that it therefore succumbed to foreign domination (see Ch. 1.14). To a modern reader there seems to be a contradiction in Arngrímur's admiration for the freedom of the common-wealth period and his submissive royalism when writing about his own time, but of course he was obliged to tailor his patriotism to his position as a Lutheran clergyman in the Danish kingdom.

Some people would say that Arngrímur created a new myth about Ice-land to replace the ones he attempted to refute. Anyway, it was predominantly through *Crymogæa* that European scholars became aware of the existence of the medieval cultural heritage of Iceland.

However, as early as during his trip to Copenhagen to have the *Brevis Commentarius* published Arngrímur made Danish scholars aware that Icelandic manuscripts contained information on the early history of Scan-dinavia. This was no small news in Denmark, because a Swedish historian had recently written a history of the Swedish dynasty, tracing it back to the grandson of Noah and thus taking it much further than the history of the Danes. In the hope of restoring the balance, Arngrímur was hired to collect information in Iceland about the ancient Danish kingdom, and a saga of the Danish dynasty is now preserved almost exclusively through his retelling of it in Latin.[10]

This was the beginning of a lively interest in medieval Icelandic texts among Scandinavians in the 17th century.[11] It soon emerged that Iceland-ers could read these manuscripts without any special training. In 1658, for instance, a twenty-two-year-old Icelander, Jón Jónsson, who later adopted the name Jón Rúgmann, set off for Copenhagen to appeal to higher au-thorities against his expulsion from the Latin school at Hólar. At this time a war was raging between Denmark and Sweden, and the ship was cap-tured by the Swedes. They found some parchment manuscripts in Jón's luggage and immediately saw that this man might be of value as a reader of manuscripts. So they sent him to the University at Uppsala, where he was taught to translate manuscripts into languages the Swedes could understand, and he later obtained a permanent post in Sweden as a trans-lator and interpreter of old Norse texts.

Modern philologists would probably make various criticisms of Jón Rúgmann's interpretations, as well as those of his exact contemporary Þormóður Torfason, who resided in Norway and was appointed a royal historiographer there. The decisive step towards a solid, empirical treatment of Old Norse texts was made by another Icelander, of a younger generation, Árni Magnússon, who became a professor of

---

[10] *Íslenzk fornrit* XXXV (1982), xix-xxvii, 3-38.
[11] Andersson (1964), 1ff.

Danish antiquities in Copenhagen in 1701.[12] In 1702-12 Árni stayed in Iceland and travelled around the country collecting information for a large land register, to which we shall return in the next chapter. On his travels he collected all the manuscripts that he could get, either buying them or accepting them as gifts and borrowing for copying those that the owners would not part with – these he returned late or not at all. Unlike most earlier collectors, Árni sought not only handsome books but any scrap or fragment that he could lay his hands on. During the winter, he stayed at the see of Skálholt, where he had ample time for study. After his return to Denmark, his collection of manuscripts and books was carried on thirty packhorses from Skálholt to Hafnarfjörður, and shipped to Copenhagen.

After his return from Iceland Árni spent his life studying Icelandic manuscripts, though without doing much publishing. He did not edit a single saga or write a single book about his main subject. The most important part of his scholarship consists of short comments on the manuscripts and their content, written on small slips of paper which he inserted into the books. These remarks are of immense value because Árni was the first in the field who exercised the minute precision which is the hallmark of philology. From a later viewpoint his slips are therefore much more valuable than many an elegant publication. On the other hand, he did not make good use of the opportunities for making medieval Icelandic literature known to the outside world.

In 1728 a fire broke out in Copenhagen and burned down half of the city. Ironically the event has become better known in Icelandic than in Danish history, because it put the bulk of the medieval Icelandic manuscript treasure in acute danger. Árni refused to have his collection removed from his house until the fire had reached the end of the street where he lived. Then four or five carriages of books and furniture were removed before the rescuers were forced to leave the house. Árni is reported to have pointed at the books left on the shelves and said: "There are books that will never and nowhere be found until doomsday." Afterwards, however, it appeared that most of the parchment manuscripts had been saved; twelve containing sagas are supposed to have been lost, but the texts of all of them are preserved in other manuscripts. On the other hand, hundreds of paper manuscripts, most of Árni's printed books and a huge amount of documents were lost. One manuscript, containing the only text of part of the *Saga of the Slayings on the Heath*, Árni had borrowed from Stockholm for copying. His scribe, Jón Ólafsson, had already copied the text, but now both the original and the copy were burnt. After the fire Jón wrote the text down from memory.[13]

---

[12] The basic work on Árni Magnússon's life and works in Danish is *Árni Magnússons levned og skrifter* I-II (1930). Már Jónsson (1998) has written Árni's biography in Icelandic.

[13] *Complete Sagas of Icelanders* IV (1997), 67ff.

Árni Magnússon has often been blamed for being careless with his manuscript treasure, but it should be said in his defence that he was not the worst. The University Library, though situated further away from the origin of the fire than Árni's house, lost all its Icelandic manuscripts but one, and this was saved because Árni Magnússon had borrowed it.

Árni Magnússon bequeathed his collection, together with all his property which he had acquired through marriage to a Norwegian widow, to the University of Copenhagen. The legacy was used to found the Arnamagnæan Institute in Copenhagen, which for the next two centuries was the centre of Icelandic studies. However, after its separation from Denmark, Iceland demanded that these national treasures be returned home. After a few decades of deliberation and discussion, Denmark yielded with outstanding generosity. In 1971 a treaty was concluded between the two countries, whereby all medieval Icelandic manuscripts that could not be considered to belong to the cultural heritage of other nations (such as manuscripts of kings' sagas) were to be transferred to Iceland.[14] In addition, two of the most precious Icelandic manuscripts from the Royal Library in Copenhagen were transferred, the *Codex Regius* of Eddic poetry, and *Flateyjarbók*, the largest of all Icelandic manuscripts, containing mainly kings' sagas. These two manuscripts were formally delivered in Reykjavík on 21 April 1971. In Reykjavík the Arnamagnæan Institute (Stofnun Árna Magnússonar á Íslandi) was founded, and it is now the centre of philological studies in Iceland.

[14] See Sigrún Davíðsdóttir (1999) for a study of the manuscript case.

2.14 People and Production around 1700

The 17th century ended with a number of bad years, in both farming and fishing; annals report minor winter famines annually in 1696-9.[1] In 1700 these problems were discussed at the Althing, but no urgent help was claimed; the result was a supplication that the regional governor took with him to the king, asking for one of the two law-men to be allowed to sail to Denmark in the next year to discuss the problems of Iceland with the sovereign. Frederik IV graciously granted this, and in 1701 Law-man Lauritz Gottrup, the promoter of the enterprise, set off to Denmark (Gottrup was probably the only law-man ever to be of Danish birth – he had moved to Iceland in the service of the monopoly trade). One of the consequences of his mission was the new price list of 1702, mostly a re-enactment of the pre-1684 list and more favourable to Icelandic producers than the one covering the period 1684-1702 (see Ch. 2.10).

Another consequence of Gottrup's mission was the appointment of a committee of two men to investigate the economic and social conditions of the country. The Crown, it seems, was beginning to take an interest in what it really was that it owned up in the far north, and even how conditions in the dependency could be improved. This second measure was to engender a unique collection of information about the demography and economy of Iceland at the turn of the 18th century.

The commissioners were two Icelandic theologians, Árni Magnússon, recently appointed professor of Danish antiquities in Copenhagen (see Ch. 2.13), and Páll Vídalín, sheriff and vice-law-man. In the absolutist fashion, they were intended to investigate and write proposals on practically everything that could be thought of concerning the administration and economy of Iceland. However, three of their tasks are of importance here: a census and registers of livestock and land.

The census was drawn up in 1703 and was intended to register the name, age and social status of every person. The commissioners instructed

---

[1] Þorvaldur Thoroddsen (1916-17) has collected evidence about the weather and consequences of bad years throughout the history of Iceland. A further elaboration is provided by Páll Bergþórsson (1987). Jón Steffensen (1975), 341-425, provides a survey of famines and scarcity diseases in Iceland.

the sheriffs on this, and the sheriffs in turn instructed their communal overseers in each commune. The result is a beautiful testimony to the effectiveness of the Icelandic administration. The census is preserved without a single commune missing – hardly even a farm, as far as we know – and everywhere women, children and paupers are registered in the same way as the pillars of society. Only some 500 individuals have been found to be registered twice. Icelanders like to think that this census is, in some sense, the first in the world where a population was counted using their names. Rivals are said to be some 17th-century censuses from French Canada, remnants of a mostly lost census from England and Wales, and a Norwegian count of males in rural areas only. However, if we want to nourish our vanity, we can contend that nowhere in the world has a register of a whole people down to the last man been preserved that is older than the Icelandic census of 1703.[2]

Also in 1703 a count of livestock was made, in some places together with the census and elsewhere separately. The original reports are missing from a number of communes and even whole districts, and it is not known if they were ever compiled.[3] However, total numbers from each district and the whole country were written into a description of Iceland by Treasurer Skúli Magnússon in the late 18th century, perhaps taken partly from the land register, which is described below. These numbers have been used in official statistics and will also be used here.

The land register made by Árni and Páll was not the first in Iceland. A few more or less comprehensive land registers had been written in 1681-97, but these contain only lists of farms with standard information such as ownership and rent; the relevant content of all of them was edited in one volume.[4] The land register of Árni and Páll contains, besides this kind of information, a detailed description of each farm (including deserted farms), its real and possible livestock, and an account of its merits and drawbacks. It took from 1702 till 1714 to compile and has been published in eleven volumes, although the whole eastern part of the country, Múlasýslur and Skaftafellssýslur, is missing.[5] This is an invaluable source of information which has yet to be exhaustively examined by historians.

When duplications have been excluded from it as far as possible, the 1703 census proves Iceland to have had 50,358 inhabitants. Knowing that the census followed a number of hard years, we can assume that the population was not at its highest; the age division in the census also indicates a population of around 55,000 in the second half of the 17th

---

[2] The census is published in *Manntal á Íslandi árið 1703* (1924-47). The information has been tabulated in *Hagskýrslur Íslands* II:21 (1960).

[3] Haraldur Sigurðsson (unpubl. 1991), 11-17.

[4] Björn Lárusson (1967). See also Björn Lárusson (1982).

[5] Árni Magnússon and Páll Vídalín I-XI (1913-43). The twelfth volume is a register (1990) and the thirteenth a collection of documents concerning the compilation (1990).

century.[6] In 1703 there were 1,202 women for every 1,000 men in the country. This great difference was not due to a higher number of births of girls than boys. On the contrary, among babies in their first year there were 217 boys and 216 girls. But among one-year-olds the girls were already more numerous, a difference that increases almost constantly throughout the age-groups. The difference is thus due to a higher mortality rate for males of all ages. This characteristic of the sexes is omnipresent, but it was more evident in Iceland than in most societies, because the infant mortality was unusually high – maybe around twice that of England at the same time. Even in reasonably mild periods in the late 18th century and for parts of the 19th century, more than one-third of all children died in their first year. The reason for this was predominantly a custom – known elsewhere in Europe in the early modern age, though scarcely on such a scale as in Iceland – of not breast-feeding babies. Thus the society unconsciously practised an effective population check through feeding babies with cow's milk, which is far too salty for infants.[7]

Another population check consisted in a low proportion of married people and a high age of marriage. In 1703 only 46% of men and 43% of women aged twenty and above were or had been married. In the 40-59 age-group the corresponding number was 73% for men and only 58% for women. Thus without contending that all people wish to marry and have offspring, it is easy to see that a large part of the population was deprived of these possibilities by social conditions. Of course this situation created a high rate of illegitimacy – some 10% in the late 18th century and up to 20% in the last quarter of the 19th. Nevertheless, marriage was the main determinant of fertility.[8]

The basic reason for the abnormally high number of unmarried people must be the difficulty in supporting a family, so let us turn to the economic basis of society. In 1703, practically the whole population had farming as their main occupation. The number of those listed with occupations that would belong in the class of civil servants today was only about 300 and skilled labourers numbered just over 100; most of the members of both these classes also ran a farm. There were seventy-six schoolboys and only five commercial managers. Within the farming occupation, it was estimated later in the century that 30% of farmers had fishing as a sideline in the spring or in both winter and spring. This must apply only to those who went fishing from their homes; a much larger proportion of farmers must have attended the fishing season in late winter or sent their farm-hands there (see Ch. 2.4).

[6] Helgi Skúli Kjartansson (1975).
[7] Gísli Gunnarsson (1983b); Loftur Guttormsson (1983a); Helgi Skúli Kjartansson (1989b).
[8] Gísli Gunnarsson (1980).

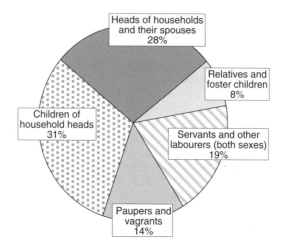

Fig. 2.14-1 Division of the population by household status, 1703.
Source: Hagskinna (1997), 137 (table 2.15).

Within the farming community some 14,000 individuals belonged to the class of farmers and their wives, while 10,000 were servants of both sexes (including a few stewards, stewardesses and casual labourers). This amounts to an employer: employee ratio of 58:42. Other occupational groups cannot be classified as accurately. Thus there were almost 6,000 children aged fifteen and older at their parents' homes. They were no doubt workers – even children as young as six or seven worked. But they would rarely have received wages, except for food and clothing, and their work could be seen as a contribution towards running, sometimes even improving, a property they might take over themselves. Paupers were also to some extent workers, and they were extremely numerous in 1703: 6,800 living at the homes of farmers and 400 vagrant beggars.

Although it was not strictly illegal for servants to marry, they were generally not supposed to do so. It would hardly have been proper to propose to a woman without being able to offer her the status of a housewife of some kind. And if a fertile woman was tempted to accept a man who could not offer that, she could expect her children to be brought up as paupers, which was definitely something to be avoided. Therefore it was basically the number of habitable farms, parts of farms or cottages that restricted the number of households in the country.

In 1703, there were 8,191 homes, just over 7,000 with a man as a head of the household and some 1,100 with a woman. They are classified in four categories, which no doubt overlap somewhat in reality:

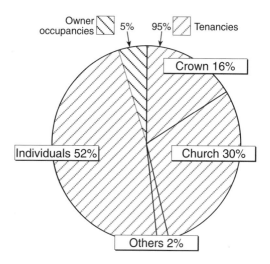

Fig. 2.14-2 Ownership and occupation of landed property, *c*.1700. Proportions are calculated according to value, not number, of farms. *Source*: *Hagskinna* (1997), 262 (table 4.3), 264 (table 4.5).

(1) Farmers on main farms (*lögbýli*), male and female, numbered 5,915. This applies to farmlands that had definite boundaries, a hayfield and grazing land of its own. The farms, however, were not so numerous. In 1695/7 only some 4,030 main farms were inhabited (incredibly close to the number of self-sufficient farmers six centuries earlier (see Ch. 1.7)), so that almost 4,000 families must have lived at two-family farms (*tvíbýli*).

(2) Outlying farms (*hjáleigur*) were inhabited by 1,181 families. They were parts of farms, rented out separately, usually with their own houses and own hayfield, but with a grazing field in common with the main farm.

(3) Cottages (*þurrabúðir, tómthús*) were inhabited by 343 families. They were either completely without the right to any farmland or so restricted that the cottars inevitably had their maintenance from another occupation, in most cases fishing.

(4) Lodgers (*húsfólk*) numbered 752, with almost an equal amount of men and women. Most of them (508) were single people, probably living in the houses of other families, but having in some way a more independent status than servants.

Around the beginning of the 18th century, approximately half of the landed property was owned by individuals. Of the other half, the Church (the bishoprics, benefices and private churches) owned about two-thirds and the Crown one-third. In spite of this unusually large proportion of private property, 95% of the farmers were tenants. Around 45% of the inhabited land was owned by individuals who rented it out. These large landowners made up the group from which the Icelandic officials were largely recruited, the real ruling class of Iceland (see Ch. 2.12).

It is disputed, however, to what extent this ruling class was distinct from the rest of the population, and I shall try to portray the situation as objectively as possible, although I definitely have my opinion on the issue. Of forty-nine secular officials (mainly sheriffs) at two distinct points of time, 1730 and 1780, twenty-eight (57%) were the sons of officials (lay and clerical), eighteen (37%) the sons of Icelandic farmers and a further three were sons of Danes. Fractionally more of the sons of these officials became officials than farmers. Some 62% of their daughters were married to officials and 38% to farmers.[9] These farmers were of course the top layer of the farming class, rich landowners who were no doubt also related to officials in other ways. But, then again, some of the fathers who were officials themselves were sons of farmers, and it can be assumed that all farmers also mixed with less wealthy ones, who might again be related to tenant farmers and cottars. The scale of ownership of the landed property thus formed a complete spectrum from those who owned no land or only a negligible part of a farm, to those who owned up to fifty farms. There was an immense difference in status and opportunities between the two ends of the scale, but it is my contention that there was no sharp divide between them.

The same applies to the bottom of the social ladder. Since the servants were mostly unmarried – and the majority of them probably did not have service as a lifelong occupation (see Ch. 3.12) – they were, while in their posts, what historians call "socially unfruitful". Therefore the servant class inevitably consisted largely of the offspring of farmers and their wives.

The rural society of Iceland seems to have been socially mobile compared with most European rural societies of pre-industrial times. This again is reflected in geographical mobility. In the 18th and 19th centuries farmers seem rarely to have stayed at the same farm throughout their farming years.[10] Both kinds of mobility, social and geographical, again contributed to creating a relatively homogeneous culture, a practically complete absence of dialects in the Icelandic language and only vague dividing line between high and low culture.[11]

From the figures above it can be deduced that around 7,100 households made their living predominantly from their own farming. According to the livestock numbers in Table 2.14-1, each home had on average three and a half cows, twenty-four ewes and sixteen wethers. The most important product was milk, preferably from cows throughout the year and from ewes in the summer. The milk was mostly consumed in the processed form

---

[9] Gustafsson (1985), 78-80.

[10] Loftur Guttormsson (1989b).

[11] Gunnar Karlsson (1995), 53-8.

Table 2.14-1 LIVESTOCK IN ICELAND IN AND SHORTLY AFTER 1703.

	Total	*Per farming household*[*]
Milking cows	24,467	3.45
Heifers	3,876	0.55
Bulls and geldings	2,977	0.42
Calves	4,540	0.64
Ewes	167,937	23.67
Wethers	111,057	15.65
Goats	818	0.12
Horses, male	11,897	1.68
Mares	8,871	1.25
Horses, unbroken	6,141	0.87

[*] i.e. of a farmer on a main farm or an outlying farm: 5,915 + 1,181 = 7,096.
Sources: Skúli Magnússon (1944), 105; *Hagskinna* (1997), 279 (table 4.13).

of butter, *skyr* (curds made from skimmed milk) and whey. Wethers were particularly important as wool producers, although they were also kept for meat and tallow. Horses were mainly used as means of transport in these times and did not yield any consumable products, although horsemeat was to become a common food later.

Talking about food, fish should not be forgotten. It has been calculated from late 18th-century estimates that 63% of the total fish catch was consumed in Iceland.[12] We know approximately how much was exported in the period when the estimate was made.[13] From this it can be deduced that home consumption amounted to some 300 kilos of unprocessed fish per person per year. This may seem like an absurdedly high amount, but in fact represents only some 40 kilos of stockfish, or 110 grams per day.

For the remaining *c*.37% if the fish catch, and a part of the wool, meat and tallow, which was exported, the most important item of import was grain. Comprehensive information about imports is available for the year 1655 and again for 1753.[14] The import of cereals (mainly rye and barley) seems to have grown in this century-long period from 714 to just over 1,000 tons per year, which amounts to some 13-20 kilos per person. Other imports were almost exclusively timber, textiles, fishing gear and horseshoes. Our first rough estimate of sources of energy by food categories applies to the year 1770. Then it is assumed that some 90% came from domestic products of animal origin and 10% from imported products of vegetable origin. Almost 50% came from milk, 20% from fats and 10% each from fish, meat and cereals.[15]

[12] Gísli Gunnarsson (1983a), 27; Gísli Gunnarsson (1987), 43n.
[13] *Hagskinna* (1997), 420-6 (table 10.3). Calculated from quantities of stockfish and (dry) salted fish 1761-80.
[14] *Hagskinna* (1997), 434-5 (table 10.5).
[15] Guðmundur Jónsson (1997), 52.

In these estimates no account has been taken of food gathered directly from nature, which may have been quite considerable. Trout and salmon were caught in lakes and rivers; eggs were collected, birds hunted, dulse gathered. Most important of these wild yielders was the Iceland moss (*cetraria islandica*, in Icelandic *fjallagrös*), a lichen that grows on inland heaths. It looks extremely unappetizing – brownish and dry, like a shrivelled piece of skin. But it is rich in carbohydrate (70%), demands no processing before being stored, and can be kept for years in a dry place. I personally salivate when I think about it cooked in milk.

The numerical information given above indicates that the Icelanders did not have to go hungry in the 18th century. However, like all averages, they no doubt conceal a lot of scarcity. Iceland was definitely not among the rich and fertile farming countries, but as the home of 50,000 people it had the advantage of being big. That was a great help, although it did not always suffice to keep the 50,000 alive, as we shall see later (Ch. 2.17).

2.15 Educational Revolution without Schools

The centre of the mercantilist state of the 16th and early 17th centuries looked upon its subjects first and foremost as sources of income and military strength. The absolutist state certainly inherited that view; however, as time went on, it developed a previously unknown interest in the thinking, knowledge and behaviour of the general public. In the first instance, this new interest seemed to be more concerned with the welfare of people in the afterlife than in this one. Nevertheless, preparing for an afterlife inevitably comprises a certain cultivation of this one, and it is therefore also of interest from a secular point of view.

In Denmark this new interest emerged under the name of Pietism, which originated in Germany in the 17th century and was above all an attempt to reinforce the Lutheran Reformation – to complete what had been left undone. This applied particularly to education. Although Luther and his contemporary reformers had intended every individual to become able to attain direct contact with God through reading Holy Scripture, in reality this did not go beyond teaching people the knowledge that was considered necessary for salvation. The easiest way to achieve that aim was to make children learn by heart Luther's catechism (which was available in print in Icelandic) and for that purpose genuine literacy was not necessary, nor was it demanded by the authorities, at least not in Iceland.[1]

Still, when a thorough study was finally made of it in Iceland, promoted by Pietism, literacy was by no means rare. In 1741 a Danish clergyman named Ludvig Harboe, accompanied by his Icelandic assistant Jón Þorkelsson, was sent out by the central authorities to Iceland to investigate Christianity and the standard of education. They travelled around the country for four years and wrote reports which are invaluable sources for the cultural situation in Iceland in the mid-18th century.

In the diocese of Hólar in the Northern Quarter, children were tested before a pastor or a deacon in each parish, in Harboe's presence. Unfortunately the age of the children is not stated in the reports, but there are indications that they were normally between twelve and seventeen. The

---

[1] The introduction of literacy in Iceland has been studied thoroughly by Loftur Guttormsson, in Danish (1981), in Icelandic (e.g. 1989a) and in English (1990). The upbringing of children in the absolutist age is discussed more generally by Loftur Guttormsson (1983b).

result was that somewhat more than half of the children in the diocese could read. In the diocese of Skálholt the clergy were asked about the status of literacy in their parish, among adults as well as children, and the exact numbers of literate and illiterate individuals were written down. The result showed that less than half of the people in the diocese were able to read. In the east (Múlasýslur and Austur-Skaftafellssýsla), about 41% were reported to be literate. In the south and south-west (Vestur-Skaftafellssýsla to Borgarfjarðarsýsla) the proportion of literate people was between 23 and 32%. In the west (Mýrasýsla to the Western Fiords) the standard was again slightly higher and more varied, between 32 and 50%.[2]

From the diocese of Hólar, little material is available for control. But from the Skálholt diocese nine parish registers from all three quarters of the diocese, written in 1748-63, indicate that the rate of literacy among all parishioners aged fifteen years and over was some 53%. It was considerably higher among men than women – the ratio was 65:43 – but age and social status were of importance also, so that "daughters" were considerably more literate than male servants, not to mention paupers.[3]

It might be simplest to explain the seemingly higher standard of literacy in the north in terms of the age difference between those under enquiry, which would indicate that literacy levels were rising sharply in the young generation. This may well be true, and there are other indications, particularly differences in literacy in different age-groups at a slightly later point (younger people more literate than the older ones), which indicate that literacy was already on the increase when Harboe made his investigation.[4] Other explanations have also been mooted, especially the book publishing of Bishop Guðbrandur (see Ch. 2.9) and his successors at Hólar, whereas no printing press was active in the diocese of Skálholt until 1685.[5]

Another factor, which may also explain why the literacy levels were higher in the east than the south, is the late winter fishing season in the south and south-west. In parts of the country where the fishing season only drew a small number of people, if any, more people were available to teach children in winter and there was more time to practise reading. This was true mainly of the north-east and east.

However, all these explanations may be superfluous, because Harboe's reports are hardly accurate or reliable enough to serve as the basis for definite conclusions about different standards of literacy. Still, it would hardly be too adventurous to conclude from them and other evidence that around half of the Icelandic population was literate in the mid-18th century.

Harboe's investigation was followed by a number of official regulations about education, Christian observance, domestic discipline and the

[2] Hallgrímur Hallgrímsson (1925), 4-54; Loftur Guttormsson (1981), 158.

[3] Loftur Guttormsson (1981), 147-9; Loftur Guttormsson (1990), 29-30.

[4] Loftur Guttormsson (1981), 146-7.

[5] Steingrímur Jónsson (1989), 95-104.

registration of parishioners and clerical services, most or all of them drafted by Harboe himself.[6] Here a policy for introducing general literacy in Iceland was formed in a way that was entirely different to that in Denmark and Norway. There schools formed the nucleus of primary education, but in Iceland parents were made responsible for the literary education of their children, in reading and Christian knowledge. Pastors were to visit every home in their parishes twice a year and, among other tasks, supervise what the children learned. Even beggars and vagrant children were not to be left out. If no household member was able to read, the pastors were recommended to press parents or other adults to go through with the children the little that they knew every day. If that did not help, the children should be placed in the homes of people who could teach them, against which the need of parents for their labour was to be no valid objection. Alternatively literate servants would be hired to teach them. The confirmation of illiterate children was prohibited. In accordance with this policy, hardly any primary schools operated in Iceland until the 19th century, and then only on a small scale (see Ch. 3.13). Very little evidence exists of a school that operated in the Westman Islands from 1745 till the late 1750s. A so-called school, established by a bequest of Jón Þorkelsson, Harboe's assistant, and run with eight to sixteen children at Hausastaðir, near Bessastaðir, in 1791-1812, was more an orphanage than a school.

Daily religious services in households were prescribed in one of Harboe's regulations, and pastors were authorized to command the heads of families to buy suitable books for them. It seems to have become a dominant custom in Iceland to hold such a service every night through the winter, but in the summer only on Sundays.[7] This proved a fortunate arrangement, not only for the Christian faith of the population but also for its linguistic and literary taste. The sermon book that dominated at Sunday services for more than a century, written by Bishop Jón Vídalín and first published in 1718-20, belongs to the classics of Icelandic literature for its rich language and colourful style.

Harboe's educational policy seems to have been quite effective. A report from the bishopric of Skálholt, 10-18 years after Harboe's visit, indicates that literacy had risen to 63% from the 36% in Harboe's report.[8] Of course these numbers must not be taken as exact, since we can never know the standard of literacy referred to. However, church registers from the 1780s clearly show an ongoing development. By then around 90% of the population aged twelve and over seem to have been literate, the remaining 10% being mainly elderly and disabled people.[9]

[6] *Lovsamling for Island* II (1853), 435-73, 505-29, 532-9, 566-88, 600-20, 636-40, 648-68.

[7] Hjalti Hugason (1988), 294-6.

[8] Loftur Guttormsson (1981), 158.

[9] Hallgrímur Hallgrímsson (1925), 60-70.

On the other hand, Harboe's revolution was restricted to religious observance, and it was undemocratic in so far as all emphasis was laid on the
receptive art of reading and none at all on the expressive one of writing. The
double process of the secularization and democratization of literary culture
took place in two distinct steps, despite their overlapping to some extent.

The art of writing seems to have been rare among common people in
the second half of the 18th century. Thus in 1787 a clergyman complained
that communal overseers could write little more than their own names and
were unable to fill in the reports on the status of farming that were required
of them.[10] There were mostly five overseers in each commune, and one
would expect that the best educated farmers would have been chosen for
the posts. However, sometime between the late 18th and mid-19th centuries, the art of writing made a breakthrough among men. The ensuing
development will be taken up for dicussion later (Ch. 3.13).

A secular literary tradition had, of course, been present in the country
since the Middle Ages, and a few secular books had been printed in Iceland before the mid-18th century; among them was the law-code *Jónsbók*,
published in Hólar in 1578, the *Book of the Icelanders*, the *Book of Settlements* and a few more sagas published at Skálholt in 1688-90. The minutes
of the Althing were printed for the first time in 1696. However, it was only
when a printing press was established outside the control of the bishops
on the island of Hrappsey in Breiðafjörður in 1773 that the publication of
secular works really took off. The press was active for twenty years and
printed about eighty books, most or all of them of secular content, while
the printing office at Hólar continued to have a monopoly of printing religious works.

In 1795 the printing press of Hrappsey was bought by a society that
had been established for this purpose and was called the Educational Society of Iceland (Hið íslenska landsuppfræðingarfélag). It was initiated and
soon presided over by the young and ambitious Magnús Stephensen, son
of Governor Ólafur Stephensen. Magnús was a law-man in north-western
Iceland and the most outstanding proponent of the Enlightenment in the
country. He was to run the printing press at different places for almost four
decades, finally at the former monastery site Viðey. He ran the book publishing mostly as a private enterprise and published a lot of his own books,
since he was a person of strong will and had a burning interest in educat-
ing his fellow countrymen. On the other hand his literary taste and style
have not been valued highly by posterity.[11] His influence is difficult to
evaluate, especially as literary activity in Icelandic also increased greatly
in Copenhagen during this period and in a way took the lead (see Ch. 3.2).

---

[10] Loftur Guttormsson (1983b), 165–6.
[11] The most recent work on Magnús Stephensen is by Ingi Sigurðsson (1996).

2.16 The Birth of Reykjavík

The expedition of Árni Magnússon and Páll Vídalín (see Ch. 2.14), as well as Harboe's mission (see Ch. 2.15), no doubt signify a previously unknown reformative interest in Iceland on behalf of the central government in Copenhagen. However, that interest was restricted to reforms within the old order – on the one hand traditional farming and on the other Christian salvation, but by the mid-18th century a new kind of thinking began to influence Iceland. This was the idea of absolute novelties – of introducing on a large scale something that had never existed in the country. In a way it was the idea of modernization, although in a specifically Icelandic version: for example, an urban nucleus, decked fishing vessels and watermills had been known in Europe since the Middle Ages, but in Iceland were absolute novelties. Although these attempts at reform were to prove rather unsuccessful, they stirred the stagnant society and gave rise to a movement that was to turn into a process of modernization, though much later.

One of the first projects was to explore the nature of this big and inaccessible country using modern scientific methods. In 1749 a Danish lawyer and polymath, Niels Horrebow, who had been dismissed from the Supreme Court after an embezzlement scandal, was sent to Iceland to do field research into the nature of the country. Horrebow stayed in Iceland for two years and wrote a book about his observations, which was published in Danish in 1752. In it he followed in the footsteps of Arngrímur Jónsson in correcting false statements about Iceland in foreign literature (see Ch. 2.13), probably with greater success because the book was also published in German (1753), Dutch (1754), English (1758) and French (1764).[1]

However, other men were to get the opportunity to carry out the first thorough scientific exploration of Iceland. When Horrebow had been in the country for two years, some influential people in Copenhagen discovered that two Icelandic students had studied natural history there and also travelled in Iceland to collect manuscripts for the Árnamagnæan

---

[1] The English translation is entitled *The Natural History of Iceland*. It is said to contain the most laconic chapter in any book. Under the heading "Concerning Snakes", (p. 91), it reads: "No snakes of any kind are to be met with throughout the whole island." The reason for this is that the translator has abbreviated the original text without altering the chapter division. In the original the chapter is much longer because Horrebow refutes the explanation of another author for the absence of snakes in Iceland.

Institute. During their travels they had memorably challenged the traditional view of Iceland's nature by ascending the volcano Hekla, which, according to them, no one had dared to do before. One of them was Eggert Ólafsson, a well-known poet though not one held in very high esteem in the 20th century. The other was Bjarni Pálsson, a student of medicine and later the first director of public health in Iceland. When the qualifications of these young men were discovered, Horrebow was called home and they were sent to Iceland instead, where they carried out their investigations over six years. The result was published in a two-volume report, written by Eggert and published in Danish (1772), German (1774-5), and French (1802). An extract entitled *Travels in Iceland* was published in English in 1805. More than any other single work, this laid the basis for solid knowledge of the geography of Iceland, and for posterity it is an invaluable historical and ethnographical source.

Another much more extensive attempt at modernizing Iceland was also partly a consequence of Horrebow's stay there. In 1750-1 he wintered at Bessastaðir, with the newly-appointed treasurer of Iceland, and the first Icelander to occupy that post, Skúli Magnússon. Skúli was an energetic man determined to utilize his position to help his country, and during the winter he and Horrebow had long discussions and probably agreed that Iceland needed regeneration of agriculture, factory-run wool-processing, forestry, fishing on decked vessels and fish-processing with salt instead of drying. All these ideas had been suggested before; what was new about Skúli was that he wanted action as well as words.[2]

At the Althing of 1751 he established a joint-stock company, together with about half the Icelandic secular officials. In all thirteen men, most of them sheriffs, promised to contribute 1,550 rdl., which amounted to the price of some 350 cows or twenty reasonably good units of farming land. The company never received a formal name, but in Danish it was usually called De nye Indretninger (the New Enterprises), which according to the custom of the time was transformed rather than translated into Icelandic with the word *Innréttingar*.

After the meeting of the Althing, Skúli sailed to Copenhagen, and stayed there the winter. He was well received in the Danish colleges; his proposals were exactly in tune with what the government was engaged in elsewhere – promoting industry in remote parts of the realm – and the textile industry was generally accepted as the best vehicle of industrial development. So Skúli was promised 10,000 rdl. to get the project off the ground and three lots of farm land owned by the Crown. These lots were all close to Bessastaðir and Viðey, where Skúli had his residence. Two of them, Effersey and Reykjavík, were at or close to the trading harbour which was usually called Hólmurinn (the Islet); the third, Hvaleyri, included the

[2] Skúli Magnússon's biography is written by Jón Jónsson Aðils (1911). The most recent survey of his enterprise in Reykjavík is by Lýður Björnsson (1998).

trading harbour of Hafnarfjörður. Skúli bought two decked fishing vessels and named them Frederik's Wish and Frederik's Gift, honouring Frederik V who had been so generous. Furthermore, he bought timber for houses and implements for wool-processing, and hired fourteen Danish and Norwegian farming families to teach Icelandic farmers to grow grain. In the summer of 1752 Skúli sailed home with his ships, had the goods landed at Hólmurinn and began to plan the building of a row of one-storey timber houses with high attics along the path that lay between the farm-houses of Reykjavík and the shore. That path later received the name Aðalstræti (Main Street).[3]

At this time Reykjavík was just a farm, but a major one, with a church and six outlying farms. In the 1703 census there were twenty-one inhabitants at the home farm and forty-eight at the outlying farms. There is no indication that Skúli chose Reykjavík for his enterprise because of the evidence of old sagas that it was where the first permanent inhabitants of Iceland had lived (see Ch. 1.1). His only reasons seem to have been proximity to the harbour and the administrative centres of Bessastaðir and Viðey.

In the houses built at Reykjavík small workshops were set up for spinning wool and weaving cloth, twisting ropes and tanning hides. For the more energy-demanding fulling, a water-mill was built on a river a few miles away. Some seventy workers of both sexes were engaged at the workshops when the activity was at its height. The ships were sent out fishing from Hvaleyri in Hafnarfjörður and used for transport between Reykjavík and Copenhagen. The foreign farmers were placed in the homes of well-off farmers around the country. Sulphur was mined for export. In all this Skúli himself acted as director.

Most of these experiments were distressingly unsuccessful. Within a few years all the farmers had left, and there is no evidence of any Icelander pursuing the attempt to grow grain. The wool and skin industry was run at a heavy loss. Perhaps the project was too ambitious from the start – lacking an internal market the industry had to produce for export, and there it had to compete with the technically highly developed woollen industry of Europe. Another optimistic attempt to improve the Icelandic economy was to damage the wool industry seriously. In the 1750s an experimental sheep farm was established not far from Reykjavík, but rams imported to the farm from England a few years later brought with them scab, which proved lethal to the Icelandic stock. It so seriously damaged Icelandic sheep farming that it could only be exterminated by the slaughter of all sheep and a change-over of stock in the diseased areas in the 1770s. The

---

[3] A multi-volume history of Reykjavík is to be published, but as yet only the period from around 1870 has been covered, by Guðjón Friðriksson I-II (1991b-4) and Eggert Þór Bernharðsson I-II (1998). For an older history of the town see Klemens Jónsson I-II (1929). Much information can also be found in two collections of lectures, *Reykjavík í 1100 ár* (1974) and *Reykjavík miðstöð þjóðlífs* (1978).

result was that the workshops could not even get the wool they needed for production. The company was supported repeatedly by the Crown until the original investment had been multiplied at least sixfold.

Royal officials in Copenhagen grew tired of this seemingly endless loss, and in 1764 they forced Skúli to accept the merger of the *Innréttingar* and the trading company which was about to take over the Iceland trade from the Crown (see Ch. 2.10). The former owners of the *Innréttingar* became partners in the trading company, but within a short span of time most of them had sold their shares, and the enterprise gradually shrank. However, the woollen industry in Reykjavík lasted longer than the trading company. When the Crown took over the Iceland trade again in 1774, the *Innréttingar* went with it, and the Crown seems to have run the workshops longer than it ran the trade. In 1799 they were sold to two Danish merchants, who were probably engaged in trade in Reykjavík at the time. In a census taken in 1801 there were still fifteen individuals in the town with occupational titles such as weaver, spinner and wool sorter, but a letter written two years later, testifies that the workshops had been closed down completely.

The *Innréttingar* did not transform Icelandic society as Niels Horrebow and Skúli Magnússon had hoped. Nor did various other attempts at introducing something new, especially the so-called home-workshops, which were also set up in these years. However, all this no doubt had some influence on the woollen industry, which continued to exist in every single home in the country. The only decisive effect of all these enterprises, however, is to be attributed to the *Innréttingar* alone, and that is the founding of Reykjavík, which is now the home of almost 40% of Iceland's population – more than half if we include the suburbs, which form separate municipalities. Although the *Innréttingar* was active for only half a century and never employed more than 100 people, it proved to be a sufficiently strong magnet to attract other institutions, when the incentive emerged to place them in an environment that was as close to being urban as one could get in 18th-century Iceland.

Around 1770 the first prison was built in Iceland, removing the need to send Icelandic offenders to Copenhagen to serve their sentences. In order to be able to use the labour of the inmates, the institution was placed in (or close to) Reykjavík. There a small stone house was built, the first one in the town and one of the first in the whole of Iceland (it was preceeded by Skúli Magnússon's residence in Viðey). In this way the workshops attracted an official institution with its own employees.[4] In the 1810s the prison was abolished and the house was turned into a residence for the governor of Iceland. Since then it has housed the upper echelons of the governing system within Iceland, and is currently the office of the prime minister. With our poverty as regards old buildings it is considered one of the most precious cultural monuments in Reykjavík.

[4] Björn Þórðarson (1926).

2.17 Catastrophe

The 18th century was a time of contrasts in Iceland. On the one hand, it was an initiating period of optimistic, progressive, future-oriented thinking, after the predominantly backward-looking tendency of the previous century. On the other hand, it was in the 18th century that Icelandic society suffered its worst disasters since the plague epidemics of the late Middle Ages (see Ch. 2.5).

The first of these came in 1707 in the form of a smallpox epidemic which raged through the entire country for the next two years. No comprehensive information has been preserved about the deadliness of the epidemic, but contemporary annals record the numbers of dead in individual parishes and communes. If these numbers are compared with the population figures for the same areas in 1703 (see Ch. 2.14), around a quarter of the population appear to have died in the epidemic – 26.4% to be exact. If this evidence is representative, the population was reduced from some 50,000 to 37,000. The damage was in fact more serious than these numbers indicate, because the epidemic mostly killed people under the age of forty, those born after the previous epidemic in 1670-2. It was somewhat less harmful to children than to young adults, but it is said to have killed almost all pregnant women.[1]

The second major shock of the 18th century was a famine in the 1750s. Around 1750 there began a period of unusually cold weather and widespread pack ice which, besides closing the fishing grounds, always carries cold weather with it. Thus already in 1751 a valley in the north-east, Vopnafjörður, with 357 inhabitants in 1703, was practically devastated; most people became vagrants, indicating that the livestock must have died; even the pastor could not sustain himself at the parsonage. Most of the inhabitants of Vopnafjörður seem to have saved their lives by leaving, since "only" twenty-three are said to have died from hunger in the whole district of Norður-Múlasýsla in that year. The following years were no better, and bad catches of fish added to the dire situation. In 1755 pack ice lay off the northern coast from late winter until September. In the autumn of 1755 the volcano Katla, in the southern Mýrdalsjökull glacier, erupted and caused severe damage from ash and floodwater. In 1756 the pack ice reached the southern coast, the Westman Islands and Reykjanes. After that the weather improved, but many people must have suffered severe shortages, since a large proportion of the livestock was obviously dead. According to the most recent estimates, the population of the country was reduced

---

[1] Jón Steffensen (1975), 295-308.

by some 5,800 between 1751 and 1758, from just over 49,000 to little more than 43,000.[2]

Twenty years after the end of the famine, the population is considered to have passed the 50,000 mark again, but only half a decade later Icelandic society was faced with the most severe catastrophe of the 18th century, not in terms of the number of deaths it caused but as a threat to livelihood in the country generally.[3] It began on Whitsun morning, 8 June 1783, in the district of Vestur-Skaftafellssýsla, in an area called Síða. In clear and calm weather people noticed a dark cloud rising in the north, behind the mountains. In a short time the cloud had reached the inhabited area and a layer of black ash covered the ground. Since May earthquakes had been common, but they were now almost continuous and accompanied by thunderous noise. Two days later the River Skaftá dried up and another two days later a lava flow came down its course and began to cover farmlands. Named after this river, the eruption is called "Skaftáreldar" (*eldar* is the plural of *eldur*: fire).

It soon appeared that the ash was extremely poisonous. On 14 June heavy rain fell, so foul-smelling that people with chest trouble could hardly breathe. Birds were found dead, all iron rusted, grass began to wither and the feet of animals became yellow and sore. The same day dark cloud was also seen in Eyjafjörður in the north and subsequently it spread over much of the country. People from Síða who climbed the mountains saw twenty-two fires in a fissure near a hillock called Laki.

Soon people began to flee from the farms nearest to the lava flow, and one farm after the other was overwhelmed by the lava. People tried to get away with their property, but had to leave much of it behind. One farmer managed to collect his eighty ewes, intending to drive them to a secure place, when the lava swept over the group, and nothing was left of it. On Sunday, 20 July, a church service was due to take place at the former convent farm Kirkjubæjarklaustur, but when the pastor, Jón Steingrímsson, and his congregation arrived the flow had approached to within only a few miles of the farm and the mist was so dense that the church could hardly be seen from the farmhouse. Nevertheless, the pastor conducted his service as usual, and no one showed the least sign of fear sitting in the church. Afterwards people saw that the flow had stopped and piled up exactly where it was when the service had begun. This was related by Jón Steingrímsson himself who, in his autobiography written after the catastrophe, vividly depicted these incredible events.[4] The end of the lava flow can still be seen today, a few miles from Kirkjubæjarklaustur.

[2] Guðmundur Jónsson (1994), 157.
[3] These events are discussed thoroughly, in Icelandic with summaries in English, from both a geological and a historical viewpoint, together with a collection of original sources, in *Skaftáreldar 1783-1784* (1984).
[4] Jón Steingrímsson (1913-16), 177. For a more exact account of this episode and of the eruption, in an English translation, see Jón Steingrímsson (1998).

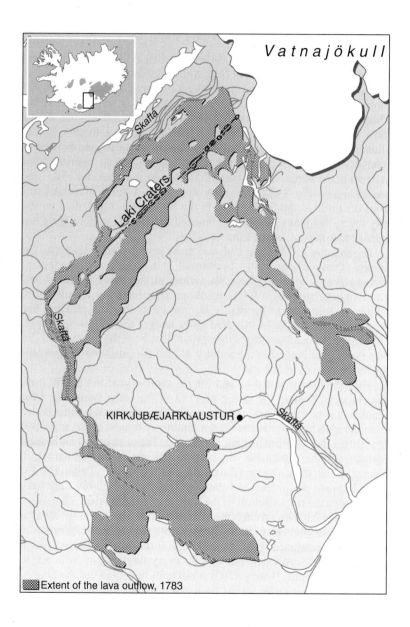

Map 2.17-1 Scene of the Skaftá eruption, 1783.

In October the lava flow began to decrease, and in February 1784 fire was seen in the Laki craters for the last time. The eruption left an area of 580 km.² covered with lava.

However, the eruption in Síða was only the beginning of the calamities. The preceding winters had been cold, with much snow in the north so that stores of hay, which provident farmers kept from year to year, were largely consumed. The winter of 1783-4 was still very cold, with pack ice off the coast from the new year. Little hay was in store from the summer, and in some places it proved to be poisonous, probably from fluorine which is often found in volcanic ash. Usually the late winter, spring and even early summer comprised the period of shortage, but now people began to starve to death in the north-easterly part of the country in December 1783. Impoverished people flocked from the eruption area in the south-east and from the north to the fishing area in the south-west. Many died on the way there, and many others who reached the fishing stations were too exhausted to survive over-eating fresh fish.

The summer of 1784 was bad, and many people were feeble after the hunger of the previous winter. In addition, in the central southern region, in Rangárvallasýsla and Árnessýsla, serious earthquakes occurred in August and destroyed some 400 farmhouses. They had to be rebuilt before winter, to some extent inevitably in time taken from haymaking. For all these reasons people still died from hunger the following winter, although the climate had begun to improve. However, the summer of 1785 was favourable in most of the country, so that the survivors' housekeeping began to recover.

Thus the famine lasted on and off for about a year and a half, from December 1783 until the spring of 1785. It was soon named the Mist Famine, due to the constant mist caused by the eruption. The mist is also considered to have partly caused the famine by poisoning the grass and preventing the sun from heating the ground. The mist spread far beyond Iceland, and there are those who believe that it caused a bad harvest in France, which in turn caused the shortage of bread and inflation that led to widespread discontent, and thus the Revolution of 1789 may have been among the consequences of the Icelandic "Skaftáreldar".

When the bad news from Iceland reached Copenhagen in the autumn of 1783, it was too late to do anything before winter, but a collection of money was organized there. Almost 10,000 rdl. were collected, which would have sufficed to buy one ewe for every single person who was to die from the famine. However, it was not until July 1784 that the king issued a decree on the transport of grain to Iceland for free distribution and free distribution of fish by the trade monopoly, which in these years was run by the Crown itself. Some of the money collected was sent to Iceland to help impoverished people buy new livestock. However, all this seems to have been of limited help. Just as much fish was exported from Iceland in

1784 as in the previous years. The money collected amounted in the end to 46,000 rdl. but only a small part of it was used as intended. When Iceland had recovered so well that there seemed no obvious need for the money, a fund was established and used for diverse purposes in the interest of Iceland. On the whole the state failed lamentably to react to the catastrophe. The officials in Iceland had few resources at their disposal and were slow to seek help from Denmark. The Danish authorities were remote and badly informed.

It is not easy to determine the population loss in the Mist Famine. Not only famine but also a disease raged in the country, called in contemporary sources "*landfarsótt*", a common term that can refer to any epidemic. However, since plague can be excluded at this time, no known epidemic would under normal circumstances cause more than a fraction of the mortality of the famine years. But if a disease which is not normally lethal kills a large number of people because of their debilitated condition, as seems to be the case here, this must be seen as the cause of their death. No known epidemic could be so lethal, because smallpox also raged in Iceland in 1785-7. Contemporary sources keep mortality numbers from the smallpox clearly distinct from the *landfarsótt*, and state that the smallpox killed 1,500.[5] In all, the population of Iceland decreased by just over 10,500 from the end of 1783 to the end of 1786 – from 49,753 to 39,190, to be precise.[6] So the victims of the famine cannot have been much less than 10,000, or close to one-fifth of the whole population.

Even the severely reduced population had far less livestock left per person than before the famine. In 1785 a general count of livestock in Iceland took place, and it shows that the number of cows and horses was about half of what it had been in 1703 (see Ch. 2.14), ewes about 30% and wethers 12%. But it could be an almost incredibly quick process to restore farming in the old Icelandic society, when the climate was tolerable. In this case young people must have soon begun to exploit the possibilities for early marriage which the farmland left by the dead offered to the survivors. In 1791-5 the population growth averaged 1.32% per year (almost double that of the relatively prosperous period 1736-50), and in the late 1790s it rose to 1.67%. In 1801, in the first reliable census since 1703, the population had reached 47,240 – still some 3,000 less than at the beginning of the century. Most of the farms devastated by the lava flow in Vestur-Skaftafellssýsla were sooner or later rebuilt.

[5] Jón Steffensen (1975), 311-13.
[6] Guðmundur Jónsson (1994), 158; *Hagskinna* (1997), 54 (table 2.2).

2.18 From Factory Village to Administrative Centre

As was to be expected, the official reaction to the Mist Famine was somewhat contradictory. On the one hand, the Danish authorities even contemplated transplanting the whole population of Iceland to the heaths of western Jutland, which people were beginning to see as cultivable land, or to some other place in the Danish kingdom.[1] On the other hand, the monopoly trade was abolished in 1786-8. Partly, of course, this was a surrender to the bankruptcy of the Crown-run trade after the hard years, but the new trading system also included a plan of organized urbanization in the country.

Trade between Iceland and other countries was to be free to any citizen of the Danish Crown, except those who lived with monopolized trade themselves (Faroe, Greenland, Finnmark in Norway and the overseas colonies of Denmark). Only ships owned by Danish citizens could be used, and no direct trade between Iceland and countries outside the kingdom was permitted. Six Icelandic trading harbours were to be turned into trading towns, whose citizens were granted certain privileges, such as exemptions from taxes and the licence to engage in trade anywhere in a large area. Thus citizenship in Akureyri gave rights to run trade at any harbour in the Northern Quarter. This urban planning proved to have little success, and all the prospective trading towns were to lose their privileges again, except Reykjavík, which was slowly developing into a small urban nucleus.

When the town of Reykjavík was officially founded by a royal decree of 18 August 1786, the trading houses had already been moved from the harbour at Effersey into Reykjavík. But the introduction of so-called free trade meant that more than one trading firm could be active in the town simultaneously, which was already happening in the 1780s. Around 1807 some five shops were run in Reykjavík, four of them owned by Danes, besides a few minor traders, who were mostly Icelanders.[2]

Another and more important factor that contributed to the emergence of Reykjavík was the administration of the country, both ecclesiastical

[1] Anna Agnarsdóttir (1993), 28, 37-9.

[2] Sigfús Haukur Andrésson II (1988), 492. This two-volume work is the most comprehensive study of Icelandic trade between 1774 and 1807.

and secular. In the earthquakes in southern Iceland in 1784 (see Ch. 2.17) all the houses at Skálholt collapsed except for the church. The see had already lost most of the livestock, which had been kept at the home farm, and obviously its tenants were not able to pay much rent. Nevertheless, the bishop stayed at Skálholt with his servants through the winter, but no school was held there. In the following year a decision was made to sell the farm of Skálholt and all the landed property of the see, to move the residence of the bishop and school to Reykjavík and to pay his salary and the running cost of the school from the Danish treasury. Thus the see of Skálholt was abolished after seven centuries of operation (see Ch. 1.6). A schoolhouse was quickly erected in Reykjavík, but the bishop had to manage on his own in the following years. Bishop Hannes Finnsson, who succeeded his father in 1785, bought Skálholt himself and lived there for the rest of his life, until 1796.

The reason for this arrangement was not only the bankruptcy of the see of Skálholt. At this time economic liberalism was a dominant policy in Denmark, although absolutism was in full force in the constitutional area, and freehold of land was generally considered to be beneficial. Therefore the see of Hólar's turn also soon came. In 1801 it was abolished and the two bishoprics, and the two schools, were united in Reykjavík. The school was to leave the town again and have a stay at Bessastaðir for four decades, 1805-46, where it is believed to have had its cultural heyday, at least in comparison with the status of society in general.[3] But thereafter it was firmly stationed in Reykjavík again.

The Althing was still held at Þingvellir annually until the end of the 18th century, now only as an appeal court (see Ch. 2.12). Some kind of shelter, a mixture of house and tent, had been built in the 1690s to accommodate the Law Council, and in the second half of the 18th century a small timber house had been raised for this purpose. Complaints about leakages and draughts in the house are a regular occurrence in the minutes of the Althing in the 18th century. Sometimes the idea of moving the Althing or dividing it into two courts, one for each law-man, was also contemplated, but all remained the same. So it did not seem to portend anything new when Law-man Magnús Stephensen in 1798 declared that he had become so sick and weak from staying in this windy hovel that he could not finish the court case in question – which he did at his home a few weeks later. But, apart from two sentences that were passed at Þingvellir three days later, this was the end of the Althing at this historical place. Before the next session Governor Ólafur Stephensen (Magnús's father) decided on his own that the session of 1799 should be held in Reykjavík, where the building of the Latin school was available during the summer holiday. The same was done in 1800.

[3] For study in Swedish of the Bessastaðir School, with emphasis on its theological education, see Hjalti Hugason (1983).

In the mean time a committee of four, including Magnús Stephensen, had been appointed in Copenhagen to consider the arrangement of schools and jurisdiction in Iceland. In accordance with its report, a royal decree was issued in 1800, whereby the Althing was abolished and a new High Court (*Landsyfirréttur*) established in Reykjavík with three professional judges. The posts of law-men were abolished and their incumbents turned into a president of the court (Magnús Stephensen) and one of its two assessors. The court convened for the first time on 10 August 1801. The High Court had exactly the same place in the judiciary system as the Althing had before, between the local courts of sheriffs and the Supreme Court in Copenhagen. The great step forward was that it convened not once but regularly, at least six times in each year.

The new president of the High Court, Magnús Stephensen, opened it with a speech in which he severely attacked the opinion that the Commonwealth period had been the golden age of Iceland:

Besides, I willingly leave the imagination of happiness to those who associate it with the first four centuries of freedom and independence, and hold material prosperity in higher esteem than internal quiet and peace, protection of life and property, and everything else that is required for true happiness. Still more willingly I leave it to whomever wants, after more than five centuries, to dream about the greater happiness that Iceland would probably have enjoyed under its old own government, and preserved until now, than it has enjoyed under the kings of Norway and Denmark. I also leave it to them to think of convenient ways of calming down and clearing out the old riots, tumults, robberies and killings and extinguishing all murderous arson, which would still probably have been practised had the same freedom and anarchy reigned as before.[4]

This speech shows that the modernization of Iceland as part of the Danish realm had a passionate advocate in Magnús Stephensen. No less does it show that Magnús felt he had opponents to contend with on the issue. He obviously reckoned that some people in Iceland would see the replacement of the Althing at Þingvellir by an ordinary appeal court in Reykjavík as sabotage of some great values. However, such a view does not seem to have found expression, and perhaps it hardly existed any more. Events that took place in Iceland a decade later would indicate that Magnús was fighting against a dying opposition (see Ch. 3.1), although it was to be revived before long (see Ch. 3.2).

By the beginning of the 19th century the chief officials of the administration within Iceland were gradually gathering in Reykjavík. Skúli Magnússon's successor as treasurer, a Dane named Paul Michael Finne, probably lived in Reykjavík from the beginning of his career in Iceland in 1794. At least he was living there with his wife and son, brother-in-law and four servants in 1801, according to the census of that date.[5] Two years

---

[4] Björn Þórðarson (1947), 40-1. My translation.
[5] *Manntal á Íslandi 1801. Suðuramt* (1978), 399.

later the post of treasurer was united with the newly-established office of town bailiff (*bæjarfógeti*, the urban equivalent of a sheriff). An official health service had been started in Iceland with the post of director of public health (*landlæknir*) in 1760. His residence was at first a few miles from Reykjavík, at Nes on the Seltjarnarnes peninsula. In 1804-7 the Danish occupant of the post preferred to live in Reykjavík, but officially the residence and the adjoining pharmacy were not moved into the town until 1834. In 1806 a Dane, Frederik Christopher Trampe, became governor. He owned a house in the town and preferred living there rather than in his official residence at Bessastaðir. A few years later, as has already been mentioned (Ch. 2.16), the Reykjavík prison-house became the new official residence for the governor. By that act the royal administration in Iceland was formally stationed in the town.

In the 1801 census the Reykjavík which was about to become the administrative centre of Iceland had 307 inhabitants.

2.19 "A Desperate Land"

The idea that life in Iceland had degenerated since the first centuries of settlement was widespread from the 16th century onwards, if not earlier. It thus formed the backbone of Arngrímur Jónsson's historiography (see Ch. 2.13). The idea is no doubt at least partly imported; this was the essence of the European Renaissance, which in the German-Nordic world became mainly known as Humanism, of which Arngrímur was definitely one of the most outstanding proponents in Iceland. The advocate of Enlightenment, Magnús Stephensen, tried to challenge this view and replace it with general progressive thinking, as we saw in the last chapter, but even he did not doubt that life had been more prosperous in the Commonwealth period than later. His challenge consisted only in valuing the peace and security of the absolutist period more highly than the prosperity of earlier times.

The degeneration theory acquired new meaning and content during the struggle for Iceland's independence in the 19th and early 20th centuries, when degeneration was connected with the loss of national freedom in the 13th century. This meant that the theory could be used as a promise of a more prosperous life in the future, if the country reclaimed its autonomy. No one expressed this thought more vividly than the poet Jónas Hallgrímsson in the early 19th century, for instance in the poem *Gunnarshólmi*, from which the title of this chapter is taken. In this poem Jónas describes an event in *Njal's Saga*, in which the saga hero Gunnarr has been sentenced to outlawry but on his way to the ship happens to look back, and returns home because his homestead looks so beautiful to him. In the 19th century people still pointed out the place where Gunnarr returned (as we still do), which was a grassy knoll or holm called Gunnarr's Holm (Gunnarshólmi), in an area that has been ravaged by a certain Cross River. Jónas tells the story of Gunnarr and ends by making the Holm a symbol of hope for his people:

> *For Gunnar felt it nobler far to die*
> *than flee and leave his native shores behind him,*
> *even though foes, inflamed with hate and sly,*
> *were forging links of death in which to bind him.*
> *His story still can make the heart beat high*
> *and here imagination still can find him,*

> *where Gunnar's Holm, all green with vegetation,*
> *glisters amid these wastes of devastation.*
> *Where fertile meads and fields were once outspread,*
> *foaming Cross River buries grass and stubble;*
> *the sun-flushed glacier, with its snowy head,*
> *sees savage torrents choke the plains with rubble;*
> *the dwarves are gone, the mountain trolls are dead;*
> *a desperate land endures its time of trouble;*
> *but here some hidden favor has defended*
> *the fertile holm where Gunnar's journey ended.*[1]

As things were to develop, increased self-rule went hand in hand with economic progress, particularly in the early 20th century (see Chs 3.15 and 4.1-4.2). In this way the theory was confirmed by experience and obtained an increasingly secure place in Icelandic historiography. Even scholars like the Danish ethnologist Kirsten Hastrup, who have more or less abandoned the idea of an early golden age,[2] have relied heavily on the theory of degeneration.[3] Even though Icelandic scholars have stopped blaming Norwegian and Danish authorities for the misfortunes of Icelandic society, misfortune is conspicuously present in most of their interpretations.[4]

However, doubts have recently been raised over this interpretation of Iceland's history. Thus it has been maintained that "The period between 1550 and 1800 can be seen as the golden age of the rural society of Iceland, a peaceful period, when the peasant society lived under the protection of the Danish king, without any major challenges."[5] Of course, there is every reason to treat the degeneration theory with caution. The image of Iceland's history looks suspiciously like traditional world history, with a glorious antiquity (which in Iceland happened to be in the Viking Age and the high Middle Ages), dark Middle Ages (in Iceland *c.* 1400-1800) and restoration (19th and 20th centuries). Or, if we prefer, it looks like any romantic story. It should also be recalled, as has been mentioned earlier (Ch. 1.7), that the myth of a past golden age seems to be universal. Therefore, it is necessary to ask more critical questions about the alleged degeneration than have usually been raised in Icelandic historiography.

First, it must be acknowledged that the concept of general degeneration presupposes that the quality of human life has some common denominator, which makes its different aspects calculable in relation to

---

[1] Jónas Hallgrímsson (1996-7). Translated by Dick Ringler in the verse form of the original.

[2] Hastrup (1984), 250-2.

[3] Hastrup (1985), 157-242 and (1990), e.g. 280-95.

[4] See, for example, Gísli Gunnarsson (1983a), 168-77.

[5] Árni Daníel Júlíusson (1996), 395. My translation from Danish. See also Árni Daníel Júlíusson (1998).

each other. Much disagreement about the merits of different periods inevitably relies on different evaluations of the aspects of life – for instance, on the value of freedom as against security. Thus the renowned literary historian Sigurður Nordal said in defence of the Saga Age as compared with later times: "Deplorable but true is the fact that a considerable measure of overt violence which people dare oppose is more tolerable than injustice parading as a stable and equitable system of government."[6] There is, of course, little hope of general agreement on such a statement, let alone on the evaluation of the concrete historical facts to which it refers.

Nevertheless, we conceive mental images of historical periods which are based on historical facts, and there is no way to determine when, in the transition from individual facts to general pictures, we leave the sphere of scholarship and enter that of imagination. Therefore I propose to move slowly and carefully from one end of the spectrum to the other. First, I shall discuss two relatively delimited questions that are of central interest in this connection, those of population number and climate. Then I shall consider the question of deterioration more generally, albeit with reference to definite and very earthy aspects of life, and with a somewhat heavy emphasis on economic standards. I shall not consider the (from our viewpoint) obvious degeneration of literature, since I look upon the heyday of old Icelandic literature in the Middle Ages as one of those rare historical exceptions.

As mentioned earlier (Ch. 1.7), some scholars have argued that the population of Iceland was some 40-100% larger in the high Middle Ages than it was at the first census in 1703. Others have been of the opinion that, since Iceland was first inhabited, the population was restricted to approximately 50,000. All these estimates, and even those that put the number as low as 40,000 in the Middle Ages, echo the theories of the Scottish demographer Thomas Malthus, which presume that the means of sustenance inevitably restrict the growth of population. Apart from that, the idea of a population ceiling of 50,000 is obviously based on the actual development in the 18th century, when the population underwent three major checks, which happened to occur every time it approached or reached the 50,000 mark (see Ch. 2.17).

Malthus's hegemony has been challenged considerably in recent decades by the opposite view that agricultural societies do not normally succumb to population pressures, but react to them by more effective use of the land.[7] This opinion has recently begun to influence the debate in Iceland. In the case of 18th-century Iceland it has also been pointed out that the three population checks were too different to support a general rule.[8] It can hardly be a law that a population undergoes a check in the

---

[6] Sigurður Nordal (1990), 95.

[7] Boserup (1965), 116-18.

[8] Árni Daníel Júlíusson (1990).

form of either a smallpox epidemic, a famine caused by cold climate, or a famine caused (at least partly) by a volcanic eruption, every time it reaches a definite number. Instead it has been suggested that for centuries the population growth of Iceland was mainly restricted by epidemics. It is known that in sparsely populated and relatively isolated islands contagious diseases tend to enter as epidemics that attack and kill many adults. On continents these same diseases are endemic and mainly attack children, who are much more resistant than adults and therefore survive and attain lifelong immunity.[9] This can be suitably applied to Iceland, where measles caused a lethal epidemic as late as 1882.

Thus the theory of an absolute population ceiling in the 18th century and earlier has been challenged, although we cannot say that it has been disproved. It could be suggested that the population check normally occurred through the recurrent cold and wet spells. After all, three famines reduced the size of the Icelandic population in the century-long period from the late 17th to the late 18th century (see Chs 2.14 and 2.17). The smallpox epidemic of 1707-9 may just have prevented such a check earlier than when it actually took place, in the 1750s, or made that one somewhat less lethal than it would otherwise have been.

In the following century the capacity of Iceland was put to the test again when the population number passed the 50,000 mark and I leave it to readers to determine whether that test supports or dispels the theory of a population ceiling (see Ch. 3.8).

One argument that has been brought against the population ceiling is that by modern standards Iceland must have been able to sustain more livestock than the 35,000 cattle, 280,000 sheep and 27,000 horses that were there in 1703, and hence it could have sustained more people.[10] It is too early to judge this statement, but inevitably it leads us to the important question of climate during the centuries of alleged deterioration.

Before the beginning of regular measurements of temperature in Iceland in 1845 (see Ch. 3.7), we have two main kinds of sources about climate in the country. One consists of the written records of the weather from year to year, where only the information about drift-ice proves to be sufficiently concrete to be used for long-term comparison. The Icelandic meteorologist Páll Bergþórsson has compared the average temperature, according to recorded measurements, from 1845 until the present, with the frequency and duration of drift-ice off the coasts from year to year over the same period. The conclusion was that the drift-ice curve mirrored the temperature curve so well that the temperature curve could be extended past 1845 as a reflection of the drift-ice curve. The general result is that the period from about 1200 to the 1920s saw an unbroken spell of cold climate,

[9] McNeill (1979), 133-7. See also Árni Daníel Júlíusson (1990), 150.
[10] Árni Daníel Júlíusson (1996), 168-263; and (1998), 77-86.

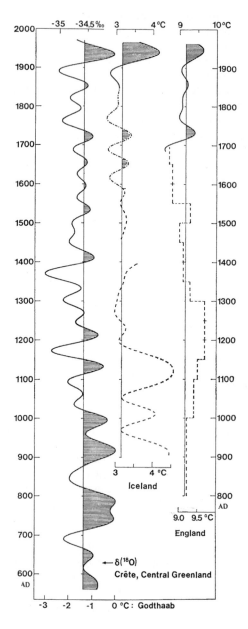

Fig. 2.19-1 Estimated average temperature in Greenland, Iceland and England. From Dansgaard *et al.* (1975), 25.

compared with the time before and after. There are great fluctuations within this period, and for the first two thirds of the 15th century even a daring scholar like Páll Bergþórsson has not even ventured to draw a curve, because of lack of information. But no long time span can be said to be much worse than all others, except perhaps the second half of the 18th century, and no definite line of development can be discerned through the period.[11]

The other important source on climate is the core of the Greenland ice cap, which reaches much further back than the colonization of Iceland and shows a clear deterioration of temperature in the 11th century (see Ch. 1.7). Concerning the dark ages of Iceland, the ice-core generally supports the Icelandic evidence in spite of certain deviations. No period seems to have been colder in Greenland than the 14th century, especially its second half. Next to it come the second halves of the 12th and 19th centuries, which in Greenland proved considerably colder than the second half of the 18th. But the sudden and decisive change towards a warmer climate in the early 20th century occurs at about the same time in Iceland as in Greenland, which greatly supports the argument for taking the ice-core evidence seriously as a source on temperature in Iceland.[12]

The conclusion is that the climate was generally much colder in the centuries under discussion than during the first centuries of habitation – leaving open the question of the exact timing of the change – and in the 20th century. Climate can therefore be seen as a factor contributing to economic relapse, which means that we may hold on to the degeneration theory, while abandoning (if we want to) the purely nationalistic interpretation of devastating foreign oppression.

Concerning evidence about the standard of living, nothing can be more direct than the physical stature of people. According to measurements of skeletons and of living people carried out around the middle of the 20th century, the average height of Icelanders was as follows:[13]

	Number in sample	*Men cm.*	*Women cm.*
Before *c.*100	39	172.3	161.2
11th century	55	172.0	158.7
1650-1800	30	169.2	153.3
1952-4	1,630	176.8	163.7

Although these results are based on rather small numbers, they certainly indicate that the conditions of life were considerably better during the first centuries of habitation than in the 17th and 18th centuries.

[11] Páll Bergþórsson (1987), 211-16.

[12] Dansgaard *et al.*, (1975).

[13] Jón Steffensen (1954-8), 280-8 and (1975), 263-4, 426-33.

The same can be deduced from the habitation of people. The 10th- and 11th-century farmers in Þjórsárdalur built themselves main halls of some 50 m.², besides a smaller living-room (see Ch. 1.7). These houses appear to have been provided with latrines – where a number of people could even sit simultaneously.[14] Although they have not been excavated in Þjórsárdalur, there is no doubt that bathrooms were common – clearly they were saunas of some kind in which stones were heated in a stove and steam was produced by sprinkling them with water.

In the late Middle Ages people seem to have begun using the bathrooms for sleeping in, probably because they were the only rooms at the farms that could be heated, and in the 19th century "bathroom" (*baðstofa*) had become the normal word for the main living-room of the house, where most people worked in the evenings and slept at night.[15] All the rooms of the house complex were gradually built narrower than before, which no doubt means that they were also lower. At the same time the main corridor uniting the individual rooms became longer, and thereby also darker, in order to conserve as much warmth as possible. The house developed into a cluster of individual chambers, separated by thick walls of stone and turf, covered with thick turf roofs, and only partly with boarded roof, walls and floor. Among the stories told in Europe that angered self-respecting Icelanders was that they lived underground, in caves or holes in the earth. I suspect that some modern Icelanders would agree with these foreigners if they entered an ordinary farm house of those times. No bathrooms were used for bathing any more – many people probably never bathed. The dung channels in the cowsheds, or just open ground, were used instead of latrines.[16]

Amusements seem to have been rare also. Dance was condemned by the Pietist authorities of 18th-century Denmark and, unlike all the other peoples in the realm, the Icelanders seem to have submitted to the ban and given up dancing for more than a century.

However much we attempt to revise and leave behind the heritage of nationalism, it is not easy to abandon the idea that Icelandic society degenerated in fairly general terms from the early settlement until the 18th century. There are objective indications that the material standard of living fell considerably. Convincing arguments also speak for the widespread sense of diminished ambition, self-esteem and joy of life.

---

[14] Sveinbjörn Rafnsson (1977), 79-81.

[15] Arnheiður Sigurðardóttir (1966), 69-79. See also Chapter 3.12.

[16] For housing in Iceland since the late Middle Ages, before modernization, see, for example, Stenberger, ed. (1943), 269-306. For an excellent survey that covers earlier as well as later times, see Hörður Ágústsson (1987).

PART III

A Primitive Society Builds a State

1809-1918

3.1 An Abortive Revolution

If Marx was right in his contemptuous remark on the rule of Napoleon III in France, that everything of great importance occurs twice in history and the second time as a farce,[1] the farcical replica of the great French Revolution occurred in Iceland in 1809: a Danish prisoner of war in England, serving as an interpreter for an English trading expedition to Iceland, seized power in the country and promised to grant the inhabitants independence as well as democracy.[2] This was, of course, made possible by the Napoleonic wars, in which the English attack on Copenhagen in 1807 had compelled Denmark to side with France against Britain. In the autumn, eighteen of the forty-one ships that had sailed to Iceland in the summer were captured on the way back and ordered to sail to England. Among those captured was one of the very first Icelandic merchants and shipowners since the introduction of so-called free trade, Bjarni Sivertsen from Hafnarfjörður. In London he made a great effort to secure continued trade with Iceland, with the help of Sir Joseph Banks, the influential president of the Royal Society, who had led a scientific expedition to Iceland in 1772.

While in London Bjarni Sivertsen also met a Danish prisoner of war on parole, Jørgen Jørgensen, and aroused his interest in Iceland. Although Danish by birth and nationality, Jørgensen had sailed on British ships and his sympathies seem to have been more on the British than on the Danish side. He now joined the group of Englishmen, whose most prominent member was Sir Joseph Banks, which advocated the annexation of Iceland by Britain. In 1808 Jørgensen met a certain Samuel Phelps, who ran a soap factory in Lambeth and had run out of fats for his soap production. Jørgensen told him that Iceland produced tallow for export but, because of the war, had difficulty in exporting it. So around New Year 1809 Phelps sent a ship to Iceland with Jørgensen as an interpreter.

This expedition was unsuccessful, mainly because in Iceland the trading season was during the summer. However, as the trade prognosis was

---

[1] Marx and Engels I (1969), 398 ("The Eighteenth Brumaire of Louis Bonaparte").
[2] McKay (1973); Anna Agnarsdóttir (1989). The most comprehensive study in Icelandic is Helgi P. Briem (1936), but Anna Agnarsdóttir (1979, 1989) has a convincing revision of many of his arguments.

favourable, Phelps decided to make another attempt the following summer and prepare it better this time. He secured the protection of the British Navy for his Iceland trade, and in June a British sloop-of-war was sent to Iceland. On his arrival there the captain forced the Danish governor, Frederik Christopher Trampe, to sign a treaty whereby British citizens were granted the unlimited right to trade in the country.

A few days later Phelps himself, accompanied by Jørgensen, appeared in Reykjavík, where they saw no sign of the trading convention. When they found that Trampe had a prohibition on trade with the British on pain of death still posted up, they decided to use force. On Sunday 25 June, after church, some thirteen armed men stormed the governor's house, captured him and took him on board their ship. Apart from Governor Trampe, only four Danish civil servants were resident in Reykjavík: the bailiff, the sheriff of the surrounding district and two policemen. That was about the whole Danish force in the country. The English sailors are said to have met the bailiff in a Reykjavík street and told him to keep to his home, which he seems to have done. The sheriff and the two policemen are hardly mentioned in connection with the coup. No Icelander had been appointed to any office that obliged him, rather than any other law-abiding citizen, to prevent the arrest of the governor. It is said that Trampe asked people not to try to rescue him, and evidently no one did so. Danish rule in Iceland was overthrown by the capture of one single person.

While the manufacturer turned to his trade with the natives, the rule of the country was entrusted to Jørgensen, a task he obviously enjoyed. The very next day after Trampe's arrest he issued two proclamations, both of them in Danish and Icelandic, and had them posted up in Reykjavík. In the first he declared that all Danish authority in Iceland was abolished. A curfew was imposed on Danish citizens in the country and on Icelanders in the service of Danish mercantile houses. All firearms, daggers and ammunition were to be surrendered. On the other hand native Icelanders, royal officials included, were promised good treatment, provided they did not disobey any of these orders. Thus Jørgensen made a clear distinction between Danes and Icelanders.

The second proclamation was partly the draft of a constitution for Iceland, which was to become an independent country under British protection, with its own legislative body and its own flag. Later, Jørgensen gave himself the title of "all Iceland's protector and supreme commander on sea and land", but his rule was only to be temporary until the population could elect representatives to their parliament.

After this, Jørgensen began to look for support among Icelanders. One of the judges of the High Court in Reykjavík took over the post of regional governor of the Southern Region, which had been a part of Trampe's office. A group of eight Icelanders became Jørgensen's bodyguard and rode with him through the Western Region and to the village of Akureyri in

Reykjavik in 1810, the year after Jørgensen's coup. From George Mackenzie's book, *Travels in the Island of Iceland*, 1811.

the north to secure his power in the country. Most Icelandic officials decided to stay in their offices under Jørgensen's rule: the judges of the High Court, the bishop, the director of public health, the regional governor of the Western Region and most of those sheriffs whom Jørgensen managed to contact. Only the regional governor of the North-Eastern Region and five sheriffs honoured their official oaths to the Danish king and resigned.

The reason why people were so obedient to Jørgensen was probably that they assumed he was backed by the British government. But it soon became apparent in Iceland that this was not the case and everything that he had proclaimed about British protection was his own invention. Early in August a British warship came to Iceland to assess the situation. At first the captain, Alexander Jones, was not sure what to do; maybe he thought that Phelps and Jørgensen were acting secretly on behalf of the British government. The captain even attended a ball given by the "supreme ruler". However, Jones finally managed to drag out of Phelps that he and Jørgensen had acted entirely on their own. A little later contact was established between the captain and the president of the High Court, Magnús Stephensen, who asked the captain to remove the usurpers from the country. Finally, on 22 August, a treaty was signed between Phelps and Captain Jones on the one hand and, on the other, Magnús Stephensen and his brother Stefán Stephensen, the regional governor who had abdicated. Jørgensen was thereby removed from office and the rule of Iceland was temporarily handed over to the Stephensen brothers. Governor Trampe was set free, but rather than resuming his office, he chose to sail to England to demand restitution for the wronged Icelanders and himself. In the next year a new governing board was appointed by Trampe, who was still in London, and its appointment was confirmed by the Danish Crown. Thus Danish authority over Iceland was firmly restored before the war had come to an end. Britain never found the effort to seize Iceland from Denmark worth making, however easy it might have been.

Shortly after his arrival in England, Jørgen Jørgensen was detained for breaking his parole. However, he was to continue leading an adventurous life, sometimes in the secret service of the British government. Later he was taken as a convict to Australia, where he went on a number of expeditions.[3] His observations on the life and customs of the Aborigines in Van Diemen's Land have recently been discovered and published.[4]

Jørgensen's coup in Iceland was entirely caused by external factors, and it had no discernible consequences in the country. For two decades after 1809 no signs can be found of any wish among Icelanders for autonomy. Afterward, they contemptuously nicknamed Jørgensen "the

[3] Hogan (1891).
[4] Plomley (1991).

Dog-Days King", since his rule coincided roughly with the period of the calendar year called the dog days. Nevertheless, there are two reasons why the coup of 1809 is worth remembering. First, like the story of the Reformation (Ch. 2.8), it reveals clearly how utterly defenceless the Danish administration in Iceland was if even the most feeble form of violence was exercised against it. Secondly, and more important for later history, the episode offers an exceptionally clear indication of the absence of political nationalism or democratic ideas in Iceland at this time. Although people seem to have had little trouble in accepting Jørgensen's rule, there is little sign of any enthusiasm for his message. This became particularly evident when he was removed and no one lifted a finger to defend the newly-acquired independence or prospects of democratic rule. People simply did not care who was the formal head of the country, as long as the Icelandic officials were free to run business as usual.[5] Still there is no reason to doubt that the Icelanders preserved their strong feeling of ethnic identity, which they had acquired in the Middle Ages or the Viking Age (see Ch. 1.10). At least among the more educated strata of society, that feeling had been strongly refreshed by the new interest in Iceland's cultural heritage since the 17th century (see Ch. 2.13). Thus the Icelanders of the early 19th century offer a good example of a people with a clear ethnic identity but no sense of political nationalism.[6]

The same remarkable indifference can be seen five years later, when Norway was severed from the Danish Crown by the peace treaty after the war, and suddenly became one of the most democratic states in Europe in a personal union with Sweden. Although the three old dependencies of the Norwegian Crown – Iceland, Faroe and Greenland – remained under Denmark, no Icelander uttered a word about this, as far as we know, except one who was resident in Norway. Thus the 550-year-old union of Norway and Iceland was dissolved, and the Icelanders seemed not to feel affected by the separation in any way. Apparently, no one in Iceland wished to follow Norway into the new arrangement in the hope of a more autonomous status or more democratic government. To apply a metaphor which was about to become popular in Europe at the time, Iceland was fast asleep. Applying a more recent terminology, we definitely had an Icelandic *ethnie* in the 1810s but there was still no Icelandic nation. This, however, was going to change radically during the next forty years.

---

[5] Gunnar Karlsson (1995), 38-9.

[6] See the discussion in *Nations and Nationalism* II:3 (1996), 357-70, and works referred to therein.

3.2 Romanticism and National Awakening

In early 19th-century Germany and Denmark it became a generally acknowledged fact that the true essence of things was concealed in their origin and past development. This attitude, which is sometimes called historicism and sometimes seen as a part of the Romantic movement, was bound to nourish among Icelanders an increased self-esteem and, among other nationalities, an enhanced interest in their country. Thus the Danish linguist Rasmus Christian Rask became particularly interested in the Icelandic language, which he saw as the original common language of the Scandinavian peoples. At the same time he looked upon the language and literary culture of modern Iceland as being one and the same as in the Middle Ages to his own day. This led to the strange conclusion that the language called Icelandic had been spoken all over Scandinavia in the Middle Ages and the Viking Age, even before Iceland was discovered and colonized.

When Rask visited Iceland in the 1810s he found that the language was seriously threatened by Danish influence, particularly in Reykjavík and other trading stations. He therefore forecast that within 100 years no one would speak Icelandic in Reykjavík and within 300 years it would be extinct altogether. To resist this trend, Rask instigated in 1816 the establishment of the Icelandic Literary Society (Hið íslenska bókmenntafélag), mainly with the purpose of publishing books, both medieval and modern, in Icelandic. The society was divided into two departments, one in Copenhagen and one in Reykjavík. The Copenhagen department, mainly kept going by Icelandic students and intellectuals, was the more active one throughout the 19th century and published, often with official support, large scholarly works, such as five volumes of medieval Icelandic documents[1] and another five volumes of contemporary Icelandic statistics.[2] In a way the Literary Society was an embryonic academy for Iceland.

Not until the 1830s did this cultural movement have a political counterpart.[3] Here the impulse came from Germany. Since the Middle Ages,

---

[1] *Diplomatarium Islandicum. Íslenzkt fornbréfasafn* I-V (1857-1902).

[2] *Skýrslur um landshagi á Íslandi* I-V (1858-75).

[3] For a basic work on the beginning of Iceland's struggle for autonomy, until 1851, see Aðalgeir Kristjánsson (1993).

Denmark's king had been the duke of two duchies to the south of Denmark, Slesvig and Holstein. Slesvig had a mixed population of Danish-and German-speaking people, but Holstein was exclusively German and a member of the Confederation of German States established in 1815 after the defeat of Napoleon. Almost throughout Iceland's struggle for independence, its successes and disappointments came to be closely related to developments in the duchies. This was not surprising since it was in fact one and the same process: the dissolution of the multi-ethnic Danish empire into nation states.

In the charter of the Confederation of German States it had been decreed that in all the states a consultative assembly should be established. However, in the following fifteen years, political calm prevailed all over the Danish realm. So King Frederik VI felt no need to fulfil this promise until, in the wake of the July revolution in France in 1830, a wave of upheavals and constitutional changes swept through Germany, and German politicians started to press King Frederik to grant the Holsteiners their rights. At the same time a Slesviger caused some panic and earned himself a year in prison by suggesting a common constitution for Slesvig and Holstein in a personal union with Denmark. Then the Danish Crown decided that it was time to do something. It did not seem feasible to discriminate against the subjects of Denmark, so the Crown decided in 1831 to establish four diets in the realm, one for Holstein, one for Slesvig, one for Jutland and one for the archipelago of Zealand, Funen and the smaller islands. This assembly was also to represent the other islands that were considered to be Danish: Iceland and Faroe. On the other hand Greenland, with its Inuit population, was never mentioned in this connection, any more than the Danish colonies in the West Indies.

This arrangement had probably been devised in the Danish Chancery in order to make Iceland's share as substantial as it could possibly be. But by then demands had already been raised for a completely different organization. In 1831 a Danish nobleman, Count Holstein of Ledreborg, published a booklet on the proposed diets and declared his support for the plan to establish four assemblies, the only exception being that it might be right to establish a separate assembly for Iceland. His argument in favour of this idea refers to unnamed travelogues where it was related that the inhabitants of this country still missed the old political institutions which once were their sign of honour. This statement reveals where Holstein, who was not known for any particular interest in Iceland, had got the idea. A Scottish clergyman, Ebenezer Henderson, had travelled around Iceland in the 1810s in order to distribute Bibles. Before his expedition he had stayed in Denmark, studied Icelandic and read Icelandic sagas. He seems to have imbibed rather romantic ideas about the old Icelandic Althing, since he maintained in his journal from Iceland – what is scarcely borne out by other sources – that the population of Iceland deeply regretted the abolition of the Althing in 1800. Parts of Henderson's journal were later printed in a Danish periodical, where Count Holstein may have become acquainted with his ideas.

Count Holstein's proposal may well have had some influence in Denmark, but among Icelanders there were people who needed no help to see the establishment of the diets as an opportunity to restore the old Althing at Þingvellir. As early as 1829 an Icelandic law student in Copenhagen, Baldvin Einarsson, had started an annual, which was mostly written in dialogues that were said to take place at Þingvellir, the old site of the Althing. The title suggests an interest in the Althing, although the editor explained it in a way that sounded politically more innocent.[4]

However, when the king announced his intention to establish the diets, Baldvin was quick to reveal his interest in the restoration of the Icelandic Althing in letters to his friends in Iceland. He also wrote a long essay on the representation of Iceland and had it published in 1832 as a booklet in Danish and an article in his periodical *Ármann* in Icelandic. Baldvin argued that the explicit aim of the diets – to awaken the spirit of the nation – would, in Iceland's case, never be reached by the representation of two or three men in a Danish assembly. Furthermore, such a representation would be restricted to officials because of their knowledge of Danish, and officials were exactly the people to whom the king already had access as advisers. Therefore, the right solution was a separate assembly in Iceland, to be held at the sacred site Þingvellir.

By this time the idea of an Icelandic assembly had already gained considerable ground among Icelandic officials in Iceland. When, in the autumn of 1831 and the following winter, they were consulted about the arrangement of Iceland's representation in the diet of the Danish Islands, they demonstrated an almost total lack of interest, but proposed two alternatives. One group, among whom was the sixty-nine-year-old Chief Judge Magnús Stephensen, did not want to know of any representation at all. They were content with the unrestricted monarchy as it was. Another group of officials proposed an assembly in Iceland. The most prominent and best-known member of this group was the regional governor in the North-Eastern Region, Bjarni Thorarensen, who is now considered one of our major poets and the first adherent of Romanticism in Icelandic poetry.

This interest in a separate Icelandic assembly did not affect the Danish Chancery, but because the officials in Iceland showed no interest in making arrangements for the election of Iceland's representatives, the Crown appointed two representatives for the country to the diet of the Danish Islands, which convened for the first time at Roskilde in 1835. One of them was the Danish governor of Iceland and the other an Icelander who

---

[4] The annual was called *Ármann á Alþingi* which might be translated as "Guardian at the Althing" and refers to the place-name Ármannsfell (Ármann's Mountain), close to Þingvellir. For a biography of Baldvin Einarsson, see Nanna Ólafsdóttir (1961).

served as a royal archivist in Copenhagen. Thus the very first step towards democratic development in Denmark threatened to incorporate Iceland perhaps more closely than the absolute monarchy had ever done.

Baldvin Einarsson did not live to see his proposals ignored. He died in 1833 as the result of an accident and was mourned by his friend Bjarni Thorarensen with an elegy typical of the new Romantic view in Icelandic poetry, where the country and the people form a whole.[5] Bjarni wrote:

> *Iceland's*
> *evil fortune*
> *is in no want of weapons.*
> *Fire from within,*
> *flooding rivers,*
> *lay waste large districts.*[6]

However, Baldvin's precedent was to be followed only some two years later by four Icelandic students in Copenhagen, when they founded the annual *Fjölnir* and took up the agitation for restoration of the Althing. In the first issue a poem named "*Iceland*", by one of the editors, Jónas Hallgrímsson, forms a kind of a programme for the periodical. The poet starts by addressing his country:

> *Iceland, fortunate isle! Our beautiful, bountiful mother!*
> *Where are your fortune and fame, freedom and virtue of old?*
> *All things on earth are transient: the days of your greatness and glory*
> *flicker like fires in the night, far in the depths of the past.*
> *Comely and fair was the country, crested with snow-covered glaciers,*
> *azure and empty the sky, ocean resplendently bright.*
> *Here came our famous forebears, the freedom-worshipping heroes,*
> *over the sea from the east, eager to settle the land.*
> *Raising their families on farms in the flowering laps of the valleys,*
> *hearty and happy they lived, hugely content with their lot.*
> *Up on the outcrops of lava where Axe River plummets forever*
> *into the Almanna Gorge, Althing convened every year.*

Later the poet returns to the present and asks:

> *How have we treated our treasure during these six hundred summers?*
> *Have we trod promising paths, progress and virtue our goal?*

And his answer is:

> *Comely and fair is the country, crested with snow-covered glaciers,*
> *azure and empty the sky, ocean resplendently bright.*

---

[5] See Þórkatla Óskarsdóttir (1982), 78-106.

[6] Bjarni Thorarensen (1935), 160. My translation in the verse form of the original, which is one of the two metres of Eddic poetry (see Ch. 1.2).

A Primitive Society Builds a State, 1809-1918

Ah! but up on the lava where Axe River plummets forever
into the Almanna Gorge, Althing is vanished and gone.
Snorri's old site is a sheep-pen; the Law Rock is hidden in heather,
blue with the berries that make boys – and the ravens – a feast.
Oh you children of Iceland, old and young men together!
See how your forefathers' fame faltered – and died from the earth![7]

In the historical tradition of Iceland, *Fjölnir* has occupied a central position as a vital organ of Iceland's nationalist movement. However, it may be difficult to define its contribution exactly. Only nine volumes of the annual were published in thirteen years, 1835-47. It raised hardly any new political demands; in that field it followed the lead of Baldvin Einarsson's annual.[8] It was written in a fresh and sometimes aggressive tone and managed to attract considerable attention in Iceland, although it cannot be called popular. No evidence exists of the distribution of the first volumes, but in the years 1843-5, 300-400 copies of volumes 6-8 went on sale in Iceland and Copenhagen.[9] This may seem ridiculously few, but in a society with limited access to printed texts, where books were read aloud in large homes and loaned from farm to farm, an annual with a print-run of 300 copies could have had more influence than a widely circulated daily newspaper does nowadays.

However, what has earned *Fjölnir* its remarkable reputation in Iceland is probably, first and foremost, the poems of Jónas Hallgrímsson, where childish joyfulness, humour, pure lyric and burning patriotism form a unity that has fascinated successive generations of Icelandic readers. If *Fjölnir* made no major contribution in political demands and agitation, it certainly did so in poetry, and perhaps that was exactly what was needed in order to unite the Icelandic people at that time and build up their self-image. Maybe Jónas's great political contribution was to give his people something Icelandic to love – together.

---

[7] Jónas Hallgrímsson (1996-7). Translated by Dick Ringler in the verse form of the original.

[8] Ragnheiður Kristjánsdóttir (1996), 153-61.

[9] Aðalgeir Kristjánsson (1972), 84-6.

3.3 Jón Sigurðsson and the New Althing

During the late 1830s the idea of more extensive internal rule in Iceland gained increased support.[1] In 1837-8 a group of Icelandic officials and leading farmers, instigated by top officials, signed a petition for a consultative assembly stationed in Iceland. Danish governors in Iceland also began to see the advantage of a stronger and more centralized government within the country. In 1837 Governor L.A. Krieger, on leaving his post in Iceland, suggested the establishment of a cabinet in Reykjavík, with a governor and two ministers, which was to make possible the transfer of a larger part of the administration of Iceland to the country. His successor, Governor C.E. Bardenfleth, suggested a realistic middle course between an elected assembly and a permanent cabinet. Based on his proposal a Committee of Officials was established by royal decree in 1838, composed of ten Icelandic officials. It was to convene in Reykjavík every other year for a maximum of four weeks.

The first issue that was submitted to the first session of the committee, in June 1839, was the mode of electing the representatives of Iceland to the Roskilde Assembly. The committee drafted an election law, but with a familiar lack of interest in the matter it proposed that for the time being the king should kindly appoint Iceland's representatives.

The draft had scarcely begun its slow course through the colleges of the Danish Crown when, in December 1839, King Frederik VI died and was succeeded by his cousin Christian VIII. He had been elected king of Norway during the short-lived uprising there in 1814, and had been suspected of liberal tendencies ever since. However, he was unable to make any liberal move in Denmark because it would have been bound to include a decision concerning the duchies, which would displease either his nationalist Danish subjects in Slesvig and Denmark proper or his equally nationalist German subjects in Slesvig and Holstein.

However, it seemed safe to make a small gesture towards the remote speakers of the ancient Danish language. So on 20 May 1840 King Christian went against the proposal of his own Chancery, which suggested that everything should remain the same concerning Iceland's representation

---

[1] The subject of this chapter is discussed in Aðalgeir Kristjánsson (1993), 48-115.

at Roskilde. Instead the king ordered the Chancery to ask the Committee of Officials in Reykjavík to consider whether it would not be suitable to set up a consultative assembly in Iceland, which would be named Althing and would convene at the meeting place of the former Althing, Þingvellir.

Almost simultaneously with this important decision, the Icelandic group of nationalists in Copenhagen acquired a new leader. This was Jón Sigurðsson, born on 17 June 1811, the son of a clergyman from Hrafnseyri in the Western Fiords.[2] He had gone to Copenhagen in 1833 and chosen as his main subject philology, the usual training received by Latin school teachers. In Jón's first years in the city the editors of *Fjölnir* were busy preparing the first issue of their journal. However, we hear very little of Jón in politics for years, until in 1840 he suddenly abandoned his university studies and entered the political arena in full force. At first he attempted to take over the *Fjölnir* group and have the journal change its name in order to rid itself of whatever bad reputation that it had. When this plan failed, Jón and a group of followers established a new annual journal, *Ný félagsrit* (New Society Papers), which first appeared in 1841.

In the ensuing years, while the Committee of Officials accepted the royal offer of an Althing and the colleges considered its arrangement, lively discussion on the issue took place among the politically active Icelanders, mostly in Copenhagen. They were practically unanimous in arguing for a more democratic structure of the assembly than either Icelandic or Danish officials had planned. They demanded as general a franchise as possible, although no one yet mentioned women in this connection. The penniless Icelandic students in particular were eager to avoid any financial limits on eligibility. On the other hand, they disagreed bitterly on the location of the assembly. The more romantic *Fjölnir* group was convinced that the national spirit of Iceland would not be properly awakened anywhere except at Þingvellir, whereas Jón Sigurðsson and his group wanted the Althing to form the nucleus of an Icelandic capital in Reykjavík. The *Fjölnir* group replied that Reykjavík was largely a Danish town, dominated by Danish merchants and their servants. Jón Sigurðsson retorted that the Althing would help to make it Icelandic.

The dispute spoiled the joy of victory for young men, who were full of altruistic love for their country. When it was clear that Reykjavík had conquered, the poet Jónas Hallgrímsson wrote a poem in which he described the assembly as a meeting of ravens on a hillock, instead of the hoped-for meeting of hawks on a rock, referring to the ancient Law Rock at Þingvellir (see Ch. 1.3). On the other hand, the dispute is highly revealing about the conflicts that lurked within the nationalist movement in Iceland, as is

---

[2] A short biography of Jón Sigurðsson by Hallgrímur Sveinsson (1996) has been published in English. The five-volume biography by Páll Eggert Ólason (1929-33) is still, though sorely dated, the most extensive study of the struggle for independence in Jón's times.

probably the case with nationalism anywhere. The wish to preserve and enliven old national characteristics was represented by the Þingvellir group, while the equally ubiquitous urge to begin the process of modernization was the force behind Jón Sigurðsson's opinion. Personal letters make it clear that Þingvellir enjoyed majority support in the country. But Reykjavík was supported by most of the officials, who maybe did not look forward to residing in tents at Þingvellir during the Althing session. There was no building there which could accommodate the assembly, and it seems that no one expected a building to be built in the near future. In Reykjavík, on the other hand, a large and handsome building for the Latin School was under construction. Since the Althing was intended to convene in the summer, during the school's vacation, this provided excellent accommodation for the Althing sessions, and the representatives from rural areas would normally be able to find lodging with friends and relatives.

A royal decree on the arrangement of the Althing was issued in March 1843.[3] It was to be composed of twenty-six members; twenty of them elected and six appointed by the Crown. The franchise was limited to men, aged twenty-five years or more and of a certain minimum social status, and gave voting rights to approximately 3-5 % of the population (see Ch. 3.14). Eligibility for election was limited in the same way with regard to property and to those aged thirty or more. The assembly was to convene every other year, on the first weekday of July, and sit for four weeks. The electoral term was six years, so that an election gave the right to attend three sessions.

The first election was held in 1844 and gave ten farmers, three clergymen, two secular officials, three additional academics and the steward of the Latin School the right to attend the first session of the Althing. (This makes only nineteen because in one constituency, the Westman Islands, no one proved to have the right to vote.) The king appointed one of the regional governors, two High Court judges, two clergymen and one local sheriff. These men held the first Althing session, which convened in Reykjavík on 1 July 1845.

Jón Sigurðsson was elected to the Althing in the constituency of his home district in the Western Fiords. By that time he already had a reputation among a considerable part of Iceland's population as leader, probably because of his articles in *Ný félagsrit*. After the first Althing session people in the district of Þingeyjarsýsla started a collection of money to support him, and the representative of the district wrote to him: "I have almost become tired of telling one person after another about you, including such details as how large your hands or feet are."[4]

This ingenuous adoration may have worn with time, and Jón could not altogether avoid disappointing some of his fellow countrymen. However,

<hr>

[3] *Lovsamling for Island* XII (1864), 469-525. Text in Danish and Icelandic.
[4] See Gunnar Karlsson (1977a), 30-2. My translation.

he was to stay at the forefront of Icelandic politics for more than three decades until the first important milestone was reached, in 1874. Five years later he died before the struggle was taken up again, but he has remained ever since one of the most powerful symbols of Icelandic identity.

Jón lived all his adult life in Copenhagen, where he never had a permanent occupation but lived on scholarships, which he received mainly for philological and editorial work of various kinds. He made an important contribution to research in Icelandic history, taking a leading role in editing medieval documents, with the first volume of *Diplomatarium Islandicum*. Jón's political messages reached Iceland in *Ný félagsrit*, which was published almost every year for more than three decades. In Copenhagen he kept contact with every new generation of Icelandic students, the future élite of Iceland. The weekly gatherings at the home of Jón and his wife Ingibjörg Einarsdóttir were renowned within the Icelandic diaspora in the city.

Jón Sigurðsson was by no means a typical 19th-century national hero. He was not an extreme nationalist and for his time, was rather devoid of romanticism. Above all, he was a protagonist of modernization, democracy, human rights and economic progress. There seems to have been an incredible gap between Jón's outlook and that of his Icelandic followers, many of whom were very traditionalist, as we shall see later (Ch. 3.8). Jón's career was not typical for a leader of a liberation movement either. He was never arrested for his political activity or spent a single night in prison. On the contrary, for most of his life he was sustained by rather generous research grants from various scholarly institutions, more or less funded by the Danish treasury.[5]

The early 1840s saw Iceland make two major gains in the initial formation of its political existence. First, the establishment of a separate consultative assembly for 58,000 people in Iceland, while parallel assemblies elsewhere in the realm represented at least six times that number,[6] was a clear recognition of Iceland's separate status. Second, the appointment of a national leader was an important step towards the formation of a nationalist, political movement in the country.

---

[5] Guðmundur Hálfdanarson (1997b)
[6] Bergsøe I (1844), 362-3.

3.4 The Search for Status in a Constitutional Monarchy

In 1848 a new wave of revolts swept through Europe and led to the February Revolution in France. In the Danish monarchy the wave released forces that had been swelling under the cover of absolutism.[1] In March the German representatives at the two consultative assemblies of Holstein and Slesvig held a common meeting and sent a deputation to Copenhagen to demand a common constitution for the two duchies. Their aim was a unified German Schleswig-Holstein within the Confederation of German States, but in a personal union with Denmark. As soon as news of this meeting arrived in Copenhagen, the leaders of the national-liberal movement convened a meeting of more than 2,000 and demanded a common constitution for Denmark and Slesvig. Thus the nationalists on both sides, German and Danish, agreed to a political divorce but only on condition that they had the bilingual Slesvig as their share.

On the following day, 21 March, a large gathering of Copenhageners, led by the city council, marched to the royal palace and demanded the appointment of new ministers who enjoyed the confidence of the people. The king, Frederik VII, who had come to power in January that year, replied that his old ministers had already resigned. On the following day a new cabinet was appointed with generous representation of the liberal-nationalists, and the king declared himself a constitutional monarch. Such was the peaceful end of the most absolute of all the absolute monarchies in Europe.

Events took a less peaceful course in the duchies. Even before the new government had given the German deputation its uncompromising reply that Denmark and Slesvig would be united under one free constitution, a revolt broke out and a three-year war ensued.

To Icelanders who were influenced by the double movement of nationalism and democracy, this development could obviously raise high hopes.[2] At the same time, though, there lurked the danger that a democratic form of government would tend to incorporate Iceland in a way

---

[1] Oakley (1972), 170-9.

[2] The development in Iceland, until 1851, is related by Aðalgeir Kristjánsson (1993), 123-426.

which the old one had never done. It is the nature of the democratic nation state to affect its citizens, both politically and culturally, much more than the absolute monarchy had ever done. At any rate, the question that was bound to emerge was: what would Iceland's status be within the constitutional Danish monarchy?

Jón Sigurðsson, who was already widely acknowledged by his fellow-countrymen as their political leader, was the first to give a definite answer to this question. In 1848 he wrote a long article in his annual, *Ný félagsrit*, where he put forward the opinion that the sovereignty over Iceland reverted to the Icelandic people when the king relinquished it. When Iceland had submitted to the Norwegian Crown in 1262-4 (see Ch. 1.14), the Icelanders submitted to the king alone and not to the Norwegian people. In course of time the Danish Crown had succeeded the Norwegian as a party to the treaty, but that did not change the nature of the union. So when absolutism, which had been accepted in Iceland in 1662, was abolished, the country would regain the status it had enjoyed, according to the Old Covenant of 1262, as a separate polity under the Danish king, but in no way subject to the Danish people (see Ch. 2.1). On this basis Jón proposed a legislative parliament in Iceland and a government of four persons who would stay in Copenhagen in turn, one at a time.

In real terms this amounted to a plan for an Icelandic state in a personal union with Denmark. However, Jón Sigurðsson never used the term 'state' of Iceland, perhaps because it seemed too challenging or too arrogant when referring to a population of only 60,000, who were mostly poor peasants and farm-hands.

When Jón Sigurðsson used a medieval document as evidence of the political rights of Iceland, he had a close precedent in the German Schleswig-Holsteiners: they had based their demands for unification of the duchies on a 15th-century treaty, where it was decreed that they should be united for ever.[3] Nevertheless, Jón's idea was ingenious, and was to form the theoretical basis of Iceland's demands for autonomy for seventy years.

At home in Iceland a few democrats reacted to the news from Copenhagen and to Jón Sigurðsson's message by convoking, in the summer of 1848, the first free political meetings which were meant to represent the whole Icelandic people, the first in Reykjavík and the second at Þingvellir. Although only attended by some twenty men each, they were the beginning of democratic political activity in the country. During the following years it became the custom to hold a meeting at Þingvellir each summer, and for some time a kind of political organization grew up around these meetings, with a local committee in each district, which at the same time formed a constituency to the Althing, and a central committee in Reykjavík. This was the first political organization in Iceland.[4] It did not, however,

---

[3] Sverrir Kristjánsson (1981), 196-217.
[4] Gunnar Karlsson (1977a), 70-3.

develop into a political party, since it was meant to represent the Icelandic people as a whole.

The most important consequence of the political meetings in Iceland in 1848 was the royal declaration of 23 September. In a formal reply to the Reykjavík meeting the king declared, in the verbose style of the absolute monarchy, that it was not his intention to finalise decisions regarding Iceland's constitutional status within the realm until the Icelanders had been given a chance to speak on the matter at their own meeting in the country.[5] The distinctiveness of Iceland was thus clearly acknowledged.

In this year also the government offices in Copenhagen were reorganized in accordance with the new system of government, and the Chancery and Treasury substituted by modern ministries. In this reorganization, a separate Department of Icelandic Affairs was set up under the Ministry of the Interior. Its first director was an Icelander, Brynjólfur Pétursson, well known for his liberal and nationalistic opinions, and a former member of the editorial board of *Fjölnir*.

It would have been in line with Jón Sigurðsson's theory for Iceland to have refused to be represented at the Constitutional Assembly that convened in October to compose a constitution for a democratic Denmark. However, the national-liberal Icelanders took a more cautious line; Jón himself, Brynjólfur Pétursson and three other Icelanders accepted the king's appointment to the Assembly, as there was no time to organize elections in Iceland, and used the opportunity to see to it that Iceland was not included explicitly in the Constitution. In this they were completely successful; in the Constitution, which was sanctioned by the king on 5 June 1849, the word Iceland does not occur.

All this seemed extremely promising for Icelandic national-liberals. However, when the National Assembly, which the king had promised in his letter of 23 September 1848, finally convened in Reykjavík in the summer of 1851, the political tide had turned in Denmark, as elsewhere in Europe. Most of the revolts of 1848 had petered out or been overcome in various ways. The war in the Danish duchies had ended with Danish victory, after the German powers – Prussia and Austria – had withdrawn their support of the rebels. However, the programme of the Danish national-liberals – to unite Denmark and Slesvig – had proved to be unrealizable and they were therefore rapidly losing their influence in Danish politics.

As might be expected in this political climate, the proposal which the Danish government made to the Assembly was worlds apart from the expectations of 1848. A few days after the start of the Assembly, a Danish warship arrived with a troop of twenty-five soldiers, who were stationed in Reykjavík while the Assembly was sitting. The ship also carried a bill proposing a "law on Iceland's status in the organization of the state and on

[5] *Lovsamling for Island* XIV (1868), 185.

elections to the Danish Parliament in Iceland". According to the bill, the Constitution of Denmark, which was attached to the bill, was to be valid in Iceland, with an exception concerning the legislative power, and Iceland was to get six seats in the Danish Parliament. Legislative power in internal Icelandic affairs was to remain with the king (in real terms, his Danish ministers), with the participation of the Althing which it already had – namely consultative power – or might be granted later. It was added that such participation would be similar to the self-rule which regional authorities in Denmark were to be granted. An exception was the right to levy taxes on Icelanders and appropriate money from the exchequer of Iceland, which was dependent on the decision of the Althing.

The members of the Assembly were astonishingly slow to react to this proposal. On 24 July when the Assembly had been sitting for almost three weeks, the royal representative, Governor Jørgen Ditlev Trampe, announced that the king intended to have the Assembly dissolved no later than 9 August. However, it was not until two weeks later, on 6 August, that a committee majority had an alternative bill finished and prepared in print. This laid out a constitution for a practically independent Iceland, based on Jón Sigurðsson's proposals of 1848. The country was to have no governing body in common with Denmark except the king and the succession law, with other affairs subject to mutual agreement. The only formal submission of Iceland to the Danish state was to be the attendance of one of the Icelandic ministers at the Council of State in Copenhagen.

On 9 August the members of the Assembly were called to a meeting. Governor Trampe took the floor and announced that the bill proposed by the committee was such that the Assembly had no authority to discuss it. After that, he declared the Assembly dissolved. The secretary at this meeting was a young Icelandic poet of the Romantic school, Benedikt Gröndal. He was obviously a faithful adherent of Jón Sigurðsson's party, because he did not stop recording as soon as the governor had dissolved the Assembly, as an obedient secretary would have done. Instead he wrote down in elegant handwriting a description of the event, which has become widely known and celebrated in the nationalistic history of Iceland.

[*Governor:*] And I declare in the name of the King (*Jón Sigurðsson*: May I have the floor to defend the actions of the committee and the Assembly? *Speaker*: No) that the Assembly is dissolved.

Jón Sigurðsson: Then I protest against this procedure.

Governor (as he and the Speaker stood up and walked away): I hope that the members of the Assembly have heard that I have dissolved it in the name of the King.

Jón Sigurðsson: And I protest in the name of the King and the people against this procedure, and I reserve for the Assembly the right to complain to the King about this act of illegality.

Then the members of the Assembly rose and most of them said as if with one voice:

We all protest!

While this was going on, the Governor and the Speaker slowly left the room, and when they were out of the door one of the members shouted:

"Long live our King, **Frederik the Seventh**!", and the members joined him with one voice.

The members then left the meeting room.[6]

Although no vote was ever taken in the Assembly from which the degree of support for the two alternative bills could be deduced, there is no doubt that an overwhelming majority supported Jón Sigurðsson's faction. In

Jón Sigurðsson – well-known from a quite early age for his snow-white hair.

[6] *Alþingistíðindi* 1851 (1851), 413-14. My translation.

all, forty-three representatives sat in the Assembly, thirty-seven elected and six appointed by the king. After the meeting a protest note to the king was signed by thirty-six members, thirty-five elected and the other a royal appointee. On the other hand, only five members, all royal appointees, came to a banquet to which the governor invited them after the meeting. So it can be concluded that thirty-six members supported Jón Sigurðsson's policy, five accepted the policy of the government and two must be considered neutral.

There is hardly any reason to doubt that the elected members represented the opinions of the higher strata of society, down to the average farmer. The thirty-six-man strong opposition included eleven farmers. This is the first time that it can be ascertained that the common man in Iceland had adopted the nationalism which had so clearly been absent during Jørgen Jørgensen's revolt four decades earlier (see Ch. 3.1).[7]

As an acknowledgement of the new mood in Iceland, the Danish troops stayed in Reykjavík through the following winter. The government also tried to suppress the movement by forbidding all officials who had opposed the royal proposal at the Assembly to sit in the Althing in the future. Two officials who had been appointed temporarily to their posts were fired, and one of them never held an official post again. In Iceland's struggle for autonomy, a stalemate ensued for two decades. Nevertheless, the events of the years 1848-51 spelt a defensive victory for Icelandic national-liberals. This can be seen if we compare Iceland with the Faroes, where no one reacted to the revolution of 1848 with demands for self-rule, no royal pledge was given to the Faroese and no national assembly was held. In 1850 Faroe was formally incorporated into the Danish state when a law was enacted on the election of Faroese representatives to the Danish parliament.[8]

---

[7] Gunnar Karlsson (1995), 38-42.
[8] Debes (1982), 35-43.

3.5 The Danish Side

It is impossible to blame the Danes for resisting the extremely radical demands of the majority in the National Assembly of 1851. For any state in 19th-century Europe to have freely granted such extensive autonomy to a country or province that was considered to form a part of it would have been seen as a clear and most inappropriate sign of political apathy.

In addition Denmark had a much more serious problem to deal with in the two duchies on its southern borders, and Danish politicians must have been anxious to avoid anything that could be understood as a precedent for a separation there. The revolution had been peaceful in Denmark proper in 1848, but in the duchies it had set off a bloody war, which Denmark had managed to win only on the condition that it did not make any changes in their status (see Ch. 3.4). In this situation Danish politicians did not want to disturb the constitutional status of any of the country's dependencies.

Nevertheless, as time went on and the Icelanders persisted, the question must have emerged in Denmark as to what was the use of retaining Iceland within the state. Therefore it is important to ask what caused the Danes to want to keep Iceland and why they nevertheless gradually gave in, even though Iceland would have been in no position to achieve its aim through violence.

Since the Danish trade monopoly had been lifted in Iceland in the 1780s (see Ch. 2.18), the Danish Crown had no major economic interests there. Although most of the foreign trade of Iceland was run by Danish merchants until the late 19th century (see Ch. 3.11), their position did not depend on political dominance; there was nothing to suggest that the competitiveness of Danish firms in Iceland would be harmed by the home rule which Iceland demanded. Icelandic farmers still paid the king's tax, which had been introduced in 1262-4 (see Ch. 1.14): 20 ells a year. A part of the bishops' quarter of the tithe went to the Crown after the Reformation, and a certain amount of customs duties were collected in Iceland. But this did not nearly pay for public expenditure in the country. Around the mid-19th century, the revenue of the Crown in Iceland was about 28,000 rdl. annually, while the expenditure was almost 52,000. The difference, 24,000 rdl., was paid by the Danish treasury.[1]

[1] Bragi Guðmundsson and Gunnar Karlsson (1988), 131-2.

From a military point of view, Iceland was a pure liability for Denmark. It was far too big and too distant to make it worth defending, and therefore it was wide open to English attack at any time.

There were no problems regarding the dividing line between Denmark and Iceland; the border was formed by hundreds of miles of ocean. The Danish population in Iceland was restricted to a handful of merchant families. In 1860 only 104 persons in Iceland (0.16 % of the population) had been born abroad,[2] which probably accounts approximately for Danes resident in the country.

It must have been predominantly a question of pride for Denmark to keep its hold on Iceland. Rasmus Christian Rask's message, that modern Icelandic was the ancient common language of Scandinavia (see Ch. 3.2), had its effect in Denmark, of course, and the wave of historicism and romanticism in the early 19th century greatly enhanced esteem for Iceland in neighbouring countries. The future leader of the Danish national-liberals, Orla Lehmann, then twenty-two years old, wrote a review of Baldvin Einarsson's booklet on the re-establishment of the Althing in 1832 and declared that in the naked mountains of Iceland

... we see our own past a gigantic monument raised over a distant time, which in severe loneliness projects into a world where everything is new and altered. Thus in the old days a number of Scandinavians emigrated there and introduced the life and customs of the old North. A life so rich in alteration and transition has, since that time, almost transformed for us the surface of the earth and its inhabitants; the mighty hand of civilization has ploughed up almost every trace of the life of these ancient times and everything that moved within it. But as if frozen between the distant icy mountains, where the storms of time never reached, it persists in almost complete purity in Iceland, so that we can see there a living past, an eloquent picture of past life.... Therefore, every Scandinavian is bound to feel affection for the Icelandic people, and we should definitely be able to find in the character, mode of life and customs of present-day Icelander, traces of our own old physiognomy, which we would look for in vain in our crumbled ruins and lifeless annals.[3]

Thus to Danish romantics Iceland was a small jewel in the Crown. In their eyes it would have been devastating to promote modern Danish culture in Iceland, which they never tried to do. The central authorities were, in general, remarkably indifferent to contemporary Icelandic culture. No compulsory school system was introduced there throughout the 19th century, although it had begun in Denmark in 1814.

In the political arena the romantic attitude towards Iceland led to some ambivalence. It was obviously right and proper to allow and encourage the Icelanders to re-establish their old Althing. It must also have been

[2] *Hagskinna* (1997), 142 (table 2.21). The number refers to people holding the common Danish-Icelandic citizenship with birthplace abroad.
[3] *Maanedsskrift for Litteratur* VII (1832), 523-4; Gunnar Karlsson (1995), 44-5.

tempting to be generous with constitutional concessions to the guardians of the ancient Scandinavian culture. On the other hand, when Iceland threatened to leave the union, the admirers of ancient culture were bound to feel hurt. Therefore, it was no wonder that the Danish attitude towards Iceland's demands was somewhat inconsistent, generous during waves of liberalism and mean during periods of conservative backlash.

Only one major attempt was made from the Danish side to contradict Jón Sigurðsson's theory on Iceland's rightful status within the realm (see Ch. 3.4). As might be expected, the author was a man who was concerned with the cultural heritage of medieval Iceland. He was J.E. Larsen, a professor of law at the University of Copenhagen and member of the board of the Árnamagnæan Institute, which preserved the manuscript collection left by Árni Magnússon (see Ch. 2.13). In 1855 Larsen published a booklet in Danish, *Om Islands hidtilværende statsretlige Stilling* (On Iceland's Constitutional Status Hitherto), putting forward arguments against Jón Sigurðsson's views. First, he said, the Old Covenant of 1262 was just like any treaty made in the Middle Ages, when one state submitted to another and they were united. Secondly, Iceland's present status could not be based on a medieval document, least of all as it would be read now, but on the development of that status through the ages. Larsen's booklet was published in Icelandic the next year, but its influence must have been negligible except perhaps that it proved once more how insolent and arrogant the Danes could be.

The same could surely be said of Jón Sigurðsson's rebuttal of Larsen's arguments, which was published in Danish as early as 1855 and in Icelandic the next year. After all, people's attitudes relied not on historical or constitutional arguments but on feelings. This did not mean that arguments were unimportant. On the contrary, since the dispute was fought with words alone and not with guns – no shot was ever fired in Iceland's struggle for independence – it was crucial to have good arguments as one's artillery.

On the other hand, since the attitude of the disputants was rooted in sentiment, Denmark was destined to lose. Since the only valid reason to want to go on "owning" Iceland was pride, it could not serve any purpose to own it against the will of its inhabitants. In a way Denmark's dilemma in the struggle with Iceland was the ever-recurring problem of unrequited love. And, as always in such situations, Denmark had no choice but to give in, slowly and gradually – though probably no more slowly than it took Iceland to became capable of having self-rule. This development, which will be described in the following chapters, is a prototype of the kind of international struggle where the weaker party inevitably wins.

3.6   Towards Legislative Powers in 1874

A decade after the unsuccessful National Assembly in Reykjavík (see Ch. 3.4), the national-liberals regained their power in Danish politics and began to look for a new solution to the problems on the southern border of Denmark. In this connection, a new step was taken to break the deadlock in the struggle about the constitutional status of Iceland.[1] In Copenhagen a government committee was appointed to prepare the separation of the official finances of Denmark and Iceland. The urge came partly from the Danish parliament, which found itself unable to have any say about the finances of the exotic little dependency in the North Atlantic. At the same time Danish parliamentarians worried about the growing deficit in Iceland's budget and wanted to make that problem of the Icelanders alone.

The committee consisted of three Danish representatives and two Icelanders – Oddgeir Stephensen, the director of the Department of Icelandic Affairs in Copenhagen and Jón Sigurðsson. In its report, which was finished in 1862, the committee agreed on two important points. Firstly, they all supported the financial separation of Denmark and Iceland and thus Iceland's autonomy in internal, financial affairs. Secondly, they all proposed that the Danish exchequer should support the prospective Icelandic exchequer with an annual allocation.

This prospective allocation was not exclusively looked at as poor relief for Iceland. In their awkward situation – that of needing financial support in order to be able to claim some autonomy – the Icelanders were lucky in so far as the support could be partly based on arguments of justice. Since the first centuries of the Christian Church in Iceland, the episcopal sees and Latin schools had been run with income from landed property that belonged to the sees. In the late 18th century and around 1800, the sees had been abolished and the two schools united (see Ch. 2.18). Then the properties of the sees had been sold and the money had been paid into the Danish treasury, which in return took over payment of the salary of the bishop of Iceland and for the running of the Latin school. Now, when this burden was about to be removed from the Danish treasury, it was

---

[1] The subject-matter of this chapter is discussed in detail by Páll Eggert Ólason IV (1932), 207-485 and V (1933), 5-262. See also Einar Arnórsson (1949), 71-211.

considered fair to demand compensation to the treasury of Iceland, which would bear it in future. The problem was that it was difficult to make this compensation high enough to cover the deficit in Iceland, let alone do anything to meet the urgent need for increased public services and measures to haston economic progress in the country.

In the committee all the Danes and the Icelander Oddgeir Stephensen agreed that Iceland needed more than it could demand and accordingly proposed an annual allocation of 42,000 rdl., which was close to the deficit in Iceland's finances. A part of this sum – they disagreed on how large a part – would be permanent and the other part temporary while Iceland's economy was recovering. Jón Sigurðsson alone tried to calculate the sum which Iceland might rightfully claim. This consisted mainly of the value of the Icelandic farms which the Crown had sold, paying the proceeds into the Danish treasury, and a share of the profit of the monopoly trade in Iceland, corresponding to the proportion of Iceland in the population of the realm. In this way Jón came to the conclusion that Iceland could make a reasonable claim on Denmark for a sum that corresponded to an annual rent of some 120,000 rdl. From this sum he subtracted 20,000 as Iceland's contributions to the Royal House and central government and proposed that the Danish treasury pay some 100,000 rdl. annually to the prospective treasury of Iceland.

This was a hopeless demand, of course; it has even been suggested that Jón made it partly in order to postpone the realization of extensive autonomy for Iceland, because he did not believe that his fellow-countrymen were ready for self-rule.[2] Whatever the case, his proposal served well the purpose of making it possible for the Icelanders to demand an allocation from Denmark and to receive it, when it came, without feeling like beggars. Along with his theory of Iceland's constitutional status (see Ch. 3.4), Jón Sigurðsson's interpretation of its right to claim recompense is one of his major contributions to the struggle for independence.

The trauma which Denmark suffered in 1864, when the Crown lost its duchies to the German powers, proved a further spur to solve the question of Iceland. This may be partly due to the coincidence that Hilmar Finsen, one of the Danish officials who lost their jobs when Slesvig became a part of Prussia, was an ambitious man of Icelandic ancestry. The Danish government had left the post of governor in Iceland vacant for some years, maybe waiting for a new institution to take its place. However, now that Finsen had been pensioned it seemed a good idea to send him to Iceland as governor.

After an abortive attempt in 1865 to conclude the financial separation alone, a government bill proposing a constitution for Iceland was submitted to the next session of the Althing in 1867. This was a big step forward

---

[2] Guðmundur Hálfdanarson (1997b), 56-7.

from the proposal to the National Assembly. Although Iceland was defined as an inalienable part of the Danish state (the Icelandic term corresponding to "state" may be somewhat ambivalent), only the paragraphs on the king in the Danish Constitution were to be valid in Iceland. Also legislative powers in all internal Icelandic affairs were to be in the hands of the Althing, together with the Crown. Apart from this, it seems to have been intended that the government of Iceland would remain practically the same as before. Iceland would have no participation in the running of common Danish-Icelandic affairs. Ministerial power over Iceland – the king's share of the legislative power and the executive power – was to rest with one of the ministers of the Danish government. The internal administration, headed by a body of one or more persons, was to come under the minister. Along with the bill, the king announced that he would ask the Danish parliament for an allocation of 50,000 rdl. annually, of which 37,500 would be a permanent contribution.

In most of its main points the Althing accepted this proposal, although it made various minor changes to the bill, mostly to make it at least less apparent that the responsible ministerial power was to remain in Copenhagen and not partly with the internal administration in Reykjavík. Governor Hilmar Finsen, who served as royal representative at the Althing, negotiated with the Althing members on these changes and clearly indicated that he would do all he could to bring about royal assent to the constitution. It must have looked as if Iceland was going to get its own legislative parliament the very next year.

This, however, did not happen. No grant of money could be allocated from the Danish treasury without the consent of the Danish parliament, so inevitably it too would have a finger in the pie. Members began to add various conditions for the allocation, and the issue was sent to and fro between the two chambers of parliament. The result was that the government rejected the proposal of the Althing of 1867, apparently because it could not secure the allocation from parliament. Then the case was submitted to the Althing again in 1869 in a form which seemed unacceptable to its members, although to a modern observer the proposal looks little different from the bill of 1867. Nevertheless, a new stalemate appeared inevitable.

This was avoided by a new minister of justice in Denmark, A. F. Krieger, who took up his post in 1870. Since the Department of Icelandic Affairs had now been transferred from the Ministry of the Interior (see Ch. 3.4) to the Ministry of Justice, the Icelandic question was his responsibility, and he decided to cut the Gordian knot and have the Danish parliament pass a law on the status of Iceland. This he managed to do and had the law passed in both chambers with an overwhelming majority. On 2 January 1871 the king sanctioned the so-called Status Act (*stöðulög*).[3]

[3] *Lovsamling for Island,* XXI (1889), 1-5. Text in Icelandic and Danish.

In all its main points the Status Act is a confirmation of those stipulations of the constitutional bill of 1867 which prescribe the relations between Iceland and the Danish state, plus an allocation of financial support to Iceland. Iceland was defined as an inalienable part of the Danish state (with the word "state" translated by a somewhat vaguer term in Icelandic), but a country with special rights. It would not participate in the rule of common affairs unless such participation was sanctioned by both countries, an arrangement that seemed practical at the time. Iceland's internal affairs were demarcated in such a way that even the most radical Icelanders would accept. The Act does not state explicitly that the Danish parliament renounced legislative power in these affairs, since it was doubtful if it ever had it, but this can safely be concluded from a special clause on the Supreme Court of Denmark. On that issue it was stated explicitly that its role as a final arbiter in Icelandic affairs could not be changed without the consent of the Danish parliament. The financial support was set at 50,000 rdl. annually, the same amount that had been offered in 1867, but now a little less, 30,000 rdl., was to be paid permanently. Finally, it was declared that the Danish parliament would stop dealing with issues concerning Iceland's internal revenues and expenditure.

The Status Act obviously opened the way for a constitution for Iceland's internal affairs to be enacted, with the mutual consent of the Danish government and the Althing or a new National Assembly in Iceland. The law, however, did not meet with any delight in Iceland. On the contrary, never had resentment been so bitter. The Althing of 1871 protested against the law and proclaimed that it was to be seen as a declaration of the Danish parliament, which set out what it was ready to offer to Iceland at this stage. On these grounds, the Althing decided to accept the financial support but reserved its right to demand more. This was the policy of Jón Sigurðsson and his uncompromising majority at the Althing, but the unusual narrowness of his majority reveals that there were more doubts than usual about this course. The proclamation that the Status Act was not binding for Iceland was passed by fourteen votes to ten; the minority consisted of all six royally-appointed members and – more revealing about the uncertainty within the nationalist group – four of those elected.

The next year the government proceeded along the same lines, when it decided to redefine the post of governor in Iceland and give it a new name, *landshöfðingi* instead of *stiftamtmaður*. The *landshöfðingi* had slightly more authority than the *stiftamtmaður*, though not to such an extent that I need give the post a new name in English. This meant an increase in administrative power within Iceland, and it stressed Iceland's special status within the state, since the post of *landshøvding* (which was the Danish form of the name) was no part of local government in Denmark. Nevertheless, this decision caused increased bitterness in political circles in Iceland, since the change was made without consulting the Althing and without support in Icelandic law. Furthermore, this indicated that ministerial power in Icelandic affairs was not on its way into the country.

All this led to a sentiment in Iceland which even threatened to surpass Jón Sigurðsson's policy in demands. In northern Iceland an intelligent farmer, Einar Ásmundsson, clearly imitating Jón Sigurðsson's way of judicial argumentation, propounded the theory that Christian IX was not the lawful king of Iceland since he had come to power under the succession law of 1853, which had never been made valid in Iceland.[4] It was Einar's intention not to secede from the Crown – hardly anyone seems to have wanted that – but to acquire a stronger position in coming negotiations. As a next step, a meeting was convened at Þingvellir in the summer of 1873, before the summoning of the Althing. The meeting was to be attended by elected representatives from all constituencies, and some of its protagonists intended that it should declare itself a constitutional assembly, which would enact a constitution for Iceland and send it to the king for sanction. It did not go that far, but much against the wishes of Jón Sigurðsson, who opted for a more peaceful line, it declared that Iceland was a separate society (*þjóðfélag*), only in a personal union with Denmark.[5]

Thus when the Althing of 1873 began to discuss the constitutional issue, a settlement seemed further away than at any previous time. But in the middle of the proceedings the issue took what was almost a U-turn. It so happened that in the next year Iceland was going to celebrate the millennium of its first settlement (see Ch. 1.1). Now the idea emerged in the Althing to ask the king to give Iceland a constitution on this occasion. This was a brilliant idea, as the political majority in Iceland had said far too much about Iceland's constitutional rights to be able to enact a constitution that would have any hope of gaining royal approval. On the other hand, it seemed better than nothing to accept the self-rule which was available and could be expected to be at least as good as the proposal of 1867. The way out of the dilemma was to accept the constitution as a birthday present, because one accepts a present before one unwraps it. So the Althing of 1873 ended in unprecedented harmony. A bill of a new, radical constitution, which everyone knew would be rejected, was passed with only two noes. Then the wish for a constitution presented by the king was passed unanimously as a second choice.

The Crown, of course, seized this opportunity to bring the dispute with Iceland to an end for the time being. On 5 January 1874 Christian IX issued a Constitution for Iceland's Internal Affairs, which was to come into force on 1 August the same year.[6] It could be seen in the constitution that the Crown had not been filled with any particular generosity on the

---

[4] Arnór Sigurjónsson II (1959), 268, 300-18; Gunnar Karlsson (1977a), 140-2.

[5] Sigurður Líndal (1959), 203-12.

[6] *Lovsamling for Island* XXI (1889), 732-57. Text in Icelandic and Danish.

occasion of the millennium, although it was in no way unexpectedly mean either. The constitution was explicitily based on the Status Act, which the Althing had rejected: it applied to the issues that were internal Icelandic affairs according to that act. In these affairs, the Althing was vested with legislative power, together with the Crown, in the same way as in any constitutional monarchy of this time. Royal powers in these affairs were, according to the letter of the constitution, to be performed by the Minister for Iceland, but it was to emerge that this post would be a sideline of the Danish Minister of Justice. Thus, ministerial power was exercised in practically the same way as before – which was to become the main point of contention in the next phase of the struggle (see Ch. 3.15). Apart from this, the constitution contained provisions on general human rights, based on corresponding clauses in the Danish constitution.

On the occasion of the millennium Christian IX paid the first royal visit to Iceland, in the summer of 1874. The celebrations were unequalled in the country, where festivities had been almost unknown.[7] Icelandic nationalists did their best to swallow their pride and conceal the fact that they had compromised in their conflict with the Crown.

Contemporary evidence agrees that the festivities in 1874 contributed greatly to filling young people with self-confidence and optimism to strive for a brighter future during the hard years to come.[8] Before we come to that, however, we must take a brief look back at the very first signs of economic and social movements in Iceland in the 19th century.

[7] Brynleifur Tobiasson (1958).
[8] Gunnar Karlsson (1977a), 381-2.

3.7 Economic Growth with Old Methods

The great process of European modernization, industrial revolution and urbanization was generally preceded or initiated by increased production in agriculture, though without any considerable technical innovations at this stage. The increase went hand in hand with population growth, whatever the connection between the two processes may have been, and the population growth at the same time provided a market for surplus agricultural products and a surplus workforce for urbanization.

In Iceland, this period of growth within the old-fashioned food production system took place during the first half and around the middle of the 19th century. In the forty years between 1815 and 1855, the population grew by 36%, from just under 48,000 to almost 65,000, which is on average 0.9% a year.[1] This is a strong population growth for an under-developed society with high infant mortality, when almost one out of three children died in their first year.

If we look at the population growth as the primary factor here, which would be a fruitful approach, we can say that population pressure thrust people simultaneously in two opposite directions, further inland and out to the fishing grounds.

The move inland took place mostly in the north-eastern part of the country, where scores of new farms were built on moorland which had been considered usable for summer grazing only.[2] At the same time, double households on established farms became more common, and farmers increased the utilization of their land by increasing the number of livestock, particularly sheep. From 1810 to 1854 the number of sheep in the country more than doubled, rising from just over 230,000 to over half a million, but the number of cattle only rose by some 25%, from under 22,000 to 27,300. It is worth noting that the increase in sheep was mainly in wethers; while their number more than quadrupled, the number of ewes only rose by some 40 per cent. Ewes were predominantly kept for the production of milk consumed at home, but wethers were reared for wool, meat and tallow,

[1] *Hagskinna* (1997), 56-8 (table 2.2). Unless otherwise indicated, the statistical material of the present chapter is based on this book.
[2] Aðalgeir Kristjánsson and Gísli Ágúst Gunnlaugsson (1990), 17-20.

which were important export goods. The increase in the number of wethers therefore indicates that the growth in farming was aimed at the market rather than for self-sufficiency.

However, cows and ewes, the kinds of livestock that were predominantly kept to produce food for home consumption, alone show that agriculture would have been able to offer each Icelander roughly the same amount of food by the end of the period under consideration here as at its beginning. While the number of cows per person decreased somewhat from 1810 to 1854 – from 0.38 to 0.30 – the number of ewes per person increased slightly, from, 3.2 to 3.5.

The sharp increase in the utilization of marginal land was, to a certain extent, made possible by the relatively limited exploitation of the land after the great famine of the 1780s (see Ch. 2.17). It is well known in Iceland that marginal land, especially at high altitudes, can yield a reasonable return for a few decades, but loses its fertility with prologed intensive use for haymaking or grazing.[3]

Furthermore, the expansion was facilitated by a relatively warm climate compared with the period before and after, probably during the whole first half of the century and certainly in the 1840s and early '50s. Air temperature has been measured regularly in Iceland since 1845, when a local merchant at Stykkishólmur in Snæfellsnes, western Iceland, took it up as a private enterprise. During the first decade, the average temperature was similar that in the second half of the 20th century. These measurements have been coupled with information about the frequency and duration of drift-ice off the coasts of Iceland (see Ch. 2.19), leading to the conclusion that this relatively warm spell started around 1840. The preceding decades seem to have been rather cool, but considerably warmer than the worst spells of the 18th and late 19th centuries.[4] There is no doubt that the warm climate during the decade and a half around the middle of the century allowed the expansion within farming to go further than it would otherwise have done.

The growth of fishing is best visible in the statistics on the increasing number of fishing boats and the larger exports of fish. Icelandic rowing-boats were classified according to the number of oars they had, which was roughly equal to the minimal number of ordinary fishermen on board. Table 3.7-1 shows how the fishing fleet grew from 1810 to 1851 by 2,595 oars, or 28%. In addition to this number, were a helmsman on the bigger boats and sometimes a few more men aboard. Thus it can be estimated from a number of cases that each oar employed *c*. 1.3 men.[5] So the increase in crew places on fishing boats seems to amount to some 3,400. Furthermore, this was the

---

[3] Hákon Bjarnason (1942), 29-30.

[4] Páll Bergþórsson (1987), 211-14.

[5] Lúðvík Kristjánsson III (1983), 205-6.

initial period of fishing on decked vessels, which, however, numbered only 25 in 1853 (see Ch. 3.10) and employed scarcely more than 250 fishermen.

Table 3.7-1 INCREASE IN NUMBER OF BOATS AND
ESTIMATED NUMBER OF OARS, 1810-51

Types of boats	1810	1851
8-10 oars	233 × 9 = 2,097 oars	262 × 9 = 2,358 oars
4-6 oars	1,116 × 5 = 5,580 oars	1,184 × 5 = 5,920 oars
Smaller	805 × 2 = 1,610 oars	1802 × 2 = 3,604 oars
Total	9,287 oars	11,882 oars

Source: Jón Jónsson (1994), 18-19.

If we try to estimate how important this increase of crew places at sea was on a national basis, it must first be taken into consideration that fishing was only rarely a year-round occupation. Most fishermen were farmers and their farm-hands, who only went to sea during the fishing season in late winter and spring (see Ch. 2.4). I assume that each job on a fishing boat amounted to one-third of a full-time occupation, so that 3,400 crew places make no more than 1,130 jobs. However, if we assume that these men were breadwinners making a contribution that amounts to sustaining and employing (for fish-processing and services of various kinds) a family of seven each, including themselves, then the increase in fishing could explain the sustenance of almost half the population growth.

Statistics for fish exports seem to show an even larger growth than the number of boats. In 1806 the export of the two most important products, stockfish and salt fish, amounted to 695 metric tons, but by 1855 it had risen to 3,852 tons. These numbers are not directly comparable, as the export of salt fish increased much more than that of stockfish, and salt fish is more than twice as heavy when it has been processed. As Table 3.7-2 shows, in 1806, fish processed for export can be estimated to have weighed about 4,000 metric tons unprocessed, but, in 1855, the amount had risen to some 16,000 tons. The total catch had not increased as much, since domestic consumption hardly increased more than the corresponding population growth. If we use the same estimate as in Chapter 2.14, the domestic consumption was equal to 300 kilos of unprocessed fish per head per year. Then the conclusion, as set out in Table 3.7-2, is that the total catch had doubled in the period, which is considerably more than the increase in the fishing fleet would suggest.

Table 3.7-2 EXPORT OF FISH AND ESTIMATED TOTAL CATCH, 1806 AND 1855 (*tonnes*)

	Export		Conversion	Unprocessed	
	1806	*1855*	*factor*	*1806*	*1855*
Stockfish	373	494	× 7.7	2,872	3,804
Salt fish	322	3,358	× 3.73	1,201	12,525
Total	695	3,852		4,073	16,329
Domestic consumption				14,027	19,453
Estimated total catch				18,100	35,782

Sources: *Skýrslur um landshagi* I (1858) 79, 579, and *Hagskinna* (1997), 428 (table 10.3). For conversion factors see *Hagskinna* (1997), 305, and Jón Jónsson (1994), 50.

It is evident that the period from the 1810s to the 1850s was characterized by growth in Iceland, not only in population but also in standards of living. This is also manifest in a strong increase in foreign trade. Import of food grew considerably; between 1819 and 1855, the import of rye and rye meal increased from 20 to 33 kilos per person. However, the increase was much greater in the luxury commodities of the time. The import of tobacco rose from less than a pound to one and a half pounds per person, of spirits (*brennivín*) from 1.5 to 6 litres per person, coffee beans and sugar from practically nil to 7 pounds of each item.[6] This must have been a period of growing optimism, and it is reasonable to assume that it contributed to the build-up of self-confidence that was needed to make the population of Iceland adopt Jón Sigurðsson's nationalist policy (see Ch. 3.4). It would have also been reasonable to assume that the society would take the step into modernization proper, industrialization and rapid growth of towns in the second half of the century. This, however, proved not to be a straight forward process, as we shall see in the next chapter.

[6] *Hagskinna* (1997), 442-3 (table 10.5), 544 (table 10.20); see also *ibid.* 56-8 (table 2.2).

3.8 The Crisis in Rural Society

During the 18th century the population of Iceland passed, or verged on, 50,000 three times, a fact that forms the main basis for the theory that Iceland, with its old economic structure, could not sustain more than that number of inhabitants (see Ch. 2.19). Whether this is true or not, the population in the 19th century rose much higher than 50,000. By 1855 it had reached 65,000 (see Ch. 3.7) and by 1870, 70,000. To this the adherents of the theory of an absolute population ceiling of 50,000 might reply that such strong population growth could be accommodated in the relatively good years of the 1830s and 1840s, but caused serious problems as soon as sheep-farming began to meet new adversities in the late 1850s.[1]

The adversities were of two kinds. One of them was an epizootic of scab, passed on four English lambs that were imported to improve the Icelandic breed in 1855.[2] In the next years scab raged through the southern and western parts of the country, reaching as far as Mýrdalur in the central south and Húnavatnssýsla in the north-west, killing a large proportion of the sheep and making some of the survivors useless.

The scab soon became the hottest political issue in Iceland, since people disagreed over whether it should be eliminated by cure or by the complete extermination of sheep and change of stock in the diseased areas, in the same way an earlier case had been dealt with in the 1770s (see Ch. 2.16). The disagreement started to overlap with the constitutional issue, since Jón Sigurðsson became one of the leading proponents of cure, thus supporting the policy of Danish authorities, while there was certainly a majority for extermination in Iceland, especially – but not by any means solely – in the areas where the epizootic had not arrived. In 1859 Jón came to Iceland, together with the chief veterinarian of Denmark and two other Danish vets, with unlimited authority to do anything that they considered necessary to extinguish the epizootic. By this action Jón risked his position as the political leader of Iceland, which was revealed by the fact that in 1859 he lost his seat as speaker of the Althing – by one vote.

---

[1] The crisis and its social and political consequences are discussed by Guðmundur Hálfdanarson (1991), 101-65. For the development of family and household structure, see also Gísli Ágúst Gunnlaugsson (1988).

[2] Þorvaldur Thoroddsen III (1919), 401-11; Páll Eggert Ólason IV (1932), 49-115.

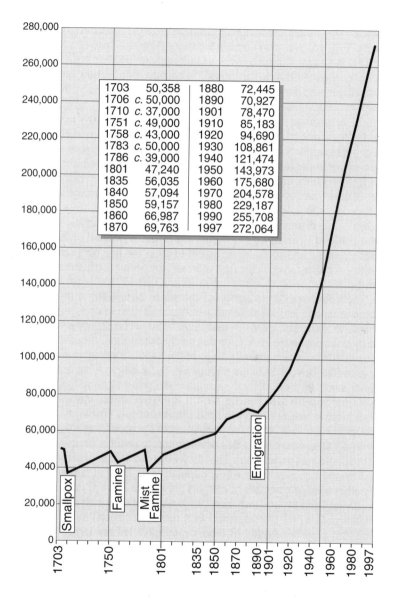

1703	50,358	1880	72,445
1706	c. 50,000	1890	70,927
1710	c. 37,000	1901	78,470
1751	c. 49,000	1910	85,183
1758	c. 43,000	1920	94,690
1783	c. 50,000	1930	108,861
1786	c. 39,000	1940	121,474
1801	47,240	1950	143,973
1835	56,035	1960	175,680
1840	57,094	1970	204,578
1850	59,157	1980	229,187
1860	66,987	1990	255,708
1870	69,763	1997	272,064

Fig. 3.8-1 Population development, 1703–1997. *Sources: Hagskinna* (1997), 49 (table 2.1), 54 (table 2.2); *Hagtölur mánaðarins* (1998); and other sources referred to in this chapter.

The statistics show a reduction of the sheep stock in Iceland by almost 40%, from more than half a million in 1854 to just over 300,000 in 1859. Still, this number conceals the more dramatic facts of a reduction by 85% in Rangárvallasýsla, 78% in Gullbringu- and Kjósarsýsla, and 75% in Árnessýsla and Borgarfjarðarsýsla.[3] One may wonder how famine was escaped in these districts – it can perhaps best be explained by their proximity to the best fishing stations.

The other most important source of difficulty was partly responsible for the reduction of the sheep stock. A serious deterioration of climate set in at approximately the same time as the scab reached its peak, in 1859. According to the temperature measurements in Stykkishólmur (see Ch. 3.7), 1859 was the coldest year hitherto recorded, with an average temperature of 0.94°C. An overall average for the first fourteen years in Stykkishólmur (1845-58), was 3.48°C, while the next eleven years (1859-69) averaged 2.36°C.[4] The difference of 1.12°C may not seem very dramatic to people who are used to much higher temperatures, but in Iceland such a difference is crucial and could be sufficient to cross the line between life and death – for sheep even in the first year, and for people too in the second or third.

The collective consequence of increased population numbers, the sheep epizootic and a colder climate was a decline in opportunities for people to marry and establish their own homes. The situation was made still worse because the generation that reached the normal age of marriage – around thirty – was unusually large in the 1860s. That again was due to a wave-like movement in the population, according to what is known as Sundt's law. In these years the second wave resulting from a population explosion after the Mist Famine (see Ch. 2.17) was around thirty years old.[5] Thus in the decade between 1850 and 1860 the twenty-five/thirty-four age-group grew by 45%, while the population of the country as a whole grew by 13%.[6] One would expect this development to result in a relative growth of the domestic servant class. That, however, did not happen; they remained around a quarter of the whole population for most of the century. On the other hand, the number of paupers grew from 2.1% of the population in 1850 to 5.6% twenty years later.[7] In general the unemployment of able-bodied people was not accepted as a reason for social support at this time, but a greater supply of labour may have led the farmers to set a higher standard for those that were accepted as able-bodied workers.

---

[3] *Skýrslur um landshagi* II (1861), 854-6.

[4] *Hagskinna* (1997), 37 (table 1.1).

[5] Helgi Skúli Kjartansson (1975), 126-9.

[6] Guðmundur Hálfdanarson (1986), 461. See also Guðmundur Hálfdanarson (1987), 31.

[7] *Hagskinna* (1997), 211 (table 3.4).

Rural society, led by its representatives at the Althing, reacted strongly and in a largely reactionary way to this problem. But, before we consider this reaction, we must take into account that it had been a dominant policy in Iceland over the centuries that all adults who did not run a farm of their own should serve as domestic servants in the homes of farmers (see Ch. 1.8).

The threats to this general rule were basically of two kinds. On the one hand, people tended to form their own homes without access to land, as cottars (*búðsetumenn, þurrabúðarmenn, tómthúsmenn*), normally making a living from fishing. On the other hand single people, mostly men, constantly tried to make a living as free labourers (*lausamenn*). In 1783, the status of free labourers had been forbidden altogether. Living as cottars was never forbidden completely, but in 1808 it was decreed that in future cottars must prove that they had access to sufficient land to feed a cow or six ewes, and a vegetable garden.[8] Thus, relying entirely on fishing as a means of subsistence was in principle forbidden.

As discussed in Chapter 2.4, there were mixed motives behind these restrictions. In the 19th century, it even looks as if it was considered to be a social and educational necessity for people to spend a part of their lives in domestic service.[9]

When the social ties had been knotted as firmly as this, the crisis within rural society around 1860 could hardly be met with more of the same kind. The only obvious way to reduce the expenses of poor relief in the future, within the old economic system, was to limit procreation. At this time, marriages were restricted in Iceland in the same way as in Denmark: those who had received poor relief as adults needed special permission from the communal authorities to enter marriage. The second and third sessions of the consultative Althing, in 1847 and 1849, discussed proposals of further limits on marriages of poor people, but in these years of prosperity and optimism they were rejected by an overwhelming majority. In 1859, on the other hand, the Althing passed by sixteen votes to nine a petition to the king asking him to issue a law that forbade the marriage of "notorious squanderers, drunkards and good-for-nothings", unless their communal authorities permitted it or their best men guaranteed that they would not be in need of poor relief for the next three years. The Danish government refused the petition out of hand, which did not prevent the Althing from discussing the issue in the following sessions and trying again, equally unsuccessfully, with a petition for even stricter limitations on marriages in 1865.[10]

---

[8] *Lovsamling for Island* IV (1854), 683-6; VII (1857), 192, 195.

[9] Guðmundur Hálfdanarson (1995), 769-70.

[10] Jón Blöndal and Sverrir Kristjánsson (1954), 18-22.

The extreme conservatism displayed by the Althing in its reaction to the crisis is the main basis for a theory propounded by the Icelandic historian Guðmundur Hálfdanarson that Icelandic farmers allied with liberal academics, such as Jón Sigurðsson, in their demand for independence, chiefly because the farmers wanted to protect Iceland from what they saw as the dangerous influence of Danish liberalism. Thus, in Guðmundur's opinion, the struggle for national freedom was partly fought to prevent individual freedom.[11]

This ingenious idea turns Iceland's struggle for independence on its head in a way which would appeal strongly to our post-nationalist age. And there were people, though as far as we know only in the adverse 1860s, who expressed their wish to be free from Denmark in order to be able to introduce strong conservative measures in Iceland.[12] It is also true that, in 19th-century Iceland there was a striking discrepancy between bold and novel nationalism, on the one hand, and reactionary social policy, on the other. However, there is hardly sufficient evidence to conclude that social conservatism was the major force behind the nationalism of Icelandic farmers. In Iceland, and probably in all European rural societies that came to know liberalism and nationalism, there was a constant conflict between the secure old and the tempting new alternatives, between the fear of innovation and the wish for a better life.

In Iceland this conflict was mirrored in a slow and hesitant abolition of the social restrictions described above. As late as 1887 the Althing passed, by a large majority, a bill which put even more restrictions on the establishment of cottages. In the conservative atmosphere that reigned in Copenhagen at this time (see Ch. 3.15), the bill was ratified by the king. However, by this time the society was changing so fast that it is doubtful if a law of this kind could be enforced any more. On the other hand, under pressure from Denmark, the law on service duty by single people was somewhat eased in 1863. From then on, servants of twenty-five years or older could buy themselves a licence to become free labourers. The price was not far from one year's wages for servants of either sex. In 1894 the price was lowered considerably, and all people over thirty could receive the licence free. By this law the service duty seems to have been abolished in practice. Still, as late as 1907 the Althing passed a new law on free labourers and cottars, where the restrictions of the earlier laws were eased, but not abolished altogether. The principle of labour bondage has, in fact, never been abolished legally in Iceland, although it is no longer printed in the official collection of valid law.[13]

---

[11] Guðmundur Hálfdanarson (1991), 27, 99-100, 155-7, 161; Guðmundur Hálfdanarson (1995), 765-74.

[12] Guðmundur Hálfdanarson (1991), 155; Gunnar Karlsson (1977a), 439.

[13] Jón Blöndal and Sverrir Kristjánsson (1954), 22-33; Guðmundur Jónsson (1981), 33-42, 63-4, 70-3.

The social reality had abolished the law before the legislator had the spirit to do so.

The crisis of overpopulation in Iceland's countryside was not solved by restrictions but by two outlets, which opened at approximately the same time and let out an approximately equal number of people in the period before industrialization. One of the outlets, which we shall deal with first since it ended first, was emigration to America. As to the other, there is no better term in English than urbanization, however badly the word 'urban' fits the squalid fishing villages that received the surplus population from the Icelandic countryside.[14]

---

[14] See Guðmundur Hálfdanarson (1995), 775.

3.9 Emigration

As already mentioned, the population of Iceland remained remarkably homogeneous in the ethnic sense, over the centuries (see Ch. 3.5). Correspondingly, there was no Icelandic population anywhere outside Iceland, apart from the tiny colony in Copenhagen and a few Icelanders scattered around Denmark for various reasons. In 1870 only 299 inhabitants of Denmark were reported to have been born in Iceland. By 1900 this number had risen to 743, or approximately 1% of the population of Iceland.[1] Although people born to Danish parents in Iceland are included in this number, there cannot have been many, so, roughly speaking, this must refer to the Icelandic element in Denmark's population.

For this reason it must have been a rather remote possibility for Icelanders to emigrate, even when they heard news of the great exodus that was to take more than 50 million Europeans to the New World in the century between the Napoleonic wars and the First World War. However, this great movement gradually came closer to Iceland; in the 1860s it reached Scandinavia in full force, and in the end it induced more than 2 million Scandinavians to leave their home countries and head for America. Most came from Sweden and Norway; from Denmark just over 300,000 emigrated, about 14% of the Danish population in 1890.

In general the exodus from Iceland to America imitates the same movement from Europe, in the typically microscopic style of Iceland, in having heretics as its pioneers.[2] Around the middle of the 19th century two young apprentices from the Westman Islands were converted to Mormonism in Copenhagen, and on their return home founded a group of Mormons in their home island. From there the first five Icelandic emigrants sailed to America in 1855, heading for their promised land in Utah. They were later followed by a few more Mormons, but of course the emigration to Utah could not be the start of any major movement and is only remembered as a curiosity.

The same can probably be said about the next move. Around 1850 a group of people in the north-eastern district of Þingeyjarsýsla began to

---

[1] *Statistisk tabelværk* V A: 4(1904), 9*, xxxviii.

[2] The story of Icelandic emigration and the Icelandic settlements in North America has been written in Icelandic by Þorsteinn Þ. Þorsteinsson and Tryggvi J. Oleson I-V (1940-53). There is a short survey in English by Helgi Skúli Kjartansson (1992). See also Helgi Skúli Kjartansson (1977, 1980).

plan emigrating to Greenland, which originally seems to have been modelled on the Viking Age colonization there (see Ch. 1.4), which was well known to Icelanders from the sagas. The bad year 1859 (see Ch. 3.8) gave a new impulse to these ideas, which soon took a different course. The farmer Einar Ásmundsson, who was later to question the right of Christian IX to rule over Iceland (see Ch. 3.6), had spent a year in Copenhagen and was a man of unusually broad outlook. He assumed the leadership of an emigration society and pointed out to its members that it was not advisable to emigrate from one cold country to another still colder. No, the country to emigrate to, in Einar's opinion, was Brazil. A circular has been preserved in which he describes and compares the three countries which he cited as possible destinations: Canada, the United States and Brazil. It is tempting to quote his description of Brazil as evidence of the knowledge and attitudes which could be found among 19th-century farmers in Iceland:[3]

The third country, the empire of Brazil, lies in the southern part of America, south of the equator. It is of approximately the same size as, or even bigger than, the United States of North America, so that no state in the world is bigger except Russia and China. The inhabitants of Brazil descend from Portugal and speak Portuguese. That is, the white ones, who are not much more than one million in the whole country. Around five million people are black, brown and mixed. But most of them are unfree and slaves of the whites, all of whom are considered chieftains or noblemen although they have nothing but their colour to boast of. The country is sparsely inhabited, as can be deduced from the population number, since it is not even a quarter of that of the United States. Still, Brazil on the whole is a better country than the United States; indeed it is, all things considered, one of the very best countries in the world. Winter never comes there, and many kinds of fruits and vegetables grow excellently. Nowhere else in the world are there such forests, and many excellent kinds of wood grow in them. On cultivated land one can grow an abundance of coffee, sugar cane, cotton, tobacco, rice, maize and so on. In some parts of the country there are plains without forest cover, with large herds of wild cattle and horses, but in the whole country there is a lot of game and birds. Many metals are found in the earth – in some places particularly gold and silver, also jewels. Brazil is about five times further away than Copenhagen.

On reading this one might wonder why everyone did not take the next boat to Brazil. Actually few of its readers did, but in 1873 a group of more than thirty people made their way there from northern Iceland via Copenhagen, and some of their descendants are still aware of their origin and have recently visited Iceland.

While the northerners were considering whether they should set out for Greenland or for Brazil, some people from the south moved to the United States, without initiating any major movement. That was to arise in the north in 1873 the same year as the Icelanders landed in Brazil, also from Þingeyjarsýsla.

[3] Arnór Sigurjónsson I (1957), 326-7. My translation.

From this time until 1914 the names of 14,268 emigrants have been registered.[4] The list is mainly based on two types of sources: parish registers and the lists of emigrants made at the offices of Icelandic sheriffs. If these sources had been compiled and preserved perfectly, they would form a complete duplicate: every emigrant would be listed in both. Therefore, from the number of emigrants missing from one of them or the other, it can be estimated how many must be missing from both and thus from the list altogether. In addition, from 1900 onwards Canadian immigration statistics specify Icelandic immigrants and prove that they were considerably more numerous than the Icelandic sources indicate. In this way it has been estimated that approximately 17,000 Icelanders emigrated to America in the period 1870-1914. On the other hand, it has been calculated from population growth figures between censuses, minus natural growth, that the total net emigration from Iceland in the period was not far off the number in the list. Some 2,000 people seem to have returned to Iceland.[5] Therefore, the recorded 14,268, gives quite a good idea of the population loss from Iceland, and these individuals, who are listed by name, will also form the basis for most of the statistical information presented here.

They amount to 20% of the population of Iceland in 1887, when approximately half of them had emigrated. This number may not be quite as dramatic as it seems at first sight, since more individuals lived in Iceland in the emigration period altogether than in any single year of that period. Therefore, the 14,000 were "taken from" a considerably higher number of people than the population number at any one point of time. Just over 100,000 children were born in Iceland in the emigration period, 1870-1914, so that about 170,000 individuals lived in the country for some part of the period or all of it,[6] but only a proportion of them spent their whole life within the period. It can be roughly estimated that the population of Iceland between 1870 and 1914 corresponds to 90,000 whole lifespans, which leads us to the conclusion that some 15% of them left the country for America.

Emigration from Iceland is unique in that most went to Canada, whereas from most or all other European countries the majority went to the United States. This was partly due to the late beginning of emigration from Iceland after the Canadian authorities had begun to promote emigration in cooperation with the Allan Line, which already had an agent in Iceland in 1873. Contrary to most European countries, this promotion campaign was successful in Iceland, because emigration was only just about to start from there and Icelandic emigrants had no relatives in the United States to help them take the first steps. Besides, Canada offered its immigrants what the Icelanders were after: land to live on and even a separate settlement.

[4] Júníus H. Kristinsson (1983).
[5] Helgi Skúli Kjartansson (unpublished material borrowed from the author).
[6] *Hagskinna* (1997), 161 (table 2.34).

Map 3.9-1 The heartland of the Icelandic settlement in Manitoba, Canada. Gimli, with a name from Norse mythology, was the capital of New Iceland.

In Iceland emigration to America was connected from the beginning with ideas about an Icelandic society in the New World. In 1874 a twenty-four-year-old Icelandic journalist appeared before the United States President Ulysses Grant to prepare him for a request for an island off the coast of Alaska, which would be closed to others and to which the whole Icelandic population could move.[7] The plan came to nothing, but in the next year Canadian authorities reserved a colony on the western shore of Lake Winnipeg for Icelanders alone and named it New Iceland. It was practically uninhabited by Europeans but sparsely populated by Native Americans.[8] However, the land of New Iceland proved rather barren; only a minority of the Icelandic immigrants ever settled there and many of them quickly left. Within a few years the town of Winnipeg, much further south, had the largest settlement of Icelanders in America.

Thoughts of abandoning Iceland completely – quite unrealistic in practice, of course – were originally kindled by political grievances after the enforcement of the Status Act in 1871 (see Ch. 3.6). On the other hand, emigration came to be strongly condemned by Icelandic nationalists, who saw it as virtual treason against the fatherland. Thus many people no doubt left the country with a feeling of guilt, which may have made immigrants of Icelandic origin more attached to their old country than others. They travelled with so much of Iceland in them.

Although the Icelandic emigrants were no doubt pulled by the favourable offers of the Canadian authorities, they were of course also strongly

[7] Hjörtur Pálsson (1975), 42-3, 76-80, 100-1, 127-8.

[8] Gerrard (1985) has written about the colonization of New Iceland in English. See also Kristjanson (1965) and Lindal (1967).

pushed by the situation in Iceland. An eruption of the volcano Askja in 1875 spread a layer of ashes 10-20 cm. deep over large districts in the east and played a decisive role in sending 1,190 people to America the next year, compared with fifty-nine the previous year. Then, in the 1880s, a spell of cold weather set in, with the years 1881 and 1882 far below 2°C on average in Stykkishólmur, and the period 1881-7 was similar to that of 1859-69 (see Ch. 3.8), with an average temperature in Stykkishólmur of 2.42°C.[9] In the four-year period 1886-9, over 4,200 recorded emigrants left the country, more than a quarter of the total.[10] This wave of emigration, together with an epidemic of measles in 1882, created the last period of decreasing population in Iceland's history, from 72,445 in the 1880 census to 70,927 in 1890.

In general the lack of variety in opportunities forced Icelanders to emigrate. Women appear to have reacted to this impetus more strongly than in most countries. While the excess number of men among emigrants threatened to disturb the sex ratio on both sides of the Atlantic, women were in a narrow majority among the Icelandic emigrants: 50.67% as against 49.33% men. To a certain extent, this peculiarity can be explained by an unusually high excess number of women in Iceland (see Chs. 2.14 and 3.12), added to the high proportion of emigration of whole families. But it must have been partly caused by the almost total lack of light industry and reasonably paid services in an urban environment, which received an increasing number of women in the more urbanized parts of Europe.

Although no new Iceland was born in the New World, for decades the West Icelanders (*Vestur-Íslendingar*), as they are still called in Iceland, for decades lived much of their social and cultural lives in Icelandic. In many areas they had their own congregations, with Icelandic clergymen, and their separate societies. They published a number of periodicals and books in Icelandic, most of them in Winnipeg. For decades two weekly papers were published there, carrying the nationalistic titles *Lögberg* (Law Rock) and *Heimskringla* (after Snorri Sturluson's kings' sagas); only in the second half of the 20th century were they united under the compound title *Lögberg-Heimskringla*. It is still published, mostly in English now, although many people of the older generation still speak Icelandic fluently.

---

[9] *Hagskinna* (1997), 37-8 (table 1.1).

[10] Júníus H. Kristinsson (1983), xx-xxi (table 1).

3.10 The Age of Decked Fishing Vessels

If America relieved the overpopulated Icelandic countryside of some 14,000 individuals (see Ch. 3.9), we can assume that the villages around the coast of Iceland, including Reykjavík, received a slightly higher number in the same period. In 1904, before any considerable growth can be attributed to the mechanization of fishing (see Ch. 4.1), just over 20,000 people, a quarter of the population, lived in urban nuclei of fifty or more inhabitants. Unfortunately, no statistical information is available about their number until 1889, when they were just over 9,000, 13% of the population.[1] However, judging from the growth of Reykjavík alone, from little more than 1,000 inhabitants at mid-century to almost 4,000 in 1890, we may assume that the bulk of the villagers in 1904 were, or were descended from, people who had left a country farm in the second half of the 19th century. At any rate, these 20,000 individuals were the pioneers of urbanization, who tried their luck "on the gravel" (*á mölinni*), as used to be said in Iceland, before the encouragement of mechanization.

Two changes at the coast were particularly important in making this enterprise possible in the second half of the 19th century. One was expansion in trade, which was touched on in Chapter 3.7 and will be the subject of the next chapter. The other was the introduction of decked vessels in fishing.

For centuries fishing off Iceland had been pursued in open rowing boats (see Ch. 2.4). On such vessels fishing tours were mostly restricted to one day, so that only shallow fishing banks could be utilized, which inevitably made fishing an unstable and hazardous industry. In the 17th century according to annals, it could happen that the share of each fisherman of a crew after a whole fishing season of three or four months was fewer than two fish. On the other hand, in good fishing years the share could reach 1,000-2,000 fish. Bad weather and drift-ice could prevent fishing for a month. In 1685 twenty boats are reported to have been lost and 174 men drowned. In 1700 165 men – 0.33% of Iceland's population – were drowned on the same day.[2]

---

[1] *Hagskinna* (1997), 90 (table 2.7). This work provides most of the statistical material referred to in the chapter.

[2] Jón Jónsson (1994), 61-4.

As early as the 15th century, English fishermen had fished on larger, decked vessels off the coasts of Iceland (see Ch. 2.6). For centuries, however, Icelanders only occasionally attempted to use decked boats, mainly driven by sail and not oarsmen, for fishing. One of these attempts was made by the previously mentioned Icelandic merchant Bjarni Sivertsen in Hafnarfjörður at the beginning of the 19th century (see Ch. 3.1). However, this industry grew slowly and irregularly. Three periods can be distinguished in its development. Until the 1850s most decked vessels were stationed in the Western Region, in Snæfellsnes and the Western Fiords. In 1853 there were reported to be 25 decked fishing boats in the country, 19 of them in the west. In the 1850s, the north entered this industry with vigour, particularly the Eyjafjörður district. In 1858 the overall number was 66-35 in the North-Eastern Region and 26 in the Western Region. In this period the decked boats were predominantly used for catching shark, which had to be sought fairly far out into the Arctic Ocean. In the late 1860s and '70s, a new centre of gravity emerged in the south-west, with an emphasis on cod fishing; in 1887, the overall number was 86, divided almost equally between the three regions. During the 1890s the number of decked vessels went up to 140, and the addition was almost equally divided between the Reykjavík area and the Western Fiords. In addition to the growing number, the new boats were usually much bigger than the older ones. Some of the early decked vessels were nothing but twelve- or ten-oar rowing-boats with a deck put into them. These newer boats were up to 90 gross registered tons (GRT), with the space under the deck divided into a hold for keeping the catch and a cabin with bunks and a stove.[3]

After the beginning of the 20th century the decked fishing boats gradually disappeared, but that development is difficult to follow, as more or less satisfactory auxiliary engines were put into the boats that remained in use.

The last period of decked-boat fishing – roughly the last three decades of the 19th century, coinciding approximately with the governor period in political history (see Ch. 3.15) – was by far the most important in the development of the society. Therefore, we predominantly refer to these years when we talk about the age of decked vessels (*skútuöld*) in Icelandic history.

This somewhat pompous term may easily promote the overestimation of the decked boats. It would be dubious to call their age the start of modernization in Iceland. Rather, it is a part of the growth of industries with old methods, which was described in Chapter 3.7 with the first half of the century in focus. No new techniques were introduced in the decked boats. Technically, there had been nothing to prevent the Icelanders from

---

[3] For a comprehensive work on fishing on decked vessels in Iceland, see Gils Guðmundsson I-V (1977).

beginning fishing of this kind, after the English model, as early as the 15th century. Even the fishing gear was almost exclusively a simple hand-line. Nets and long-lines, which were well known on the open boats, were not considered suitable for decked vessels.

Furthermore, the decked vessels far from replaced the open boats, although they were not a pure addition to them either. In Chapter 3.7 we calculated that in 1851 the fleet of open boats had almost 12,000 oars, which amounts to over 15,000 crew places and some 5,000 year-round jobs. In 1900, using the same method, one comes down to 8,400 oars, *c.* 11,000 crew places and some 3,600 year-round jobs. At the same time, the crew members on decked vessels numbered just over 2,000.[4] Even if we assume that they all had a year-round occupation as fishermen, the rowing boats still provided 80% more jobs than the decked vessels. Moreover, the open boats seem to have brought twice as much fish ashore, even at the height of the fashion for decked vessels. In 1900, which was not an exceptional year in any way for catches, the open boats caught some 42,000 tons and the decked vessels 23,000 tons of demersal fish (mainly cod and haddock).

Still, even though the decked boats did not bring modernity to Iceland in a technical sense, they contributed greatly to doing so socially. They were the first large-scale enterprises in the country, run by a single employer with a hundred or more employees. The merchant Ásgeir Ásgeirsson in Ísafjörður in the Western Fiords owned up to sixteen boats at the same time, which must have employed some 220 crew. Pétur Thorsteinsson in Bíldudalur, also in the Western Fiords, ran eighteen boats, when he was at his best; they must have had about 250 men in their crews. In 1904 Geir Zoëga in Reykjavík ran seven boats of the largest kind, 80 GRT on average, with 125 ordinary deck-hands on board.[5] In addition to this, all these men were engaged in fish-processing – an industry of greatly increasing importance – fish export and other trade. In this way, the decked fishing boats brought capitalism to Iceland.

It was also an important innovation that the decked boats could follow the shoals of fish along the fishing grounds, from the southern and southwestern coast in late winter, to the west in the spring and north in the summer. They were often fishing for around half the year. A part of the other half could be used for maintenance of ships and fishing gear, besides other work for the firm, so that many of the shipowners could provide their fishermen with a year-round occupation. In this way the decked boats created a professional class of fishermen for the first time after a thousand years of fishing off the shores of Iceland.

The capitalist mode of production created, of course, previously unknown conditions for class conflict. Except for a small and short-lived

---

[4] *Hagskinna* (1997), 310, 313 (tables 5.2 and 5.3).

[5] *Landshagsskýrslur* 1906 (1907), 24.

union of typographers in Reykjavík in 1887-90, the first trade unions emerged in the fishing industry on the decked vessels.[6] In contrast to the origin of labour unions in most countries, the employers took the lead in this development, when the owners of decked boats in the Reykjavík area founded an association in 1894 with the purpose of keeping down the wages of their employees. A leading person in this enterprise was the bank director Tryggvi Gunnarsson, former director of the trading society Gránufélag (see Ch. 3.11), a man who was always inclined to act rather than let things happen. The deck-hands responded with a union, which they called Báran (The Wave), in the same year and announced their wage demands. The skippers stepped in as mediators, both parties gave in and the first formal wage contract was made in Iceland. In the next years a number of seamen's unions were established in other fishing stations, modelled on Báran and given the same name – Báran no. 2 and so on. However, only a few of these unions survived the technical revolution in fishing after the end of the 19th century. Most of them dwindled away and new unions were established in their place, as we shall see later (Ch. 4.3).

The increase in fish products brought about by the decked vessels was sufficient to make them give a permanent top position among export goods, which introduced their overwhelming importance in exports in the 20th century. The last time that the value of agricultural products was greater in exports than that of marine products – some 2.3 million krónur[7] as against 2 million – was in 1876. In 1900 marine products were sold for 5 million krónur, besides 2 million for whale products, which were exclusively owned by Norwegians, while agricultural products sold for 1.8 million.[8] In a number of ways this immense increase in export earnings made foreign innovations possible in Iceland, although the next great novelty in the modernization process, the mechanization of fishing, does not seem to emerge directly from the decked-boat fishing. Some of its profit no doubt went into paying for trawlers and motor-boats, and a number of former decked-boat owners had a share in the trawler industry, but no large-scale employer in decked-boat fishing was to play a leading role in the new mechanized industries.

---

[6] Ólafur R. Einarsson (1969) describes the origin of the labour movement in Iceland. Ingólfur V. Gíslason (1990) provides a survey of the organization of employers.

[7] When the króna (pl. krónur, Danish krone) was introduced in Denmark and Iceland instead of the rigsdal, in 1875, two krónur corresponded to one rigsdal. That, however, tells us nothing about the relative value of the rigsdal and krónur further back in time, or since the Second World War (see Ch. 4.12).

[8] *Hagskinna* (1997), 430-2, 504-13 (tables 10.4 and 10.17).

3.11 Freedom of Trade and the Cooperative Movement

The Danish monopoly trade in Iceland had been lifted in the wake of the Mist Famine in the late 1780s (see Ch. 2.18). Foreign trade in Iceland was then restricted to the subjects of the Danish king, which, of course, allowed Icelanders to participate in their foreign trade themselves. However, the trading stations left by the monopoly trade were mostly bought by Danes, since there was neither the capital nor trading connections in Iceland for taking over the trade at that time. When, in 1814, Norway left the kingdom and Norwegians thus lost the right to trade in Iceland, foreign shipowners were permitted to apply for licences to sail to Iceland, but they were required to pay a tariff that made foreign trade in Iceland impracticable.

As time went on, many of the trading stations in Iceland fell into the hands of large Danish firms, which ran trade at a number of harbours. Thus for decades the Copenhagen firm Ørum & Wulff ran most of the trading centres in the north-eastern and central-eastern part of the country, from Húsavík in Þingeyjarsýsla to Djúpivogur in Suður-Múlasýsla.[1] The only possible competition came from non-resident merchants, who were only permitted to trade from their ships at authorized trading harbours for four weeks at a time. In 1855 there were fifty-eight shops at twenty-five places in the country. Of these, twenty-six were owned by merchants who were resident in Iceland and thirty-two by foreigners, in the sense that their residence was abroad (at this time there was no particular Icelandic citizenship that could be used to distinguish between Icelanders and foreigners). These numbers certainly exaggerate the Icelandic part of the trade, since most of the shops run by people resident in Iceland were probably very small. Thus nine of them were situated in Reykjavík, where there were also five shops owned by foreigners, in a village of some 1,300 inhabitants and a rather limited hinterland of rural areas.[2] The large central shops or trading stations, which sold any goods that were available in the country and received for them all kinds of exportable products, were at this time mostly owned by Danes.

---

[1] Þorkell Jóhannesson (1958), 57-67.
[2] *Skýrslur um landshagi* I (1858), 588-9.

Usually import and export were run in common at each trading station, by the same firm and at the same place. In practice, most of the trade was pure barter, where no money was present, although the prices had been calculated in money since 1776 (see Ch. 2.10).

This description applies exclusively to foreign trade. Internally, trade had been run in Iceland throughout the centuries, largely between inland farmers, who had butter, tallow, woollen clothes and even meat to sell in exchange for dried fish from those who lived predominantly on fishing. However, this kind of trade was mostly carried on directly between the two kinds of producers/consumers. No statistics are available about it, and no one has yet studied it thoroughly. In the 19th century, a part of this trade went through the hands of merchants, but no information is available about its volume.

Free trade with all countries and by the citizens of any country was on Jón Sigurðsson's political programme from the start and, since people were, of course, constantly discontent with the condition of the trade, this policy may have played an important part in his early popularity in Iceland.[3] The case was discussed at the first session of the Althing and every session thereafter, and in the National Assembly of 1851 a bill of free trade was the only one to be completed, with a petition to the king.[4] In 1854, the Danish Parliament enacted a law on sailing and trade in Iceland, which was to secure practically equal rights for the citizens of the Danish kingdom and foreigners from 1 April 1855.[5] Foreign trade was restricted to authorized harbours, which in practice meant that shops could only be established where there was at least a remote possibility of mooring a ship.

The new law seems to have had an immediate effect. Already in 1856 almost 30% of the tonnage of cargo ships arrived in Iceland from countries other than Denmark, a proportion that did not rise considerably until the 1870s.[6] These numbers do not indicate the participation of non-Danish firms in Iceland, since the ships may have been more or less in the service of Danish trading firms. Nevertheless, the direct contact with countries other than Denmark opened up possibilities for new business contacts.

One of these possibilities was the export of horses and sheep to Britain, which was begun on a considerable scale in the 1870s. This, especially the sheep trade, played a decisive part in transferring foreign trade into the hands of the Icelanders themselves.[7] Another part in that development was played by the social initiative of Icelandic farmers. Therefore

---

[3] Gunnar Karlsson (1977a), 32.

[4] *Alþingistíðindi* 1845 (1845), viii; 1847 (1847), xi; 1849 (1850), ix; 1851 (1851), vi, 409-12.

[5] *Lovsamling for Island* XV (1870), 611-23. Text in Danish and Icelandic.

[6] *Skýrslur um landshagi* III (1866), 574-83; V (1875), 822.

[7] Sveinbjörn Blöndal (1982).

we must first take a quick look at their attempts to improve their lot in the trade.

In the first round, these attempts were restricted to forming groups who went together to the merchant with common price demands for their products. As early as 1795 a formal agreement was concluded and signed by the clergymen and communal overseers in the eastern district Norður-Múlasýsla on negotiations with the local merchant about pricing. However, the merchant seems to have repelled the attack,[8] and in the coming decades associations of this kind are mentioned only occasionally. But, after the middle of the 19th century, at least in Suður-Þingeyjarsýsla, it seems almost to have been a custom in some communes, especially those that were not close to trading harbours, for farmers to combine in order to negotiate with the merchant and try to make the merchants at Akureyri and Húsavík compete for their products.[9]

As might be expected, the merchants learned to meet the demands of the farmers, partly by forming their own informal associations against them, but perhaps more by meeting their price demands by marking up the prices of foreign goods. This may be the reason for the extremely high pricing of both Icelandic and foreign goods in the shops of Iceland for much of the 19th century. Often the merchants bought Icelandic products for a higher price than they could expect to get for them abroad. The losses – all the merchants' expenses together with their profit – were met with sometimes more than a 100% mark-up on foreign goods. In pure barter, where money was only a unit of calculation, it mattered little how high the numbers written into the ledger were, as long as the balance between sold and bought goods was kept reasonable. On the other hand, the unnatural pricing explains a constant lack of money in circulation in Iceland, while Iceland and Denmark had a common currency. It was an evident loss for a merchant to buy Icelandic goods for 10 rdl. in money, take them to Denmark and get perhaps only 9 rdl. for them there. Therefore the merchants did all they could to avoid paying with money, and with shops so few and far between they could get away with quite a lot.

The second round of attempts at the improvement of trade on behalf of Icelandic farmers was started in 1869, when a group of people in the Eyjafjörður area bought a French ship that had been stranded there, with a view to restoring it for sailing abroad. Shares were sold to local clergymen and farmers, who proved to be not quite as penniless as one might expect (see Ch. 3.12). A self-educated farmer from the district and an unusually active man, Tryggvi Gunnarsson, later a bank director, assumed the post of director of the enterprise, and the result was a large trading company, called Gránufélag, with shops in most trading places in the north-eastern

[8] Sigfús Haukur Andrésson (1981), 129-34.
[9] Gunnar Karlsson (1977a), 245-58. This book is the main source for the story of the cooperative movement told in this chapter.

and eastern part of the country.[10] This was imitated in other districts, but all these joint-stock companies failed after a few years. The Gránufélag alone survived for some decades, but in fact it was owned by Danish wholesalers, who were the creditors of the company. Thus this bold attempt to get the foreign trade into Icelandic hands became in reality a Danish-ruled enterprise.

The third round was free from this danger of Danish dominance, since from the beginning it was connected more with Britain than with Denmark and started more modestly and carefully. Every now and then the attempt had been made in Iceland to found small purchasing societies and order goods directly from Denmark. In this way the abnormal mark-up on foreign goods could be circumvented, and this could pay off well for those who had money and acquaintances in Copenhagen to do the purchasing. But most farmers had neither.

It was here that the export of living sheep came to the farmers' aid. British buyers of sheep who came to Iceland would pay in hard cash – silver and gold. This money could be used to send abroad and order goods; or, more simply, one could form a society and negotiate with the buyer to bring English meal, salt and other goods in his ship to Iceland to exchange for sheep. The next step was for the society itself to export the sheep through agents in Britain and buy in exchange goods ordered by its members. Finally, the society could order goods which its leaders thought their members would like and sell them in its own shop.

This was the development of a small purchasing society, Kaupfélag Þingeyinga (Purchasing Society of Þingeyjarsýsla), which was founded in the commercial area of Húsavík in 1882. It seems to have been founded for practical purposes only, but in a bitter struggle with the local factor of Ørum & Wulff at Húsavík, who tried to exclude its members from all trade, the leaders of the society turned their activity into an ideology. They discovered that without knowing it they had entered the international cooperative movement, which was traditionally attributed to Robert Owen and the weavers of Rochdale in northern England. The purpose of the society was no longer proclaimed to be better prices but a democratization of trade. "Commerce is the right of any individual, so important that it cannot be entrusted to any particular class," wrote a young farmer in the leading group. "Trade can come under the general social rule that everyone has the right to vote on, and trade is no mystery, but a social activity which any mature person can understand and participate in."[11]

In the 1880s a number of similar trading societies were established in other districts, mostly with sheep export as the principal concern. Many of them called themselves *kaupfélag*, which thus became the usual term for a

[10] The activity of this society is described in detail by Þorkell Jóhannesson and Bergsteinn Jónsson II and IV (1965-90).

[11] Gunnar Karlsson (1977a), 315-16. My translation.

cooperative. They modelled their arrangement more or less on Kaupfélag Þingeyinga and shared its agent in Newcastle, England. In this way a co-operative movement emerged in Iceland. When in 1896 sheep imports from Iceland were made impracticable in Britain by over-strict hygiene require-ments, the movement had become strong enough to survive the blow. After the beginning of the 20th century the cooperative societies formed the Federation of Icelandic Cooperative Societies (Samband íslenskra samvinnufélaga), which was to develop into the largest economic concern in the country, a position it held well into the second half of the 20th cen-tury until it suddenly collapsed in the 1980s.

The origin of the societies explains why the cooperative movement in Iceland acquired some unusual features. Since it grew up in rural districts, where trading was mostly by barter, the same societies had to cater for selling products and buying consumer goods. They had to unite the roles of producers' and consumers' cooperatives, which formed two distinct movements in most other countries, including Denmark. For this reason also the cooperative movement in Iceland was not allied to socialism but to the liberal, agrarian Progressive Party (see Ch. 4.4).

The cooperatives, together with the growth of the fishing villages in the age of decked vessels, brought the bulk of foreign trade in Iceland into the hands of Icelanders. In 1903 there were 262 shops in Iceland – 216 owned by Icelanders and forty-six by people resident abroad.[12] This gives an inaccurate picture of the situation, partly because some of the coopera-tives may not have run a shop at this time, although they engaged in foreign trade. Nevertheless, the numbers are right in giving the idea that the dominance of Danish firms in Icelandic trade was no longer a problem. The trade was not democratized on the scale that the advocates of Kaupfélag Þingeyinga dreamed of, but the nationalist goal of trade in the hands of Icelanders was largely reached in this period.

---

[12] *Landshagsskýrslur* 1904 (1904-5), 257-8.

3.12 Standard of Living

It was definitely not true that ancient Nordic culture in Iceland had been kept deep-frozen for centuries as the young Danish romantic Orla Lehmann maintained in the 1830s (see Ch. 3.5). On the other hand, Iceland was still throughout the 19th century a primitive, underdeveloped society. And since it was in its last phase as such and the sources allow us to be much more explicit and accurate about the life of the common people in this period than at any time before, it is worth taking a last look at the mode of living and different living standards of the Icelanders before they plunged into the turmoil of modernization.[1]

The Icelandic countryside must have shown little more sign of human habitation in the 19th century than it had done for centuries. Most of the houses were overgrown with grass and scarcely looked different from natural hillocks in the landscape. However, some farmers in this period began to build more of the individual chambers, which the ordinary farms consisted of, with timber gables facing the pavement in front of the houses. Some farmers even moved the *baðstofa*, which had traditionally been at the very back of the cluster, to the front row. Thus originated in the late 18th and 19th centuries the gabled farmhouse, with a straight front row of timber gables and a self-assured look that promised cultural and social renaissance;[2] this short-lived kind of farmhouse became the image of traditional Icelandic houses for 20th-century national romanticism in Iceland.

To the romantic picture also belongs a rectangular vegetable garden in front of the farmhouse. This too was a 19th-century novelty, and scarcely typical even then. The only traditional cultivation consisted of a grass field surrounding the farm which was somewhat greener than elsewhere, because the grass enjoyed the benefit of manure and was, in some farms, fenced off with a low wall to keep the livestock out. This was the *tún*, the most precious part of the farmland, which yielded hay for the cows.

There were hardly any man-made roads in the country, but gradually the hooves of horses and cattle had formed narrow paths. Only in the last decades of the century did roads begin to be built for carriages, and in the 1890s bridges were built across two of the largest rivers flowing from

---

[1] For a basic work on the ethnology of Iceland, mostly relying on 19th-century evidence, see Jónas Jónasson (1934). More comprehensive studies are published in the unfinished collection *Íslensk þjóðmenning* I, V-VII (1987-90).

[2] Hörður Ágústsson (1987), 289-95.

The image of an Icelandic 19th-century farm. Tapestry embroidered by Þórdís Egilsdóttir, 1937.

the glaciers to the south coast, which later proved able to carry cars and were in use until the mid-20th century.

Throughout the 19th century a large majority of Icelanders lived in turf houses, no better than those that were described in Chapter 2.19. The trade union leader and writer Tryggvi Emilsson describes the *baðstofa* that his family moved into in 1916. It had an earthen floor, turf walls and turf ceiling, which were only partly covered with timber.[3] Even in Reykjavík, there were 140 houses in 1865 made of turf and only seventy-six of timber, while six were built of stone.[4] In 1910 when statistical information is available about the whole country, over half of the dwelling-houses were still made of turf, 40% were made of timber and less than 4% of stone or concrete.[5]

Within the class of turf houses, living conditions were widely different. Two neighbouring farms at Eyjafjörður in the central north around 1880 exemplify this. On Kambur there was one *baðstofa* of 11 m.[2] (100 sq. ft), where six adults and four children lived, although adult single men may have slept in the so-called front-house (*framhús*), which was approximately 10 m.[2]. There was also a kitchen of 10 m.[2], a pantry of 6 m.[2] and a small hut for keeping manure, which was used as fuel. All these houses were connected by a narrow corridor; the cowshed alone was behind the kitchen,

[3] Tryggvi Emilsson (1976), 167.

[4] Gísli Ágúst Gunnlaugsson (1982), 95.

[5] *Hagskinna* (1997), 373 (table 7.3). In this chapter, as previously, this source will be used without further references.

so that the cow (or maybe there were two) had to make its way through it on its way in and out. On the farm Grund, on the other hand, two families of twenty-two individuals in all lived in seven rooms, besides kitchens and pantries for each family.[6] In all the living-rooms (not kitchens and pantries) the ceiling, walls and floor were probably covered with timber. A well-built turf house of this kind was not necessarily a worse dwelling than any other. I myself did not live in a turf house for longer than a month and was unfortunately too young to remember much about it. But in my youth, in the 1940s and 1950s, I sometimes visited such houses, which were dry, warm, clean and reasonably bright.

The space allocated to individuals was, of course, different in traditional housing. In the better-off homes the farmer and his wife had a private room, in others not. Apart from that it was customary for the whole household to live practically all their indoor life in the *baðstofa*, often with two sharing each bed – most likely an adult and a child. Thus the indoor private space of an adult domestic servant could be restricted to little more than half a bed and, above it, a narrow shelf, formed naturally where the roof met the wall. As if to carry the lack of privacy to the extreme, it was customary to sleep naked. It must be added, though, that the lighting in the *baðstofa* made nudity less evident than we might imagine. In the 19th century glass gradually came to replace the membranes made from after-births of cows in the windows; and for lighting, paraffin lamps were just beginning to challenge primitive fish-liver-oil lamps.

Timber houses originated in the villages and in the 19th century were mostly restricted to them. These houses were not altogether a progressive step. Many of them were badly insulated, and fuel was used sparingly for heating, so that they were often colder in the winter than turf houses. In addition, it proved difficult to keep timber houses water-proof in the windy rains of southern and western Iceland. Therefore corrugated iron was a welcome novelty when it began to be imported, in the 1880s,[7] and it is still a notable characteristic of the older parts of Icelandic towns and villages, sometimes painted with bright, strong colours.

Considering the abundance of stone in Iceland, stone houses were introduced amazingly late. In the second half of the 18th century a few official buildings were built of stone, but stone-cutting was practically unknown in Iceland until after the building of the Althing house in Reykjavík around 1880. A few Icelanders then learned the craft from Danish masons, and some small stone dwelling-houses were built in Reykjavík. However, stone did not become very popular as a building material in Iceland, and was finally overtaken by concrete in the 20th century.

For people who had never known any habitation except a sparsely populated countryside, where even latrines were not considered neces-

[6] Bragi Guðmundsson and Gunnar Karlsson (1988), 86.
[7] Pétur H. Ármannsson (1987), 148.

sary, it inevitably took time to learn what was needed in a town. In the 19th century Icelanders had definitely not learned this, as the English traveller John Coles observed when he went there in 1881:

I do not remember having seen an uglier town than Reykjavik; the houses are of all sizes, colours, and shapes; not a tree is to be seen, and no definite plan seems to have been followed in laying out the streets; should the place grow much larger the town surveyor will have a difficult job before him, as beyond the existing streets, the houses have been built anywhere, so that to extend a street in a straight line it would necessitate the pulling down of several houses. The ugliness of Reykjavik is not, however, its worst feature, for I am bound to confess that the entire absence of anything like sanatory [sic] arrangements makes itself very apparent, even to the most unobservant, and is absolutely shocking to the untrained olfactory nerves of the stranger; in some places, the stench of decayed fish and other abominations was so dreadful that they powerfully reminded me of a Chinese settlement in a Californian mining district.[8]

The truth of this description is confirmed by many native Icelanders of the period. By this time, however, Christian IX had visited the town and celebrated the millennium of Iceland's settlement (see Ch. 3.6). On that occasion a small garden had been laid out around the first statue in Iceland, a copy of one portraying the Danish-Icelandic sculptor Bertel Thorvaldsen, made by himself and presented by the Copenhagen city council.[9] Reykjavík was beginning to prepare itself for its function as a state capital.

Moving closer to the individual, Icelanders dressed mainly in clothes made from Icelandic wool, knitted and homespun; hides were used for shoes and oilskins. However, some changes can be seen here too. Just as in housing, Iceland acquired its national symbol in clothing in this century. Sigurður Guðmundsson, an Icelandic painter educated in Copenhagen, designed a national costume for both sexes, based partly on traditional costumes and partly on his own taste and opinion of how people had dressed in the Saga Age. The men's costume did not catch on, but the women's gained immense popularity and is still worn on most festive occasions.[10] In the second half of the 19th century the import of textiles and clothing almost tripled in value, which was no different from imports in general.

From written sources one might conclude that the Icelanders were obsessed with food, especially fatty foods, butter, tallow and fatty meat. This, of course, is a concomitant of life in a cool, wet climate with poor houses and inadequate clothing. In this period, large-scale starvation is not recorded; the last famine occurred in 1803, in the third bad year in succession, when 119 people are recorded to have died from pure hunger

---

[8] Coles (1882), 7.

[9] Guðjón Friðriksson (1991b), 28-9.

[10] Elsa E. Guðjónsson (1967, 1969); Margrét Guðmundsdóttir (1995b).

and 450 in all from hunger and diseases derived from the shortage of food.[11]

Of course, many people suffered greatly from hunger after this, and no doubt some individuals died of it. The increasing number of paupers (see Ch. 3.8) was generally considered to be a serious threat to society, and they met with strong condemnation. The system of maintenance had an inbuilt tendency towards the harsh treatment of paupers. They were normally provided with lodging at a home in the neighbourhood, which in return received payment from the commune. To minimize the cost the paupers were sometimes auctioned to those who offered to accept them at the lowest price, which of course tended to be the people who spent least on their maintenance and extracted the most work from them.

In individual cases the condemnation of paupers could take the form of cruelty and even torture. One such case was that of Sæmundur Stefánsson, born in 1859 and brought up as a pauper because his parents could not afford to marry, although they had three children together. According to Sæmundur's memoirs, he slept on hay, wrapped in an old sail with a piece of turf under his head. He walked barefoot and for years was beaten almost daily. At the age of eight he was no bigger than a three-year-old, and was "discovered" by a visitor who complained to the communal overseer, and it must be said in defence of the community that the overseer reacted to the complaint and had the boy removed to a farm where he was helped to recover.[12]

In general, however, the inhabitants of Iceland seem to have taken in quite a normal amount of nutrition and would have been envied for their diet by a majority of contemporary Europeans. Most of their food consisted of milk products, fat, meat and fish, while the common people in Europe lived mostly on an unvarying diet of cereals. It has been estimated that in Iceland the proportion of food of animal origin went down from 90% to just over 50% during the 19th century.[13]

Apart from basic needs like food, the deprivation of family life for people like Sæmundur Stefánsson's parents must have been the greatest evil experienced by the poor. The status of domestic servant was not supposed to be lifelong, but to last for a period between childhood and one's entry into farming. For men this was not far from reality. In the almost wholly rural district of Rangárvallasysla around the middle of the 19th century, close to 80% of the men had acquired the status of householders before the age of forty.[14] For women the chance of becoming housewives was much smaller, because they were considerably more numerous than men (see Ch. 2.14).

[11] *Saga Íslendinga* VII (1950), 404.

[12] Sæmundur Stefánsson (1929), 7-11.

[13] Guðmundur Jónsson (1997).

[14] Guðmundur Hálfdanarson (1993), 25.

However, people of both sexes normally entered marriage late because of the shortage of opportunities to establish one's own home. In the mean time, most people were forced to spend their best years in the service of others. Unfortunately we have only scattered evidence about wages in this period, but what we do have indicates that the annual wages of male domestic servants rose from the equivalent of approximately 45 krónur in the mid-century to some 120 krónur by the end of the century, while the wages of female servants rose from the equivalent of 15 to 60 krónur. In real wages the rise amounts to a doubling for men and a little more than this for women. No fall in wages can be discerned in the crisis of the late 1850s and '60s – perhaps because they were so low anyway – but most of the rise took place in the relatively prosperous 1890s. In addition to wages domestic servants received free food, lodging and clothes – at least working clothes. Many authors of the period estimated the costs of keeping servants, and most of them concluded that the wages were 15-25% of the overall expenses of keeping a male servant and 10-15% in the case of a female.[15]

Most authors agree that people worked long hours in the haymaking season from July to September. Some cite as much as 16-18 hours a day, others 12-16. In the fishing season, working hours varied according to weather and catches, from zero to 18 hours. Otherwise men do not always seem to have worked very hard, but working hours for women were normally longer, since they were supposed to dry and repair the working clothes of the men for the next day, after the men had finished their work. Even helping men pull off their outer clothes was among the tasks of women.[16]

For the population in general, it has been estimated that, in 1900, it spent 55% of its income on food, 13% on housing, 14% on clothing, 10% on other goods and 8% on services. This indicates that most people could afford very little other than necessities, but not that all people were poor. There were doubtless a number of farmers who managed to save money or invest in land. When the trading society Gránufélag was established around 1870 (see Ch. 3.11), the equivalent of 22,500 krónur in share capital was collected within three years from 450 shareholders in Eyjafjörður and Þingeyjarsýsla, an area with just over 1,400 households.[17] This means that every third householder in the area could spare on average a sum of 50 krónur, if they found the enterprise worth it. Of course, this was the area that had enjoyed good business in shark fishing since the mid-century (see Ch. 3.10), but too few were engaged in that to explain the number of shareholders.

However, there were a few wealthy people in the country. The richest merchants, such as Ásgeir Ásgeirsson in Ísafjörður, who owned up to

[15] Guðmundur Jónsson (1981), 31-9.

[16] Guðmundur Jónsson (1981), 29-30, 48-52.

[17] Þorkell Jóhannesson and Bergsteinn Jónsson II (1965), 137.

sixteen decked fishing vessels (see Ch. 3.10), controlled more property than anyone else, but we do not know how much of it was net wealth. However we do know how much the bishop of Iceland in 1866-89, Pétur Pétursson, owned. He did not live in any great luxury in his two-storey house in Reykjavík, with ten rooms, including the bishop's office, but he was married to the daughter of a wealthy farmer and made a return on the wealth by lending money. When he died he left behind 80,000 krónur.[18] This was an amount that would have sufficed to buy 800 cows at that time or to pay the annual wages of 2,000 female servants. This is not very impressive compared with the really rich in larger societies, but quite a lot considering the poor population of Iceland.

---

[18] Þorvaldur Thoroddsen (1908), 272-3, 281-2.

3.13 Education

When the message of nationalism reached Iceland, obligatory education, which consisted only of reading and a basic knowledge of Christianity, was the responsibility of the parents, under the supervision of the local pastor (see Ch. 2.15). According to contemporary sources, this arrangement succeeded in enabling most people to read; most men and some women could also write. One author, describing the mid-19th century, states that writing and arithmetic were considered to be suitable accomplishments for intelligent men, reading for men of average abilities and for women. He adds that many adult people feared that it would distract youngsters from their work if they paid too much attention to learning, and many young people learned to write behind their parents' backs. Memoirs contain a number of stories of children who cut themselves feathers for writing with calf's blood on slips of old private letters.[1] The child or teenager yearning for education and stealing time to practise writing or to read books is an indispensable part of the traditional story of progress in Iceland, and it has no doubt been told to many a lazy pupil in order to urge him or her to work harder. There is doubtless some truth in these stories, although some elements sound somewhat incredible: calf's blood, for example, was not often available at an ordinary farm. And, of course, these stories are not equally true about everyone; those who had never longed for learning naturally did not write their memoirs or urge on lazy pupils.

In fact, Icelanders seem to have relied rather heavily on their home education and been remarkably indifferent to the call of modern times for the formal education of the common people. The introduction of compulsory school attendance for children in Denmark in 1814 produced no equivalent in Iceland throughout the century. The only legal reform in this area was made as late as 1880, when writing and arithmetic were added to reading as educational requirements for all children.

Nevertheless, educational institutions for children were founded, mainly through private or social initiatives, in many places in Iceland in this period. A primary school was established in Reykjavík in 1830 with eighteen pupils, the only school in Iceland in the period where teaching seems to

---

[1] Gunnar M. Magnúss (1939), 77-8. This is the basic work on primary education in this period, although it is sorely dated. Legislation on education at all stages is described by Guðmundur Finnbogason (1947).

have been mostly in Danish. But in 1848 the school was suddenly abolished when the Danish governor in the town decided to annul the custom of townsmen giving the school 1% of the peat they dug up.[2] After that, Reykjavík did without a primary school for over a decade, until in 1862 one was established by special legislation. Meanwhile, in 1852 a school had started which served in common two fishing villages on the south coast, Eyrarbakki and Stokkseyri, and in the 1870s more villages followed suit.

In the rural areas permanent schools would have been useful in only a small number of places; except for boarding-schools which might have been a practical solution, but would have been considered unacceptable for financial reasons. The problem was solved by the itinerant school (*farskóli*). This form of schooling was known in Denmark but acquired much greater popularity and tenacity in sparsely-populated Iceland.[3] It is not known exactly when itinerant teaching started there, but it was at least known in Þingeyjarsýsla in 1866, when a general district meeting recommended this form of education, and in the 1870s we have a number of records of itinerant teaching in the district. Most of the teachers were local men, many of whom had never been to school themselves.[4]

The itinerant school was held in private homes of a reasonable size. Children from the nearest farms might walk to it daily, but others stayed at the farm while the school operated, often for three or four weeks at a time. Sometimes the teacher lived on the farm, but in other cases he or she moved on with the school to another reasonably spacious farmhouse and kept a school there for another three or four weeks. In this way teaching could be a winter-long occupation, but during the short Icelandic summer it was – and partly still is – a remote idea.

In the late 1870s, when the country had acquired its own treasury, it soon began to support primary education financially: first only the permanent schools of the towns and villages and later also the itinerant ones. That was all the state authorities did to encourage the education of children, until at the turn of the century preparation began for extensive legislation, which was finally passed in 1907. Part of the preparation was a thorough status report, made in the winter of 1903-4.[5] The most striking revelation was perhaps that even in the age-group 10-13, where school attendance was considered to be most appropriate,[6] only 60% attended any kind of school, permanent or itinerant – one-third of them, though, for less than a month during the whole winter. Of the 60% who entered a

[2] Klemens Jónsson I (1929), 251-2.

[3] Loftur Guttormsson (1992).

[4] Gunnar Karlsson (1977a), 368-70.

[5] Guðmundur Finnbogason (1905).

[6] Guðmundur refers to this group as 10-14 years. However, if we compare the number, according to him (p. 39) with *Hagskinna* (1997), 125 (table 2.11), it is evident that Guðmundur includes only four year-groups of children, not five.

school, 80% attended itinerant and 20% permanent schools. This was the status of formal, primary education at the beginning of technical modernization in Iceland, and it corresponds roughly to the division of the population between rural areas and urban nuclei at that time (see Ch. 3.10).

The education law of 1907 introduced compulsory school attendance in urban areas, and the demands on youngsters aged of fourteen were increased to the extent that it became, in most cases, impracticable to do without more or less formal teaching in rural areas also. This does not mean that the itinerant school disappeared. In the rural areas, more pupils attended itinerant schools than permanent schools until around 1960.[7]

Secondary education, meaning preparation for the priesthood and university education, had a long tradition in formal institutions, and it was also much better catered for in Iceland in the 19th century than primary education. The Latin school that moved back to Reykjavík from Bessastaðir in 1846 (see Ch. 2.18) was supposed to take six years, but even the first class demanded prior knowledge in Danish, Latin, Greek, geography and arithmetic. Thus a gap existed between the compulsory primary education and the secondary stage, which could only be filled by private education. Often the teaching was provided by local clergymen, who used it to increase their income. However, many parents found this to be a cheaper way of education for the first two years than to attend the school, so many pupils took an entrance examination for admission into the third class. Around ten students graduated from the school annually in the 19th century.[8]

The bridging of the gap between primary and secondary education was not institutionalized completely in this period (1809-1918). Nevertheless, most innovations in formal education took place somewhere in between these two stages, in various kinds of occupational schools. The governor period, 1874-1904, saw the beginning of a number of such schools. Women's schools, prepared girls to become housewives and also offered considerable general education; the first was established in Reykjavík in 1874. The first farming school was established in 1880 and three more later in the decade. Practical secondary schools (*gagnfræðaskólar*) and adolescent schools of various kinds were founded, the first in 1880. One of them opened the first teachers' training department in 1892. Some of those schools attempted to imitate the successful Danish folk high schools, but on the whole such schools never became rooted in Iceland. A navigation school was established in Reykjavík in 1891, and technical training was available in Reykjavík at evening courses more or less regularly from 1869 onwards. However, no regular craft school was established till 1904.

---

[7] *Íslenskur söguatlas* III (1993), 137.

[8] *Hagskinna* (1997), 856 (table 18.11).

It would be tempting to attribute this sudden expansion in formal education to the financial independence bestowed by the constitution of 1874, and it may well be that financial support, or hope of such support, encouraged people to start new schools. But only one of these schools, a practical secondary school at Möðruvellir in the north, was established by law and run by the Icelandic treasury. A contributing factor may be the establishment of district committees in 1872 (see Ch. 3.14) which established and supported some of the schools, particularly farming schools and those for women. But these new schools reflect above all a determination among Icelandic individuals to start the process of economic modernization and catch up with neighbouring countries, a determination that did not bear much fruit until the 20th century.

Graduation from the Latin school gave access to the priesthood until 1847, when a theological seminary was established in Reykjavík. Later, in 1876, a medical school was also established there. Apart from that, university education was sought in Copenhagen, where Icelandic students enjoyed the privileges of free lodging at a students' hostel and financial support, which could cover food and even other necessities if the student was thrifty (which not all were). If we consider the idea of Iceland's separation from Denmark in these times, hardly anything would have been as irreplaceable as free and certain access to the University of Copenhagen. After the theological seminary in Reykjavík had been established, the largest group of Icelandic students in Copenhagen enrolled in the faculty of law. However, in the 19th century an increasing number began to venture into other disciplines, such as philology, natural history, history and even engineering.

The nationalist movement of the governor period, which we come to later (Ch. 3.15), had as part of its programme the provision of university education in law in Iceland. Icelandic legislation would be the focus, and the correct theory of the country's constitutional status would be taught. Repeatedly the Althing passed proposals for either a law school or a university, where the existing schools be united and a faculty of law added to them. But each time the Danish government refused to sanction the law, giving various reasons for its refusal.

From a modern viewpoint, this interest in university education may seem somewhat far-fetched, while the more basic parts of the educational system were still so primitive. However, nothing shows more clearly the dominant portion of the nationalist movement in the political life of Iceland at that time. Icelandic historians today may disagree over whether the lack of interest in popular education was due to the primitive status of the society, which had not yet learned to appreciate schooling, or to the success of informal, individual home tuition in the rural areas. Icelandic culture in fact contained a strange mixture of extreme primitiveness and a self-assurance that was not completely unfounded. This mixture sometimes confused foreign visitors to Iceland, among them John Coles who, at a farm in Þingeyjarsýsla in 1881, met a man in his twenties from a neighbouring farm:

He stood for some minutes eyeing me with a half-puzzled expression on his face; then, entering the room, greeted me so warmly that we might have been friends of 20 years' standing. He forthwith sat down and began instructing me in his own language, and, from the few words of English he spoke, appeared to consider himself a professor in ours – and a very dirty professor he was; his hands and face were grimed with dirt, and his clothes were in the same state as his person. But he was so good-humoured and delighted with his lame attempts at English, that it was impossible to be annoyed at his attentions. In a short time he proposed that we should cement our friendship in a convivial cup.[9]

The Englishman does not seem to have considered where such a peasant had managed to pick up those few English words. Actually he may well have been able to read an easy English text, although his spoken English sounded laboured, and he therefore provides evidence of the free, individual learning that could be found in Iceland in this period.

Popular reading societies became common in the 19th century: in some parts of the country, people who had never entered a school began to get hold of books in foreign languages, mainly Danish, and learned to read them, mostly by their own efforts. In 1903-4 there was a reading society in a majority of communes, which on average owned some 200 books each. This does not tell the whole story because in some societies the books were sold to individuals once they had circulated among the members. Approximately one book in every seven was in a foreign language.[10]

Self-education seems nowhere to have been as developed as in Þingeyjarsýsla, where Mr Coles met the dirty professor, partly perhaps because the district was far from the fishing grounds that were worked in the winter season, so that most men stayed at home then and had ample time for studying (see Ch. 2.15). In one commune, Mývatnssveit around Lake Mývatn, with less than 400 inhabitants and probably no one with higher education except the pastor, a reading society was established in 1858. In the early 1870s it began to buy books in Danish, and in 1885 owned around ninety titles in that language, some 200 volumes in all. Many were popular Danish magazines and instructive works on agriculture. But in the same commune an educational society was established in 1875, which, among other things acted as a society for reading foreign books, and in its book list one finds works like John Stuart Mill's *The Subjection of Women* in a Danish translation. In other cases we hear of individuals or small groups of people who began to make their way to the local clergyman and borrow

---

[9] Coles (1882), 87.
[10] Guðmundur Finnbogason (1905), 33-5, 60.

books from him or even ask him for help in ordering foreign books from abroad.[11]

It is difficult to say how widespread and how influential this self-educating movement was. All we can say for sure is that there were young men in the rural districts of Iceland (women are rarely mentioned in this connection) who managed to establish contact with foreign, educated circles without the intervention of educational institutions. This can, for instance, be seen in the development of the ideological basis for the cooperative in Þingeyjarsýsla, mentioned earlier in Chapter 3.11.

[11] Gunnar Karlsson (1977a), 354-76; Sveinn Skorri Höskuldsson (1970).

3.14 Democracy for Farmers

When Icelandic farmers and future farmers began to contemplate whether their trading society did not in fact mean democratization of trade (see Ch. 3.11), it clearly indicated an attitude that as far as we know, was new in 19th-century Iceland. It meant that these men had themselves been democratized. What we traditionally call Iceland's struggle for independence (*sjálfstæðisbarátta*) is a double process of state formation and democratization. It has been customary in Icelandic historiography to stress the former component, a view that clearly mirrors the dominant 19th-century attitude (see Ch. 3.8). Here we shall attempt a different approach and stress the importance of democratization by discussing it separately.

In this connection one should not forget that the Danish absolute monarchy was, even by the standard of the time, unusually centralized. Formally all state power originated in the king, and in reality most of it originated in his loyal officials (see Ch. 2.12). All power came from above and was exercised down the social scale. Therefore, any measure of a popular vote or popular initiative in social affairs, however imperfect, is of vital importance here because it marks a reversal of the direction of power. When this reversal had taken place, it was easier to increase the flow and move its origin further down the social scale.

When the Althing was established by royal decree in 1843, the franchise was restricted to two groups of men:[1] first, farmers who either owned at least a small farm (10 hundreds) or held a lifelong lease from the state or the Church of an average farm (20 hundreds); and secondly, townsmen who owned a house of timber or stone, valued at 1,000 rdl. or more. The age limit was twenty-five years, and the franchise was, although not explicitly stated in the decree, restricted to males. It has been estimated that these rules gave voting rights to some 3-5% of the population. Just over half were excluded because of their youth and a quarter because of their sex. Of the remaining quarter, only 15-20% were enfranchised. Thus 80-85% of adult men were excluded for financial and social reasons.[2]

These rules, however, probably did not reflect the dominant ideas in Iceland of the dividing line between the sovereign individual and the

---

[1] The organization of the Althing is described in detail by Einar Arnórsson (1945).

[2] *Hagskinna* (1997), 124-6 (table 2.11). See also Einar Laxness (1995), i–r, 58; Gunnar Karlsson (1977a), 18-19.

dependent one. In the elections to the National Assembly in 1851, more liberal rules were used, and in 1857 almost equally liberal rules were enacted for elections to the Althing. According to the law of 1857, the electorate to the Althing can be divided into four categories of males aged twenty-five and older. First, all farmers who paid taxes "to all estates" – that is to the state, Church, pastor and commune. This meant that practically all self-sufficient farmers were enfranchised. Secondly, officials and graduates from university or a theological seminary. Thirdly, burghers – men who had bought a certificate that allowed them to run trade or industry at a trading centre, provided they paid at least 4 rdl. in tax to their commune annually. Fourthly, cottars who paid at least 6 rdl. in tax to their commune. This time it was explicitly stated that those who had received poor relief and neither paid it back nor had the debt remitted were disenfranchised.

These rules gave voting rights to some 8-10% of the whole population, hence more than half of adult males were excluded for financial and social reasons. In practice this meant that the electorate consisted of farmers. In all constituencies except Reykjavík and perhaps the Westman Islands, farmers, including those who lived more or less from fishing, could decide the result of elections. In most constituencies, they decided it practically alone. Also, from the very beginning farmers occupied a considerable portion of parliamentary seats. At the first session of the Althing they made up just over half of the elected members (see Ch. 3.3). However, it was not until 1879 that a farmer, Jón Sigurðsson at Gautlönd in Þingeyjarsýsla, received a major post at the Althing when chosen speaker of the Lower Chamber – the first non-academic to reach a top position in Icelandic politics.[3]

Laws on voting rights were not altered substantially until 1915. Throughout the 19th century there seemed to be complete agreement between the Copenhagen authorities and the nationalist majority in Iceland that those enfranchised by the law of 1857 were the proper representatives of the whole Icelandic people. On the other hand, as urban industries grew, wages rose and fishing increased, in the 1890s and at the beginning of the 20th century, the restrictions based on tax-paying affected fewer people as more and more people became tax-payers and more townspeople, especially cottars, were included in the chosen group of electors.

Even though the right to vote was so restricted, it was, until after the turn of the century, not even exercised by as many as half the voters. In the first elections to a legislative Althing in 1874, which were also the first for which we have complete statistics, only 20% participated. From then on, participation rose to 53% in 1902 and to 76% in the 1908 elections (see Ch. 3.17).[4]

---

[3] Gunnar Karlsson (1977a), 441-6.
[4] *Hagskinna* (1997), 877 (table 19.1).

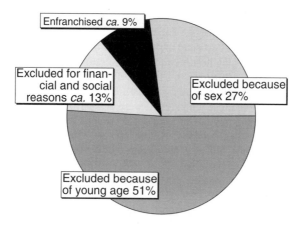

Fig. 3.14-1 The franchise, from 1857 onwards, calculated from the census of 1860. The same proportions are generally valid throughout the 19th century. *Source: Hagskinna* (1997), 124-6 (table 2.11), 877 (table 19.1).

However, one must be careful about interpreting the meagre participation exclusively as a sign of lack of interest in politics. To begin with, there was only one polling station in each constituency, and it could take a day's travel to reach it. This explanation has a limited value, because electoral meetings were only marginally better attended than elsewhere in Reykjavík and the Westman Islands, where distances were a small hindrance.[5]

The lack of interest in elections, compared with our times, can partly be explained by the lack of opposed political parties and indeed the lack of any basic disagreement in politics. In all elections until 1900 the nationalist movement, led first by Jón Sigurðsson and later by Benedikt Sveinsson, enjoyed an overwhelming majority in most constituencies. Often it was evident that the former representative would be re-elected; if not, the leading group of the district would probably have picked his successor. Attending an electoral meeting was like going to a boring general meeting in a society, knowing that the retiring executive committee already picked their successors, when one is reasonably content with their choice.

The interest in politics can be found not in elections but in public meetings where policy was discussed.[6] From the very beginning of the Althing, it was customary to send petitions from the constituencies, signed by a

[5] *Landshagsskýrslur* 1912 (1913), 112-13.

[6] This survey is mostly based on Gunnar Karlsson (1977a), 33-49, 69-123, 149-58, and takes more account of the constituency of Suður-Þingeyjarsýsla than others, although an eye has also been kept on other parts of the country. See also Gunnar Karlsson (1972a), 59-70.

number of voters, and sometimes by people who were not even enfranchised. In the 1850s, the leading groups in some constituencies began to hold annual district meetings, which, to a certain extent, were successors of the organization that grew up in preparation for the National Assembly of 1851 (see Ch. 3.4). At these meetings petitions to the Althing were signed by those present, and usually by them alone. Therefore these petitions had fewer signatures than was customary earlier; on the other hand, one is more confident that those who signed were actively participating in politics. The third stage developed after 1874 when it gradually became the custom to hold a so-called pre-parliamentary meeting (*þingmálafundur*) in every constituency before each session of the Althing, where a number of resolutions were passed and the minutes from the meeting were sent to the Althing. These meetings were often attended by more people than election meetings.

Thus it can be said that, in contrast to our times, when almost all enfranchised people in Iceland elect representatives but few of us ever participate in devising political programmes, in 19th-century Iceland more people dealt with political policy than with elections. Admittedly it was often maintained, no doubt rightly, that the will of the people as expressed in petitions and resolutions was ready-made by the Althing representative, who used it as a justification for his own policy. Nevertheless this was a political activity, and it no doubt secured some control for the voters.

In addition to the pre-parliamentary meetings in the constituencies, the nationalist movement convened a national meeting at intervals at Þingvellir. There the will of the entire nation was supposed to emerge and guide the Althing representatives in their decisions.

An important step towards democracy was made in 1872, when a new law on local government in Iceland was enacted.[7] The Icelandic commune (*hreppur*) had been ruled by local farmers, the overseers (*hreppstjórar*), one or more in each commune, since the Commonwealth period. In the 19th century they were supposed to share their power and responsibility with the local pastor. The communal overseers had originally been elected by the farmers, but in the period of absolutism they were appointed by the regional governor, sometimes after nomination by the local farmers. In 1872 some form of democratic government was introduced in three stages at the local level. In the communes a committee of three to seven members (*hreppsnefnd*), headed by an executive chosen from the committee members by themselves, took over the organization of poor relief and other tasks which the commune ran as a community. Only the communal overseer kept his role as a deputy of the sheriff. The district committees (*sýslunefndir*), who formed the next stage, have already been mentioned in connection with the schools (see Ch. 3.13). They were composed of

[7] The basic works on local government are those by Þórður Eyjólfsson (1952) and Lýður Björnsson I-II (1972-9).

representatives from the communes and headed by the sheriff. Finally, the district committees elected members to regional councils (*amtsráð*), which were headed by the regional governors. The electorate for the communal committees was approximately the same as for the Althing; here also the democracy of farmers reigned.

At the same time Reykjavík acquired its own democratic government. A council had been elected in the town since the 1830s, but in 1872 it was reorganized and attained a similar power in communal affairs to that of the communal committees and district committees. In the second half of the 19th century three other trading centres – Akureyri, Ísafjörður and Seyðisfjörður acquired the status of a town (*kaupstaður*) with a similar form of government to that of Reykjavík. This meant that the stages of commune and district were united; they were communes outside districts and had a sheriff of their own, who, strangely enough, was often the same person as the sheriff of the surrounding district.

Some rules of personal freedom had been enacted in Iceland based on the Danish model in the 19th century, but the constitution which Christian IX presented to Iceland in 1874 established basic human rights: freedom of opinion in speech and print, freedom to establish associations and hold meetings, the inviolability of property and home, religious freedom.

Proceeding from the constitution, democracy entered the Church in the 1880s.[8] Elected committees were founded to run the affairs of parishes and districts under the supervision of provosts, together with the pastors and provosts. A law was passed that made it possible for congregations to take over the running of local churches. A way was opened for individuals to leave their congregation, if they did not like their pastor, and enrol in another one. People who did not belong to the National Church were given legal status – for instance, the possibility of entering a civil marriage and founding their own congregations. Finally, the election of vicars was introduced, admittedly with some restrictions, but nevertheless more democratic than the system that we live with in Iceland now.

One more component of the development of democracy was the emergence of free associations. Formal associations founded in Iceland before the beginning of the 19th century could probably be counted on the fingers of both hands, most of them established by officials. But during the 19th century founding a society became the dominant way of addressing a problem.[9] Of the first free associations founded and run by common people, some have already entered our story: the reading societies (see Ch. 3.13) and the trading societies (see Ch. 3.11). A little later came farming societies of individual communes or districts, some of which were called progressive societies (*framfarafélög*) and did not only deal with farming

[8] Magnús Jónsson (1952), 25-44.
[9] Ample examples are provided by Hrefna Róbertsdóttir (1990) and a number of works listed in her bibliography.

in a narrow sense. Philanthropic societies started in the last quarter of the century; one of the first was established by women in Reykjavík in connection with the unveiling of Bertel Thorvaldsen's statue in 1875 (see Ch. 3.12) and called Thorvaldsensfélagið (the Thorvaldsen Society). Temperance societies had been attempted earlier, and in the 1880s the International Order of Good Templars obtained a secure foothold in the country. In the Scandinavian countries religious movements were among the first popular associations, but in Iceland they arrived late; hardly any are mentioned before the Salvation Army came to Reykjavík in 1895.[10] At about the same time, the labour movement was emerging (see Ch. 3.10).

Of course, the democracy of free associations was not restricted to farmers. On the contrary, perhaps the initiative of townspeople came into its own there more than anywhere else, while the farming class dominated the political system. In Reykjavík alone, 113 societies have been listed which were established between 1840 and 1900.[11]

The press was a little of both; it was an "urban" initiative, but strongly dominated by politics and most likely the views of farmers, who formed the bulk of subscribers. A small monthly paper published in Reykjavík in 1846-9 and called *Reykjavíkurpósturinn* marks the beginning of newspapers in Iceland, although historical tradition has usually given that status to the more influential, longer-lived and more nationalistic *Þjóðólfur*, which started in 1848. From then on, the publication of papers was uninterrupted, and soon it was not restricted to Reykjavík; papers were also published in Akureyri, Eskifjörður, Seyðisfjörður and Ísafjörður in the 19th century. Most of the papers were issued from every fortnight to twice a week; daily papers only existed as attempts until the 1910s. Usually the papers were private enterprises, owned and run by their editors. Like any paper, they had two principal roles: to disseminate news, foreign and domestic, and to present opinions. Both of these roles were vital in the preparation for modernity, which was the theme of the late 19th century. In their second role, the papers were an important part of the democratization process. Together with the Althing, it was in the papers that common people – non-officials – acquired for the first time a voice that was heard right across the society.

[10] Pétur Pétursson (1983), 99-130.
[11] Hrefna Róbertsdóttir (1990), 124-7.

3.15 Struggle towards Home Rule

Iceland's struggle for independence from Denmark centred around the nationality of two major bastions of political power. One was the legislative assembly passing legislation on Iceland's internal affairs. The other was ministerial power in these same affairs: the right to advise the king and take responsibility for his decisions concerning Iceland. At the National Assembly of 1851 the disagreement on these institutions was complete: the Danish proposal stipulated that Danish authorities should legislate on Icelandic affairs (apart from decisions on finance) and that members of the Danish government should serve as ministers of Iceland. The majority of representatives, led by Jón Sigurðsson, replied with a demand for an internal legislative parliament (the Althing vested with legislative power) and an Icelandic government within Iceland (apart from an emissary in Copenhagen). The meeting was dissolved with disagreement on both points (see Ch. 3.4).

The constitution of 1874 was a compromise in which Iceland was granted the first-mentioned demand, the legislative parliament, but had to concede the other and accept that a Danish government minister should occupy the post of minister for Iceland. It was therefore on this issue that the next round in the struggle for independence turned. Because of the development of the struggle it is useful to see the "Icelandization" of ministerial power as combining three components: first, the minister for Iceland should be resident in Iceland; secondly, he should be an Icelander by nationality; and thirdly, he should not act within the Danish Council of State.

The struggle was taken up again in 1881 in a new handsome stone building in the centre of Reykjavík, which the Althing had been extravagant enough to build for itself.[1] By this time Jón Sigurðsson was dead, and Benedikt Sveinsson, a sheriff in Þingeyjarsýsla, took up the case and proposed the election of a committee to write a proposal for an amendment of the constitution. The case was not resolved in this session or in the next one, in 1883. Interest in the issue in the Althing still seemed rather limited. Then in 1884 a new wave of interest in the constitutional issue, and perhaps in politics in general, arose in Iceland. In that year no less than three attempts were made in three distinct parts of the country to

[1] The basic work on the struggle for independence after 1874 is Björn Þórðarson (1951). The interpretation presented here is partly also in Gunnar Karlsson (1972a).

establish political parties.[2] They all advocated radical nationalist policies, which can be deduced from the names of two of them, even if one only knows that the Icelandic term for a people/nation is *þjóð*: Þjóðfrelsisfélag (National Liberation Society) and Þjóðlið Íslendinga (the Icelandic National Front). But these associations also stood for some of the liberal, democratic, social-radical, although not socialist, attitudes, that characterized the leftist parties (*Venstre*) in Denmark and Norway. It seems therefore likely that the new political interest in Iceland was inspired by the bitter struggle between the left and right in Scandinavia in these years, maybe not least by the parliamentary victory of the Leftist Party in Norway in 1884, when it formed a government for the first time.

However, the time of political parties had apparently not arrived in Iceland. All these attempts failed, but the fruit was reaped by the informal nationalist movement under Benedikt Sveinsson's leadership, who had no interest in the leftist demands for increased democracy and social justice. This movement purported to speak for the whole nation, in the same way as it had done in Jón Sigurðsson's days. In the decade to come, it concentrated on the revision of the constitution, and is therefore referred to as the Revision Movement (endurskoðunarhreyfing) in Icelandic history.

One of the leaders of the movement, Jón Sigurðsson at Gautlönd, speaker of the Lower Chamber, convoked a meeting at Þingvellir a few days before the Althing session of 1885. There the Althing was called upon to propose a thorough revision of the constitution. The Althing followed the recommendations of the meeting in its main points and passed a proposal for constitutional revision. A national council was to be established in Iceland, with a regent (a substitute for the king) and up to three ministers.

The proposal did not arise out of interest in a royal figure in Iceland. On the contrary, that figure was looked upon as a necessary evil, proposed in order to be able to move ministerial power to Iceland. As a parliament committee put it: either one must have an image of the king at the minister's side in Reykjavík or an image of a minister at the king's side in Copenhagen. They preferred the first alternative, probably because it was the only way to guarantee that Icelandic affairs were decided on outside the Danish Council of State and thus kept separate from Danish affairs. One could be reasonably sure that the proposed revision would secure the "Icelandization" of ministerial power in all its above-listed components. The separation of the ministerial power of Iceland from the Council of State was probably considered a matter more of symbolic value than of political power. However, symbolic value is not necessarily a small thing. Symbols are important to everyone who accepts their symbolic value, and they were particularly important to 19th-century nationalists.

---

[2] Gunnar Karlsson (1977a), 158-78.

The revision became the main issue in all sessions of the Althing for a decade. For various reasons the amendment was not passed in every session, but in 1885 and 1893 it was. It called for the dissolution of the Althing, parliamentary elections and an extra session in the following year (1886 and 1894). The amendments were also passed at the extra sessions, but, in accordance with the recommendation of his conservative government, the king refused to sanction the proposals, arguing that such an alteration would violate the union of the state.

The Revision Movement had many characteristics of a political party. It had a number of individual issues on its programme, all of which aimed for the increased autonomy of Iceland. They wanted to oblige merchants running shops in Iceland to have permanent residence in the country, to abolish the role of the Danish Supreme Court as the highest appeal court in Iceland and to establish a law school or a university in Iceland (see Ch. 3.13). The Revisionists tended to preach their policy as a patriotic ideal, and their opponents even felt compelled to defend themselves against charges – perhaps not often expressed directly – of treason to their fatherland. This gave the Revisionists an extremely strong position for a time, but did not prepare them well for the compromise that would in the end be an inevitable condition for any success in the constitutional issue.

In the 1890s one can discern growing discontent with the stagnant policy of the Revisionists. This change of attitude might have been partly due to the influence of Scandinavia; in both Denmark and Norway the polarization of the 1880s was now retreating and practical objectives came to the forefront in politics. The economic situation was also improving in Iceland in the 1890s; the treasury appeared to have extra means available for practical enterprises, if only there were some central institution that had the capacity and vitality to organize something. At the same time the rural representatives in the Althing, who had usually been most interested in keeping national expenses as low as possible, were about to nurture an interest in technical improvements, especially in communication, not least because many of them now had a new interest in commerce as leaders of the local cooperative. In this situation what was evidently needed was a minister of Icelandic affairs who did not consider these affairs a minor sideline but was ready to work actively for progress in Iceland.

The first man to realize how to exploit this situation was a young member of the Althing, the philologist Valtýr Guðmundsson, who was resident in Copenhagen and held the post of lecturer in Icelandic history and literature at the university. He began on his own to search for a compromise between the Danish government and the members of the Althing. The result was a new proposal for constitutional change, which Valtýr advanced at the Althing of 1897. It looks absurdly insignificant in comparison with the extensive constitutional revision. Concerning the main issue, the nationality of the minister, it only laid down that he was responsible to the

Althing and had the right to attend its meetings. However, Valtýr main-tained – and managed to convince at least a considerable part of his fellow countrymen – that this meant more than one might assume. The minister would be obliged to attend the Althing sessions. He would have to spend months every other year journeying to and staying in Iceland, and there-fore he could not have other ministries to cater for. He would also have to be able to speak Icelandic, which would secure his Icelandic nationality. On the other hand, his residence in Copenhagen and his sitting as a member of the Danish Council of State would remain as before. Thus only one component of the ministerial power of Iceland was to be Icelandized – the nationality of the person occupying the post.

This idea met with a harsh response in Iceland, not only from the Revi-sionists but also from a considerable part of the top officials, who joined forces with their former opponents against Valtýr. A group of Reykjavík officials was popularly called the "Governor Clique" and was said to be ruled by the Icelandic governor, Magnús Stephensen, grandson of Stefán Stephensen, one of the few Icelandic officials who did not submit to Jørgen Jørgensen's rule in 1809 (see Ch. 3.1). Magnús may have been the real ruler of the country at this time and was no doubt strongly opposed in his heart to Valtýr, although he could not react officially against a proposal that enjoyed the goodwill of the government. It is clear that the Governor Clique saw Valtýr as an upstart (he was actually of humble origin, the ille-gitimate son of a district secretary and a member of a radical group of Icelandic students in Copenhagen in the 1880s). Everyone was convinced, probably correctly, that he was aiming at the post of minister himself and would lead a new clique to power in Iceland.

This argument could not, of course, be used against Valtýr in open debate. At the beginning his opponents turned vehemently against his proposal to accept a constitutional change which did not exclude the minister for Iceland from sitting in the Danish Council of State; this was said to amount to accepting that Iceland was a part of the Danish state. However, as practical views gained more ground and after the death of the prophet of principles, Benedikt Sveinsson, in 1899, this argument in-creasingly lost its appeal. Then Valtýr's opponents shifted their programme towards the importance of having the minister resident in Iceland and assumed the name Home Rule Party (Heimastjórnarflokkur).

Of course, there were people who looked forward to the power change that Valtýr was assumed to be proposing. Therefore he acquired the sup-port of a few of the most radical politicians, among them Skúli Thoroddsen, who had been dismissed from his office as a sheriff in Ísafjarðarsýsla, obviously – though not formally – for his political activity, which included acting as the shadow editor of a radical paper called *Þjóðviljinn* (The People's Will).[3] But the party of Valtýrians (Valtýingar) consisted above

[3] A biography of Skúli Thoroddsen has been written by Jón Guðnason I-II (1968-74).

all of those who were most anxious for practical progress. Thus the usual party division of the time, with a conservative (right-wing) and a liberal (left-wing) party, did not emerge in Iceland until a couple of decades later (see Ch. 4.4).

The Althing was almost equally divided between the parties. In 1900, a general election suggested that the electorate was also equally divided. At the Althing session of 1901 the Valtýrians had the upper hand only because one of their opponents was prevented from attending. However, after they had got their proposal through the Lower Chamber, before it had been passed in the Upper Chamber, the news arrived that the Leftist Party had finally been commissioned to form a government in Denmark. This was seen as a radical change of regime, and in Iceland it was seen to increase the likelihood of a better bargain. Still, the Valtýrians decided to stick to their programme and also passed in the Upper Chamber a bill that envisaged an Icelandic minister for Iceland, resident in Copenhagen.

This was of course a hopeless situation for the Valtýrians, and the Home Rule Party won a landslide victory in elections for the extra session of the Althing in 1902. The new Danish government allowed the Althing to choose whether it preferred the minister to reside in Copenhagen or in Reykjavík, and of course it chose Reykjavík; even the Valtýrians voted for it. At the same time, though, the government gave the Althing a bitter pill to swallow. The proposal for the constitutional amendment said that the minister should "whenever necessary go to Copenhagen and submit to the king, in the Council of State, laws and important decisions of government". Attached to the proposal was a message which said that not a word in it might be altered if it were to be sure of royal sanction. Thus for the first time ever the Althing acknowledged explicitly that Iceland was a part of the Danish state. And it did so with one dissenting vote only.

Ironically the constitutional change that included this belated formal incorporation of Iceland into the state instigated nothing less than the decisive victory of Iceland in its struggle for independence, together with a large step in the development of democracy. It was important enough to get a ministry within Iceland, but even more important was the fact that the new minister would inevitably be chosen by the parliamentary majority of the Althing. The Danish Venstre had so long fought for government by parliamentary majority at home that they could by no means resist it in Iceland – and scarcely had reason to want to either. Home rule gave the Icelandic electorate an opportunity to have, through the Althing, some say in who was to rule the country as a minister, which no doubt made the Icelandic ministers more anxious to please the electorate than their Danish predecessors had been.

Thus the first Icelandic minister, the poet, lawyer and leader of the Home Rule Party, Hannes Hafstein, opened up a new period in Icelandic history on 1 February 1904, when he entered his humble ministry with its fourteen employees, in the building that had been built as a prison but had housed the supreme rulers within Iceland since 1820 (see Ch. 2.16).[4] At the same time the post of governer was abolished, and the so-called governor period (*landshöfingjatími*) in Icelandic history, which had been introduced by the constitutional changes of 1871-4 (see Ch. 3.6), came to an end. However, before we turn to the characteristics of the new period in Part IV, we must follow the double development of democracy and state formation through two more steps: the liberation of women and the acquisition of formal autonomy in 1918.

[4] Agnar Kl. Jónsson (1969) I, 14-58.

3.16 Liberation of Women

As in any other traditional European society, Icelandic women were largely excluded from the most basic human rights. They could aspire to no executive roles in the political system; higher education was barred to them, and so in consequence were the professions for which such education was required. Major decisions about their personal life, property and marriage were out of their hands. In this chapter we see how Icelandic women gained a legal status equal to men in these three areas, not separately but mostly in chronological order. The story of how and when women acquired real equality with men is not covered in this book, but some of it will be taken up in Chapter 4.13.

Formal equality mostly emerged in a period of seven decades from 1850 to the early 1920s.[1] For the sake of convenience it can be divided into three phases, which of course overlap to some extent. The first, spanning from around 1850 to the early 1880s, is mostly based on a common conviction within the male-dominated rural society that women could at least in some capacities take on a role that was somewhat equal to men's. The second, from the 1880s until around the turn of the century, formed part of the left-wing, liberal movement which was mentioned in the last chapter, without enjoying the support of any particular women's movement and with rather limited participation by women. The third phase, in the first two decades of the 20th century, was characterized by an active struggle by women, often in organized associations. As might be expected, this phase proved to be the most effective.

When people began to send petitions to the newly-established Althing, it was common, at least in the constituency of Suður-Þingeyjarsýsla, that more people than the voters alone signed the petitions; the main rule seems to have been that all farmers and none but farmers were eligible to sign petitions. In Iceland it was quite common for women without husbands to run farms; they were mostly widows, who were inevitably numerous in a society dependent on fishing. In Suður-Þingeyjarsýsla there were at this time twenty-five women farmers (not including cottars) out of some 400 farmers in all. In 1845, the first year of the Althing, a few single female farmers in the district signed petitions. Some of these were copied at the Althing,

---

[1] For basic surveys of this development, see Gísli Jónsson (1977); *Ártöl og áfangar i sögu islenskra kvenna* (1998).

273

and in the copies the female names were changed to male ones; for example, Valgerður Eiríksdóttir is copied as V. Eiríksson and Guðrún Guðnadóttir as G. Guðnason, and once as Hallur Grímsson, obviously a male name. When I noticed this, I first thought that Hallur must have been Guðrún's household manager and that the copyist had known that. But no one with this name is to be found at her farm or in the neighbourhood; it must have been invented by a scribe at the Althing in his good-natured attempt to save the peasants of the north from the embarrassment of not knowing that politics was for men only.[2]

The very first dealings of the Althing with women's issues also seem to indicate a relatively liberal attitude. In these years the government used to ask the Althing generally which recent Danish law it wanted to have enacted for Iceland. Among them was a new Danish inheritance law, which kept in principle the old rule, valid both in Denmark and Iceland, that a man inherited twice as much as a woman. The new Danish law only added the exception that parents were free to decide that their daughters would inherit as much as the sons. But the Althing unanimously asked the king to enact for Iceland perfect equality for men and women in matters of inheritance. In 1850 this was done, so that Iceland established equal right to inheritance seven years before Denmark.

Admittedly this may have made rather little difference, since all women, except widows, were obliged to have a legal guardian to rule their property. However, in 1861 the first step was made towards the right of women to rule their property when it was enacted, this time in accordance with Danish law, that single women should acquire personal autonomy at the age of twenty-five, the same age as men. Husbands were still the legal guardians of their wives.[3] Presumably the clause obliging women to obtain the consent of their parents or guardians before marrying ought to be considered having been abolished by this law, when they had reached the age of twenty-five. This issue has not been much discussed in the historiography of the women's movement, perhaps because it is clear that in this area not so much the law as convention and moral rules predominate.

The first taste of franchise granted to Icelandic women seems to have been based on the rural attitude that a woman became almost the equivalent of a man if she took on a man's role. In 1882 the king sanctioned a law which the Althing had passed unanimously the year before and gave franchise in communal elections to widows and other single women who ran farms. The proposer was a farmer in his late forties who had never entered a school and was not, as far as we know, in touch with any foreign radical movements.

[2] Gunnar Karlsson (1977a), 42-3.
[3] Bragi Guðmundsson and Gunnar Karlsson (1988), 30-1.

Still older – in his early sixties – and equally devoid of formal education was the farmer who instigated women's rights to attend higher education. It should be noted, though, that he had recently married a much younger woman when, at the Althing session of 1885, he tabled a bill giving women equal rights to men at the Latin school, the theological seminary and the medical school. The bill was not passed, but it led to a royal decree, issued the next year, allowing women to graduate from the Latin school and the medical school, although at the theological seminary they were supposed to take a special examination which did not give them the right to become pastors or even to preach in a church.

The liberal left-wing movement which flourished in Scandinavia in the late 19th century was basically a moral one; it took on the role of reminding their societies of the ideals of human rights, which they had adopted nominally, but without paying attention to all the logical consequences. The largest group of people that had been left out in these libertarian developments were women, and their cause was taken up strongly by the leftists. One of their most outstanding prophets in Denmark, Georg Brandes, translated John Stuart Mill's book *The Subjection of Women*. A classic Scandinavian expression of this movement is Henrik Ibsen's play *A Doll's House*.

Among Icelanders demands for the liberation of women seem to have gained ground almost simultaneously in two groups in the early 1880s: among radical students in Copenhagen and in the rural community in Þingeyjarsýsla. A young lawyer who had just returned home from the university gave a lecture in Reykjavík in 1885 "On the Freedom and Education of Women".[4] The next year his colleague Skúli Thoroddsen established the radical paper *Þjóðviljinn* in Ísafjörður and made it an organ of the cause of women. The political association the Icelandic National Front, which was established in Þingeyjarsýsla in 1884 (see Ch. 3.15), had the equality of men and women on its programme, and a few women occupied minor posts in an extremely complicated organization, which the association had imitated from European secret societies.

From these two centres of agitation, Ísafjörður and Þingeyjarsýsla, petitions signed by 100 women were sent to a Þingvellir meeting in 1888, calling upon it to support freedom for women. But it is typical of this period that although nobody seems to have resisted the demand, the meeting only passed a vague and rather insignificant resolution on the issue. The cause of women did not meet much hostile response among men in these years, but like most other social issues it was overshadowed by the nationalist struggle against Denmark. Thus, the draft constitutions of the 1880s and 1890s never went further than to decree that women could be granted the franchise by simple law, without a constitutional amendment.

[4] Páll Briem (1885).

Bríet Bjarnhéðinsdóttir, leader of the Icelandic movement for women's rights. Bríet is wearing a traditional Icelandic costume – not the one that Sigurður Guðmundsson designed (see Ch. 3.12) but a type which became more popular in the 20th century.

Although this phase was dominated by men, it saw the emergence of the woman who was to personify the struggle for women's liberation in Iceland. In 1884 Bríet Bjarnhéðinsdóttir, then aged twenty-eight, moved to Reykjavík. Born in Húnavatnssýsla in the north in 1856, she had graduated from a women's school after one winter's study. In her first year in Reykjavík she noticed that the newspaper *Fjallkonan*[5] showed unusual interest in the cause of women, so she ventured to offer the editor an article which she had drafted at the age of sixteen. It was printed in 1885, and is said to be the first article by a woman even published in Iceland. It was published under a pseudonym, but two years later Bríet summoned the courage to give a public lecture in Reykjavík on women's rights.[6] However, Bríet did not proceed directly to the forefront of a liberation movement. Instead she married the editor of *Fjallkonan*, had two children and largely withdrew from the public scene for years.

In the meantime the third phase of liberation set in with the establishment of the Icelandic Women's Society (Hið íslenska kvenfélag) in 1894. Originally, its main purpose was to support the desire of Icelandic women to study at the proposed Icelandic university (see Ch. 3.13). It also dealt with the franchise issue, and collected thousands of signatures on a petition to the Althing demanding total equality with men. The leader of the society was Þorbjörg Sveinsdóttir, a midwife in Reykjavík and Benedikt Sveinsson's sister, but after her death in 1903 the society appeared to give up the struggle for female rights.

A few years later, in 1906, the International Woman Suffrage Alliance (IWSA) held a meeting in Copenhagen, and Bríet Bjarnhéðinsdóttir was invited, maybe because since 1895 she had edited a magazine for women, *Kvennablaðið* (The Women's Paper). The next year Bríet organized the establishment of an affiliated society in Iceland, the Women's Rights Association of Iceland (Hið íslenska kvenréttindafélag, later Kvenréttindafélag Íslands) and was its leader for two decades.[7] In the years that followed, things began to happen. In 1907-9, the franchise in communal elections was extended to married women, although female servants were still left out. In 1908 a women's list, with four names, stood for election to the town council in Reykjavík. It won the highest number of votes of all lists, almost 22%, and all four candidates were elected to a council of fifteen.[8]

Before women acquired the franchise for the Althing, a decisive step was taken in the other main area of inequality. As a minister of Iceland, Hannes Hafstein had opened the modern secondary school for girls, which till 1904 had been the Latin school. In 1911 Hannes, when no longer

[5] Literally 'Mountain Woman', a poetic female image of Iceland.

[6] Bríet Bjarnhéðinsdóttir (1888).

[7] The story of this association is told by Sigríður Th. Erlendsdóttir (1993).

[8] Auður Styrkársdóttir (1994), 48-51.

serving as a minister, submitted a private member's bill on the equal rights of men and women to attend all educational institutions, to receive scholarships, to graduate and to assume any profession.

The discussion of this bill revealed more scepticism among the members of the Althing than at any previous time, and a few of them used the opportunity to amuse themselves and their colleagues. One former spokesman of leftist liberalism, the leader of the Þjóðfrelsisfélag in Reykjavík in 1884 (see Ch. 3.15), remarked that "it would be rather inconvenient in Austur-Skaftafellssýsla [a district divided by a number of deep and broad rivers] if the sheriff were to give birth when she was called upon to investigate a criminal case or issue a sentence of imprisonment or if she went into labour while travelling between her annual communal meetings".

He received the reply from one of his colleagues that men were no more guaranteed against indisposition than women; male sheriffs could catch pneumonia and male doctors rheumatism, which was more problematic than childbirth since these were diseases that could come suddenly and unexpectedly. The bill gained an overwhelming majority at the Althing, and in the Lower Chamber was finally passed by sixteen votes to five.

The same Althing session, in 1911, passed an amendment of the constitution, which, together with other changes considered in the next chapter, gave the franchise at national elections to women and hitherto disenfranchised men, on equal terms with others. The disagreement here was not mainly about the female franchise, but about the franchise of domestic servants of both sexes. In the end, though, they were included. Only those who had received poor relief and had neither paid it back nor had the debt remitted were excluded, and so remained until the 1930s.

This amendment was postponed for a few years, because the Althing and the Danish government could not reach agreement on the wording of the clause determining where the minister of Iceland should submit Icelandic affairs to the king (see Ch. 3.17). Meanwhile serious doubts about the franchise began to haunt the Althing members. When the issue was taken up again in 1913, the franchise of the new groups of voters – women and servants – was restricted to those aged forty and over. These age-limits were to be lowered by one year annually, so that the then normal age-limit of twenty-five would be reached after fifteen years from the amendment being enacted. In this form the amendment was ratified by the king on 19 June 1915, which is traditionally celebrated as the breakthrough of women's rights in Iceland, although the law entailed that women then aged twenty-five still had to wait until 1923 for their franchise – by then, they would be thirty-three and the age limit would have come down to thirty-two. As it turned out, they did not have to wait that long. In 1920 a new constitutional amendment was enacted in view of the new status of Iceland in 1918 (see Ch. 3.17). By then the Althing had seen that the new electorate would not cause any major coup in Icelandic politics, and it abolished special age limits for it.

After this alteration the most formidable legal obstacle to equality was the control of common property in marriage. In 1900 a major stage had been reached when the liberty of husbands to dispose of common property without the consent of their wives was greatly limited and women were entitled to control their private property and their own income. This law has not been included in any of the phases of women's liberation here, since it was submitted by the Danish minister of Iceland and based on recent Danish law. The final step, on the other hand, was undoubtedly a consequence of the liberation movement in Iceland. In 1923 a new law introduced practically complete equality in the rule over property in marriage.

In the first decade of the female franchise women's lists were common in both local and national elections, and such a list brought the first woman into the Althing in 1923. This was Ingibjörg H. Bjarnason, head-mistress of the Women's School in Reykjavík. However, she apparently felt that she could have more influence within a political party and entered the Conservative Party, one of the predecessors of the new Independence Party (see Ch. 4.4), to the great disappointment of some of her electors. Thereafter women's lists were rarely attempted until after the parties had begun to lose their political hegemony in Iceland in the 1980s (see Ch. 4.13).

3.17 Towards Autonomy in 1918

The period of 15 years between 1 February 1904 and 1 December 1918 is marked off in Icelandic history as the home rule period, and to an outsider its political history seems extremely complicated. This is partly because the political configurations of the period, the parties in formation, were extremely unstable. Seven "cabinets" were in power in these years, six ministers of Iceland and finally one coalition government.[1] The essential content of the political system and the matters of dispute that defined these configurations also seem rather remote to most of us. The relation to Denmark continued to absorb the attention of politicians, and particularly the issue on which Iceland had been forced to give in when it achieved home rule: the duty of the minister to enter the Danish Council of State in order to have Icelandic affairs sanctioned by the king. This was the very point that defined the status of Iceland as part of the Danish state.[2]

Icelandic society progressed rapidly in these years, mainly through the mechanization of fishing, as we see later (Ch. 4.1), and the Icelanders found it ever more difficult to be reconciled to the formal status of their country as a part of the Danish state, however free they were to rule themselves – there was scarcely any disagreement between the Danish and Icelandic authorities in these years on any matter except the form of government. Although we must accept that formal status is important, this situation makes the political life of Iceland appear especially anachronistic from the modern point of view. It was caught in the formal constitutional terms of the 19th century, while society was moving rapidly into modern capitalism, dominated by economic considerations which became particularly adverse during the First World War.

The main object of politics called for party divisions that were not, as was mostly the case in the other Nordic countries, between left and right. All the Icelandic parties stood for rather cautious liberal, progressive attitudes. They also espoused nationalism, but it was on the tendency to be demanding or compliant *vis-à-vis* Denmark that the parties marked themselves off from each other. We can see these divisions as forming a

---

[1] The basic work on the administration of Iceland after 1904, and a considerable part of Icelandic politics, is Agnar Kl. Jónsson I-II (1969).

[2] The basic account of the struggle for autonomy is still Björn Þórðarson (1951), 129-385.

vertical line, where the most demanding are at the top and the most compliant at the bottom.

When Hannes Hafstein came to power in 1904, his Home Rule Party was definitely further up the vertical line of politics than its opponent, the Valtýrians. On the other hand, a third group was formed by those who refused to accept the clause of Council of State in the constitutional amendment and thus outbid the Home Rule Party in demands. They called themselves the Country Defenders (Landvarnarmenn) and had only one member of parliament in 1904, but in the next years they gained much support among the younger generation.

However these party relations proved unstable. The opposition in the Althing soon began to get at Hannes from above, by presenting itself as more nationalistic than he was. When he made a contract with a Danish telegraph company concerning a patent to lay an underwater telegraph cable to Iceland and run it for a definite period, he was accused of giving preference to a Danish firm instead of using wireless (then in its infancy) to get into contact with the outside world. When it became known that his appointment had been countersigned by the Danish prime minister, he was accused of accepting the status of a member of the Danish government (this was proved wrong when the government resigned in 1905 but Hannes continued in his post without receiving a new appointment).

So Hannes Hafstein was pressed to show his patriotism, and indeed it was high time to clarify the nature and organization of Iceland's status by replacing the Status Act, which had never been formally accepted by the Althing as valid, with a new union treaty. Hannes managed to get so far that in the spring of 1908 a Danish-Icelandic committee sitting in Copenhagen, consisting of politicians from government and opposition parties, drafted a new treaty defining Iceland's status within the Danish realm. This proposal, commonly called the Draft (*Uppkastið*), was supported by the whole committee except one of the Icelandic representatives, Skúli Thoroddsen, the editor of *Þjóðviljinn*, who had joined forces with Valtýr Guðmundsson because of his opposition to the governor and his clique in Reykjavík (see Ch. 3.15). The disagreement between the committee majority and Skúli Thoroddsen is most apparent in Article 1 of the Draft, where the majority proposal defined Iceland as "a free and independent, inalienable country", but Skúli's proposal defined it as "a free and autonomous state". Thus the disagreement was mostly on the question of formal statehood for Iceland.

Two representatives from the opposition party supported the Draft, so that its acceptance in Iceland seemed fairly secure, in spite of Skúli Thoroddsen's divergence. However, they greatly miscalculated the feelings of Icelanders. The practical solutions of the 1890s were no longer in fashion. Young people were now flocking into youth organizations, which adopted the double role of most nationalist movements: to preserve national traditions – old or recently invented – and to modernize society. The struggle for autonomy, which had been fought predominantly with juridical arguments, now entered the arena of sentiment more openly than before. Symbolic values obtained higher ratings; thus for the first time a special Icelandic flag – a white cross on a blue background – came into use without any warrant in law or ordinances.

An episode in Reykjavík during the summer of 1913 epitomised the new atmosphere. The captain of a Danish warship had an Icelandic flag confiscated from a one-man rowing-boat in the harbour, on the grounds that this flag was not allowed on vessels belonging to the Danish state. As soon as this became known in the town, Danish flags, which had been hoisted to greet Danish ships in the harbour, disappeared, and more and more Icelandic flags were hoisted in their place. This was followed throughout the day by various demonstrations, which were actually the first to take place in Iceland's struggle for independence.[3]

In an atmosphere that could create such an uproar, the Draft was doomed. In parliamentary elections in September 1908, its supporters obtained only 43% of the vote and nine seats, while the opponents had 57% and twenty-five seats. Although Hannes Hafstein could nominate six of his followers for royal appointment, his majority was lost, and when the Althing convened in February 1909, it passed a vote of no confidence in him. By this time the opposition had united into a party called the Independence Party (Sjálfstæðisflokkur) – not to be confused with the present-day party of the same name – which took over and nominated a new minister.

In the following years, an attempt was made to improve the formal status of Iceland within the realm by an amendment to the constitution. The Danish government agreed to replace the clause about the Danish Council of State (see Ch. 3.15) with a provision that the king would decide where the submission of Icelandic affairs was to take place. Everyone knew that he would decide on the Danish Council of State, and in Iceland the majority were willing to accept that. But would the royal decree on this be issued as an Icelandic affair, countersigned by the Icelandic minister, or as a common Danish-Icelandic affair, countersigned by the prime minister of Denmark?

It took over a year to reach an agreement on this question, but finally it was done and the constitutional amendment was ratified by the king on 19 June 1915. This amendment was no great step towards independence, but it was an important milestone in the development of democracy. Not only did it introduce a general franchise for both sexes (see Ch. 3.16), but it abolished the royal appointment of six members to the Althing. After the introduction of rule by parliamentary majority in 1904, the royal appointment had even ceased to be a guarantee of conservative support, and was

[3] Agnar Kl. Jónsson (1954-8).

now an absurd anomaly since it gave the minister at any time six extra followers in the Upper House of the Althing. Furthermore, the constitutional amendment allowed an increase in the number of ministers in Iceland and thus opened the way to forming coalition governments, which ever since 1917 has been the dominant means of securing majority governments in the multi-party system of Iceland.

At the same time as he ratified the constitutional amendment, the king issued a decree that allowed the use of the Icelandic flag within Iceland and in its territorial waters. However, to avoid similarity with the Greek and even the Swedish flags, a red cross was inserted into the middle of the white cross on the blue background.

In these years the pride and joy of Iceland, probably more than anything else, was its fleet of oceangoing ships – trawlers, and two new steamers which had been bought by the newly-established Steamship Company of Iceland (Eimskipafélag Íslands). It is not surprising, therefore, that the question of the relationship with Denmark was taken up by the Althing in 1917 in the form of a resolution requesting the king to give the Icelandic flag the status of a marine flag. When the prime minister of Iceland mentioned this in the Danish Council of State, the Danish prime minister and the king preferred to take up the whole issue of the union of Iceland and Denmark. Proceeding from that point, a Danish-Icelandic committee met in Reykjavík in the summer of 1918 and in little more than a fortnight came to a conclusion about the arrangement of the future union of the countries. The proposal was passed in both the Danish and Icelandic parliaments and in a plebiscite in Iceland, and came into force on 1 December 1918.

By this treaty Iceland became a separate state in a basically personal union with Denmark whereby, of course, all problems with the Danish Council of State were solved. Common Danish-Icelandic affairs mainly concerned the Crown and rules of succession, external affairs and mutual rights of citizens of one state in the other. The Supreme Court in Copenhagen was to remain the final appeal court of Iceland until Icelandic authorities decided otherwise, which they did in 1920 by elevating the High Court in Reykjavík to the status of Supreme Court. The annual contribution of the Danish treasury to Iceland (see Ch. 3.6) – which was no longer of much importance – was abolished and replaced by a fund designed to promote cultural connections between the countries. After the end of 1940 either of the parties could express a wish for a revision of the treaty. If no new agreement could be reached within three years, either could terminate the treaty. Finally it was decreed that Denmark would notify other countries that Iceland was an independent state and that it was neutral and had no defence force. Thus began Iceland's twenty-two-year period of declared undefended neutrality.

Why was Denmark suddenly so generous to Iceland? First, at the end of the First World War the self-determination of peoples was the order of the day. Even Denmark itself was preparing to reclaim northern Slesvig through a plebiscite, which led to a reunion of a large part of the Danish-speaking population there with Denmark in 1920. Secondly, Iceland was not the same as it had been. Not only had it developed considerably, but during the war it had assumed self-rule on an unprecedented scale. Although both Denmark and Iceland were neutral and remained out of the hostilities, the connection between the countries was largely broken, and the Icelandic authorities were forced to negotiate on their own with Britain and the United States for the import of necessities to the country.[4] After this Denmark could not say to Iceland that it was unable to rule itself. Thus Iceland became one of the group of European states that gained independence in the wake of the First World War.

[4] See Sólrún B. Jensdóttir (1986).

PART IV

The Great 20th-Century Transformation

4.1 Industrial Revolution in Fishing

In November 1902 a two-horsepower (h.p.) motor, burning paraffin, was installed in a six-oar rowing-boat called the *Stanley* at Ísafjörður in the Western Fiords. The engine had been bought from Denmark for 900 krónur and was accompanied to Iceland by a sixteen-year-old boy who put it into the boat and taught its helmsman how to operate it. In the following winter season the boat had little success because of unfavourable weather and bad catches, according to the helmsman's account, but in the spring season, after Easter, it fished well and attracted serious attention from neighbouring fishermen when it went out on two fishing trips in one day.[1]

This was not the first time that motor power was used in Iceland. The first internal-combustion engine was bought by an Icelander to drive a printing press in Reykjavík in 1899 (some would say this was typical of Iceland). Steam engines had been used by Icelanders at least since the 1890s, mainly in the small cargo ships run by the largest trading firms.[2] Icelanders had also been acquainted with mechanization, in the form of both steam and internal-combustion propulsion, as used by foreign fishermen and whalers in their waters. Nevertheless, the installation of an engine in the *Stanley* in 1902 began a new era in Icelandic history, since the successful mechanization of the Icelandic fishing fleet, which was to modernize the whole society and form the economic basis for the Icelandic welfare state followed from it.[3] Twelve years later, in 1914, the number of motor boats under 12 GRT gross registered tonnage had reached 400, while larger motor vessels, apart from trawlers, numbered twenty-three. In 1930 the corresponding numbers were 787 and 224, while the number of rowing-boats had fallen from over 2,000 in 1900 to 170.[4]

Trawler fishing had first become known to Icelanders around 1890, when English steam-driven trawlers began to sweep the fishing grounds off the coasts with those huge sacks of net they called trawls.[5] In the 1890s

---

[1] Árni Gíslason (1944), 291-302.

[2] Jón Þ. Þór (1988), 99.

[3] For a generel survey in English of the development of Icelandic fishing in 1900-40, see Sigfús Jónsson (1980).

[4] The main source for statistical information is still, as before, *Hagskinna* (1997); these figures appear on p. 311 (table 5.3). Below, this source will be used repeatedly without further reference being made. The role played by central government in the economic transformation of Iceland is discussed thoroughly by Guðmundur Jónsson (1991).

[5] The basic work on British trawler fishing in Icelandic waters until 1916 is Jón Þ. Þór (1992).

they caused a serious problem for the fishing community around the southern part of Faxaflói by trawling over nets laid by local fishermen. On the other hand, the English were so fastidious that they only collected plaice, haddock and halibut. The cod that got into their trawls were thrown back into the sea. Some Icelanders began to collect the fish the English did not want, sometimes for no payment, sometimes in exchange for goods like alcohol or tobacco. This at least was the story told by the opponents of this trade, which was seen by many Icelanders as extremely humiliating. Some suggested that the foreign intruders should be warded off by rowing out to the fishing grounds with large rocks and dropping them overboard where they would damage the trawls. Others concluded that the only sensible solution for Icelandic fishing was to start trawling also.

The first attempt to run trawler fishing off Iceland was made in 1899 by an Englishman who had settled in Hafnarfjörður.[6] The name of the ship was *Utopia*, which was prophetic because the enterprise came to nothing and was abandoned that same autumn. Other attempts made in the same year and the succeeding ones were all based on foreign capital and equally unsuccessful. Trawler fishing that succeeded and was at the same time truly Icelandic was begun in 1905, when a company owned exclusively by Icelanders bought a trawler named *Coot* from Scotland and operated it at a good profit from Hafnarfjörður for more than three years, most of the time with an all-Icelandic crew. When the *Coot* ran aground in 1908 and the company was dissolved, there were already others in the business. In 1907 a new company called Alliance had a trawler built for it in Britain named the *Jón forseti* (President Jón) – the common appellation of Iceland's national hero Jón Sigurðsson.

With Alliance the remarkable Thor Jensen entered the trawler industry. He was a Danish immigrant in Iceland who had come to the country as a teenager in the service of a Danish trading firm. Later he started his own business, and was a merchant and owner of decked ships in Reykjavík when he launched Alliance. In 1912 Thor and his family established a new trawler firm, Kveldúlfur, which was to dominate the industry until the time of the Second World War.

The same year, 1912, also saw the breakthrough of trawler fishing off Iceland. The number of trawlers grew from ten to twenty, and their share of the country's entire catch passed 20%. After that the industry grew considerably, though somewhat irregularly. In 1930 the number of trawlers reached forty-one, its highest level before the Second World War. Two years earlier the last decked sailing vessel had disappeared from the list of fishing ships.

Thus the mechanization of the Icelandic fishing industry took place between 1902 and 1930. In this period the annual catches grew from some

---

[6] For an account of the origin of trawler fishing off Iceland up to 1917 see Heimir Þorleifsson (1974).

80,000 to 400,000 tons, while the number of people engaged in fishing increased by some 50%. Fish-processing developed more slowly; the dominant mode of processing cod throughout that time was dry-salting, performed in a labour-intensive way without much mechanization. Herring, the second most important fish caught in the period, was mostly salted into barrels or rendered into oil, which yielded a by-product of meal for animal food. Official statistics show almost a trebling of the numbers engaged in fish processing during the first three decades of the 20th century. However, these numbers are unreliable, since the statistics only count heads of households (including households consisting of one person only), and fish processing was to a large extent the job of married women and teenagers.

The transformation of the Icelandic fishing industry has all the characteristics of an industrial revolution, with a great and rapid growth of production brought about by new techniques that increased productivity. The transformation is generally considered to have taken place at this time – 30-50 years later than in Denmark – because of a new influx of foreign capital. A bank, Landsbanki Íslands (the National Bank of Iceland), had been established in Iceland in 1886. It was exclusively under official ownership and issued special Icelandic banknotes, guaranteed by the Icelandic treasury and with the same value as the corresponding Danish currency. By the end of the 19th century many people were finding this source of credit insufficient. So in 1904 a new bank was established completely under foreign – mostly Danish – ownership and given the sole right to issue banknotes in Iceland. This was Íslandsbanki (Bank of Iceland), which operated until 1930 and became the most important source of loan capital for the emerging trawler fishing.[7]

It has been estimated that the owners themselves contributed, on average, a little less than half the price of the trawlers that were bought before 1917. Most of the balance came from Íslandsbanki, but many of the loans were soon repaid, because the industry proved extremely profitable, once the initial difficulties had been overcome. *Jón forseti* cost 153,000 krónur in 1907, of which Íslandsbanki lent 54,000 and the Landsbanki 16,000. Both these loans, and even double that sum, according to the account of Thor Jensen, had been repaid from the profit of the enterprise before the end of 1910.

In assessing the importance of foreign capital, one must remember that the transformation of fishing off Iceland was based on technical innovations that were very new when introduced there. Although the steam engine had been used in ships for more than half a century, the trawl did not come into general use until the 1880s. It was about this time that the first internal-combustion engines were produced, and their use in fishing boats was an absolute novelty at the turn of the century. Indeed no industry in Iceland could have been mechanized to the extent that fishing

[7] The basic work on Íslandsbanki is Ólafur Björnsson (1981).

was before these new machines came into use, the country being devoid of all metals, timber or any of the precious natural resources that sustained 19th-century industrialization.

On the other hand, when the right kind of fishing gear and machines to power ships were available, fishing proved an excellent field for industrialization in this backward society. The absence of a communication system within the country was relatively unimportant, since the fish were brought ashore and exported from the shore again. A revolutionary change was made in communication with the outside world in 1906 when a telegraph line, initiated by the new Home Rule government, was opened between Iceland and Europe (see Ch. 3.17). A large-scale fishing industry could scarcely have been run without being able to order salt, spare parts for engines or herring barrels from abroad more rapidly than the speed of mail-ships. The lack of any proper harbour was, of course, a considerable obstacle, and the first major effort to build one was started in Reykjavík in 1913.

How Icelanders learned to operate machines in a country where the wheel had hardly been discovered is still something of a mystery. A few had apparently had some experience at whaling stations that had been run by Norwegians at a few places in the Eastern and Western Fiords for a few years. Apart from that, most of the necessary knowledge must have been acquired by experience – sometimes no doubt painful and expensive – together with the inventiveness possessed by some people with little formal schooling.

Although Hafnarfjörður was the cradle of the trawler industry, it came to have by far the most influence in Reykjavík and contributed greatly to the growth of the town in the 20th century. In 1917 twenty trawlers were registered in the country, seventeen of them in Reykjavík. It has been estimated that each trawler employed about forty men on a year-round basis. If each man supported a family of five – this was the normal way of thinking at the time, although other family members made their contributions in various ways – each trawler provided for 200 people, and hence more than 20% of the 15,000 inhabitants of Reykjavík lived off the trawler fisheries. Other fishing stations thrived using motor boats. Thus the population of the Westman Islands quadrupled, growing from some 600 to 2,400 between 1900 and 1920, without a single trawler being run from there.

Technical innovations in one branch of industry do not, of course, create an industrial revolution in a society without being linked to other economic activities. The development of Iceland seems to accord well with the type of economic growth described by Canadian and American economists in terms of the staple theory and the export-base model.[8] These theories apply to economic growth originating in one major industry that produces goods for export from an internal natural resource. The

[8] Sigfús Jónsson (1980), 23-54.

distribution of this growth has been described as taking place through three kinds of linkages from the export sector: backward linkage to the production of goods needed by the staple industry, forward linkage to the further processing of the goods produced, and final demand linkage to the production of consumer goods for those who make a living in the staple industry.

In Iceland backward linkage from fishing does not seem to have been important during the period of breakthrough before 1930, except perhaps in the import trade, since most of the equipment used for fishing was imported. In forward linkage the processing of fish provided much work on the coast, and the rendering of herring for animal feed involved new techniques. Furthermore, the freezing industry made a humble start in the 1930s.

However, the most important linkage in this period seems to be to the production of consumer goods, not least in agriculture, which then for the first time acquired a considerable domestic market for its surplus products. Thus the increase of urban population and of its purchasing power was a condition for a process of modernization that was to start within agriculture, although on a much smaller and slower scale than in fishing. The story is told of a grown-up farmer's son in southern Iceland who in 1925 bought a wheelbarrow and took it home to his father's farm. The old man looked at the thing and said: "This is no doubt a good tool for those who know how to use it."[9] It was not until the 1950s that tractors replaced horses as the common yielders of energy in hay production, which is the essence of Icelandic farming.

Other kinds of production of consumer goods grew slowly, although for instance a few wool-processing and textile factories had been established since around the turn of the century.[10] In 1930 our omniscient *Hagskinna* tells us that only about 3,300 household heads were engaged in manufacturing other than fish processing, i.e. a little less than 7% of the workforce in the country. Almost half of this group were engaged in the manufacture of textiles, clothes, shoes and skins.[11]

Nevertheless, the first three decades of the 20th century were a period of rapid economic growth in the society as a whole. In 1901-13 the average annual growth of gross domestic product (GDP) per capita was 3.2%, while the corresponding figure in sixteen comparable members of the future Organization for Economic Cooperation and Development (OECD) is 1.8%. For the period 1913-50 the figures are 2.2% for Iceland but 1.3% for the same sixteen countries.[12] The Icelandic economy rapidly caught up with its earlier-developed neighbours.

[9] Björn Þorsteinsson (1982), 13. My translation.
[10] Magnús Guðmundsson (1988), 19-46, 109-30.
[11] *Hagskinna* (1997), 220 (table 3.9).
[12] Magnús S. Magnússon (1993), 114.

4.2 Modernization of Life

The economic growth described in the last chapter led to a metamorphosis of daily life. Instead of living under turf roofs and in almost wild nature, the typical mode of living came to be in a house built of timber or concrete, standing on at least some kind of street. The urbanization process, which started in the late 18th century (see Chs 2.16 and 2.18), now began to be reflected in population numbers. In 1904, the year before the trawler *Coot* arrived in Iceland, a quarter of the population lived in urban nuclei of fifty or more inhabitants (see Ch. 3.10). In the early 1920s this proportion passed 50%, and in 1930 almost 60% of the population were urban by the same definition. At that time, still using the dividing line of fifty inhabitants, Iceland seems to have been the most highly urbanized of all Nordic countries.[1]

The growth of towns and villages was by no means welcomed by the whole society: the "flight from the countryside" was commonly seen as a serious threat, not only to the rural areas and their need for labour, but to the entire society, the national culture and even the nation's physical and moral standards.[2] The theory of the superiority of rural to urban life was well known in Europe at this time and mixed variously with fashionable ideas of human eugenics,[3] but it can be assumed to have had an unusually strong appeal in Iceland, with its complete lack of traditional urban culture and extraordinarily rapid urbanization.

Apart from the movement from the countryside to the towns and villages, the transformation of daily life naturally took place within both kinds of settlements. Country life became more like urban life, though not everywhere equally rapidly. When my family was compelled to move from its tenant farm in 1943, the year when the ninth child was born, we moved to a farm with a turf house consisting of one living-room (a traditional *baðstofa*) and a kitchen, pantry and corridor. There was no running water into the house for consumption or out of it for sewage, no sink, and no latrine of any kind. Such primitive housing was unusual by then, but it was by no means unique. In 1940, 23% of houses in rural areas were still made of turf.

---

[1] *Hagskinna* (1997), 90 (table 2.7); Gustafsson (1997), 224. Only *c.* 2.3% lived in urban nuclei of between fifty and 200 inhabitants, so that it makes little difference where the dividing line is drawn.

[2] The subject is treated thoroughly by Ólafur Ásgeirsson (1988).

[3] See Unnur B. Karlsdóttir (1998).

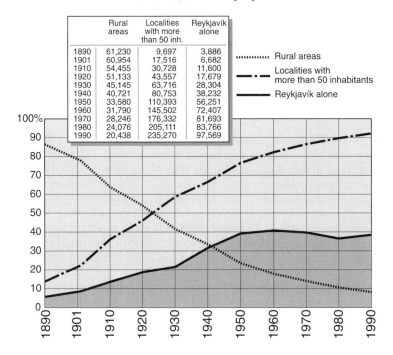

	Rural areas	Localities with more than 50 inh.	Reykjavík alone
1890	61,230	9,697	3,886
1901	60,954	17,516	6,682
1910	54,455	30,728	11,600
1920	51,133	43,557	17,679
1930	45,145	63,716	28,304
1940	40,721	80,753	38,232
1950	33,580	110,393	56,251
1960	31,790	145,502	72,407
1970	28,246	176,332	81,693
1980	24,076	205,111	83,766
1990	20,438	235,270	97,569

Fig. 4.2-1 The urbanization process, 1890-1990. *Source*: *Hagskinna* (1997), 120 (table 2.9), 123 (table 2.10).

In the urban areas the heyday of timber houses such as those described in Chapter 3.12 came to an end shortly after 1915, when a fire broke out in the centre of Reykjavík and burned down twelve houses. After this event it was forbidden to build timber houses in Reykjavík larger than 75 m². Although this was decided for Reykjavík only, timber houses soon went out of fashion elsewhere too. It was really not until the 1970s that people began to rediscover the charm of one- or two-storey timber houses.

The timber houses were replaced by concrete ones built according to a method developed in Iceland in the late 19th century (although it was known elsewhere). Timber shuttering is erected for the entire walls, and later for ceilings, in which the houses are cast.[4] In the 1920s, which was on the whole a prosperous time for Iceland, a whole quarter of handsome one- and two-storey concrete houses was built in Reykjavík. The Althing of 1929 was so optimistic that it passed a law[5] forbidding the installation of apartments in the basements of new houses in towns and villages and

---

[4] The development of the method is described by Guðmundur Hannesson (1943), 240-60, who also gives a good account of the history of housing in Iceland.

[5] *Stjórnartíðindi* 1929 A (1929), 190-1.

arranged for the gradual elimination of all existing ones. This programme of course came to nothing in the depression of the 1930s (see Ch. 4.5), but by 1940 concrete houses had become just as common in the towns as timber ones, while in the villages timber houses were still more than twice as common. In this period also, a large part of the centre of Reykjavík was being built up of three- or four-storey concrete buildings for shops and offices. The central streets were laid with asphalt and the pavements with concrete slabs.

Even in Reykjavík, drinking-water was brought from wells within the town until 1909 when the waterworks was established. By then the first sewers had already been laid, but after 1909 it became unavoidable to have a closed sewer in every street. In 1904 the first hydroelectric power station in Iceland came into service in Hafnarfjörður. It was privately owned and provided sixteen houses in the town with electricity for lighting, besides the carpenter's shop of the owner. Reykjavík chose another way and had a gasworks for lighting and cooking opened in 1910. The first hydroelectric power station for Reykjavík was finished in 1921 on a river which was then outside the town but now runs through it.

The first proper household expenditure survey was made in 1939-40, but a rough estimate is possible from 1914 onwards. At that time the average family was thought to spend almost half its income after tax on food (49%), 17% on housing, 15% on clothing, 6% on fuel and heating and 13% on other expenses. These consumption habits did not seem to change drastically before the Second World War. By 1939 the proportion spent on food had fallen to 43%, while that on housing had risen to 20%. Other changes were negligible, and "other expenses", where one would expect to see signs of more varied and luxurious consumption habits, had gone up by only 1%. If we used the same categories to describe consumption in Iceland in the 1990s, "other expenses" would amount to more than half. Transport, mainly the private car, takes up almost 20% of all consumption, approximately as much as food. So we see that the Icelanders of the first half of the 20th century were, by our standards, thrifty people who spent most of their income on what we would call basic necessities. The wealthy minority was so small that it had little impact on the averages.

Where food consumption was concerned, no major changes took place before the Second World War either. The trends of the 19th century (see Ch. 3.12) proceeded at a similar pace, but now sugar was the most important single factor in the change and increased its share in the total consumption from 7% (of nutrition value, not price) at the turn of the century to 14% in 1938. Mainly for this reason, and because of increased consumption of margarine, the share of imported foodstuffs grew from 46 to 54% and food of vegetable origin from 48 to 58%.[6] The introduction

[6] Guðmundur Jónsson (1997), 52.

of potatoes, which came about gradually in the late 19th and early 20th centuries, seemed to make surprisingly little difference to total food consumption. However, there is no doubt that potatoes became practically indispensable as a part of every meal in Iceland in the period under discussion here. In the novel *Salka Valka* by our Nobel Prize winner Halldór Kiljan Laxness, people in a poor fishing village in the interwar years were told the gospel of socialism. They were sceptical, but "of course it was not the first time they had heard incredible stories told; for example, that Jesus, a man as poor as a rat, had fed five thousand people with a small loaf, a still smaller piece of fish, and no potatoes at all."[7]

Without implying that the old rural society was freer from social problems than the new urban one, it is safe to say that the transformation demanded – and introduced from abroad – new solutions to social problems. One of these was the founding of charitable societies, which also mark an epoch as they provided the first platforms for the social and political influence of women, long before they were enfranchised to the legislative assembly. Among the first was an Icelandic division of the World Women's Christian Temperance Union, normally called Hvítabandið (White Ribbon) in Icelandic, established in 1895. Although its basic aim was temperance, it took on many other charitable tasks and even built a small hospital in Reykjavík in the 1930s and pressed the town council to receive it as a gift a decade later. One-third of the money for a state hospital, opened in Reykjavík in 1930, was raised by women. In this way Icelandic women found their way of bringing about a solution to a problem which was peculiarly theirs, having to cater for sick people in their homes because of the lack of appropriate institutions.[8]

The need for new social organizations also appeared in the religious area.[9] As already mentioned (Ch. 3.14), the National Church enjoyed almost complete hegemony in rural Iceland in the 19th century. On the other hand, the towns and villages in the decades around 1900 proved to be quite a fertile soil for religious movements, and a Lutheran Free Church, the Salvation Army, the Young Men's Christian Association (YMCA), Seventh-Day Adventists and various spiritualist societies struck roots in the country. The National Church was hardly ever threatened by any of these movements; throughout, it enjoyed more than 90% adherence among the population, although church attendance may have dwindled. On the other hand, the Church was effectively invaded by spiritualism, particularly in the person of Haraldur Níelsson, professor of theology at the University of Iceland from 1911 to 1928, for decades a large part of its clergy were avowed spiritualists.

Among new social movements, none was stronger than that against alcohol. By modern standards alcohol consumption does not seem to have

[7] Halldór Kiljan Laxness (1936), 278.
[8] Margrét Guðmundsdóttir (1995a), 200-5.

been very great in the 19th century; in 1881-5 it amounted to 2.36 litres of pure alcohol per person annually. However, in this society only a minority drank; very few women or male teenagers ever did, and many adult males must have been excluded through poverty, so alcohol consumption may have been quite considerable among better-off adult males. If all the alcohol is supposed to have been consumed by the enfranchised minority at the time (see Ch. 3.14), each person imbibed some 25 litres of pure alcohol per year.

Anyway, drinking was considered a serious problem, and temperance societies were already active in Iceland before the middle of the 19th century. After the arrival of the International Order of Good Templars (IOGT) in the 1880s, the annual alcohol consumption went down from 2.36 to 1.5 per person, which of course was partly a consequence of the bad years of the early and mid-1880s (see Ch. 3.9). But in the more prosperous 1890s consumption did not reach the level of the early 1880s, and in fact never did so until the 1970s.

The triumph of the Good Templars went on until in 1908 complete prohibition was approved in a plebiscite, with a majority of about 60%.[10] The import of alcohol was forbidden from the beginning of 1912 and all sale of it from the beginning of 1915. At first the prohibition seems to have been reasonably successful, although what could be imported for medical reasons was no doubt considerably abused. Then after the First World War Spain threatened to put high tariffs on Icelandic salt fish if Iceland did not lift the prohibition on Spanish wines. In 1922 the Althing gave in and made an exception in the prohibition law for wine with up to 21% alcohol content. The import and sale of the wine was entrusted to the state, thus introducing the state monopoly of the alcohol trade, which is still valid in Iceland.

The Spanish wines were perhaps a minor gap in the bulwark against alcohol, especially since there was little tradition of wine drinking in Iceland, but more gaps were to open up later. People gradually learned the art of distilling their own spirits, which seems to have been practically unknown at the beginning of the prohibition period. Also improved communication must have made smuggling easier. Finally, in 1933, the abolition of the prohibition was approved in a plebiscite by 58 to 42% of the votes. On one kind of alcoholic drink only was the prohibition retained, namely beer which was considered more likely than other drinks to attract the young. To the astonishment of many foreign visitors, the ban on beer was not lifted until 1989.

[9] A thorough study is provided by Pétur Pétursson (1983).

[10] The story of the prohibition has been told by Arnar Guðmundsson and Unnar Ingvarsson (1993).

4.3 The New Working-Class Movement

As mentioned earlier (Ch. 3.10), it was in the 1890s that decked ships created for the first time in Iceland the conditions for employees to unite in wage negotiations against united employers, although their unions were too restricted to this declining sector of fishing to develop into a general trade union movement. The Báran departments in Reykjavík showed their last signs of life in 1909-10; only in the southern villages of Eyrarbakki and Stokkseyri did Báran unions, established in 1903, develop into viable unions of workers and seamen.

In the late 1880s and 1890s groups of skilled workers made a few attempts to form trade unions, most of which proved abortive. The first union of this kind that survived was the Icelandic Typographers' Union, established with twelve members in Reykjavík in 1897 and operated as such until it was recently united with other unions in the area of book manufacture. Even unskilled workers in the small towns of Akureyri and Seyðisfjörður formed short-lived unions in the late 1890s.[1] Thus the utilization of unions in the struggle for a better life was well known in Iceland before the turn of the century, but the urge does not seem to have been strong enough to overcome the hindrances such enterprises inevitably meet with.

In 1906 a new start was made in Reykjavík when the bookbinder Pétur G. Guðmundsson launched a new paper called *Alþýðublaðið*[2] in which he proclaimed the policy that workers should price the commodity they sold, their labour, just as merchants priced their goods.[3] Further, the paper announced the establishment of a new union of workers in Reykjavík, to be named Dagsbrún (Daybreak). When it was established in January 1906, 384 workers signed its charter and by the end of the year members

---

[1] Ólafur R. Einarsson (1969).

[2] The word *alþýða* will occur frequently in this chapter and in the following one. It is composed of the prefix *al-* (all) and *þýða*, related to *þjóð* (people), and means originally "the general people" or "common people". The organized working class adopted the word to describe itself, so it will alternatively be translated as "people" and "labour (class)".

[3] For survey of the development in Reykjavík until 1916, see Ólafur R. Einarsson (1974). A year-by-year survey covering the period 1875-1934 is provided by Gunnar M. Magnúss (1967).

numbered almost 600 or approximately a quarter of all male workers in the town.[4] Yet, there was some reluctance in this initiative. This appeared in, among other things, the choice as chairman of Sigurður Sigurðsson, an agronomist in the service of the Agricultural Society of Iceland. Whatever he may have thought about the interests of urban labourers in 1906, he clearly expressed his support a few years later for farmers in their resistance to wage rises in agriculture.[5]

Dagsbrún was also rather moderate in its wage demands. At the inaugural meeting it passed a by-law which decided that working hours should be from 6 o'clock in the morning till 6 in the evening, which meant eleven hours of work daily. The wages were set at 25 aurar (0.25 krónur) an hour in the winter and 30 aurar an hour in the summer, which was around the top level of wages at the time.

The following years were relatively prosperous, and Dagsbrún managed to raise wages, without major conflict, to 35 aurar an hour in 1913. This would have meant an income of almost 1,200 krónur a year if the worker had constant employment, but temporary unemployment was common, and an investigation performed in Reykjavík in the spring of 1913 led to the finding that a working-class family earned on average only 738 krónur a year,[6] that is, some 75% of the full-time wage of a worker earning 30 aurar an hour.

In 1906-8 a number of labour unions were established, *inter alia* of unskilled workers in Hafnarfjörður, Ísafjörður and Akureyri. When a confederation of trade unions was launched in 1907, eleven unions were invited to join. However, the time did not seem ripe for a strong and active labour movement. *Alþýðublaðið* ceased publication in 1907, and the country-wide Labour Union held its last meeting in 1910. It has been suggested that the constitutional struggle against Denmark in these years (see Ch. 3.17) attracted too much attention to allow any other social or political struggle to take place in the country, and it was indeed tempting in those years to see all Icelanders as being united in a fight against a common opponent.

For this reason it was fortunate for the labour movement that a Danish employer gave it the occasion to embark on a major wage struggle as early as 1913. A contractor from Denmark who undertook the building of the harbour in Reykjavík refused to abide by the new wage agreement of Dagsbrún and the employers in the town of 35 aurar an hour, and offered the workers 32.5 aurar unless they made a special agreement on working hours. A group of workers called for a strike in a proclamation which stressed the national dimensions: "The foreigner who manages the

[4] Magnús S. Magnússon (1985), 184.
[5] Ólafur Ásgeirsson (1988), 33-4.
[6] *Ingólfur* XI (1913), 147 (16 September).

harbour work intends to oppress Icelandic workers". The strike lasted two months and ended in a complete victory for the workers and the first written wage agreement that Dagsbrún made.

In 1913 working-class women also began a wage struggle. At their first meeting, held by the Women's Rights Association and its chairman Bríet Bjarnhéðinsdóttir (see Ch. 3.16), it was decided to send all the major employers in the town a letter and ask them to restrict the working hours of women to ten a day and to raise their wages from 15 to 20 aurar an hour. The letter was signed by 250 women, but the employers did not respond. Then in the autumn of 1914 a union of female workers in Reykjavík named Framsókn (Progress) was established by sixty-eight women, and soon there were around 100. Its first chairwoman Jónína Jónatansdóttir, was not strictly working-class, since she was the wife of a carpenter who ran his own business.

A decisive step was taken in the development of the labour movement in 1915 when a group of trade unions began to publish a new organ, also called *Dagsbrún*, under the editorship of Ólafur Friðriksson who, in his home town of Akureyri, had established the first social-democratic society in Iceland earlier the same year. Ólafur had lived for years in Denmark where he became acquainted with the social-democratic movement, and was the first devoted socialist (in fact with some anarchist tendencies) who was active within the movement in Iceland. It was he above all who gave it political content.

Also important in this process was a young teacher in Reykjavík, Jónas Jónsson, often named Jónas Jónsson from Hrifla after his birthplace, Hrifla in Þingeyjarsýsla. It was Jónas who persuaded Ólafur to come to Reykjavík and take up the editorship of *Dagsbrún*.

Although neither Ólafur nor Jónas had ever been sailors, they were both active in the establishment later in 1915 of the Reykjavík Union of Deckhands (Hásetafélagið), which was to become one of the strongest trade unions. As early as 1916 the union held out for a two-week strike of the trawler fleet because of a disagreement over premiums paid to the sailors for fish liver. The result was almost a doubling of the liver price paid to the sailors. Apart from that, the most urgent task of the Union of Deckhands was to get the working hours on board the trawlers reduced. If the catches were good, most skippers forced the crew to work continuously day and night, even for 60-70 hours, before they were allowed five or six hours' sleep. No agreement could be reached on this issue, and finally, in 1921, a law was passed stipulating a minimum rest period of six hours in every twenty-four on the trawlers.

The constitutional amendment of 1915 extended the franchise to workers, irrespective of the taxes they paid (see Ch. 3.16). Although this may not have greatly increased the number of urban working-class voters, since the tax threshold had not been high, the amendment no doubt helped to raise the expectations of workers for political influence. In January 1916 workers submitted their own list of candidates for local elections in Reykjavík and won an impressive victory, obtaining 46% of the vote and three representatives out of five.[7]

On 12 March 1916 the final step was taken towards a country-wide organization of the working-class movement. The representatives of seven unions met in Reykjavík and established Alþýðusamband Íslands (ASÍ – the Icelandic Federation of Labour) was to act simultaneously as a political party under the name Alþýðuflokkur (Labour Party). The key figures in its foundation had been Jónas Jónsson, who drafted its stipulations, and Ólafur Friðriksson, but neither of them assumed the presidency. Its first president was Ottó N. Þorláksson, who had been among the initiators of Báran in 1894. But at the first regular meeting of the union in the autumn he was already succeeded by Jón Baldvinsson, who occupied the post for twenty-two years until his death in 1938. Jón Baldvinsson, a typographer by craft, was a moderate social democrat and a convinced supporter of the conservative view, common in Iceland between the wars, that the migration of people to the urban areas should be restricted as much as possible in order to improve the lot of those already there.[8] His opinions did not make the coexistence of revolutionary communists and moderate social democrats in the labour movement any easier.

The organization of the employers was simpler than that of the workers; it was not until 1934 that they united into the Confederation of Icelandic Employers (Vinnuveitendafélag Íslands, later Vinnuveitendasamband Íslands, and now Samtök atvinnulífsins).[9]

The labour movement had to face the double task of convincing the working class of the feasibility of joining the movement, and of pressing the employers to acknowledge it as a negotiating partner. It has not yet been investigated thoroughly how and when the movement accomplished this. However, it seems clear that only a minority of the working class was organized before the 1930s. On the other hand, the employers seem on the whole to have already accepted in the 1910s or early 1920s that negotiating with the unions was the best way of keeping labour relations tolerable. Wage disputes were officially acknowledged in 1925 when a law on mediation in labour disputes was passed. It did not legalize strikes, but assumed that they might take place and set out what a state mediator should do if they did.

Still it was not until 1938 that extensive legislation on labour unions and labour disputes was enacted. Then individual union members were

[7] A fifteen-man town council was elected for the first time in 1908 (see Ch. 3.16). After that, until 1930, one-third of the council was elected every other year.
[8] Ólafur Ásgeirsson (1988), 40-2, 60-2.
[9] For a study of the subject in English, see Ingólfur V. Gíslason (1990).

obliged to obey legally accepted resolutions and agreements made by their unions. The latter were legalized as trading partners, each within its area, and all individual agreements between employers and employees that clashed with the collective agreements were made invalid. Strikes and lockouts were explicitly allowed, and employment of blacklegs was forbidden.[10] By this law the labour organization was formally incorporated into the governing system of Icelandic society, where it has remained ever since.

[10] *Stjórnartíðindi* 1925 A (1925), 171-4 (no. 55); 1938 A (1938), 130-9 (no. 80).

4.4 A New System of Political Parties

In Chapter 3.17 it was suggested that the political configurations of the Home Rule period should be viewed vertically, with the most demanding parties in the struggle for independence at the top and the more compliant ones further down. The constants in this system from 1908 onwards were the Independence Party at the upper end and the Home Rule Party at the bottom. Various splinter groups and short-lived alliances arose for shorter periods.

The union treaty of 1918 was so satisfactory for Iceland that it brought the struggle for independence practically to an end. Iceland obtained all the power that it wished for, and the more formal symbols of independence, such as a prince of their own, could only be obtained after twenty-five years. Thus the ideological basis of this vertical party system came to an end in the middle of the period when Iceland was taking on the class divisions of an industrialized, capitalist society (see Ch. 4.1). So naturally the system was replaced by a new one which, like the party systems in all the nearby countries, was predominantly based on class divisions and is traditionally seen as forming a horizontal spectrum between left and right.

In the late 19th and early 20th centuries the three Scandinavian countries, which Iceland inevitably tends to see as its models, all developed a party system dominated by the Social Democrats, with a relatively weak right-wing party, one or more rather small liberal-central-agrarian parties and a small isolated communist party. As we shall see, Iceland came in roughly the same period to have a party system that was similar in form but very different in proportions. In Iceland this new system came to be composed of four parties, which have dominated Icelandic politics with incredible stability since the 1930s. However, this stability has depended on centres of gravity placed differently from the Scandinavian systems.

The Labour Party, established as the political arm of the Icelandic Federation of Labour in March 1916 (see Ch. 4.3), was the first to base its existence on a particular class, and presented itself as the left wing of a future horizontal party system.[1] But of course, the party could not completely escape having a place on the vertical line, where it inevitably suffered from being at the very bottom as the most Denmark-friendly party. The reason for this was, first, the contention of the entire socialist working-class movement

[1] For a short survey of the history of the party, see Helgi Skúli Kjartansson (1987).

of Europe that class divisions were more important than national divisions. Further, in accordance with that contention, the party had good contacts with Danish Social Democrats, and indeed received considerable financial support from them from 1919 onwards. How decisive an influence the Danish Social Democrats had on their Icelandic sister party is disputed among historians.[2]

Next in the new party system came the agrarian-liberal Progressive Party (Framsóknarflokkur).[3] Unlike the electorate that the Labour Party appealed to, farmers had formed the bulk of Icelandic voters from the beginning, and of course they did not need a party while that situation lasted. The party was established by eight Althing members in December 1916 and January 1917. Its support came from three sources. One was a Farmers' Party (Bændaflokkur), which had been in existence in the Althing since 1912, although its members had simultaneously participated in the "vertical" parties. The second group had been formed mainly by Jónas Jónsson from Hrifla, who was preparing not only the establishment of a working-class union and a labour party (see Ch. 4.3) but also an agrarian-liberal party. He was a man of ambitious plans who did not stop at creating a single party but wanted an entirely new system of three parties: in this he chose to be in the middle, in a liberal party which would enjoy the support of a fairly large social democratic party. The third component of the Progressive Party came from the Independence Party, which was in the process of dissolution for reasons we need not consider here.

Many a follower of the Progressive Party may have looked upon it exclusively as an advocate of agrarian interests within a society undergoing rapid urbanization. But in the eyes of Jónas Jónsson it was predominantly a liberal party and a faithful supporter of the cooperative movement, which had been introduced to Iceland by farmers (see Ch. 3.11) and was still largely confined to rural areas, with most of its shops in trading villages and most of its trade with farmers. Around this time the Federation of Icelandic Co-operative Societies (SÍS) was building up what was to become the largest concern in the country, with branches in import, export, manufacture and shipping. The Progressive Party lived in close symbiosis with this great economic power, which helps us understand the strong position of both in a society where the importance of agriculture and rural life was fast receding.

The right wing of the new system was to find its focus in a party named the Independence Party (Sjálfstæðisflokkur), but not until several years

---

[2] Ólafur R. Einarsson (1978, 1979); Stefán F. Hjartarson (1989), 99, 115-16, 129; Þorleifur Friðriksson (1990), *passim*.

[3] For an insider's story of the party, see Þórarinn Þórarinsson I-III (1966-87). A more detached view is provided by the biography of Jónas Jónsson by Guðjón Friðriksson I-III (1991a-3).

[4] The story of the first fifteen years of the Independence Party has been written by

after the older party of that name had disappeared.[4] When the left and central wings of the new party system were emerging, the Home Rule Party formed the centre of gravity of its right wing. In the 1919 general elections it received almost 30% of the vote and 26% of the parliamentary seats. In the next elections in 1923, an alliance of the party and what remained of the old Independence Party, called the Citizens' Party (Borgaraflokkur), attained 53.6% of the vote and more than half the seats. Now a period of complicated alliances and merging and splitting of parties took place on the right, which ended with the founding of the new Independence Party in 1929. In the following year the party won 48.3% of the vote in general elections to the seats of the nationally elected members of parliament who had succeeded those appointed by the Crown (see Ch. 3.17).

Thus the right-wing party of Iceland did not originate as a conservative, upper-class party of landowners and top officials like many right-wing parties in Europe. Instead it was the main heir of both the major parties in the old vertical system, the Home Rule Party and the Independence Party. Thus it became the political home of the average nationalistic and even 'non-political' Icelander. Its name was said to refer to the independence of both the nation and the individual. The party refused to be a class party but maintained that it united all classes, which in fact it managed to do unusually well. Apart from urban employers, most of whom supported the party, it enjoyed the support of a considerable part of the farming class and urban workers. In a way the Independence Party resisted the left-right party system, but it could not escape occupying a place on the horizontal spectrum any more than the Labour Party could avoid being a part of the vertical one. It was – and is – a right-wing party because other parties see themselves as being to the left of it.

The fourth party of the system was established under the name of the Communist Party (Kommúnistaflokkur Íslands), but through two successive mergers with splinter groups from the Labour Party it has twice changed its name – first to the Socialist Party (Sameiningarflokkur alþýðu, sósíalistaflokkurinn) and later to the People's Alliance (Alþýðubandalag).[5]

After the Russian Revolution of 1917 most democratic countries in Europe had their own communist parties, positioned to the left of social democrats. In Iceland the communists coexisted uneasily with the social democrats within the Labour Party throughout the 1920s, until the congress of the Federation of Labour in November 1930 – which simultaneously served as a party congress – when a separation proved inevitable. Until

---

Magnús Jónsson (1957). For a study of the origin of the party, see Hallgrímur Guðmundsson (1979), and of its first years, Svanur Kristjánsson (1979). A survey in annalistic form is provided by Hannes Hólmsteinn Gissurarson (1989).

[5] The story of the communist movement until 1934 is given in Þór Whitehead (1979). After that, no comprehensive work is available about this arm of Icelandic politics, until the account of the People's Alliance by Óskar Guðmundsson (1987).

then the congruence of union and party had not been strictly enforced, so that members of parties other than Labour were allowed to participate in the Federation. Now the Federation leaders decided to end this abuse in order to prevent the separation of the two branches of activity. They proposed an amendment to the regulations, which prescribed that no one could take on any task for the union, not even attend the congress, without a prior commitment to follow and support the political program of the Labour Party. The amendment was passed by 52 votes to 15, whereupon the communist minority walked out and established the Communist Party.

This led to a bitter dispute in the labour movement. The Communists gained the upper hand in a few trade unions, which were then immediately expelled from the Federation, leading to new unions under the rule of social democrats being established in their place. This was, of course, thought to be extremely unfortunate, not least in times of deep depression, when maximum solidarity was needed to prevent a fall in wages. Therefore, increased pressure for the reunion of the two working-class parties began to be felt. A further urge came from the Soviet-ruled Comintern, when in 1935 it changed its policy and recommended its member parties to join forces with social democratic parties against the growing threat of fascism. Together with a decisive election victory for the Communist Party in 1937, where it gained 8.4% of the vote and three members in the Althing, a strong sentiment arose for reunion. This was not realized, but a large group of the Labour Party, led by the parliamentary member Héðinn Valdimarsson, united with the Communists in 1938 and together they established the Socialist Party.

Although Héðinn was to leave the party in disillusion, when it refused to condemn the Soviet invasion of Finland in 1939, the Socialist Party did well in the coming years. In general elections in October 1942 it gained ten seats (18.5% of the vote), while Labour won only seven (14.2% of the vote).

From then until 1991 the Icelandic Labour Party found itself in the unpleasant situation of having a larger party to its left. In 1956, when the Socialist Party's almost unconditional confidence in the unpopular Soviet Union was about to reverse this situation, Labour was split by the departure of a left-wing group led by the president of the Federation of Labour, Hannibal Valdimarsson, to cooperate with the Socialists. Together they formed the People's Alliance, which was turned into a political party in 1968. At the same time the Socialist Party was abolished.

Within the new system the parties originated in two ways. The centre and right-wing parties, the Progressive Party and the Independence Party, were established as parliamentary parties and only gradually turned into mass parties, building up constituency branches. The two working-class parties were established by groups that had no representation at the Althing but were sooner or later to acquire their members of parliament. Thus all the parties developed into a similar organizational pattern.

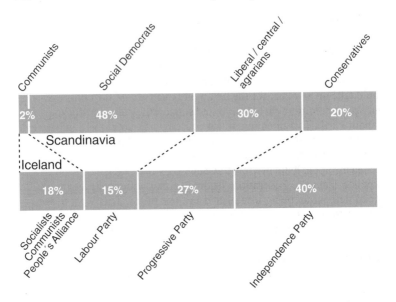

Fig. 4.4-1 Iceland's class-based party system by the end of the inter-war years, compared with its Scandinavian counterpart. For Iceland the proportions are based roughly on the average of two parliamentary elections held in 1942, and are fairly representative of the following years. For Scandinavia they are based on the surprisingly similar results of the elections in Norway in 1936 and Denmark in 1939. The strength of the parties is calculated as a proportion of the total support for the four main forces only, omitting other parties.

They also had their own organs, although the forms of ownership differed. Two of these were daily papers from the beginning (meaning papers published six days a week, as is still normal in Iceland). *Morgun-blaðið* (The Morning Paper) had been published since 1913 and became the main organ of the Independence Party, and *Alþýðublaðið* was published by the Labour Party from 1919 onwards. Others developed into daily papers: *Tíminn* (The Time) for the Progressive Party, and *Þjóðviljinn* (The People's Will – the name given to it by Skúli Thoroddsen's widow) for the Communist Party and its successors. One more daily paper, *Vísir* (Sprout), was published as an afternoon paper in Reykjavík. Thus for more than four decades after the Second World War the capital had no fewer than five daily papers.

No party within this system has ever attained an absolute majority in both chambers of the Althing – a condition for forming a one-party majority government. Therefore almost all governments in Iceland since the introduction of cabinet government in 1917 have been either short-lived minority governments or coalitions.

As for the form of coalitions, the interwar period can be divided into two. During the first decade, 1917-27, the coalitions were usually led by the right-wing parties or alliances that originated in the Home Rule Party and ended in the new Independence Party. In 1927-42 the Progressive Party led all governments. Although the party did not usually enjoy more than 25-30% of the total vote, and always less than the Independence Party, it was usually the largest parliamentary party, with around 40-50% of members. The reason for this was that the Progressive Party was strongest in rural constituencies, which were in the process of relative depopulation and hence highly overrepresented in the Althing.

In 1927 the Progressive Party formed a minority government supported by the Labour Party. Jónas Jónsson was one of the three members of this government, as a minister of justice as well as health, education and culture. Though not prime minister, he was the strong man of the government and saw the new coalition as a decisive shift of power in Iceland from the aristocracy to the common people. Jónas was also an enterprising minister and made good use of the prosperous late 1920s. Thus what was perhaps the most effective educational institution in 20th-century Iceland, the State Radio, was established by his Ministry of Education. He also had a number of lower secondary schools built in rural areas, the so-called district schools (*héraðsskólar*). Their purpose was partly to stop the "flight from the countryside", but they actually made a greater contribution to the development of Icelandic society by preparing young country boys and girls for a future life and occupation in urban surroundings.

Jónas was a controversial political figure. For instance, after a lengthy quarrel in which he was engaged with most of the medical profession, the director of a newly-established mental hospital in Iceland declared that he was insane, whereupon Jónas immediately fired him. Jónas usually got the better of his opponents, but this deprived him of popularity. Thus this extremely able man found himself politically isolated from about 1932 for the rest of his long life, even within his own party, although he served as its chairman until 1944.

In 1934-9 the Progressives and Labour formed a coalition, called the Government of the Working Classes (Stjórn hinna vinnandi stétta). This was a replica of the "red-green" alliances in Scandinavia in these years, with the difference that there the labour parties had the leadership and were supported by the liberal-agrarian-centre parties, but here the leadership was in the hands of the far stronger Progressive Party. In 1939 the Independence Party was taken into the coalition in a so-called "National Government" (Þjóðstjórn), which nevertheless excluded the Socialists, and was in power until 1942. It was thus the task of the Progressive Party to steer Iceland through the Depression, which is the subject of the next chapter.

4.5 The Depression in Iceland

In the summer of 1930 the assumed millennium of the Icelandic Althing was celebrated at Þingvellir in the presence of Christian X, a number of foreign dignitaries and more than a quarter of the entire population of Iceland. This was a proud young nation reminding the world of its existence, as well as its cultural heritage. The event was the culmination of a period of prosperity and optimism, which had lasted in Iceland practically uninterrupted since the end of the First World War. Although Iceland had been removed from the harassments of the war, it could not escape an average annual inflation rate of 27% from 1914 to 1920, resulting in big cuts in real wages. By the end of this period the Icelandic króna was no longer equivalent to the Danish krone, although roughly their rates remained the same until the Second World War. After 1920 a period of declining prices set in – much more so in foreign goods than in Icelandic exports. Wages also fell but not on a comparable scale, so that the decade saw progress and rising living standards.

The worldwide Depression, which is traditionally said to have started with the great crash on the New York stock exchange in October 1929, put an end to this.[1] Already before the end of 1930 the effects of the Depression began to be felt in Iceland through a decreasing demand for Icelandic exports and hence falling prices. The total value of Icelandic exports fell from 74 million krónur in 1929 to 48 million in 1932, and was not to rise again to the pre-1930 level until after 1939. In these years Icelandic exports were made up of roughly speaking 90% marine products and 10% agricultural, so that the fall in export values hit these industries first and fishing hardest of all.

Difficulties in selling fish products for acceptable prices led the trawler owners to stop fishing periodically when it seemed least likely to pay off. Although agriculture was also hit, proportionally a much larger part of its market was within the country. Therefore agriculture was threatened by both falling export prices and the reduced purchasing power of the urban population, who were suffering from growing unemployment.

The recession within the fishing industry naturally caused widespread unemployment in the fishing towns and villages. Unfortunately there is

---

[1] A popular history of the Depression in Iceland is by Kjartan Jónasson (1986), but only its first volume has been published, covering the period until 1932. As before, *Hagskinna* (1997) is the main source of statistical information in this chapter.

little information about unemployment, particularly before the Depression years, but it is known that seasonally it had long been endemic, especially in December and January. In Chapter 4.3 above, it was calculated, admittedly on a rather meagre statistical basis, that in 1913 the average income of a working-class family in Reykjavík amounted to only three-quarters of the total annual wage of a male worker. Numbers registered by the trade unions in Reykjavík indicate that the seasonal unemployment rate in the town could reach 10-14% of the workforce in the worst years, even during the prosperous 1920s. In the Depression years, unemployment in Reykjavík ranged seasonally between 3 and 10%, according to official statistics – the unemployment figures collected by the trade unions are sometimes much higher, and show more than 20% in the autumn of 1932, a level never exceeded. In the early winters of 1935 and 1938 these numbers were down to 8-10% again.[2] This may not seem extremely serious by modern standards, but unemployed workers had no right to benefits and thus their situation was widely different from now.

The available statistics are practically restricted to Reykjavík, but the situation probably varied greatly in other towns and villages, from one place and season to another. There are revealing accounts of extreme shortages in some fishing villages – although they may not be literally true. It is said that the government decided to help the inhabitants of a fishing village in the east to start growing potatoes on a large scale and sent them seed-potatoes and timber for fences (supposedly on loan). But the villagers were so desperate that they burned the fence posts to cook the seed-potatoes.

Apart from such extreme cases, the problem of unemployment was dealt with mainly by two kinds of solution, which inevitably leads us back to the capital.

One of these was charity, which in Reykjavík was predominantly run by the Christian congregations. They ran soup-kitchens where people could get meals to eat on the spot or take home to their families. The other solution was public work, financed jointly by the state and local authorities. It was restricted to men and allocated to unemployed breadwinners according to their supposed need. The relief work of Reykjavík was partly carried out within the town, where the workers laid streets, sewers, etc. But partly it was performed in the southern lowland called Flói, where the workers dug ditches intended to drain new farmland – supposedly in order to lower the number of unemployed workers in the future. The place was nicknamed Siberia by the workers, who tried to keep a sense of humour while spending cold winter weeks there.[3] It was never of any use for farming, and it was doubted whether the land was sufficiently high above the nearby river to allow drainage.

[2] Magnús S. Magnússon (1985), 153-5.
[3] Jón Gunnar Grjetarsson (1988).

Although this public work seems rather insignificant, it was important enough to cause the most serious riot in the Depression years. There are several cases of minor acts of violence in connection with the class struggle during these years, but the disturbances on 9 November 1932 at the Good Templar house in Reykjavík, colloquially called Gúttó, were the worst.[4] The town council, where the Independence Party had an absolute majority, intended to cut the number of workers in the public work scheme and lower their wages, which in the eyes of the workers was just a preamble to a general cut in wages. On 9 November this proposal was to be discussed by the council at its meeting in Gúttó. When the meeting started on the stage in the hall at 10 o'clock in the morning, the house was already packed with people, and many more stood outside where a loudspeaker had been set up. All was peaceful until after a lunch break the police tried to restrict the number of people entering the house. The crowd then began to rush in, but a few policemen armed with clubs turned on them. The intruders in turn broke tables and benches to use as clubs. At two o'clock in the afternoon, the meeting was dissolved before any decision could be made.

The Labour representatives in the council, supported by the workers, demanded that the meeting be re-convened and a decision made to keep the wages intact. They therefore tried to prevent the council members of the Independence Party from leaving the house, but the police managed to help most of them out through a cellar door. A little later the police cleared the house with their clubs, but the workers responded by throwing stones at the house. Héðinn Valdimarsson, a Labour member of the council, was seen breaking chairs and handing the pieces out through a broken window for the workers to fight with. Now the fight continued outdoors and ended by leaving the entire police force of Reykjavík disabled: twenty-one policemen were hurt, and the remaining seven had fled. The town was in the hands of the workers.

Consequently the council gave up all plans for cutting wages or restricting public work in any way. Thus not only in this case but throughout the Depression the labour movement prevented cuts in wages. The salaries of civil servants were simply decided by law at this time, and they had to suffer a cut of 15%. Apart from this, the Depression years were on the whole favourable for those in full-time employment, because deflation continued at a similar rate as before until 1934 when prices began slowly to rise again.

In spite of widespread unemployment, the urban areas continued to grow through the Depression years, which naturally led to a serious shortage of housing. In a society that had recently forbidden the installation of apartments in basements (see Ch. 4.2), people considered themselves lucky if they could get one of these, and a previously unknown kind of slum emerged on the outskirts of Reykjavík and elsewhere.

[4] The affair is described in Ólafur R. Einarsson and Einar Karl Haraldsson (1977).

The problems of the industries were also treated in two basically different ways. One way was the organization of marketing. One typical solution was the the Union of Icelandic Fish Producers (Sölusamband íslenskra fiskframleiðenda), which was given by law a monopoly on the export of salted fish to prevent fish exporters from underbidding each other.[5] In these years the marketing of agricultural products was also organized in a way that in practice gave a monopoly to dairies run on a cooperative basis by the farmers and secured a common price for milk irrespective of where and in what form it was sold. This was an immense help to the farming community, but in the long run it certainly did not create the most efficient system of production in the dairy industry.

The other way of helping production in the country was, as in other countries, by protective tariffs and other import restrictions. In this way and with a special loan fund the Depression fostered in Iceland the manufacture of consumer goods such as furniture, shoes, margarine and sweets, which would never have thrived without protection. We noted earlier that only about 7% of the workforce were engaged in manufacturing, apart from fish-processing, at the onset of the Depression (Ch. 4.1). Ten years later that number had risen to 12%.

However, none of these measures helped the country much to get over the Depression, and we find in Iceland very little evidence of Keynes's economic cure – that the state should put more money in circulation. Devaluation of the currency would seem the most straightforward solution, since the problem was essentially low export prices, but the authorities were hesitant to use this remedy. The króna followed the English pound when it was devalued against gold in 1931, but it was not devalued further until 1939.

The Depression lasted longer in Iceland than in most other countries, at least the Nordic ones. This was not so much the fault of Icelandic economists as a result of the Spanish Civil War, breaking out in 1936 and practically closing the market for salt fish. From 1935 to 1939 the export of dried salt fish went down from 39,000 to 20,000 tons and the value from 17 to 11 million krónur. The immediate responses to this varied from year to year – for instance, increased export of uncured salted fish at a lower price. After the outbreak of the Second World War in 1939 the export to Britain of fresh fish on ice for soaring prices solved the problem for a while – the future solution, frozen fish fillets, was then only in its infancy.

Thus it was the Second World War that freed Iceland from the grip of the Depression, by the demand it produced for food in Britain. It also did so by providing a new kind of employment in the country, as we shall see in the next chapter.

[5] The export of salt fish from Iceland is discussed thoroughly in Valdimar Unnar Valdimarsson I-II (1997).

The war abolished the Depression itself but not the economic system which it had introduced in Iceland, with its restrictions on economic flows of all kinds. Imports were regulated, trade with foreign currency was monopolized by state-owned banks, and loan capital was largely distributed by state-regulated funds. This of course was in no way an Icelandic peculiarity during the Depression, or during the War, but in Iceland the restrictions remained in full force for almost thirty years – 1930-60.[6] In certain areas they are still with us in Iceland, although now almost all political forces are united in trying to get rid of them.

[6] Magnús S. Magnússon (1993), 200-14.

4.6 War and Occupation

It might have been expected that Iceland would easily fall prey to fascist ideology. The pride in its old Germanic culture, a predilection for ideas that were at least related to human eugenics (see Ch. 4.2), and of course a burning inferiority complex over being among the smallest of all nations might have provided fertile soil for ideas propounded by German Nazism. And indeed one finds in Iceland, as perhaps in all countries, sentiments that are unpleasantly reminiscent of Nazism. Even imperialism reared its head in the powerless Iceland of the 1920s and 1930s, when the idea of reclaiming Greenland as an old satellite of the country (see Ch. 1.4) gained considerable support.[1] However, as a political movement Nazism never gained any foothold in Iceland, having its best results in local elections in Reykjavík in 1934 – 2.8% support. In national elections it only had candidates in a few constituencies and never exceeded 5% support in any of them, while the Communists collected more than 8% nationally.[2]

There is no doubt of the sympathy of an overwhelming part of the Icelandic population for the Western Allies in the world war that broke out on 3 September 1939.[3] Nevertheless, the Icelandic authorities were determined to remain neutral as long as they could. Even after Denmark had been occupied by Germany on 9 April 1940, Iceland turned down Britain's offer of protection.[4] On the very day of the invasion of Denmark, the British consul general in Reykjavík delivered to the foreign minister of Iceland a declaration which stated that the British government would prevent Iceland from suffering the same fate as Denmark, and hoped to have the assistance of the government of Iceland in any necessary measure for that purpose. The government replied two days later and stuck strictly to the neutrality that had been proclaimed in 1918 (see Ch. 3.17).

On the other hand the Icelandic authorities were quick to clear up the constitutional complications that might ensue from the occupation of

---

[1] Jón Ólafur Ísberg (1989).

[2] For Nazism in Iceland, see Ásgeir Guðmundsson (1976).

[3] On Iceland in the Second World War, see the dissertation by Þór Whitehead (1978). Þór has published four books on the subject in Icelandic with a common subtitle, *Ísland í síðari heimsstyrjöld*, (1980), (1985), (1995) and (1999), but as yet they only go as far as 1940.

[4] On the political and, in particular, constitutional aspect of this story, see Björn Þórðarson (1951), 455ff.

Denmark. On 10 April the Althing declared the king unable to perform his constitutional duties, which were therefore assigned to the government of Iceland, together with foreign affairs and the protection of territorial waters.

Exactly a month later, at 4.a.m. on 10 May people in Reykjavík woke to the sound of aircraft. At that time such a sound was still sufficient reason to go out and look around, and those who did saw five or six naval vessels sailing towards the harbour. No flag could be seen on the ships, and for a while people were unsure whether they were German or British. The truth became known later in the morning when soldiers began to emerge from the ships and scatter around the town. They nailed on buildings and handed to early risers in the streets a declaration, in broken Icelandic, that a British force had landed in the town in order to be there before the Germans. A group of soldiers hurried to the residence of the German consul to arrest him and found him burning some documents in his bathtub. The army occupied a number of buildings in the town and used them throughout their occupation; among them was the National Theatre, then under construction. The most impressive hotel in the centre of Reykjavík, the Hótel Borg, became the headquarters of the occupation force.

The troops were accompanied by a British minister for Iceland. He went to see the cabinet and assured the ministers that Britain would not interfere in the government of Iceland. True to its formal neutrality, the government protested at the occupation, but by the afternoon it accepted the invitation of the new minister at the Hótel Borg. In the evening the prime minister addressed the nation over the radio and asked for the British soldiers to be looked upon as guests.

Soon the forces began to erect barracks in the town, wherever they found empty spaces. They also built an airfield on the outskirts which is still used for domestic flights. Further, the troops spread all over the country and built two more airfields – in Flói and in Hornafjörður – and a naval base in Hvalfjörður. The British force consisted of approximately 25,000 men, most of whom were stationed in Reykjavík and its surroundings.

In 1940 the German army reached the English Channel, and the British authorities felt that they could no longer afford to have such a large force stationed as far away as Iceland, which was obviously in no immediate danger of invasion. Therefore the idea emerged to hand the protection of the country over to the United States, which had not yet entered the war, but did everything possible that was compatible with their neutrality (and even more) to support Britain. From Iceland's point of view, Britain could not offer much security in the long run since the danger of a German invasion of Britain was obvious. On the other hand, Iceland still held on to its neutrality and was therefore reluctant to ask for protection. The Americans were also reluctant to violate their neutrality in such a blatant way, but were beginning to see Iceland as a militarily important outpost for the future. At last an agreement was reached between the governments of Iceland and the United States, through the mediation of Britain. Iceland agreed to entrust the United States with its protection on condition that the US force would leave the country as soon as the war was over. The first American soldiers came to Iceland on 7 July 1941. The Americans brought in a 60,000-strong force, which was generally much more active there than the British, who nevertheless kept some troops in Iceland until the end of the war. The Americans built a new airfield and a large military base in the Reykjanes peninsula near the fishing village of Keflavík, and both are still operational today.

The British army already needed more labour than Iceland could provide, and thus the problem of unemployment was solved. At the same time strong inflation set in. In the first years the prices of exports rose much faster than those of imports, mainly because of the strong demand for fish in Britain, so that terms of trade improved by 40% from 1939 to 1941. Still Icelandic authorities were extremely worried about the mutually interacting rise in prices and wages. In 1939, when the króna was devalued, it had been enacted by law that the ensuing price increases should be balanced in higher wages by half or up to two-thirds, but all further wage increases were forbidden. This was the beginning of price regulation of wages, which was to play a large part in the Icelandic economy for decades (see Ch. 4.12). From the beginning of 1941 wages were fully price-regulated, according to an agreement on the labour market, but the government attempted to halt the increases by means of complicated measures such as subsidies and price control. As this proved to have little effect and the inflation went on rising, the government issued a provisional act in January 1942, freezing all wages in principle at the 1941 level. This led the Labour Party minister to leave the government in protest, but the Progressive and Independence Parties had a secure majority in the parliament and did not change their policy.

The working class replied to the wage freeze by wildcat action – short illegal strikes of relatively few people at a time, without open instigation by the trade unions. These proved so successful that the government gave in and abolished the wage freeze in September. From then on throughout the war no attempt was made to stop wage increases by law, but for some reason the inflation practically stopped in 1944. It is likely that the success of the wildcat strikes in 1942 helped greatly to establish the more militant labour party, the Socialists, as a major political platform of the working class, as was reflected in its favourable election results in the autumn of 1942 (see Ch. 4.4). This was facilitated by the organizational divorce of the Federation of Labour and the Labour Party, which was accepted at a general meeting in 1940 and came into force in 1942. In that year the Labour Party lost its status as the principal labour party of Iceland.

During the first year of occupation, while the truce between the Soviet Union and Germany was still in being, the Socialists were openly hostile to the occupation force. Besides that, a militant labour party inevitably got into conflict with the army as the largest single employer in the country. The British repeatedly complained to the Icelandic authorities at the Socialist paper *Þjóðviljinn*'s agitation against the army, but to no avail. Finally, in April 1941, the occupation force suppressed the paper, arrested the editorial staff (which consisted of only three men), and held them in prison in London until July. This was the only serious political collision between the occupation forces and Icelanders, and it was solved by Hitler's invasion of Russia in 1941, which made the Icelandic Socialists and the foreign forces considerably more tolerant towards each other.

On the other hand, social collisions were endemic throughout the war, which was not surprising when the population of a town like Reykjavík was suddenly doubled by foreigners, mostly young men, many of whom felt little sense of responsibility towards the native population. Women and even girls as young as twelve were said to have relations with soldiers, and the director of public health talked about prostitution of the worst kind. A committee nominated by the minister of justice – and composed of men only – estimated that 20% of women in Reykjavík associated with soldiers. The police were reported to have registered more than 500 women, seventy-three under the age of sixteen, who had been in close contact with them. In 1942 two homes for wayward girls were opened, but they closed the very next year. For whatever reason, concern over these contacts dwindled in the following years.

There are basically two interpretations of these concerns felt by Icelandic men, and I believe that both are valid. One is that many Icelandic girls were in great danger, and some suffered serious injury, because of the abnormal social situation created by the foreign forces. The other is that the contacts were quite natural love relationships between young men and women, which often ended in happy marriages, and that Icelandic men were simply jealous and felt themselves outmanoeuvred by the more exciting strangers.[5]

Although Iceland did not participate in any warfare, it suffered considerable casualties resulting from the war. Approximately 230 lives were lost, which was little compared to Germany or Russia but proportionally comparable to the United States.[6] Most were killed on cargo and fishing vessels sunk by German aircraft, U-boats or mines. A strict ban on all weather reports also made sailing in the North Atlantic particularly hazardous. A few Icelanders, who were painfully ignorant of the rules of war, were shot by foreign soldiers in Iceland. One tried to drive his car without permission through their camp. Another, a twelve-year-old boy, twice climbed

---

[5] See Inga Dóra Björnsdóttir (1989)
[6] Þór Whitehead (1978), 249.

into the car of a soldier. German aircraft made a few attacks on Iceland, but without causing any casualties.

On the whole, though, the coexistence of the population and the foreigners was peaceful. But the tension between them became visible when the war ended. On Victory Day in Europe, 8 May 1945, when people in other countries danced in the streets, embraced and kissed, British sailors roamed round Reykjavík and, provoked by young Icelanders, broke window-panes, turned cars upside-down and fought the police with knives and clubs.

The end of the war also created new and unexpected problems in the political arena. Because of the favourable balance of payments, and because in Iceland only the banks were allowed to own foreign currency, credits in Icelandic ownership accumulated during the war in foreign banks. In the autumn of 1944, when people began to dare to envisage the end of the war, the opposite ends of the Icelandic party system, the Independence Party, the Labour Party and the Socialists, formed a government which they called the Innovation Government (Nýsköpunarstjórn), in order to guarantee that these credits would be used to modernize the fishing industry, for the mutual benefit of shipowners and workers. The prime minister – and simultaneously foreign minister – was Ólafur Thors, leader of the Independence Party and son of Thor Jensen, the founder of the large trawler firm Kveldúlfur. This government faced a task for which it was ill-prepared.

In March 1945, two months before the capitulation of Germany, the United States government suggested to Ólafur that the US military force should be allowed to remain in Iceland permanently.[7] Ólafur knew that this would not be popular either in his own nationalistic party or among the Socialists, who, despite the temporary alliance, looked on the United States as the hotbed of capitalism. So Ólafur asked the Americans to wait, and nothing happened for some months.

In the autumn of 1945 the United States government lost patience and sent the Icelandic government a formal request for permission to have three permanent bases in Iceland – at Keflavík airport, near Reykjavík airport and in Hvalfjörður. Then a committee was appointed by the Icelandic government and the parliamentary groups to discuss their reaction. Only the Socialist representatives were firmly opposed to the request, and as all others were undecided they had their way and a definite rejection was recommended.[8] If the security of Iceland was to be the subject of international negotiation, then it should take place within the newly-established United Nations.

In spite of this result, the Americans remained in the country through the winter and the following summer, but only with about 2,000 men.

---

[7] See Þór Whitehead (1976).
[8] Kristinn E. Andrésson (1977).

Although they had promised to leave immediately after the war, it could be maintained that it had not yet ended since no peace treaty had been concluded with Germany and the United States still had a large force in Europe. British troops left Iceland in the spring of 1946.

It was not until the late summer of 1946 that Ólafur Thors made a treaty with the United States government, whereby the American army was to leave Iceland, but because of their presence in Germany the Americans were allowed to keep staff and equipment at Keflavík airport for at least six and a half years in whatever quantity was deemed necessary. At the Althing the whole Independence Party supported this proposal and the whole Socialist Party opposed it, but the Progressive Party and Labour Party split on the issue. It was finally passed by 32 votes to 19. The Socialists then left the Innovation Government in great resentment, and many more looked on the so-called Keflavík Treaty as a harmful infringement of Iceland's neutrality.

The last American soldiers left Iceland in May 1947, but an aircraft company, Iceland Airport Corporation, took over the running of Keflavík airport, where some 600-1,000 Americans were to remain.[9] The world war was over in Iceland, but the country was trapped in a new, cold war to which we shall return later (Ch. 4.10).

[9] Jón Viðar Sigurðsson (1984).

4.7 Republic

As early as 1928, all parliamentary groups in Iceland proclaimed that their parties would support the termination of the Union Treaty of 1918 as soon as possible, and no later than the end of 1943.[1] The occasion for these declarations was a question put by an opposition member, seemingly as an attack on the Progressive Party government for relying on the support of Labour, which was supposed to be unreliable in its dealings with Denmark (see Ch. 4.4). However, the Labour spokesman seems to have outwitted the questioner when he declared that Labour would support the termination not only of the Treaty but also of the personal union; the party wanted a republic. The questioner replied that he did not want to discuss the constitutional arrangement after the termination, which did not affect the personal union.

In the following years, Iceland began to prepare in various ways for taking over its own foreign affairs; thus the Althing elected a standing committee to deal with them, and from 1934 a cabinet minister was appointed to oversee foreign affairs, among his other tasks. The declarations of 1928 were reiterated by the Althing of 1937 with a unanimous resolution. In the discussion the leader of the Independence Party, Ólafur Thors, stated clearly that the question of a personal union was unrelated to that of the Union Treaty. Therefore Denmark had every reason to expect the Union Treaty to be terminated in the 1940s, but only the representatives of socialist parties seemed to want the union dissolved altogether.

The war changed the expected procedure completely. As mentioned in the last chapter, the Althing temporarily dissolved the personal union on 10 April 1940 as soon as it was known that Denmark had succumbed to German occupation. This was the real end of the 560-year-old rule of the Danish Crown in Iceland. In the next year the arrangement was made more formal, when the post of regent (*ríkisstjóri*) was established by law to take over the king's role in Iceland's constitution. To this post the Althing elected Sveinn Björnsson, a former minister of Iceland to Denmark.

This decision was strictly unconstitutional, but it is difficult to see how Iceland could have acted in a more correct way under the circumstances. On the other hand, the Althing also used the war, together with the security provided by American protection, rather incautiously, playing a

---

[1] Björn Þórðarson (1951), 422ff.

dubious game with the democratic system of government. In the spring of 1941 it decided by a resolution to postpone general elections, which were due to take place in the summer, and prolong its own mandate for up to four years if necessary.

The politicians also left the country without any stable political leadership for most of the war years. Early in 1942 the National Government resigned because of internal disagreement. The Independence Party provisionally formed a minority government supported by the Labour and Socialist Parties. The force uniting these parties was the urgent need to alter the parliamentary election system in favour of a more equitable representation between political parties; the system had greatly benefited the Progressive Party (see Ch. 4.4). To bring about the constitutional change necessary for this reform a general election had to be held, and now the politicians were so unafraid of elections that they held no fewer than two in 1942.

After the second election the political leaders were unable to form a majority government, and in the end Regent Sveinn Björnsson formed an extra-parliamentary government, which remained in power for two years without any secure political majority behind it in the Althing. The party leaders thus took a political holiday when firm leadership was most needed.

At this time also, the permanent solution of the union question inevitably came up for discussion.[2] In 1940 a professor of law at the University of Iceland and an emerging top politician in the Independence Party, Bjarni Benediktsson, expressed in print his opinions on the union issue and made it clear that he expected the personal union to be terminated at the same time as the Union Treaty of 1918. Instead of a monarchy Bjarni suggested some kind of republic.[3] From then on, no one in Iceland seems to have doubted that the personal union was a part of the Union Treaty and would disappear with it.

In 1940 voices began to be heard in Iceland that the Treaty should be abrogated and a republic established as soon as possible, in spite of the regulations of the Treaty itself. But the British government, pressed by Denmark's minister in London, dissuaded the Icelandic authorities from such an action, which they considered illegal. The principal reason for Britain's stand was a fear that Germany would blame the action on the British and use it in propaganda against them. In this round the result was three resolutions passed almost unanimously by the Althing in May 1941, at the same time as the post of regent was established. The resolutions stated that since Denmark was unable to fulfil its part of the Union Treaty Iceland had acquired full right to sever the union with it; that the

[2] Apart from Björn Þórðarson's extensive account (1951), this story has been told, with the help of documentary material not available to Björn, in Icelandic by Þór Whitehead (1973) and in English by Sólrún B. Jensdóttir (1974).

[3] Bjarni Benediktsson (1940), 33-6.

Treaty would not be renewed after the end of the war; and that a republic would come into being when the union with Denmark was dissolved. A few days later the Danish government was presented with these resolutions.

In 1942, when the United States had taken over most of the military protection of Iceland, the issue of immediate formal separation came up again, this time seemingly on the initiative of the Independence Party. Since the constitution was being amended anyway to correct the representation at the Althing, the idea of turning it into a republican constitution became more and more tempting. In the election campaign in late May and early June all the parties supported the idea. However, the United States did not like it any better than Britain had the year before, and in June President Roosevelt sent a special envoy to Iceland to prevent the plan for immediate separation from going ahead. In the summer of 1942 opposition began to emerge within Iceland also, mainly based on ethical grounds. In July sixty-one prominent Icelanders sent a petition to the Althing and asked it not to make a final decision on the country's constitutional status before the two nations could discuss the matter freely.

Thus, in 1942 two opposite camps developed in Iceland. The so-called Legal Separatists (lögskilnaðarmenn) wanted to wait for the liberation of Denmark and appealed mainly to moral standards. The Quick Separatists (hraðskilnaðarmenn) refused to wait and pointed out that the result of the war might be a German-dominated Denmark, in which case it would be safer for Iceland to have left the union already. Even though this argument cannot be denied altogether, it seems obvious that the demand for an immediate separation was mainly a vote-catching tactic by politicians who had little idea how to deal with inflation or social problems but knew from history that the independence struggle was a key to popularity. All parties and all politicians seem to have been on the look-out not to be outbid by others on the issue.

Despite this, the Americans had their way. The constitutional amendment of 1942 was finally passed with the provision that the union could be dissolved and a republic established with a simple referendum, without a constitutional amendment being passed by two different Althings. After this, confirmation was obtained from the United States government that it would not object to a separation after the end of 1943, even if Denmark could not be consulted in advance.

This set the tone for a middle course between the arguments of the Legal Separatists and the Quick Separatists, which became the final result. In February-March 1944 the Althing unanimously agreed to the establishment of the republic. Only the Labour Party, which had shown a growing tendency towards legalism since 1942, had its reservations, but it accepted the proposal on the condition that no less than three whole years – the period intended for negotiations according to the Union Treaty – should pass from the day that Denmark had been notified of the Althing resolution in May 1941 and the referendum.

King Christian X made a final attempt to reverse the process and sent a telegram to Iceland expressing his hope that a republic would not be established while Denmark was occupied. This does not seem to have had much effect. In the referendum, which took place on 20-23 May, 98.6% of the electorate voted. Only 377 (0.5%) voted against dissolution of the Union Treaty – and it should be remembered that Danish citizens in Iceland were enfranchised – and 1,051 (1.4%) against the constitutional amendment. The former opponents of unilateral separation had clearly made a decision to participate in this momentous event.

The republic of Iceland was established at the ancient site of the Althing at Þingvellir on Jón Sigurðsson's birthday, 17 June 1944. People had already begun to gather there the day before and put up their tents. Some of them woke up drenched during the night: the rain was so heavy that the Axe River flooded the camp. The rain continued for most of the day, while a gale gathered force. The military forces forbade all talk about weather on the radio, but (as the story was told in my family) the announcer at Þingvellir could not refrain from describing how the flags were "soaked by the tears of heaven".

In spite of the weather, people flocked to Þingvellir. It was estimated that 25,000 people, one-fifth of the entire population, were present at 2 o'clock in the afternoon when the president of the Althing declared the republic established. The bells of the small Þingvellir church rang out and a minute's silence followed. I was not in the crowd at Þingvellir – only my eldest sister and eldest brother went there – but the family listened to the ceremony on the radio. I remember only the silence perhaps because at that moment one of my older brothers, who had not been warned of it, came into the living-room and asked for something that he wanted.

After this the Althing meeting at Þingvellir elected a president of the republic provisionally for one year, since there was no time for the constitutional national election. The result must have been an unpleasant reminder of the fragility of the national solidarity as expressed by the minute's silence. Regent Sveinn Björnsson was elected, but only by 30 votes. The office head of the Althing got five votes and fifteen were void. The ballot was secret, but it is generally considered that opposition to Sveinn came partly from the Socialists and partly from a large minority of the Independence Party who still resented the fact that he had formed an extra-parliamentary government in 1942.

After the election, the festivities went on with speeches and addresses. The first of the foreign representatives to speak was from the United States, but the Soviet representative kept silent, obviously envisaging that the United States was about to acquire a new ally. What caused the greatest relief in the assembly was when the prime minister came to the rostrum and read a telegram containing congratulations from King Christian X.

The constitution of the republic was much the same as the previous one, with the word "king" substituted by "president". The only difference in the power of the sovereign was that the president was not even formally vested with an absolute veto against a new law. If a president refuses to sign a law, it none the less becomes valid provisionally and its permanent validity is decided on in a referendum. This has never occurred, and the presidents of Iceland have never exercised any major political power, nor have they been intended to by their voters. The choice has never fallen on a major political figure belonging to a major political party. The successors of Sveinn Björnsson (1944-52) have been, roughly speaking, of two kinds. Two have been former politicians, Ásgeir Ásgeirsson (1952-68) from Labour, and Ólafur Ragnar Grímsson (1996-) a former leader of the People's Alliance, but of course neither would have been elected if they had been seen as representatives of their relatively small parties. Two of the presidents have been known not as politicians but as cultural figures and personalities: the National Museum director Kristján Eldjárn (1968-80) and the former theatre director Vigdís Finnbogadóttir (1980-96).

4.8 Postwar Politics

The hegemony of the four political parties, described in Chapter 4.4, has remained mostly intact since the war. The Independence Party has remained the centre of gravity on the right and the largest of all parties through all elections, normally with 37-42% of the vote.[1] In spite of a decreasing rural population, the originally rural Progressive Party has in most elections kept its status as the second largest party, with 19-28% support. When it was established in 1956 the People's Alliance inherited from the Socialist Party a position on the far left of the spectrum and as the third-largest party. It has kept both in most elections, usually with 14-20% support. To its right the Labour Party has normally had 11-18% support. In the elections of 1999 a serious attempt was made to bring about a radical change in the party system. The Labour Party, the People's Alliance and the Women's Alliance formed an electoral alliance called Samfylkingin (the Alliance), but it did no more than reasonably well, with 27% of the vote. To its left a new political organization emerged: Vinstrihreyfingin, grænt framboð (Left Green Movement). Thus, in the elections the four-party system seems to have been restored rather than abolished.

The system has remained remarkably stable. It can hardly be argued that any party has been on the offensive or defensive through the period. When something extraordinary has happened, as in the 1978 elections when Labour and the People's Alliance won 22 and 23%, respectively and the Progressives only 17%, the old balance has been restored before long. On the other hand, the discrepancy between voter support and representation has been abolished in successive stages. The largest change was made in 1959 with the abolition of one/two-member constituencies, coinciding with districts (*sýslur*) and towns (*kaupstaðir*). Instead the country was divided into eight constituencies, with five to twelve representatives in each and proportional representation in all of them. This system is now being revised and still larger constituencies are being established in the more sparsely populated parts of the country. The Althing now consists of sixty-three representatives sitting in one house.

Many groups and parties other than the four permanent ones have participated in elections in the postwar years. Most have been splinter

---

[1] In addition to *Hagskinna* (1997), 878-81 (table 19.2), see *Hagskýrslur Íslands* III:31 (1995), on election results, together with newspapers for 1999.

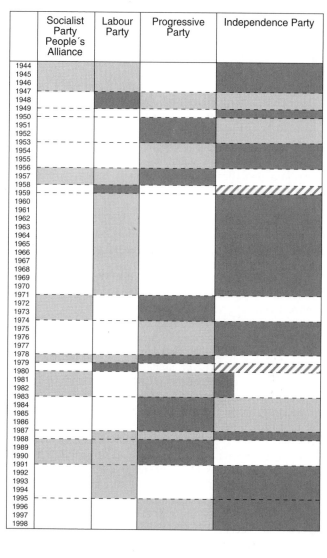

Fig. 4.8-1 Governing coalitions in Iceland, 1944–1998.

groups from one of the four parties, and some have acquired up to 10 % of the vote. But the only challenge to the four-party system that has been represented at the Althing for more than two parliamentary terms is the Women's Alliance, which has survived since 1983 and will be discussed in more detail in Chapter 4.13.

In Scandinavia it has been common for the largest party, normally the Social Democrats, to form minority governments with the permanent support of another party. After the Progressive Party government of 1929-31, which was supported by Labour, this pattern has never been followed in Iceland; therefore the party system constantly demands coalition governments. In democratic countries with a multi-party system it is usual for adjoining parties in a horizontal party system to form coalitions together. It is an exception if a party skips over a neighbouring party in search of a coalition partner. As we have seen (Ch. 4.4), Iceland mostly conformed to this rule in the interwar years, but during and after the Second World War the exceptions have been more common than the rule. In the Innovation Government of 1944-7[2] even the outer wings of the horizontal party system cooperated in a government. That has not happened again except arguably in 1980-3, but with that exception coalitions have been formed in every possible way. On the whole three coalition configurations have divided the postwar years between them.

The first consists of the right wing and centre, the Independence and Progressive Parties, which have formed coalitions that governed the country for approximately eighteen years or one-third of the postwar period at the time of writing. This grouping conforms to the rule of adjoining parties, and these two combined have nearly always enjoyed a parliamentary majority. The parties have repeatedly attempted to use this position to rule the country between them, but only twice, in 1950-6 and from 1995 up to the time of writing, did the cooperation outlast an electoral term of four years.

In spite of its apparent strength, this kind of coalition has suffered from two major weaknesses. One is the relative weakness of these parties within the labour movement. Every right-centre government has run the risk of having to deal with a united labour opposition, which has been extremely unfortunate in the unstable economic atmosphere of postwar Iceland. The other weakness of the coalition pattern is the very strength of the parties, especially in the rural constituencies. There they have formed the two principal alternatives in the eyes of most voters, which fits badly with close and lasting cooperation. However, these two parties ruled together after the 1995 election under the successful Independence Party

---

[2] As is customary in Iceland, although the prime minister resigned in 1946 the government was in power until a new one had been formed in February 1947. The basic source of information on the governments of Iceland – and indeed on the official, formal history of Icelandic politics 1904-64 – is Agnar Kl. Jónsson (1969).

leader Davíð Oddsson. They have not yet had serious difficulties with the labour movement and seem to get on better than ever before, perhaps because of the decreasing importance of the rural vote. So we may be seeing the start of a new era in Icelandic coalition politics. This is made still more likely by ongoing merger plans among the opposition parties.

Secondly, governments involving a coalition of the left wing and centre, the People's Alliance and the Progressive Party, have been formed five times in the postwar years, but their combined period only covers some twelve years. In each case these two parties have needed a third partner to form a majority government, and in three coalitions, covering about half the period, that third partner was the Labour Party. Once (1971-4) a splinter group positioned between the People's Alliance and Labour played this part, and once (1980-3) a fraction of the Independence Party did so. On the whole the instability and sometimes reluctance of the third partner has been the weak spot of these coalitions, rather than difficulties of cooperation between the People's Alliance and the Progressives.

Thirdly, the absence of Labour from two of the left-centre coalitions, and its reluctance to proceed in others, is due to a peculiar feature of Icelandic politics, which appears most clearly in the cooperation of Labour and the Independence Party. In 1959 they formed the only long-lived coalition that has been in power in Iceland, the so-called Restoration Government (Viðreisnarstjórn). It lasted uninterrupted for three electoral terms, until 1971 when it lost its parliamentary majority in elections. In 1991-5 an attempt was made to repeat the success of the Restoration Government, but this time it only lasted one term. In addition to these coalitions, the cooperation of Labour and the Independence Party includes two short-lived minority governments, formed by Labour but supported by the Independence Party, in 1958-9 and 1978-9. Thus governments based on the cooperation of parties that would be expected to form the basic opposition in the party politics of most democratic countries have ruled Iceland for approximately eighteen years during the postwar period.

In terms of a purely horizontal left-right party spectrum the Icelandic coalition system displays in two ways an outstanding peculiarity which violates the rule of adjoining parties: the relative proximity of the People's Alliance and the Progressive Party, and of the Labour Party and the Independence Party. The most important reason for this peculiarity may lie in a basic paradox that faces modern Icelandic society. On the one hand, it is so small that it must often doubt its potentiality to stand on its own feet, and is bound to feel a strong need for the cooperation and goodwill of other countries. On the other hand, its smallness also puts it in overwhelming danger of being swamped by its neighbours, their cultures and their economic systems. This applies no less to friendly neighbours than to potentially hostile or oppressive ones.

Because of this, many of the most burning and controversial questions of Icelandic politics cannot be represented by a purely horizontal party system. Therefore, the new party system, which had been modelled on that of our larger and more powerful neighbours, tended to take in the oppositions of integration versus isolation, which are basically those represented by the older party system of the period of struggle for independence (see Ch. 3.17). In this way Iceland developed a party system that was two-dimensional.[3]

The Socialist Party never fitted well into this system, since its attitude towards other countries depended on their assumed position on a left-right political axis. Nevertheless, its fierce struggle against the Keflavík Treaty in 1946 (see Ch. 4.6) no doubt set the course for a new and much more nationalistic policy. Its descendant, the People's Alliance, adopted an independent attitude towards the Eastern bloc and among the Icelandic parties became the staunchest protagonist of national values and national independence. On the other hand, in its defence of the Keflavík Treaty the Independence Party developed into a determined supporter of cooperation with the Western powers, not least the United States. Hence it became the stronghold of integration policy in Iceland, although of course there was never any talk of abandoning the formal independence finally attained in 1944.

Thus the same parties occupied the farthest extremes on both the horizontal and the vertical policy axes. On the other hand, the Progressive Party, with its roots in rural and supposedly traditional and national culture, has tended more towards an isolationist policy than the Labour Party, which after all is part of an international movement. This is the basic reason for the apparent peculiarities in the coalition configurations in Iceland. The People's Alliance and the Progressive Party, on the one hand, and the Labour Party and the Independence Party, on the other, are closer to each other on the vertical axis than on the horizontal one.

Some decisions concerning international cooperation have had the support of all political forces. Thus Iceland's participation since 1946 in the United Nations and many of its institutions has never been seriously challenged. Similarly all political parties have supported participation – together with the four mainland Nordic countries, Denmark, Norway, Sweden and Finland – in numerous Nordic institutions of which the Nordic Council, established in 1952, is the most comprehensive.[4] Other foreign policy issues have been extremely controversial. Two of them will be discussed below – the question of defence (Ch. 4.10) and that of extension of the fisheries limit (Ch. 4.11) – and in both cases we shall see clear manifestations of the vertical policy axis in action.

---

[3] The idea of a two-dimensional party system is proposed by Ólafur R. Grímsson (1982), but is developed somewhat differently here.

[4] Icelanders do not normally see their country as part of Scandinavia, although it is

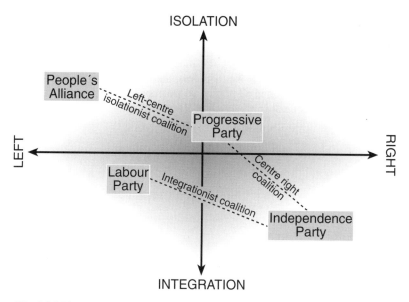

Fig. 4.8-2 The two-dimensional party system and dominant coalition configurations of postwar Iceland.

In some cases Labour has proved even more internationalist than the Independence Party, particularly over European integration towards which Iceland began hesitantly to proceed in 1970 when it became a member of the European Free Trade Association (EFTA). EFTA, established in 1960, was a major organization of states that stood outside the European Community (EC) until Britain, Denmark and Ireland entered the EC in 1973. Iceland's entry into EFTA was proposed by the Restoration Government of Labour and the Independents and passed in the Althing with their votes, and those of two opposition members, against the votes of the People's Alliance, while the Progressives abstained. Few then considered entry into the European Community but in the 1990s most of the EFTA states, including Iceland, joined the European Economic Area, while some went all the way into the EC.

This means that Iceland has now mostly a common market for goods, services, labour and capital with the whole European Union. Only fishing within the Icelandic fisheries limit and investment in the Icelandic fishing industry is reserved to Icelanders alone.

---

undoubtedly a Nordic (*norrænt*) country. In Icelandic the term Scandinavian (*skandinavískur*) does not necessarily refer to Finland either, but only to Denmark, Norway and Sweden. Apart from the five independent states, three semi-independent countries, Greenland, Faroe and Åland, participate in Nordic cooperation.

When, in the early 1990s, Sweden and Finland entered the European Community and Norway rejected membership only narrowly in a referendum, the Labour Party officially adopted a policy of supporting full Community membership, which the Independence Party and the more isolationist parties rejected. Nevertheless, there are of course supporters of European integration in all parties, so we may well have here the great controversy of Icelandic politics in the years to come.

4.9 The Welfare State

The extensive social services that developed in Iceland in the first half of the 20th century were mostly run by official institutions and were free for all. The law of 1907 institutionalizing primary education explicitly decreed that it should be delivered free of charge. From then on, free education has been the principle at all stages, paid by the state and/or the communes in various and changing ways. There have never been many private schools in Iceland, and those mostly rely on state financing.

Most medical doctors, ever since the beginning of the organized health service in the late 18th century, have been civil servants – although they were allowed to charge patients for their services – and most hospitals came to be run as official institutions, or at least were financed by taxes. Health insurance was initially run by funds with voluntary membership, but it has gradually developed into a universal state-run insurance system. This way of building up the social services of education and health care was probably modelled largely on Denmark, and was never seriously questioned in Iceland.

A few very minor measures of social insurance were introduced by law in the late 19th and early 20th centuries.[1] Already in 1890 the establishment of funds for the maintenance of old and infirm working people was enforced by law, but in reality the main purpose seems to have been to relieve the communes and thus the taxpaying farmers of the burden of supporting childless rural workers in their old age. Instead the workers themselves were taxed to finance their own old-age pension. In 1903 a law was passed on life insurance for fishermen on decked vessels – two-thirds financed by the fishermen themselves and one-third by their employers. This was gradually extended, and in 1925 a general industrial injuries insurance for most workers, except those in rural areas, was introduced, financed exclusively by the employers.

However, it was not until 1936 that comprehensive legislation on social services was enacted in Iceland. This was initiated by the Government of the Working Classes (see Ch. 4.4) and the first Labour Party minister in the country, Haraldur Guðmundsson. By this law social insurance was united in a new State Social Security Institute (Tryggingastofnun

[1] The history of welfare services in Iceland has been told in *Félagsmál á Íslandi* (1942), by Jón Blöndal and Sverrir Kristjánsson (1954) and by Stefán Ólafsson (1989, 1993).

ríkisins). The Institute was intended to operate in four departments: injury insurance, health insurance, old age and disability pensions, and unemployment benefits. However, the operation of unemployment insurance depended on the establishment of special funds, financed mainly by the workers themselves, and no trade union would establish a fund on such terms. The other kinds of insurance were financed by contributions from the state, communes and premiums, according to varying rules, and paid according to individual applications.

The arrangement was no doubt of great help for many of those who were in greatest need, but on a national scale it did not distribute a very large sum of money by the standards of later times. The expenditure of the whole system was only 1.3 million krónur in 1937 and increased to almost 10 million in 1946 (at a time of high inflation). This amounts to a constant part of the gross national product (GNP): *c.* 0. 6%, but it meant a decreasing share of total state expenditure, from 7 to 4%.[2]

The next decisive step was made on the initiative of the Innovation Government at the end of the Second World War. The Labour Party agreed to participate in the coalition in 1944 with the Independence Party and the Socialists on condition that the government introduced a system of social insurance equal to the best in the world (they probably had in mind the systems introduced by social-democratic governments in Scandinavia). A new law on the subject was enacted in 1946 and came into force at the beginning of 1947 introducing the principle of universal insurance wherever it was applicable: everyone in a given social situation was entitled to benefits without having to apply for them and without means-testing. Everyone aged sixty-seven or more was to receive retirement pension, irrespective of need. All families with four or more children (more common then than now) were to receive family benefits. At the same time the benefits paid previously were increased considerably. Thus the cost of the system rose from 10 million krónur in 1946 to 39 million in 1947, 2 % of the GNP and over 10% of total state expenditure.

The 39 million krónur only included money distributed through the State Social Security Institute. In 1947 almost double that amount, or 71 million, was counted as social security and welfare expenditure of the public sector (state and communes). In a still wider sense social affairs and services such as education, health, housing and cultural affairs cost the public sector 196 million krónur in 1947 or almost 44% of its total expenditure.

This proportion has grown slowly and not at all constantly in the postwar years. In 1990 it had reached 56%. Of course, the activity of social services has multiplied in this period: for example, between 1944 and 1990

---

[2] *Hagskinna* (1997), 703 (table 14.1), 708 (table 14.4), 737 (table 15.4), 746 (table 15.9), 787 (table 16.5). In the following, most of the statistical information, until 1990, comes from *Hagskinna*; for the following years, from the yearbook *Landshagir*.

the number of days of hospital stay increased from 400,000 to 1.3 million and pupils in upper secondary schools increased from 2,700 to 17,200. But the social services have only multiplied at roughly the same rate as other activities in the society. The system was already there by the end of the war.

However, two structural changes in the Icelandic welfare system in this period are worth mentioning. One was the introduction of unemployment insurance in 1956 as a part of the settlement after a six-week strike of general workers in Reykjavík and its neighbourhoods the previous year. The fund was financed by premiums from employers and allocations from communes and the state. The expenditure of the fund has, of course, fluctuated dramatically: during the first nine years of the Unemployment Insurance Fund it never spent more than one million krónur annually in benefits, but in 1969 it paid out 124 million. In 1990 it paid one billion new krónur, or one-twelfth of the total benefits paid by the State Social Security Institute.

The other major novelty, which was less sudden, was the day care of children under school age. In 1940 six day-care institutions with 317 children were registered in the country. No statistics are available for later developments, but in 1973 the number of institutions had risen to sixty-five and of children to almost 4,000. At that time day care was almost exclusively the privilege of children of single mothers and students, and even for them the waiting list could be long. In 1990 the number of children had surpassed 11,000, which means that about one in two children aged between one and six years received some kind of day care. Since then the number has gone up still more. If we only count the 3-5 age-group, almost 85% had day care in 1996. Most communes now consider it a priority to be able to offer day care to all parents who want it.

Day care is not free like compulsory education, but it is substantially subsidized so that the system now offers the most important kind of family benefits. Not least, it offers mothers the previously rare freedom of keeping their jobs and proceeding with their careers while their children are young. Of course, mothers have always been on the labour market in Iceland, and single mothers had few other ways of surviving. But while many housewives still stayed at home it was relatively easy to find grandmothers or other helpful women to take care of children. Nowadays, most women go to work outside their homes. In 1997, 84% of Icelandic women in the 25-64 age-group, as compared with 96% of men, had some income from work. This development necessitated the growth of the day care system, and has been facilitated by it.

It was the intention of the Innovation Government that Iceland should reach an equal footing with Scandinavia in social services. It seems as if this aim was almost achieved in the following years, measured by expenditure on welfare, including social insurance, unemployment benefits and health care. In 1950 Iceland was admittedly at the bottom among the

Nordic states, spending 6.3% of its GNP on welfare, but Norway spent only 6.5% and Sweden topped the list with 8.3%. Later however, Iceland lagged well behind: in 1987 its welfare expenditure was only 17%, while the other Nordic states had increased their to 26-36% of GNP. Only in the health service was Iceland about average, while in all other aspects it was the lowest. The difference lay partly in the lower demand in Iceland: old-age pensions and unemployment benefits were less, partly because the population was younger and because there was less unemployment. More surprising is the fact that Iceland spent less on family benefits than all other Nordic countries, while its birth rate was the highest. Of course, these numbers can never be exactly comparable, but everyone familiar with the services offered to families with young children in Scandinavia and in Iceland knows that this difference is very real. Therefore, it is of interest that the conditions in Iceland do not seem to dissuade people from having children. The connection seems to be the other way round: more babies make the need to help parents less apparent to the authorities.

In expenditure on education also, Iceland seems far behind all countries that we want to be compared with. In a comparison of thirteen states in 1984 it proved to be the last-but-one with only West Germany lower – due, it is said, to an unusually high participation by private industry in vocational and technical education.

In spite of these shortcomings one can argue that on the whole the Icelandic welfare system has been successful. The population increased by just over 100% between 1945 and 1995, from 130,000 to 268,000. Net emigration has been light; in 1961-90 it averaged only around some forty-eight persons annually. A male Icelander born in 1990 had a life expectancy of seventy-five years and a female 80.1 years – figures that are among the world's highest. The Icelander has also been growing physically: in the late 1930s the average adult male was 173.6 cm. tall and the female 159.2 cm. In the late 1980s he was 5.8 cm. and she 7.1 cm. taller. These are all healthy signs, but one may wonder whether the standard of the society can be kept up in future without the best possible education.

These tasks are basically the same in all countries. In addition each country has its own dangers to security that the welfare state has to meet in its own way. For Icelanders throughout the centuries the sea represented the most imminent danger, and the technical revolution of the 20th century has not altogether removed it. Nowadays, however, many more people die in car accidents than at sea.

On land, a volcanic eruption in the Westman Islands in 1973 was the largest natural catastrophe during the history of the welfare state in Iceland. On a night in January the earth opened only about 200 metres from the edge of a town with some 5,000 inhabitants. Within a few hours the cleft had extended almost right through the island. Luckily, nearly all the fishing fleet was in the harbour, the weather was good, and the entire island was evacuated during the night and early morning. A part of the town later disappeared under lava, and all of it was buried in black volcanic ash. After the end of the eruption in June, the town was cleaned up and later partly rebuilt. Within a decade it had almost reached its former population.

The eruption caused a mental shock to many people and great economic damage, but it took no lives and with generous help from many countries people were largely compensated for their economic losses. Afterwards it is difficult to see the traces of the eruption in the economic statistics of Iceland. Measured in casualties, snow avalanches have caused much more harm in Iceland during the last decades than the eruption. Many fishing villages were originally built on sandbanks in the fiords. When the villages expanded, houses were often built too close to mountains which can collect great masses of snow in the winter. In 1974 twelve people lost their lives in an avalanche in the eastern town Neskaupstaður. In 1995 two major avalanches in fishing villages in the Western Fiords took thirty-four lives – fourteen in Súðavík in January and twenty in Flateyri in October – and destroyed a number of houses.

It has been introduced as a principle in Iceland that people should be compensated as far as possible for all major damage caused by natural catastrophes. For that purpose special legislation has been enacted which is entirely separate from the private insurance system and the state social security system described above.

4.10 Iceland in a Cold War

The reluctance of the Americans to leave Iceland at the end of the Second World War (see Ch. 4.6) indicated a new attitude towards the country and at the same time a complete reorientation of Iceland in the political universe. Before the war it had been politically attached to Denmark but virtually within Britain's military sphere of influence. During the war the last formal ties with Denmark were broken and the United States succeeded Britain as the great power that would not let anyone else get a foothold in the country. The difference was that the British had remained quiet about their interest in Iceland in peacetime, whereas the Americans wanted to be constantly present there and found extreme difficulty in understanding what objection the Icelanders could have to their presence. In 1945 the US minister to Iceland complained to his chief about "the peculiar independence complex" of the Icelanders.[1]

In the minds of the Icelanders, on the other hand, neutrality and defencelessness were an essential part of the national self-image, closely connected to the image of independence. Iceland had, of course, always been without any reliable military defence and, further, the introduction of sovereignty in 1918 had included a declaration of undefended neutrality (Ch. 3.17). This was why Iceland rejected America's request for permanent military bases in the country at the end of the war.[2]

A further sign of America's interest in Iceland appeared in Marshall Aid, which it launched in order to revive the economies of Europe after the war and prevent the progress of communism in a poverty-stricken continent.[3] Iceland had gained immensely from the war in financial terms and lost very little that could be compensated for by money. Thus the Icelanders did not at first expect to receive any financial help through the Marshall Plan. However, Icelandic politicians and officials soon began to smell money if they bypassed the experts at the Organization for European Economic

---

[1] Þór Whitehead (1978), 306.

[2] A considerable literature exists in English on the defence issue of Iceland in the post-war years, most of it written from the American standpoint or that of their allies in Iceland: Nuechterlein (1961); Benedikt Gröndal (1971); Þór Whitehead (1998). In Icelandic the most recent and most comprehensive survey, up to 1960, is Valur Ingimundarson (1996).

[3] Gunnar Á. Gunnarsson (1996) has written most recently about Iceland's part in the Marshall Plan.

Cooperation (OEEC) and negotiated direct with the American authorities. In this way they managed to secure for Iceland almost twice as much in direct help per capita as any other country. In 1948-52 every Icelander received on average 209 US dollars, while the war-harassed Dutch came a poor second with 109 dollars.

As the Marshall dollars were streaming into Iceland, the Cold War intensified, and after the Communist coup in Czechoslovakia in 1948 the Western powers on both sides of the Atlantic decided to establish a defence union. At the beginning of 1949 Iceland was invited to participate, and in late March the founding treaty of the prospective North Atlantic Treaty Organization (NATO) was submitted by the government to the Icelandic Althing.[4] Participation was supported by the three-party government of the Independence Party, the Progressives and Labour, but the Socialists opposed it strongly and bitterly. There was also considerable opposition among the Progressives and Labour. The decision to join NATO led to conflicts which give some idea the bitterness of disagreements on the issue.

Since February the Independence Party had secretly collected together a group of young men who were to be ready to assist the police in defending the Althing should an attempt be made to prevent it from passing the treaty. At the last moment the group was put under the command of the chief of police of Reykjavík, and on 30 March, when the second and final reading on the resolution was to take place, it was secretly placed in the Althing building and issued with helmets and clubs.

At the same time the opponents held a meeting in the neighbourhood of the Althing, and when the meeting was dissolved at half past one in the afternoon, people marched on the Althing and began to throw eggs, mud and stones at the building. The Althing passed the resolution by 37 votes to 13 (ten Socialists, two Labour MPs and one Progressive opposed it; two Progressives abstained) as stones and broken glass hurtled through the room.

The attack became even more violent after the result was announced. Then the secret force of volunteers was suddenly let out and ordered to clear the square in front of the building. This of course meant a tough fight between the two groups, which did not end until the police cleared the area with tear-gas. Three policemen were seriously injured and some twelve other people needed medical help. Twenty people were later given prison terms for their part in the attack, but the sentences were never enforced.

In submitting the NATO treaty to the Althing, the government declared that it had reached an agreement with the United States that Iceland would not have to receive foreign military forces in peacetime, and when the foreign minister, Bjarni Benediktsson from the Independence Party, signed

[4] On Iceland's entrance into NATO, see Baldur Guðlaugsson and Páll Heiðar Jónsson (1976).

the NATO treaty on Iceland's behalf, he made an oral reservation to the same effect. However, this proved to be of no lasting value. In the very next year, the United States embroiled itself in a fierce war against Communist forces in Korea, and many people believed that the Third World War was near. Rumours began to spread that the Americans would station military forces in Iceland again, and on 7 May 1951 they were confirmed. Just before 5 a.m. large transport aircraft began to land at Keflavík airport, fifteen of them within an hour. In the morning the government announced that two days earlier it had made a treaty with the US government whereby the latter took over the military defence of Iceland and would be allowed to station forces in the country for that purpose. The Althing was not sitting when this happened, but all its members except the Socialists, who were considered unreliable, had been consulted in advance and had accepted the treaty according to the government. When the treaty was submitted to the Althing in the autumn, one representative of the Progressive Party abstained from voting, but only the Socialists voted against.

The Americans brought a 3-4,000-strong force to Iceland and stationed most of it at Keflavík airport. Originally the base was run by the air force, since its main purpose was to secure intermediate landings between America and Europe in case of Soviet aggression in Europe. But in 1961 the navy took over the base because it now had the new task of monitoring Soviet submarines in the North Atlantic.

The force helped to create an economic boom in Iceland after the rather depressed postwar years. While it was building up the base, it provided more than 2,000 jobs, quite well paid by Icelandic standards. A large firm of contractors, Iceland Prime Contractor Co. (Íslenskir aðalverktakar), was set up and given the monopoly of all construction work for the force; it was owned jointly by the state, a private firm of contractors and the Federation of Icelandic Cooperatives. Thus it seemed to mirror the interests of the government and its constituent parties: the Independence Party representing private enterprise, the Progressive Party supporting the cooperative movement, and both wanting to support the treasury. At one point some 15% of Iceland's foreign currency earnings came from the force. In 1956 the workforce needed at the base decreased substantially, and since then 1,000-1,800 Icelanders have had jobs created by the military force. Since 1959 its contribution to export income has usually been around 4-8%.[5]

This of course is a considerable factor in Iceland's economy, but compared to the large economic fluctuations which Iceland has had to live with, it is certainly not a vital one. In a year of good catches and high export prices for fish products, the departure of the force would not be felt

[5] Ingimundur Sigurpálsson (1976); *Hagskinna* (1997), 402 (table 9.5). The figures only go up to 1990, but nothing drastic has happened since then.

seriously except in the Keflavík area. This is important because it was by no means taken for granted in Iceland that the force had come to stay. In the first years the soldiers enjoyed practically unlimited freedom of movement in the country and were quite conspicuous in restaurants and at dances in Reykjavík. Various kinds of corruption, such as smuggling and prostitution, were said to thrive around the force. Many people feared that such a large foreign population would spoil the national culture, language and traditions. Also, rather than protecting Iceland in a nuclear war, the base was thought likely to attract an attack, which would probably kill somewhere between 2.5% and 50% of the population, depending on the weather at the time.[6]

The Socialist Party was not an acceptable forum for all opponents of the force, since it was constantly suspected of letting its communist sympathies govern its policy. Therefore a new party was established, the National Preservation Party (Þjóðvarnarflokkur Íslands), which gained 6% of the vote and two representatives (out of fifty-two) in the 1953 elections. At the same time the opposition increased in strength within Labour and particularly the Progressive Party. In 1956 the Progressives left their coalition with the Independence Party and made an electoral pact with Labour. Together they hoped to gain an absolute majority by playing on the electoral system in a rather dubious way, which is too complicated to explain here. This alliance had on its programme an end to the US military presence in Iceland but remaining within NATO. The programme did away with the National Preservation Party. However, the electoral pact did not manage to get a parliamentary majority, but after the elections it formed a government with the People's Alliance, which had recently succeeded the Socialist Party. Among other ambitious tasks, which will be discussed later (Ch. 4.11), this government promised to free the country of the defence force. This plan was soon abandoned by the Progressives and Labour, and the Soviet attack on Hungary in the autumn of 1956 was used as justification for the change of policy. But, as has recently been revealed, the government seems to have sold the issue for a much-needed and favourable loan from the United States and West Germany, raised through the agency of NATO.[7]

From then on and through the 1960s – the period of the Restoration Coalition of Labour and the Independence Party (see Ch. 4.8) – the defence treaty with the United States had a secure majority in the Althing. But among the Icelandic population the opposition did not seem to be on the retreat, and new problems arose. With the permission of the Icelandic authorities the base began television broadcasting which could be received by more than half the country's population. When this happened

---

[6] Helgi Hannesson (1980), 25.

[7] Valur Ingimundarson (1996), 293-362.

no Icelandic television existed, so that a foreign military force had the monopoly of this new and powerful medium which was entering more and more Icelandic homes. Intellectuals of all parties (except Socialists who were excluded for tactical reasons) reacted strongly against this, but the politicians did not dare to bar transmissions. Instead the Icelandic National Broadcasting Service (Ríkisútvarpið) started television broadcasting in 1966, with extremely meagre means, and only when it had been running for some years was the American television restricted to the base area.

During their long opposition period in the 1960s the Progressives adopted their anti-force policy again, so when the opposition – the Progressives, the People's Alliance and a small third party – gained a working majority in elections in 1971, they inevitably formed a government with the departure of the force on its agenda. However, only the representatives of the People's Alliance proved to be without exception wholeheartedly in favour of the policy. The termination of the treaty was postponed with the justification that the extension of fishing limits must come first (see Ch. 4.11). In 1974 the government lost its majority.

Since then no government has ever had the departure of the defence force on its programme. Even though this has been a constant plank of the People's Alliance, the party has repeatedly participated in governments that have not adopted it on their programme. This would have been impossible for the party leadership to do in the 1960s or early '70s. The departure of the Americans is no longer a priority for any political party, and the extraparliamentary movement has also been rather quiet in recent years. The dissolution of the Soviet bloc and the removal of the alleged military threat does not seem to have increased opposition to the defence force. It has come to seem more likely that the Americans would restrict their activities at Keflavík airport than that the Icelanders would turn them out.

This does not necessarily mean that the force enjoys more support than before. For a long time opinion polls gave similar results, about two-thirds for and one-third against if only those who took a stand were counted. As late as 1987 only 41% were for the presence of the force and 33% against it, which means that among those who took a stand 55% were for and 45% against. A little less than 80% supported Iceland's participation in NATO and just over 20% opposed it.[8]

There are various reasons for the dwindling opposition to the American force. Although the dissolution of the Soviet bloc has removed most of the stated justification for its presence, it has also removed some of the objections. The attraction of the base as a military target is hardly a matter of concern now, and a policy of neutrality in the interests of disarmament and world peace has little place in a world without clear polarization. But

[8] Bragi Guðmundsson and Gunnar Karlsson (1988), 329.

above all the military force at Keflavík airport is less important to most Icelanders now than it was in the period from the 1950s to the '70s because its activities have largely remained static while those of the Icelandic population of Iceland have broadened immensely. Thus the army television of the 1960s was an exciting novelty and a major force in the popular culture of Iceland. Now we can choose between three or more Icelandic television channels and countless foreign ones. No one cares whether the television channel at Keflavík airport is seen by Icelandic eyes – either its supporters or its opponents. The same applies to many kinds of goods which no doubt gave the American presence some allure in the 1950s and '60s.

This has made the base more acceptable, but at the same its status has become more vulnerable. It would be more difficult now than ever before to argue that it is indispensable, either militarily or economically. Therefore one cannot say for certain that the dispute over the American force has disappeared from Icelandic politics.

4.11 Independence Struggle on Fishing Grounds

The extent of territorial waters around Iceland was defined during the monopoly period (see Ch. 2.10), probably more with the purpose of protecting Danish merchants from the competition of foreign fishermen than of protecting fish stock. Anyway, foreigners at that time were not allowed to fish closer to the coast than 4 Danish miles or 16 nautical miles of 1,852 metres. In the 19th century, when trade in Iceland had been freed, the Danish authorities saw little reason to defend this immense area of ocean against foreign fishermen, and in 1872 issued a regulation whereby the territorial waters of Iceland were to be in accordance with international law, namely 3 nautical miles. In bays the distance was measured by a line drawn from where the bay was 10 miles wide. This decision was confirmed by a treaty between the Danish and British governments in 1901, which explicitly set out that this should be the limit around Iceland. The same rule was applied to other countries, although they were not parties to the treaty.[1]

Already at that time, British trawlers had become a serious nuisance in Icelandic fishing grounds (see Ch. 4.1), but in spite of it no protest was heard from Iceland. On the whole Icelandic leaders were remarkably indifferent towards the way the Danish authorities disposed of their fishing grounds, while simultaneously giving absolute priority to gaining their authority over the land.

This attitude did not change until the independence struggle had been completely won. Although the Danish-British treaty of 1901 could be terminated at any time with two years' notice, this was hardly ever mooted until after the Second World War. The reason may be that competition from foreign fishing did not seem very damaging in the first half of the 20th century, and the growth of the Icelandic fishing industry was mainly in deep-sea fishing, where the grounds seemed inexhaustible. All that Iceland did in the interwar years was gradually to take over from Denmark the protection of the 3-mile limit, as the treaty of 1918 (see Ch. 3.17) entitled it to do. In 1920 the state, in cooperation with a sea-rescue society in the Westman Islands, bought a Danish gunboat which was named *Þór* after

---

[1] The history of the territorial waters of Iceland, from a juridical point of view, is related by Gunnlaugur Þórðarson (1952). Jón Þ. Þór (1991) has told the story up to 1952, and Davis (1963) takes it through the 1958 extension. Björn Þorsteinsson (1976b) and Hannes Jónsson (1982) cover the whole story through the extensions.

the old Norse god of thunder. In 1926 *Óðinn*, the leader of Nordic gods, was added to the fleet, and three years later came *Ægir*, god of the ocean. When Denmark was occupied in 1940, Iceland was of course left to protect its fishing grounds alone.

During the war the waters off Iceland were practically abandoned by foreign fishing fleets, even the British who would have had the opportunity to exploit them, and catches were generally good. But soon after the war the Icelandic fishing fleet was greatly increased, partly on the initiative of the Innovation Government (see Ch. 4.6). From 1945 to 1949, the total tonnage of Icelandic fishing vessels more than doubled. At the same time foreign ships began to frequent Icelandic waters again, and apparently this soon resulted in greatly declining catches. The catches of demersal fish (mainly cod) by Icelandic ships only grew by 17% from 1945 to 1949. Another incentive to start protecting a larger section of the fishing grounds came from America, when in 1945 the US government issued a declaration that the continental shelf of the United States was subject to American jurisdiction and should be exploited by Americans alone. Nothing was said about how the shelf was to be defined – either its depth or its distance from the coast.

In 1948 the Icelandic Althing enacted the Law on the Scientific Protection of Fishing Grounds on the Shelf of Iceland whereby the ministry of fishing could decide and make regulations for extending the territorial fishing grounds off Iceland on the shelf, which was not defined. This was to be the legal authority for all consequent extensions of the fishing limits. In 1949 the treaty of 1901 with Britain was terminated. Then began the period of extensions of the fishing limits, which lasted for the next quarter of a century.

The first extension in 1950 increased the limits off northern Iceland to 4 nautical miles and, more important, the line was drawn straight across all firths and bays. This did not come into force against Britain till the following year, when the treaty of 1901 expired. Then, in 1952, the 4-mile line was drawn around the whole country. In 1958 the limit was extended to 12 miles all around the country; in 1972 to 50 miles, and in 1975 to 200 miles, where there were 400 miles or more between Iceland and the nearest land. Elsewhere the line was drawn centrally between Iceland and Greenland to the west and Faroe to the east.

During this period no international law on the extent of economic jurisdiction on the seas was valid. The United Nations repeatedly tried to reach agreement on new rules, but all attempts proved fruitless because no single rule could obtain sufficient majority support. Therefore Iceland extended its fishing limits unilaterally – as other countries did in these years – and justified the action by the need to preserve its vital natural resource. In opposition to this, foreign countries that fished off Iceland maintained that they had a traditional right to continue doing so.

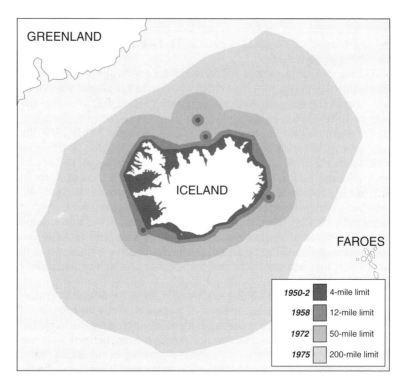

Map 4. 11-1 The extension of fishing limits around Iceland, 1950–75.

Among those countries Britain had the greatest interest in the disputed waters, and its reaction was the strongest. After the second extension in 1952, British fishing interests organized a boycott of the import of Icelandic fish into Britain, Iceland's most important market. In the preceding years 30% of Icelandic exports had gone to Britain and now this suddenly went down to 10%. In Iceland the boycott was met by increasing the freezing industry and finding new markets for frozen fish in the United States and the Soviet Union, which became Iceland's most important trading partners in the following years.

Although at first the boycott caused serious problems, it came to benefit Iceland. The fish had mostly been exported to Britain unprocessed on ice; the trawlers simply sailed to Britain after each fishing tour and sold the catch. Now Iceland was forced to develop highly technical fish processing in order to gain access to the American market, where Icelandic fish has been sold ever since as a high-quality commodity. In 1956 Britain finally realized that it had lost the struggle against the 4-mile limit and lifted the boycott, but the British fish market never regained its former importance.

While this was going on, not much more than half the fish caught in the fishing grounds off Iceland were caught by Icelanders. Britain caught almost a quarter and Germany a little less. Although Icelandic trawlers did some fishing in the waters off Greenland and Newfoundland, an urgent need was felt to protect more of the domestic fishing grounds. In 1956 a left-centre government was formed, pledging to expel the American defence force from Iceland (see Ch. 4.10) and to work on a further extension of the fishing limits. It decided to wait for the results of a UN conference on the subject in 1958, and when it failed to reach a conclusion strong pressure was put on Iceland on behalf of NATO not to extend unilaterally. The issue became increasingly intertwined with the Cold War, not least because America's best friend in Iceland, the Independence Party, was in opposition. On the other hand, the minister of fisheries, Lúðvík Jósepsson, was a Socialist and an opponent of Iceland's participation in the Western defence system.[2] He and other Socialists were suspected of pushing for the extension in order to put a wedge between Iceland and the Western alliance (in fact Lúðvík was above all the advocate of the fishing interests of the small villages in his constituency in eastern Iceland). However, the government decided to extend the limit unilaterally to 12 miles from 1 September 1958. During that night ten British warships of different types entered the 12-mile zone and British trawlers were ordered to fish in three defined areas, between 4 and 12 miles from the coast, where the warships would protect them. West German and Belgian trawlers sailed out of the zone, although their governments did not recognize the validity of the extension. The only states that recognized it before the extensions came into force were the Soviet Union and East Germany.

On the second day of the military presence the crew of the Icelandic coastguard vessel *Þór* managed to capture a British trawler that had ventured too far away from its protection vessel. The Icelanders took command of the trawler and headed for the nearest Icelandic harbour, where they intended to bring the skipper before a court as was customary in cases of fishing in territorial waters. Then a British frigate stopped the trawler and sent aboard a party of men who overcame the Icelanders. They were taken in a small boat towards the *Þór*, but the *Þór*'s captain decided to make the most of the issue by refusing to receive them. For eleven days they were kept aboard the frigate, until it sailed secretly on a dark night towards the coast near the fishing village of Keflavík. The Icelanders were made to board a small rowing-boat and row to land.

Such was the innocence of these conflicts, which the British press soon called the "Cod War" and which went on for two and a half years. In the

[2] Lúðvík represented the People's Alliance in the government, but until 1968 the Alliance was formally an electoral alliance of the Socialist Party and its ally.

mean time the Restoration Government of the Independence Party and Labour took over, more integrationist than any previous government (see Ch. 4.8). In 1961 they concluded a treaty whereby Britain acknowledged the 12-mile limit in return for minor concessions of fishing between 6 and 12 miles for three years. A more important concession made by Iceland was a pledge to submit any disagreement over further extensions of the fishing limits to the International Court of Justice.[3]

In the late 1960s a serious depression, caused by the simultaneous collapse of the herring stock and a fall in fish prices on the world market, led to pressure for further extension. In these years foreigners still fished one-third of the catches in the waters off Iceland. The Restoration parties were in a dilemma because of the treaty of 1961, but the opposition had opposed the treaty and therefore did not feel any need to take responsibility for it. Therefore the opposition parties went into the general election in 1971 with a common programme to extend the limit to 50 miles. They gained a majority and formed a government, with Lúðvík Jósepsson as fisheries minister. Abiding by their word, they extended the limit to 50 miles in 1972 and refused to submit the case to the International Court arguing that no country could accept the verdict of a foreign court concerning its vital interests.[4]

Britain reacted, as in 1958, by sending a naval contingent to the fishing grounds to protect the trawler fleet. But now Iceland brought into action a weapon developed during the earlier cod war, a kind of shears which could cut the trawls from the trawlers. This was done several times, despite attempts by the British warships to prevent it, and these attempts made this cod war fiercer than the earlier one. Several times British warships and Icelandic coastguard vessels collided, each side blaming the other. In Iceland we were of course told that the large British frigates risked sinking the small Icelandic gunboats, but pictures were shown which revealed that when the stem of the gunboat collided with the more sensitive bow of the frigate, much more damage was suffered by the frigate. In this war the victories were mainly won in the media, and both sides managed to avoid what would have been more harmful to their cause than anything else – causing the death of someone from the opposing force.

In November 1973 a truce was concluded: the British were allowed to fish in certain defined areas for two years, but they did not acknowledge the 50-mile limit and there was no agreement on what would happen at the end of the two-year period. What happened then was probably worse for the British than anything they could have dreamed of.

In these years the policy of a general economic zone of 200 nautical miles was gaining ground all over the world. In the beginning the Independence Party had led the struggle for extension but lost it for almost two

---

[3] The making of the 1961 treaty is discussed by Guðmundur J. Guðmundsson (1999).
[4] The dispute of 1972–3 has been discussed by Hart (1976).

decades because of its fidelity to Western cooperation. Now the party decided to take the lead again and went into the 1974 general election commited to extending the fishing limit to 200 miles, which covers practically all fishing grounds that can be said to belong to the Icelandic shelf. The Independence Party won a decisive victory in the election, and the government it then formed with the Progressives extended the limit to 200 miles in 1975. After this Britain could have no hope of a more friendly government in Iceland to bargain with.

A month after this last extension came into force, the armistice treaty of 1973 expired and the cod war started again in a similar way to before. This time Iceland broke off diplomatic relations with Britain (which in fact meant that the ambassador went home and the staff officially became members of the Norwegian embassy without leaving their former offices). However, a lasting agreement was now near. In the summer of 1976 the Norwegian government undertook mediation, and on 1 June an agreement was signed, giving the British permission to fish on twenty-four trawlers within the 200-mile limit for six months. On 1 December British ships left the Icelandic fishing grounds for the last time. Other countries that had not used force in Icelandic waters, although they did not acknowledge the extensions, were rewarded with concessions lasting a few years longer. Because of kinship and good neighbourliness the Faroese received more permanent concessions, which have gradually turned into mutual fishing rights. It is fair to say that in 1976 Iceland's struggle for independence where the wet part of its territory was concerned ended in complete victory in 1976.

4.12 The Fight against Inflation

Even though questions of integration versus autonomy, defence and fishing limits may have been the big issues of Icelandic politics in the postwar years, economic measures have generated many more words, more committees and more laws. The day-to-day or rather year-to-year preoccupation of Icelandic governments has been to keep the economy going.[1]

In some ways, Iceland has been more successful in this than its nearest neighbours. Thus (apart from traditional seasonal unemployment, see Ch. 4.14) we have enjoyed practically full employment for most of the postwar years. Unfortunately, because no regular unemployment insurance was introduced until 1956, no unemployment statistics covering the whole country are available from before 1957. But from then until the depression of the late 1960s those registered as unemployed never exceeded 1% of the labour force. When, in 1968, the aherring stock suddenly failed, unemployment was felt to be severe, but when we look at the statistics it appears that the highest annual average, in 1969, was 2.5%. In the 1970s, when the oil crisis led to some 5% of the labour force being idle in most European countries, the number in Iceland again fell below 1% and did not rise much higher until the end of the 1980s in a period of seriously decreasing cod stocks. It peaked at around 5% in 1994 and 1995.

Compared with the countries nearest to us, Icelandic society has been extremely sensitive to unemployment, because it has never been forced by an enduring lack of work to adopt an unemployment culture. Someone unable to find a job has found the situation less tolerable than would be the case in a society where unemployment has been endemic for decades. This has made the unemployment of each person, hiding behind the low averages, more painful than elsewhere, and compelled politicians to be more sensitive to the threat of unemployment and thus more willing to set other economic targets aside to avoid it.

A part of the price paid for almost full employment has been relatively low wages – at least compared with Scandinavia, our constant model. Icelandic workers have tended to compensate for this difference by longer

---

[1] The development of Iceland's economy is discussed by Magnús S. Magnússon (1993) and Sigurður Snævarr (1993). Statistical information is, as before, mainly taken from *Hagskinna* (1997).

working hours. Since 1972, the contractual working week has been forty hours but throughout the 1980s unskilled manual male workers worked on average at least fifty hours a week. In the same period the average working hours of all members of the Federation of Labour, male and female, was around forty-eight a week.

Another economic factor which is no doubt related to the high demand for labour is almost constant and sometimes extremely high inflation, although it is disputable which is cause and which effect. For half a century, 1940-90, inflation characterized the Icelandic economy more than anything else, and this is where its management has been least successful. During the first years of the Second World War it was around 30% a year, but thereafter it seems to have fallen to negligible figures until around 1950 when it rose again above 30%. But it is difficult to see when the inflation was genuinely stopped and when it was just kept down artificially by subsidies and other measures. However, analysis of longer periods shows that inflation fell after the war, but accelerated from the 1950s until the 1970s, and kept at roughly the same rate throughout the 1980s. The average annual rise of the general price index by decade is as follows:

	%
1941-50	14.4
1951-60	8.7
1961-70	13.4
1971-80	35.2
1981-90	35.3

These averages, of course, hide quite strong fluctuations, as Fig. 4.12-1 shows. The highest inflation rate in a single year was in 1982-3: 85.7%.

A rise in prices cannot, of course, go on for long without being compensated for in higher wages. During most of the postwar period, wages have been index-linked, and even when the government has attempted to stop wage rises by forbidding index-linkage, both the labour unions and the demand for labour by the market have tended to keep wages on a par with the price level. But higher wages increase the cost of production and thus call for higher prices, which in turn call for higher wages, and so on in a vicious circle.

Furthermore, a rise in wages increases the production cost of export goods until they cannot be sold at a profit on foreign markets. The dollars paid for a ton of fish, when changed into Icelandic krónur, do not cover the cost of fishing and processing a ton. The usual remedy for this is a devaluation of the króna, so that the bank pays the exporter more krónur for the same amount of dollars. This remedy has been used repeatedly in Iceland since 1939, as can be seen clearly by comparing the prices of

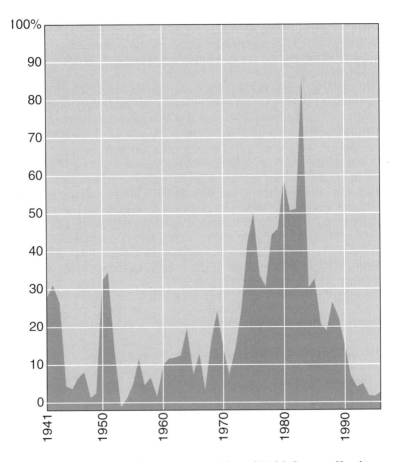

Fig. 4.12-1 Annual rise in the general price index, 1941-96. *Sources: Hagskinna* (1997), 637 (table 12.35); *Landshagir* 1997 (1997), 172 (table 12.5).

some important currencies at the end of 1938 and 1990 in "old" Icelandic krónur:

	1938	1990
US dollar	4.77	5,547
British pound	22.15	10,639
Danish krone	1.00	955

The exchange rates of these currencies are not like this now because of the change of currency that took place in Iceland at the beginning of 1981. A new króna was introduced, amounting to 100 old krónur. This was

a technical, not an economic, measure and had nothing to do with reval-
uation of the currency. A holder of 100 old krónur simply got 1 new króna
for them, and the debtor of 100 krónur had to pay 1 new króna. Nothing
changed except the number of noughts.

In fact, there was a faint hope that people might care more for their new
króna and therefore be more willing to sacrifice something to keep the currency stable. That, however, did not happen. When the new króna was
introduced, it had almost exactly the same value as the Danish krone, but,
as we see above, it had almost fallen ten years later to one-tenth of that
value.

As a remedy against inflation, devaluation is partly self-defeating, since
it increases prices on all imported goods when they are priced in Icelandic
krónur, and so helps to propel inflation – another vicious circle.

For most of the inflation period, interest rates were far below the rate of
inflation, so that interest on loans was in fact negative. People who borrowed money did not even have to pay the whole principal back. This
could be beneficial for young people in need of an apartment, and is one
reason why most people in Iceland own their homes. It was also favourable
for various kinds of private enterprise and has no doubt contributed to
much unprofitable investment. It has normally paid off in Iceland to do
rather than to leave undone, which is the basic cause of the high demand
for labour that has kept unemployment at bay.

This system of course has its drawbacks. First, it is basically unjust.
Those who have paid the cost are innocent, often elderly people who have
saved money and kept it in the bank at a negative rate of interest until it
has become worthless. Secondly, credit has become a coveted commodity, distributed by banks and investment funds that were mostly state-
owned and under political tutelage. Three political parties have "owned"
their bank directorships (the People's Alliance and the Women's Alliance
have generally been kept out of this arrangement), and have no doubt been
expected to take care of their parties' political clients. This is a system that
invites corruption. Thirdly, a society where it constantly pays to do rather
than not do and to buy rather than not buy is doomed to become stress-
ridden and competitive. "It is a strange thing about Icelanders", a foreigner
once said to me; "they are so concerned about money, yet their money has
no value."

As the above description suggests, inflation is highly addictive. Still,
it remains to be explained why Iceland was more prone to inflation than its
neighbours.[2] The basic reason is probably the uniformity of Icelandic export industries, with fish products playing such an overwhelming part
(see Ch. 4.14). Good catches and/or high prices in foreign markets cause
an increased circulation of money, which again causes an increased demand for goods and labour. Imports increase, wages rise, prices rise and

[2] This is discussed by Jón Sigurðsson (1974).

the inflation has a new injection. On the other hand, when catches are bad and/or prices low, fishing and fish processing (largely owned by the same firms) cannot be run at a profit, which necessitates devaluation of the króna, which also feeds inflation. Thus inflation tends to follow from both types of fluctuation.

A further cause of inflation is to some extent its consequence also. It probably has something to do with unprofitable investment, incited by recurrent devaluations and negative interest rates, that our industry has never managed to reach the same level of productivity as the Scandinavian countries, except in restricted areas, such as fishing and perhaps fish processing. On the other hand, we see the Scandinavian and maybe also the American standard of living as the norm. We are usually in the top league of ownership of new consumer goods such as personal computers and mobile phones.

This discrepancy between productivity and the demand of a particular standard of living has contributed to a long-standing wage dispute which has erupted in frequent and often long strikes. From the 1950s until the 1970s strikes were commonest and lasted longest among unskilled workers, where the Dagsbrún union in Reykjavík was usually in the lead. Since then civil servants have been more willing to strike, especially teachers, nurses and other employees of the health service. Wage disputes have repeatedly ended in settlements leading to immediate price rises and devaluations, starting the vicious circle of inflation over again. At the same time we are approaching the remedy that seems to have freed Iceland from that circle.

Around 1980 a general index linkage on credit was introduced. This alone did not cure inflation – rather, it had the potential to cause a rise in prices; for instance, it increased firms' credit costs and hence raised the prices of their products. However, the measure caused fewer people to become reliant on the inflation, and thus it probably contributed to the halt later on. In 1983 another step was taken when index-linking of wages was forbidden for two years. Thereafter, index-linking was entirely a matter of bargaining in the labour market, and it was never introduced fully and generally again.

Then in 1990 the decisive step seems to have been taken when the large unions – the Federation of Labour and the Federation of State and Municipal Employees (Bandalag starfsmanna ríkis og bæja) – accepted a wage rise well below the inflation rate at that time. Thus the working class sacrificed part of an expected wage rise in order to be freed from continuing inflation. This agreement, which was called the National Contract (*þjóðarsátt*), together with a relatively relaxed economic situation with a greatly reduced demand for labour in the following years, seems to have been what was needed. Iceland has since had inflation averaging around 2% – even less than its most important trading partners.

4.13 Enter Women

In the 1910s the liberation movement had in principle given Icelandic women human rights equal with men (see Ch. 3.16), but for decades this seems not to have had much effect. At the Althing, there were mostly no more than one or two women at a time, and sometimes none at all, until the 1970s. The first female doctor graduated in 1917, but the first female lawyer did so only in 1935 and the first theologian in 1945. The first female pastor was ordained in 1974. It has not been explained convincingly why Icelandic women were so slow to make use of the rights they had acquired.

However, a group of women continued to work for the cause, mainly within the Women's Rights Association of Iceland.[1] In 1930 the Association took up the struggle for equal wages, which had its first success fifteen years later. A new law on the salaries of civil servants in 1945 decreed for the first time that pay grades for women should, other things being equal, be the same as for men. This was seen at the time as a major step forward, but of course it did not secure equal pay because in many areas men and women held different kinds of jobs, and women's jobs could command lower pay than men's even though they demanded similar skills. In the private sector no law stipulated equality in pay, but in 1961 this was dealt with by a law requiring that the wages of women in unskilled labour, factories, commerce and office work should be raised in equal annual steps over the course of six years until full equality with men's wages was reached.

Just after the end of that period the radical wave of the late 1960s and early '70s, asking critical questions about all accepted forms and traditional values, reached Iceland. New types of communal household were tried by young people. Protest marches against the American force at the Keflavík base were more frequent and better attended than ever before. Associations of Trotskyists and Marxist-Lenininsts were founded. Icelandic students in Sweden occupied the embassy of their country in Stockholm, and high-school students organized a sit-in at the Ministry of Education in Reykjavík until the police threw them out. Minority groups made themselves heard more than ever before. For instance, one of the last fruits of this movement was Samtökin '78 (the Icelandic Gay Organization), an association of homosexuals of both sexes, founded in 1978, which has greatly helped to improve their rights.

[1] See Sigríður Th. Erlendsdóttir (1993).

Looking back at these years, little seems to have been achieved compared with the actual intentions of the radical wave, but in one area – the struggle for women's rights – the movement has been continually visible and quite successful. The new women's movement started in an association established in Reykjavík in 1970 called the Red Stockings Movement (Rauðsokkahreyfingin) after a Danish and, before that, American model.[2] This loosely organized pressure group had no formal governing board, and men as well as women were welcome, although women were always the majority. It agitated for anything that could possibly improve the status and increase the freedom of women. It ridiculed beauty contests as a humiliating marketing of the female body, and campaigned for free abortion and day care for children. The movement was dominated by the growing number of young educated women who were unwilling to sacrifice their careers to family life. This was a policy that enjoyed widespread support in these years, although in their attitude to the traditional family image the Red Stockings were too challenging for most people's tastes.

Support for the improved status and solidarity of women was demonstrated in a powerful way by the "women's holiday" in 1975. A number of associations and labour unions united in calling for a general strike of women (although the word "strike" sounded too radical and was not used) on 24 October in both the labour market and the home to remind society of women's contribution. The response was excellent. Work was paralysed, not only because women did not turn up but also because a number of men were left alone to take care of their children. A meeting in Reykjavík was attended by an estimated 20,000-25,000 people, around 20% of the population of the town and its suburbs.

Five years later, in 1980, the new attitude towards women won another victory, when Vigdís Finnbogadóttir, a divorcee and single mother, was elected as president of the Republic – the first woman in the world, as we maintain in Iceland, to be elected head of state in a democratic election. In fact she owed her victory to the favourable situation of competing with three men – she needed no more than one-third of the vote. But she became immensely popular in Iceland during her sixteen years in office, as well as earning widespread admiration and respect outside the country.

The victory of Vigdís of course gave great encouragement to those who wanted to move the battle into the arena of party politics. The Red Stockings could not do that because they aimed to unite people with different political convictions, although most of them inclined towards the left. Therefore the first attempt to revive the women's lists which had existed in the first quarter of the 20th century (see Ch. 3.16) was made by *ad hoc* associations, which submitted lists to local elections in

[2] For a study of the movement, see Herdís Helgadóttir (1996).

Reykjavík and Akureyri in 1982.[3] They did well and won two council seats in both places. In Reykjavík they occupied third place, with 11% of the vote after the Independence Party, which regained its absolute majority in the town with 52.5%, and the People's Alliance, which had 19%.

This promising result led to the establishment of a new political association, the Women's Alliance (Samtök um kvennalista), which participated for the first time in general elections in three constituencies in 1983. It won three parliamentary seats and 5.5% of the national vote, but 7.6% in the constituencies where it competed. This was little more than tolerably good, but victory was still to come. It has proved relatively easy in Iceland for new political groups to get considerable support, but harder for a small party to survive a second election. This the Women's Alliance did triumphantly in 1987. It submitted lists in all constituencies and won six seats and 10% of the vote. In the 1991 election, it did almost as well, but in 1995 it only scraped into the Althing with three representatives and 4.9% voters' support. The result urged the Women's Alliance to participate in an electoral alliance with Labour and the People's Alliance in the 1999 elections (see Ch. 4.8). It seems likely that the second period of special women's lists in Iceland is coming to an end.

Unlike the Red Stockings, the Women's Alliance – as the name implies – consists of women alone. Only women's names appear on its lists at elections, and only women are seen at its general meetings. The Red Stockings stressed the similarities of men and women: "women are also men" was one of their slogans, which sounds more straightforward in Icelandic than in English. The Women's Alliance has tended to put more emphasis on qualities peculiar to women, which they maintain to be useful in politics in the interests both of women and of society in general.[4]

They have not proved their case by participating in coalitions, though they have had at least one opportunity to do so, and probably more. This was perhaps the great failure of the Alliance and probably helps to explain its declining success as a political movement. Still, the Women's Alliance has no doubt been influential in Icelandic politics. They have seen to it that the attitude and interests of women have been heard on every political issue. Extensive legislation on equality has been enacted since the 1970s. Women have probably found it somewhat easier to gain influence in other parties because of the competition from the Women's Alliance. Only three women were elected to the Althing in each of the three general elections during the 1970s, but in 1983 their number went up to nine, and in 1999 to twenty-two (compared to forty-one men) or 35% of members. Since 1995 one of the four traditional parties, the People's Alliance, has had as leader Margrét Frímannsdóttir, who has served as the

<hr />

[3] A short survey of the political women's movement is given by Sigríður Dúna Kristmundsdóttir (1989).
[4] On the politics of the Women's Alliance, see Sigríður Helga Sigurbjarnardóttir (1993).

spokesperson of the newly-established Alliance (see Ch. 4.8). The city council of Reykjavík has been under the rule of a left-centre electoral alliance since 1994, and its leader – mayor of Reykjavík – is a former Women's Alliance member of the Althing, Ingibjörg Sólrún Gísladóttir. The opposition Independence Party group in the council elected a woman as its leader after its second defeat by Ingibjörg Sólrún's supporters. Finally it should be mentioned that Icelandic teenagers proved to be the most equality-minded of all European adolescents in a recent opinion poll.[5] No doubt this is partly due to the attention the Women's Alliance has constantly drawn to the issue.

In the most influential social posts women are still much more rare than in Scandinavia. At the time of writing, the government consists of twelve ministers, eight men and four women. No woman is or ever has been a director of a bank or a major investment fund in Iceland. It seems that the management of money is the male fortress which it is most difficult for women to break into. Perhaps the reason why Icelandic women have made so slow an entry into politics is the great amount of economic management inherent in the political system (see Ch. 4.12). Maybe it is true everywhere that politics ultimately consists of the distribution of money, but in Iceland it has been more obvious than in other comparable countries.

Real equality in wages is also said to be far away, even though it has been legalized for decades, because for some reason men tend to get into higher pay grades. On the other hand more girls than boys attend higher education, so it may only be a question of time before they claim their share.

---

[5] Angvik and Borries, eds (1997) B, 353.

4.14 Life is Still Fish

The young girl Salka Valka who is the heroine of Halldór Kiljan Laxness's novel, says: "When all is said and done, life is first and foremost salt fish."[1] These words have become almost proverbial in Iceland when the first half of the 20th century is under discussion. As mentioned above (Ch. 4.5), salt fish gave way to uncured fish on ice after the outbreak of the Spanish Civil War in 1936, and to frozen fish when the English fish market closed in the 1950s (see Ch. 4.11). In actual fact, relatively fewer people than before saw or touched fish except on the dinner table, but none the less it went on providing the conditions for a prosperous modern life in the country by forming the bulk of exports.[2]

As in any other Western society in the 20th century, fewer and fewer Icelandic people became engaged in production and more and more in various kinds of services, which they mostly provided for each other. Below is a rough survey of the distribution of the population of Iceland by industry in the postwar period:

	1950	1990
	%	%
Agriculture	26	5
Fishing	10	6
Manufacturing	20	19
of which fish-processing	6	6
Services and other industries	44	70

The change does not mean that production in agriculture or fishing has decreased. The number of people who live by fishing has stayed roughly the same throughout the period, and the proportion is lower in 1990 only because the total population has grown. This fact shows that with its constant proportion manufacturing, including fish-processing, has grown considerably in terms of manpower. Agriculture engaged fewer people

[1] Halldór Kiljan Laxness (1936), 283.

[2] The statistical material of this chapter is taken from *Hagskinna* (1997). Sigfús Jónsson (1984) has written a survey of Icelandic fishing in the 20th century. Apart from these, the chapter is based on sources referred to in Ch. 4.12 and, to some extent, on personal knowledge.

in 1990 than in 1950, but production has grown substantially because of increased productivity – of milk by 60% and meat by 100%. In general, the GNP per capita increased more than threefold in real terms from 1950 to 1990. This increase of course consists largely of market production replacing the old subsistence economy: when a mother hires someone to look after her child and, in turn, goes to work on the labour market herself, she increases the GNP by the wages of the person she has hired plus her own. Nevertheless, since division of labour is one of the main characteristics of modernization, the growth of GNP is no worse an indicator of modernization than any other.

It is difficult with the tools of modern economic statistics to find an indicator of the importance of fishing in the internal economy of Iceland. In 1973 (earlier figures are not easily available), fishing contributed only 7.4% to the gross domestic factor income, as the economists call it, whereas agriculture contributed 5.4%, manufacturing over 20% and trade 10%. In 1990 the proportion of fishing had gone up to 10%, agriculture down to 2.6%, manufacturing down to 17% and trade up to 13%.

One must look at export statistics to appreciate the sense in which Icelandic life is fish. From the 1940s until the late 1960s marine products usually made up over 90% of the total export value of goods, while the rest mostly consisted of agricultural products. Since the 1970s, the share of marine products has usually been 70-80%, with manufacturing products providing most of the remaining 20-30%. Around 1990 the export of goods made up approximately three-quarters of total export income, compared with the export of services (tourism, transport, work at the Keflavík base etc.). So because three-quarters of 75 is 56.25, Iceland seems to earn a little more than half of its foreign currency from fish products.

The increase in manufactured products since the 1970s is mainly due to a few attempts to strengthen the basis of the Icelandic economy by utilizing hydroelectric power. In all mountainous and rainy countries, this is a valuable natural resource, and in Iceland's case probably the third-most valuable after fish and geothermal power. Fish have been utilized since the age of settlement. Geothermal power came into extensive use for the heating of houses in the 1940s, in Reykjavík, and has constantly increased since then, especially since the oil crisis of the 1970s. Now more than 85% of the country's population have their houses heated by natural warm water. Hydroelectric power was taken into use on a small scale somewhat earlier (see Ch. 4.2), but it was not until about 1970 that the whole population had access to electricity, almost all produced by falling water.

In the 1960s a search was begun for foreign firms willing to launch energy-intensive industries in Iceland, run by hydroelectric power. The result was an aluminium smelter located in Straumsvík, south of Hafnarfjörður, opened in 1969. It was fuelled by a new hydroelectric power station on the Þjórsá river. The factory, which is owned exclusively by Swiss Aluminium, processes imported raw material and exports all its products, but the power station is in Icelandic ownership.

The establishment of the aluminium factory was a hotly debated issue in Iceland. The Restoration Government, which had closed the way to further protection of the fishing grounds (see Ch. 4.11), saw the harnessing of internal energy on a large scale, for selling to heavy industry, as a major opportunity for a radical transformation of the economic life of Iceland, but the opposition warned against the influence of huge foreign concerns in the small Icelandic economy. Thus once again Labour and the Independents appeared more integrationist than the Progressives and the People's Alliance (see Ch. 4.8). However, both camps have so far been wrong. Swiss Aluminium has not been a serious threat to the economic independence of Iceland. On the other hand, although a few other minor factories, in either shared Icelandic and foreign or exclusively foreign ownership, have since started up in Iceland, no transformation of the Icelandic economy has yet taken place. The government that came into power in 1995 eagerly sought new partners in energy-intensive industries, so that the dream of the Restoration Government may yet be realised, but if that happens the plans are bound to meet fierce opposition, this time probably from the viewpoint more of conservation of the environment than conservation of economic independence.

The left-centre government which took over in 1971 returned to reliance on fishing. At the same time as the fishing limits were extended to 50 miles, the trawler fleet was completely renewed in a few years, and a number of fishing villages where no trawlers had ever been operated were helped to get hold of one or two. At this time there was a major innovation in the construction of trawlers: instead of the old side-winders, which hoisted the trawl up the side of the ship, all the new trawlers had the trawl drawn in through an open stern. In 1971 Iceland owned twenty-four side and five stern trawlers, but in 1977, the first year after the expulsion of all British trawlers from the 200-mile zone, the number of side trawlers was down to one, while stern trawlers were up to seventy-seven. In the same period the number of smaller fishing vessels remained almost constant, around 800.

It was probably not until this time that year-round employment for both sexes became a commonplace in many fishing villages, where seasonal unemployment had been so predictable that it was not even defined as such. Catches of cod went up from year to year, and the almost complete absence of herring in these years was compensated for by immense catches of capelin.

However, new problems were not far away. Already in 1975 the Marine Research Institute issued its "Black Report", warning seriously against the overfishing of the most important stocks, particularly cod.[3] During

[3] Jón Jónsson II (1990), 116ff.

the next years fishing was restricted by prescribing days off and by temporarily closing defined areas. But in 1984 a new system of restrictions was introduced: each fishing vessel was permitted to catch a definite quota each year, in accordance with its catches in a few previous years. This system has been extended to more and more species and developed from year to year. At the same time, the quota has been increased or decreased according to the status of the fish stocks in the judgement of marine biologists.

The quota system has been a hot issue in Iceland in recent years. Its introduction meant a serious restriction of freedom, and not many seem to have foreseen that being the holder of such a restriction could become a great asset. However, it was considered necessary, in order to promote maximum productivity, that quotas could be sold – either together with ships when they were sold, or away from individual ships. It seemed the only way to direct the right to fish into the hands of those who could do it most effectively. On the other hand, this enabled individuals who had received their quota gratis to sell it for cash and, for instance, to buy a luxury car with the proceeds.

According to the law which is currently valid, the fish stocks in Icelandic waters are the common property of the nation, but it is causing increasing discontent that this common property, which has proved to be in great demand on the market, can be utilized free of charge by individuals and even sold. Consequently there are calls for the sale or hire of fishing licences, if not a general natural resource tax on all use of limited resources that seem to be the common property of all. Against this attitude the shipowners point out that any form of charge for fishing would be a burden on an export industry which is said to compete with fishing in other countries where it is not only free from such a burden but, in many cases, supported and subsidized by the state. Furthermore, the representatives of the more remote districts point out that a disproportionately large amount of fishing is carried out from those districts, and therefore a fishing charge would be socially unjust and a damaging tax on parts of the country already suffering from depopulation. Up till now only the Labour Party has adopted the policy of a fishing charge, but the issue has also caused disturbance in other political camps and will no doubt do so even more in the future.

4.15 Break and Continuity in Icelandic History

Do present-day Icelanders in their Japanese cars, with their mobile phones and buying their lottery tickets have anything in common with the first generations of people in Iceland apart from living in the same country? In other words, is there a justification for a single history of Iceland?

At first glance Icelandic society seems very modern. Almost all the buildings in the country were built in the 20th century, and the overwhelming majority are less than fifty years old and built of concrete and glass. All transport on land is by car and lorry. Aircraft are widely used to carry people between districts, and regular air transport to Europe and America has been in operation since the late 1940s. There are no railways to remind the visitor of the age before the motor-car. The man-made landscape is dominated by roads, raised somewhat above ground level to avoid snow in winter, and hayfields. Both have been created by excavators and bulldozers.

It is also easy to find Icelanders who care little about the past, and seem to live exclusively in the present and planning for the future. Most Icelanders tend to resist being seen as descendants of the Vikings, or – as Orla Lehmann observed in the early 19th century – guardians of a deep-frozen 1,000-year-old Nordic culture (see Ch. 3.5). If the tourists see something else in Iceland, they are seeing an image that has been specially put on for their benefit.

Nevertheless, we have a national self-image based on our historical heritage – the image of being a literary nation. As discussed earlier (Chs 2.9, 2.11 and 2.13), Icelandic literature was rarely above an average standard from the 15th to the 18th century. Icelanders like to believe that poetry had an important revival in the Romantic period (see Ch. 3.2), but it remains to be seen if it contained anything out of the ordinary in an international perspective.[1] In the 19th century the pioneer of modern Icelandic prose literature, the sheriff Jón Thoroddsen, wrote his two novels: *Piltur og stúlka* (Lad and Lass) published in 1850,[2] and *Maður og kona* (A Man

---

[1] The story of Icelandic literature in the 19th and early 20th centuries, until *c.* 1918, is given in *Íslensk bókmenntasaga* III (1996). The fourth volume is currently in preparation. For a survey in English of the history of Icelandic literature, see Stefán Einarsson (1957)

[2] For two translations into English, see Jón Thoroddsen (1887, 1890).

and a Woman), published posthumously in 1876.[3] There is no doubt that they belong to the genre of modern novels, but at the same time Jón was strongly influenced by the Icelandic sagas. He had a number of imitators, and around the turn of the century more competent writers began to emerge. In the early 20th century a few Icelandic writers went to Denmark to make their name as writers in Danish, and one of them, Gunnar Gunnarsson, became well known for a time in Scandinavia and Germany.[4]

However, it was not until Halldór Kiljan Laxness won the Nobel Prize for literature in 1955 that Iceland had satisfactory confirmation of its self-image as a literary nation.[5] Halldór was born in 1902 and had his first novel published in 1919. However, it was with his *Vefarinn mikli frá Kasmír* (The Great Weaver from Kashmir) in 1927 that he attracted attention as a major writer. During the following four and a half decades he wrote the eleven novels which form the bulk of his achievement, some in more than one volume. In addition he wrote short stories, poetry, several plays, an autobiographical novel in four volumes and some fourteen essay collections. But his novels from the 1930s to the 1950s are considered his best work, and all have been translated into several languages. The following are his best-known books, with their English titles and the years of their original publication in Icelandic: *Salka Valka* (1931-2), *Independent People* (1934-5), *World Light* (1937-40), *The Atom Station* (1948), *The Happy Warriors* (1952), and *The Fish Can Sing* (1958). *Íslandsklukkan* (Iceland's Bell, 1943-6) is not available in English.[6]

Halldór Laxness was a great satirist and a controversial figure, especially after he adopted strong communist sympathies in America in the 1920s. On his return home from receiving the Nobel Prize, during the depth of the Cold War, he was received by the presidents of the Union of Icelandic Artists (Bandalag íslenskra listamanna) and the Federation of Labour and a crowd of some 8,000-10,000 people, but no representative of the right-centre government uttered a word. Later Halldór abandoned his communism – if he had not already done so in 1955 – which made it easier for many of his fellow-countrymen to appreciate his genius. Afterwards it seems obvious that all the time he had been first of all a committed humanist and Icelandic patriot, who knew exceptionally well how to use humour to keep his warm feelings distinct from sentimentality.

After Halldór Laxness, Iceland has enjoyed a flourishing literary life. Since around 1980, 1,000-1,500 books have been published annually, of which 300-500 can be classified as *belles lettres*. Most of these books are

---

[3] This has not been translated into English.

[4] For some of his works in English, see Gunnar Gunnarsson (1938a and b, 1940, 1967).

[5] For a discussion in English on Halldór Laxness, see Hallberg (1971).

[6] Halldór Kiljan Laxness (1936, 1945, 1969, 1961, 1958, 1966). *Vefarinn mikli frá Kasmír* does not seem to have been translated into English. For a list of Halldór's books in the original language and translations, see Haraldur Sigurðsson (1972).

published towards the end of the year, intended for Christmas presents. No one knows how many of them are ever read by the over-worked Icelanders, but the annual book flood is a constant literary festival for those who take the time to enjoy it. The papers are full of reviews, cafés organize sessions where authors come and read from their new books, and literary people talk about little else but the books that are currently being published.

It is difficult to say what, if anything, the literary culture of contemporary Iceland owes to its medieval heritage. Of course, literature can blossom in a society without such a heritage: the Faroes of the 20th century are a case in point. In a way the achievement of Halldór Laxness and his contemporary Þórbergur Þórðarson consisted of freeing their texts from the burden of old modes of expression which were at least partly inherited from the saga tradition.[7] Poetry freed itself a little later from unconditional adherence to the old custom of regular rhyme and strict alliteration – a novelty that caused some bitter debate.[8]

On the other hand, Icelandic literary culture is obviously, for better or worse, strongly characterized by a consciousness of the literary heritage. This is nowhere more obvious than in the dominant purist language policy.[9] The basic rule is that no foreign words are used in Icelandic that cannot easily be adapted to the linguistic and morphological system of the language, and even those that can are preferably substituted by new words formed from old Norse roots.

Thus although the excavators and bulldozers were allowed to transform the Icelandic landscape in the 20th century, they were not allowed to keep their foreign names. An excavator is a *skurðgrafa*, formed by *skurður*, "ditch" and *grafa*, "digger" (literally ditch-digger), and a bulldozer is a *jarðýta*, from *jörð*, "earth" and *ýta*, "pusher" – an earth-pusher.

New words are invented not only for new objects but also for abstract concepts to which, for some reason, younger generations feel the need to give expression. Thus there were seemingly no words for sympathy and antipathy in Icelandic until the 20th century. However, there was an old word for animosity, *úlfúð*, literally "wolf's mind". By analogy, the words coined were *samúð*, "together-with mind", for sympathy and *andúð*, "against mind", for antipathy.

Sometimes, also, old words that have disappeared from use are re-invented with a slightly different meaning for new things. Thus the Old Norse word *síma*, meaning "thread", was taken into use in the form *sími* to denote telephone. It is in fact a handier word than "telephone" because it makes shorter compounds: *símaklefi*, "telephone box", and *símsvari*, "answering machine".

---

[7] Kristinn E. Andrésson (1949), 276.

[8] Eysteinn Þorvaldsson (1980).

[9] Halldór Halldórsson (1962).

Not everyone is happy with the purist language policy which, some have pointed out, entails some hypocrisy. People are not as pure as they pretend, especially since all specialized groups break the rules when speaking their own jargon. Even the academics, the very guardians of the language, who forbid the farmers to talk about "tractors" – *dráttarvél* ("pulling machine") or *dragi* is the required word – are themselves doctors and professors and use these foreign words freely. On the other hand, forming new words is a creative linguistic act which many people enjoy, and which is not altogether different from writing poetry. It seems, in a way, to keep the language more alive in people's minds than if it came to them as a ready-made system.

To a stranger it no doubt seems pretentious that a quarter of a million Icelanders should reject a word which is accepted by all other linguistic communities from California to Siberia. An even more extreme example of this peculiar self-reliance of Icelandic society over language is the policy concerning personal names, which has been dominant for most of the 20th century. At the beginning of the century it was commonly suggested that Iceland should follow the lead of all neighbouring countries by adopting family names instead of the patronymics borne by the great majority of the population. How else could a couple prove that they are married when they book in at a foreign hotel? In 1913 a new law was enacted which regulated and even encouraged the adoption of family names. But twelve years later, in 1925, the policy was reversed and the introduction of new family names was forbidden by law. Only names that had been taken up before the enactment of the law of 1913 could be used by the descendants of people who bore them in 1925.

This law was repeatedly broken – for example, by giving family names to children as second names and using them instead of patronymics – and the law has now been eased somewhat. However, the official policy is still to keep patronymics, and most Icelanders do so. Although new family names keep coming into the society – as when children have foreign fathers and Icelandic mothers – it also happens that young people reject their parents' family names in favour of patronymics. The patronymic system is also more in tune with modern demands for equality than family names: no one expects a woman to abandon her patronymic when she marries. A daughter of Fróði, who is called Hallveig Fróðadóttir, keeps her name in present-day Iceland even when she marries a man called Ingólfur Arnarson. It is the same custom that applied to the first generation of Icelanders.

Obviously Icelanders would not have stuck to this old custom of names or to linguistic purism had it not been for Icelanders' awareness of being heirs to a cultural treasure. The same could probably be said about the way they claimed autonomy over their fishing grounds, armed with nothing but their utter defencelessness (see Ch. 4.11). The strong resistance against the defence force of the world's greatest power is another effect of this awareness, although it has not (yet) gained the upper hand (see Ch. 4.10).

A more complicated question is whether 19th-century Icelanders would ever have started their struggle for independence if their ancestors had not written and preserved the sagas. Maybe they would, because of the large part that Icelandic officials always played in running their country when it was under Norwegian and Danish rule. But would they have played such a role, and done so in their own language, if they had not known of and read the sagas? There would certainly not have been a cultural revival in the 17th century if it had not been thought that there was a valuable culture to revive (see Ch. 2.13). It is no doubt true that all peoples find a golden age in their past, heroic or cultural, when they feel a need for one, and so what really happened in their past may seem of little importance. On the other hand, not all peoples feel the need to find a golden age in their past, and whether they do or not may depend to some degree on what really happened in the past. Iceland felt the need for a revival at least partly because it had unusually good material in its past on which to base it.

It is no doubt also due to this cultural heritage that the Icelanders have been blessed with neighbours who respected them enough to let them have their way at last, on both land and sea. If there is one main rule in Icelandic history, it is that victory is won by the inability to use force. The only attempt to rely on military force for its security – participation in the Western defence system – has not defended Iceland against any offensive, but has caused a bitter conflict in the country and seriously damaged the people's self-image. On the other hand, the struggle for political independence and autonomy in the fishing grounds has been won by the lack of means to exert force.

Bibliography

Adam of Bremen (1959), *History of the Archbishops of Hamburg-Bremen*, transl. with an introduction and notes by Francis J. Tschan, Columbia University Press, New York.

Aðalgeir Kristjánsson (1972), *Brynjólfur Pétursson, ævi og störf*, Hið íslenzka bókmenntafélag, Reykjavík.

—— (1993), *Endurreisn Alþingis og þjóðfundurinn*, Sögufélag, Reykjavík.

—— and Gísli Ágúst Gunnlaugsson (1990), "Félags- og hagþróun á Íslandi á fyrri hluta 19. aldar", *Saga* XXVIII, 7-62 (summary, 61-2).

Aðalsteinsson, *see* Jón Hnefill Aðalsteinsson.

Aðils, *see* Jón Jónsson Aðils.

Agnar Kl. Jónsson (1954-8), "Fánatakan á Reykjavíkurhöfn sumarið 1913", *Saga* II, 230-55.

—— (1969), *Stjórnarráð Íslands 1904-1964* I-II, Sögufélag, Reykjavík.

Agnarsdóttir, *see* Anna Agnarsdóttir.

Agnes S. Arnórsdóttir (1995), *Konur og vígamenn. Staða kynjanna á Íslandi á 12. og 13. öld*, Sagnfræðistofnun Háskóla Íslands/Háskólaútgáfan, Reykjavík (*Sagnfræðirannsóknir* XII) (summary, 204-6).

Ágústsson, *see* Hörður Ágústsson.

Alþingisbækur Íslands III, VI, IX: 1595-1605, 1640-62, 1697-1710 (1917-64), Sögufélag, Reykjavík.

Alþingistíðindi 1845-51 (1845-51), *Tíðindi frá Alþíngi Íslendínga / Tíðindi frá þjóðfundi Íslendínga árið 1851*, Reykjavík.

Andersson, Theodore M. (1964), *The Problem of Icelandic Saga Origins: A Historical Survey*, Yale University Press, New Haven.

Andrésson, *see* Kristinn E. Andrésson, Sigfús Haukur Andrésson.

Angvik, Magne, and Bodo von Borries, eds (1997), *Youth and History: A comparative European survey on historical consciousness and political attitudes among adolescents*, vol. B: *Documentation*, Körber–Stiftung, Hamburg.

Anna Agnarsdóttir (1979), "Ráðagerðir um innlimun Íslands í Bretaveldi á árunum 1785-1815", *Saga* XVII, 5-58 (summary, 56-8).

—— (1989), "Great Britain and Iceland 1800-1820", Ph.D. thesis, London School of Economics and Political Science.

—— (1993), "Ráðabrugg á dulmáli. Hugleiðingar um skjal frá 1785", *Ný saga* VI, 28-41.

—— and Ragnar Árnason (1983), "Þrælahald á þjóðveldisöld", *Saga* XXI, 5-26.

Annálar 1400-1800 I-II (1922-32), Hið íslenzka bókmenntafélag, Reykjavík.

Ármannsson, *see* Pétur H. Ármannsson.

Árna saga biskups (1972), ed. by Þorleifur Hauksson, Stofnun Árna Magnússonar, Reykjavík.

Arnar Guðmundsson and Unnar Ingvarsson (1993), *Bruggið og bannárin. Áfengisbannið á Íslandi 1915-1935*, Fróði, Reykjavík.

Árnason, *see* Vilhjálmur Árnason.

Arngrímur Jónsson, *see Purchas' Haklvytus Posthumus.*

Arnheiður Sigurðardóttir (1966), *Híbýlahættir á miðöldum*, Bókaútgáfa Menningarsjóðs, Reykjavík.

Árni Gíslason (1944), *Gullkistan. Endurminningar Árna Gíslasonar um fiskveiðar við Ísafjarðardjúp árin 1880-1905*, ed. by Arngr. Fr. Bjarnason, Prentstofan Ísrún, Ísafirði.

Árni Daníel Júlíusson (1990), "Áhrif fólksfjöldaþróunar á atvinnuhætti gamla samfélagsins", *Saga* XXVIII, 149-56.

—— (1996), "Bønder i pestens tid. Landbrug, godsdrift og social konflikt i senmiddelalderens islandske bondesamfund", Ph.D. thesis, University of Copenhagen (English synopsis, 396-8).

—— (1998), "Valkostir sögunnar. Um landbúnað fyrir 1700 og þjóðfélagsþróun á 14.-16. öld", *Saga* XXXVI, 77-111 (summary, 111).

—— *see Íslenskur söguatlas.*

Árni Magnússon and Páll Vídalín (1913-90), *Jarðabók Árna Magnússonar og Páls Vídalíns* I-XIII, Hið íslenska fræðafélag, Copenhagen.

Árni Magnússons Levned og Skrifter. Udgivet af Kommissionen for det Arnamagnæanske legat I-II (1930), Gyldendal, Copenhagen.

Arnór Sigurjónsson (1957-9), *Einars saga Ásmundssonar* I-II, Bókaútgáfa Menningarsjóðs, Reykjavík.

Arnórsdóttir, *see* Agnes S. Arnórsdóttir.

Arnórsson, *see* Einar Arnórsson.

Ártöl og áfangar í sögu íslenskra kvenna (1998), ed. by Erla Hulda Halldórsdóttir and Guðrún Dís Jónatansdóttir, Kvennasögusafn Íslands, Reykjavík.

Ásgeir Guðmundsson (1976), "Nazismi á Íslandi. Saga Þjóðernishreyfingar Íslendinga og Flokks þjóðernissinna", *Saga* XIV, 5-68 (German summary, 66-8).

Ásgeirsson, *see* Ólafur Ásgeirsson.

Auður Styrkársdóttir (1994), *Barátta um vald. Konur í bæjarstjórn Reykjavíkur 1908-1922*, Háskólaútgáfan, Reykjavík.

Baldur Guðlaugsson and Páll Heiðar Jónsson (1976), *30. marz 1949. Innganga Íslands í Atlantshafsbandalagið og óeirðirnar á Austurvelli*, Örn og Örlygur, Reykjavík.

Beck, Richard, ed. (1930), *Icelandic Lyrics. Originals and Translations*, selected and ed. by Richard Beck (incorrectly "Bech" on the title page), Þórhallur Bjarnason, Reykjavík.

Benedictow, Ole Jørgen (1992), *Plague in the Late Medieval Nordic Countries. Epidemiological Studies*, Middelalderforlaget, Oslo.

Benedikt Gröndal (1971), *Iceland: From Neutrality to NATO Membership*, Universitetsforlaget, Oslo.

Benediktsson, *see* Bjarni Benediktsson, Jakob Benediktsson.

Bergsteinn Jónsson (1964), "Fáein orð um upphaf einveldis á Íslandi", *Saga* IV, 70-86.

———— *see* Björn Þorsteinsson (1985).

———— *see* Björn Þorsteinsson and Bergsteinn Jónsson.

———— *see* Þorkell Jóhannesson and Bergsteinn Jónsson.

Bergsøe, Adolph Frederik (1844), *Den danske Stats Statistik* I, published by the author, Copenhagen.

Bergþórsson, *see* Páll Bergþórsson.

Bernharðsson, *see* Eggert Þór Bernharðsson.

Biskupa sögur II (1878), Hið íslenzka bókmentafélag, Copenhagen. See also *Byskupa sögur*.

Bjarnason, *see* Hákon Bjarnason.

Bjarnhéðinsdóttir, *see* Bríet Bjarnhéðinsdóttir.

Bjarni Benediktsson (1940), "Sjálfstæði Íslands og atburðirnir vorið 1940", *Andvari* LXV, 21-36.

Bjarni Thorarensen (1935), *Kvæði*, Hið íslenzka fræðafélag, Copenhagen.

Björn Th. Björnsson (1975), *Haustskip. Heimildasaga*, (drawings by Hilmar Þ. Helgason), Mál og menning, Reykjavík.

———— (1984), *Høstskib. Dokumentarisk roman*, transl. by Peter Søby Kristensen (drawings by Hilmar Þ. Helgason), Samleren, Copenhagen.

Björn Lárusson (1967), *The Old Icelandic Land Registers*, C.W.K. Gleerup, Lund.

———— (1982), *Islands jordebok under förindustriell tid*, Ekonomisk-historiska föreningen, Lund (*Skrifter* XXXV).

Björn Sigfússon (1934), "Veldi Guðmundar ríka", *Skírnir* CVIII, 191-8.

Björn Þórðarson (1926), *Refsivist á Íslandi 1761-1925*, Reykjavík.

———— (1947), *Landsyfirdómurinn 1800-1919. Sögulegt yfirlit*, Ísafoldarprentsmiðja, Reykjavík.

———— (1951), *Alþingi og frelsisbaráttan 1874-1944*, Alþingissögunefnd, Reykjavík (*Saga Alþingis* III).

Björn Þorsteinsson (1953), "Sendiferðir og hirðstjórn Hannesar Pálssonar og skýrsla hans 1425", *Skírnir* CXXVII, 136-64.

———— (1969), *Enskar heimildir um sögu Íslendinga á 15. og 16. öld*, Hið íslenzka bókmenntafélag, Reykjavík.

———— (1970), *Enska öldin í sögu Íslendinga*, Mál og menning, Reykjavík.

———— (1976a), "Johannes Gerechini Lodehat, biskop i Skálholt 1426-1433", *Från medeltid till välfärdssamhälle. Nordiska historikermötet i Uppsala 1974*, Föredrag och mötesförhandlingar, Almqvist & Wiksell, Stockholm, 497-506. Republished in Icelandic in Björn Þorsteinsson (1978), *Á fornum slóðum og nýjum*, Sögufélag, Reykjavík, 3-20.

Bibliography 369

—— (1976b), *Tíu þorskastríð 1415-1976*, Sögufélag, Reykjavík.

—— (1982), "Rabbað um land hillinganna haustið 1980", *Eyjaskinna* I, 13-22.

—— (1985), *Ísland*, with contributions by Bergsteinn Jónsson and Helgi Skúli Kjartansson, transl. by Preben Meulengracht Sørensen, Politikens Forlag, Copenhagen.

—— and Bergsteinn Jónsson (1991), *Íslandssaga til okkar daga*, Sögufélag, Reykjavík.

Björnsdóttir, *see* Inga Dóra Björnsdóttir.

Björnsson, *see* Björn Th. Björnsson, Lýður Björnsson, Ólafur Björnsson.

Blöndal, *see* Jón Blöndal, Sveinbjörn Blöndal.

Bogi Th. Melsteð (1907-15), "Ferðir, siglingar og samgöngur milli Íslands og annara landa á dögum þjóðveldisins", *Safn til sögu Íslands* IV, 585-910.

The Book of Settlements. Landnámabók (1972), transl. with introduction and notes by Hermann Pálsson and Paul Edwards, University of Manitoba Press, Winnipeg (*University of Manitoba Icelandic Studies* I).

Boserup, Ester (1965), *The Conditions of Agricultural Growth: The Economics of Agrarian Change under Population Pressure*, George Allen & Unwin, London.

Bragi Guðmundsson (1985), *Efnamenn og eignir þeirra um 1700. Athugun á íslenskum gósseigendum í jarðabók Árna og Páls og fleiri heimildum*, Sagnfræðistofnun Háskóla Íslands, Reykjavík (*Ritsafn Sagnfræðistofnunar* XIV).

—— and Gunnar Karlsson (1988), *Uppruni nútímans. Kennslubók í Íslandssögu eftir 1830*, Mál og menning, Reykjavík.

Briem, *see* Helgi P. Briem, Ólafur Briem, Páll Briem.

Bríet Bjarnhéðinsdóttir (1888), *Fyrirlestur um hagi og rjettindi kvenna sem Bríet Bjarnhjeðinsdóttir hjelt í Reykjavík 30. des. 1887. Fyrsti fyrirlestur kvennmanns á Íslandi*, Sigurður Kristjánsson, Reykjavík.

Brynleifur Tobiasson (1958), *Þjóðhátíðin 1874*, Menningarsjóður og Þjóðvinafélagið, Reykjavík.

Byock, Jesse L. (1982), *Feud in the Icelandic Saga*, University of California Press, Berkeley.

—— (1988), *Medieval Iceland: Society, Sagas, and Power*, University of California Press, Berkeley.

Byskupa sögur I-II (1938-78), ed. by Jón Helgason, Det kongelige nordiske Oldskriftselskab / Den arnamagnæanske kommission, Copenhagen. *See also Biskupa sögur*.

Bøgh, Anders (1997), "Margrethes statskup", *Siden Saxo* XIV:2, 2-7.

Coles, John (1882), *Summer Travelling in Iceland; being the narrative of two journeys across the island by unfrequented routes*, John Murray, London.

The Complete Sagas of Icelanders including 49 tales I-V (1997), general editor Viðar Hreinsson; editorial team: Robert Cook, Terry Gunnell, Keneva Kunz, Bernard Scudder; Leifur Eiríksson Publishing, Reykjavík

Dansgaard, W., S.J. Johnsen, N. Reeh, N. Gundestrup, H.B. Clausen and C.U. Hammer (1975), "Climatic changes, Norsemen and modern man", *Nature* CCXXV, no. 5503, 24-8.

Davíðsdóttir, *see* Sigrún Davíðsdóttir.

Davíðsson, *see* Ólafur Davíðsson.

Davis, Morris (1963), *Iceland Extends its Fisheries Limits: A political analysis*, Universitetsforlaget, Oslo.

Debes, Hans Jacob (1982), *Nú er tann stundin ... Tjóðskaparrørsla og sjálvstýrispolitikkur til 1906 – við søguligum baksýni*, Føroya skúlabókagrunnur, Tórshavn.

Derry, T.K. (1968), *A Short History of Norway*, 2nd edn George Allen & Unwin, London (1st edn 1957).

—— (1979), *A History of Scandinavia. Norway, Sweden, Denmark, Finland and Iceland*, George Allen & Unwin, London.

Desertion and Land Colonization in the Nordic Countries c. 1300-1600. Comparative Report from the Scandinavian Research Project on Deserted Farms and Villages (1981) by Svend Gissel, Eino Jutikkala, Eva Österberg, Jørn Sandnes, Björn Teitsson; Almqvist & Wiksell, Stockholm.

Dictionary of the Middle Ages V (1985), editor in chief Joseph R. Strayer, Charles Scribner's Sons, New York.

Dicuil (1967), *Dicuili Liber de Mensura Orbis Terrae*, ed. by J.J. Tierney, with contributions by L. Bieler, Dublin Institute for Advanced Studies, Dublin (*Scriptores Latini Hiberniae* VI).

Diplomatarium Islandicum. Íslenzkt fornbréfasafn, sem hefir inni að halda bréf og gjörnínga, dóma og máldaga, og aðrar skrár, er snerta Ísland eða íslenzka menn I-XVI (1857-1972), Hið íslenzka bókmenntafélag, Copenhagen and Reykjavík.

Diplomatarium Norvegicum. Oldbreve til Kundskap om Norges indre og ytre Forhold, Sprog, Slegter, Seder, Lovgivning og Rettergang i Middelalderen XIX (1914), *Aktstykker vedrørende Norges Forbindelse med de Britiske Øer* I. Kristiania.

Driscoll, Matthew (1997), *The Unwashed Children of Eve: The production, dissemination and reception of popular literature in post-reformation Iceland*, Hisarlik Press, Enfield Lock.

Eggert Þór Bernharðsson (1998), *Saga Reykjavíkur 1940-1990. Borgin* I-II, Iðunn, Reykjavík.

Eggert Ólafsson (1805), *Travels in Iceland: performed by order of his Danish Majesty. Containing observations on the manners and customs of the inhabitants, a description of the lakes, rivers, glaciers, hot-springs, and volcanoes; of the various kinds of earths, stones, fossils and petrifactions; as well as of the animals, insects, fishes, &c*, by Olafsen & Povelsen (translated from the Danish), Richard Phillips, London.

Egilsson, *see* Ólafur Egilsson.

Einar Arnórsson (1945), *Réttarsaga Alþingis*, Alþingissögunefnd, Reykjavík (*Saga Alþingis* I).

—— (1949), *Alþingi og frelsisbaráttan 1845-1874*, Alþingissögunefnd, Reykjavík (*Saga Alþingis* II).

—— *see* Jón Þorkelsson and Einar Arnórsson.

Einar Karl Haraldsson, *see* Ólafur R. Einarsson and Einar Karl Haraldsson.

Einar Laxness (1995), *Íslandssaga* a-h, i-r, s-ö. Vaka-Helgafell, Reykjavík (*Alfræði Vöku-Helgafells*).

Einar Ól. Sveinsson (1953), *The Age of the Sturlungs: Icelandic Civilization in the Thirteenth Century*, translated by Jóhann S. Hannesson, Cornell University Press, Ithaca, NY (*Islandica* XXXVI).

—— (1958), *Dating the Icelandic Sagas: An essay in method*, Viking Society for Northern Research, London.

Einarsdóttir, *see* Ólafía Einarsdóttir.

Einarsson, *see* Ólafur R. Einarsson, Stefán Einarsson, Þorleifur Einarsson.

Eldjárn, *see* Kristján Eldjárn.

Elsa E. Guðjónsson (1967), "The National Costume of Women in Iceland", *Iceland Review* V:3, 25-30.

—— (1969), *Íslenzkir þjóðbúningar kvenna frá 16. öld til vorra daga. Stutt yfirlit*, Bókaútgáfa Menningarsjóðs, Reykjavík.

Emilsson, *see* Tryggvi Emilsson.

Erlendsdóttir, *see* Sigríður Th. Erlendsdóttir.

Espólín, *see* Jón Espólín.

Eyjólfsson, *see* Þórður Eyjólfsson.

Eysteinn Þorvaldsson (1980), *Atómskáldin. Aðdragandi og upphaf módernisma í íslenskri ljóðagerð*, Hið íslenska bókmenntafélag, Reykjavík (*Fræðirit* V) (summary, 311-23).

Félagsmál á Íslandi (1942), Félagsmálaráðuneytið, Reykjavík (also included in *Saga Alþingis* IV (1956).

Finnbogason, *see* Guðmundur Finnbogason.

Finnur Jónsson (1772-8), *Historia ecclesiastica Islandiæ* I-IV. Typis Orphanotrophii Regii, Copenhagen.

Finsen, *see* Vilhjálmur Finsen.

The First Grammatical Treatise. Introduction. Text. Notes. Translation. Vocabulary. Facsimiles (1972), ed. by Hreinn Benediktsson, Institute of Nordic Linguistics, Reykjavík (*University of Iceland. Publications in Linguistics* I).

Foote, Peter G. (1977), "Þrælahald á Íslandi. Heimildakönnun og athugasemdir", *Saga* XV, 41-74 (summary, 73-4).

Friðriksson, *see* Guðjón Friðriksson, Þorbjörn Á. Friðriksson, Þorleifur Friðriksson.

Friedman, David (1979), "Private Creation and Enforcement of Law: A Historical Case", *Journal of Legal Studies* VIII:1, 399-415.

Gad, Finn (1970-3), *The History of Greenland* I-II, Hurst, London.

Gerrard, Nelson S. (1985), *Icelandic River Saga*, Saga Publications, Arborg, Manitoba.

Gils Guðmundsson (1977), *Skútuöldin*. 2nd edn (enlarged), I-V. Örn og Örlygur, Reykjavík.

Gíslason, *see* Árni Gíslason, Ingólfur V. Gíslason.

Gísli Gunnarsson (1980), *Fertility and Nuptiality in Iceland's Demographic History*, Ekonomisk-historiska institutionen, Lund (*Meddelande* XII).

—— (1983a), *Monopoly Trade and Economic Stagnation: Studies in the foreign trade of Iceland 1602-1787*. Ekonomisk-historiska föreningen, Lund (*Skrifter* XXXVIII).

—— (1983b), *The Sex Ratio, the Infant Mortality and Adjoining Societal Response in Pre-Transitional Iceland*. Ekonomisk-historiska institutionen, Lund (*Meddelande* XXXII).

—— (1987), *Upp er boðið Ísaland. Einokunarverslun og íslenskt samfélag 1602-1787*, Örn og Örlygur, Reykjavík.

Gísli Ágúst Gunnlaugsson (1982), *Ómagar og utangarðsfólk. Fátækramál Reykjavíkur 1786-1907*, Sögufélag, Reykjavík (*Safn til sögu Reykjavíkur*).

—— (1988), *Family and Household in Iceland 1801-1930: Studies in the relationship between demographic and socio-economic development, social legislation and family and household structures*. Almqvist & Wiksell, Uppsala (*Studia Historica Upsaliensia* CLIV).

—— *see* Aðalgeir Kristjánsson and Gísli Ágúst Gunnlaugsson.

Gísli Jónsson (1977), *Konur og kosningar. Þættir úr sögu íslenskrar kvenréttindabaráttu*, Bókaútgáfa Menningarsjóðs, Reykjavík.

Gísli Sigurðsson (1988), *Gaelic Influence in Iceland: Historical and literary contacts: A survey of research*, Bókaútgáfa Menningarsjóðs, Reykjavík (*Studia Islandica* XLVI).

Gissurarson, *see* Hannes Hólmsteinn Gissurarson.

Grágás. Lagasafn íslenska þjóðveldisins (1992), ed. by Gunnar Karlsson, Kristján Sveinsson, Mörður Árnason, Mál og menning, Reykjavík.

Grímsson, *see* Ólafur R. Grímsson.

Grjetarsson, *see* Jón Gunnar Grjetarsson.

Gröndal, *see* Benedikt Gröndal.

Grönvold, *see* Karl Grönvold.

Guðbrandur Jónsson (1932-4), *Frjálst verkafólk á Íslandi fram til siðaskifta og kjör þess*. Bókmentafélag jafnaðarmanna, Reykjavík.

Guðjón Friðriksson (1991a-1993), *Saga Jónasar Jónssonar frá Hriflu* I-III, Iðunn, Reykjavík.

—— (1991b-1994), *Saga Reykjavíkur. Bærinn vaknar 1870-1940* I-II, Iðunn, Reykjavík.

Guðjónsson, *see* Elsa E. Guðjónsson.

Guðlaugsson, *see* Baldur Guðlaugsson.

Guðmundsdóttir, *see* Margrét Guðmundsdóttir.

Guðmundsson, *see* Arnar Guðmundsson, Ásgeir Guðmundsson, Bragi Guðmundsson, Gils Guðmundsson, Guðmundur J. Guðmundsson, Hallgrímur Guðmundsson, Helgi Guðmundsson, Magnús Guðmundsson, Óskar Guðmundsson.

Guðmundur Finnbogason (1905), *Skýrsla um fræðslu barna og unglinga veturinn 1903-1904*, Reykjavík.

—— (1947), *Alþingi og menntamálin*, Alþingissögunefnd, Reykjavík (*Saga Alþingis* V).

Guðmundur J. Guðmundsson (1999), "'Þau eru svo eftirsótt Íslandsmið . . . '

Bibliography 373

Samningaviðræður Íslendinga og Breta í þorskastríðinu 1958-61", *Saga* XXXVII, 63-115 (summary, 114-15).

Guðmundur Hálfdanarson (1986), "Takmörkun giftinga eða einstaklingsfrelsi. Íhaldssemi og frjálslyndi á fyrstu árum hins endurreista alþingis", *Tímarit Máls og menningar* XLVII, 457-68.

―― (1987), "Aðdragandi iðnbyltingar á 19. öld", *Iðnbylting á Íslandi,* Sagnfræðistofnun Háskóla Íslands, Reykjavík (*Ritsafn Sagnfræðistofnunar* XXI), 24-32.

―― (1991), "Old Provinces, Modern Nations: Political Responses to State Integration in Late Nineteenth and Early Twentieth-Century Iceland and Brittany", Ph.D. thesis, Cornell University.

―― (1993), "Íslensk þjóðfélagsþróun á 19. öld", *Íslensk þjóðfélagsþróun 1880-1990* (Félagsvísindastofnun/Sagnfræðistofnun, Reykjavík), 9-58.

―― (1995), "Social Distinctions and National Unity: On politics of nationalism in nineteenth-century Iceland", *History of European Ideas* XXI:6, 763-79.

―― (1997a), *Historical Dictionary of Iceland*, Scarecrow Press, London (*European Historical Dictionaries* XXIV).

―― (1997b), "Þjóðhetjan Jón Sigurðsson", *Andvari* CXXII, 40-62.

Guðmundur Hannesson (1943), "Húsagerð á Íslandi", *Iðnsaga Íslands* I (Iðnaðarmannafélagið, Reykjavík), 1-317.

Guðmundur Jónsson (1981), *Vinnuhjú á 19. öld*, Sagnfræðistofnun Háskóla Íslands, Reykjavík (*Ritsafn Sagnfræðistofnunar* V).

―― (1991), "The State and the Icelandic Economy 1870-1930", Ph.D. thesis, London School of Economics and Political Science.

―― (1994), "Mannfjöldatölur 18. aldar endurskoðaðar", *Saga* XXXII, 153-8.

―― (1997), "Changes in Food Consumption in Iceland *ca.* 1770-1940", *Kultur och konsumption i Norden 1750-1950*, ed. by John Söderberg and Lars Magnusson (*Finska historiska samfundet*, Helsingfors), 37-60.

―― see *Hagskinna.*

Guðnason, *see*: Jón Guðnason.

Guðrún Sveinbjarnardóttir (1992), *Farm Abandonment in Medieval and Post-Medieval Iceland: an Interdisciplinary Study*, Oxbow Books, Oxford (*Oxbow Monographs* XVII).

Gunnar Gunnarsson (1938a), *The Night and the Dream*, transl. from the Danish by Evelyn Ramsden, Jarrolds, London.

―― (1938b), *Ships in the Sky (compiled from Uggi Greipsson's notes)*, transl. by Evelyn Ramsden, Jarrolds, London.

―― (1940), *The Good Shepherd*, transl. by Kenneth C. Kaufman, illus. by Masha Simkowitch, Bobbs-Merrill, Indianapolis.

―― (1967), *The Black Cliffs. Svartfugl*, transl. from the Danish by Cecil Wood, intro. by Richard N. Ringler, University of Wisconsin Press, Madison.

Gunnar Á. Gunnarsson (1996), "Ísland og Marshalláætlunin 1948-1953. Atvinnustefna og stjórnmálahagsmunir", *Saga* XXXIV, 85-130 (summary, 129-30).

374   Bibliography

Gunnar Karlsson (1972a), *Frá endurskoðun til valtýsku*, Bókaútgáfa Menningarsjóðs, Reykjavík (*Sagnfræðirannsóknir* I) (summary, 160-4).

—— (1972b), "Goðar og bændur", *Saga* X, 5-57 (summary, 55-7).

—— (1975), "Frá þjóðveldi til konungsríkis", *Saga Íslands* II (Hið íslenzka
bókmenntafélag, Reykjavík), 1-54.

—— (1977a), *Frelsisbarátta suður-þingeyinga og Jón á Gautlöndum*, Hið íslenska
bókmenntafélag, Reykjavík (summary, 471-5).

—— (1977b), "*Goðar* and *Höfðingjar* in Medieval Iceland", *Saga-Book* XIX:4,
358-70.

—— (1985), "Dyggðir og lestir í þjóðfélagi Íslendingasagna", *Tímarit Máls og
menningar* XLVI:1, 9-19.

—— (1986), "Kenningin um fornt kvenfrelsi á Íslandi", *Saga* XXIV, 45-77 (summary, 76-7).

—— (1988), "Siðamat Íslendingasögu", *Sturlustefna. Ráðstefna haldin á sjö alda
ártíð Sturlu Þórðarsonar sagnaritara 1984*, ed. by Guðrún Ása Grímsdóttir
and Jónas Kristjánsson (Stofnun Árna Magnússonar, Reykjavík), 204-21 (summary,
220-1).

—— (1990), *Kóngsins menn. Ágrip af Íslandssögu milli 1550 og 1830*, Mál og
menning, Reykjavík.

—— (1991), "Að ná íslenskum lögum. Um lagaákvæði Gamla sáttmála og
löggjafarvald á Íslandi í veldi Noregskonungs", *Yfir Íslandsála. Afmælisrit til
heiðurs Magnúsi Stefánssyni sextugum* (Sögufræðslusjóður, Reykjavík), 53-75.

—— (1993), "A Century of Research on Early Icelandic Society", *Viking Revalu-
ations: Viking Society centenary symposium 14-15 May 1992* (Viking Society
for Northern Research, London), 15-25.

—— (1994a), "Nafngreindar höfðingjaættir í Sturlungu", *Sagnaþing helgað Jónasi
Kristjánssyni sjötugum* I (Hið íslenska bókmenntafélag, Reykjavík), 307-15.

—— (1994b), "When did the Icelanders become Icelanders?" *Líf undir leiðarstjörnu
(Man in the North -- MAIN). Ráðstefnurit* (Háskólinn á Akureyri, Akureyri),
107-15.

—— (1995), "The Emergence of Nationalism in Iceland", Sven Tägil, ed., *Ethnicity
and Nation Building in the Nordic World* (Hurst, London), 32-62.

—— (1996a), "Plague without rats: the case of fifteenth-century Iceland", *Journal of Medieval History* XXII, 263-84.

—— (1996b), "Söguleg merking Áshildarmýrarsamþykktar", *Árnesingur* IV,
71-9.

—— (1999), "Íslensk þjóðernisvitund á óþjóðlegum öldum", *Skírnir* CLXXIII,
141-78.

—— and students of history at the University of Iceland (1989), *Samband við
miðaldir. Námsbók í íslenskri miðaldasögu, um 870-1550, og sagnfræðilegum
aðferðum*, Mál og menning, Reykjavík.

—— and Helgi Skúli Kjartansson (1994), "Plágurnar miklu á Íslandi", *Saga* XXXII,
11-74 (summary, 74).

—— see Bragi Guðmundsson and Gunnar Karlsson.

Bibliography 375

Gunnar M. Magnúss (1939), *Saga alþýðufræðslunnar á Íslandi. Hátíðarit S.Í.B*, Samband íslenzkra barnakennara, Reykjavík.

—— (1967), *Ár og dagar. Upptök og þróun alþýðusamtaka á Íslandi 1875-1934*, Heimskringla, Reykjavík.

Gunnarsson, *see* Gísli Gunnarsson, Gunnar Gunnarsson, Gunnar Á. Gunnarsson.

Gunnell, Terry (1995), *The Origins of Drama in Scandinavia*, D.S. Brewer, Cambridge (England).

Gunnlaugsson, *see* Gísli Ágúst Gunnlaugsson.

Gunnlaugur Þórðarson (1952), *Landhelgi Íslands með tilliti til fiskveiða*, Hlaðbúð, Reykjavík.

Gustafsson, Harald (1985), *Mellan kung och allmoge – ämbetsmän, beslutsprocess och inflytande på 1700-talets Island*, Almqvist & Wiksell, Stockholm (summary, 311-15).

—— (1997), *Nordens historia. En europeisk region under 1200 år*, Studentlitteratur, Lund.

Guttormsson, *see* Loftur Guttormsson.

Hagskinna. Sögulegar hagtölur um Ísland. Icelandic Historical Statistics (1997), ed. by Guðmundur Jónsson and Magnús S. Magnússon, Hagstofa Íslands, Reykjavík.

Hagskýrslur Íslands. Statistics of Iceland II:21(1960), *Manntalið 1703. Population Census 1703*, Hagstofa Íslands, Reykjavík.

Hagskýrslur Íslands Statistics of Iceland III:31 (1995), *Alþingiskosningar. Elections to the Althingi 1995*, Hagstofa Íslands, Reykjavík.

Hagtölur mánaðarins XXVI (1998), Seðlabanki Íslands, Reykjavík.

Hakluyt, Richard, ed. (1598), *The Principal Navigations, Voiages, Traffiqves and Discoueries of the English Nation, made be Sea and over-land, to the Remote and Farthest Distant Quarters of the Earth, at any time within the compasse of these 1500 yeeres ...* I. George Bishop, London.

Hákon Bjarnason (1942), "Ábúð og örtröð", *Ársrit Skógræktarfélags Íslands*, 1942, 8-40.

Hákonar saga Hákonarsonar etter Sth. 8 fol., AM 325 VIII,4° og AM 304,4° (1977), ed. by Kjeldeskriftfondet with Marina Mundt, Norsk historisk kjeldeskriftinstitutt, Oslo (*Norrøne tekster* II).

Hákonardóttir, *see* Inga Huld Hákonardóttir.

Hálfdanarson, *see* Guðmundur Hálfdanarson.

Hallberg, Peter (1971), *Halldór Laxness*, transl. by Rory McTurk, Twayne Publishers, New York.

Halldór Bjarnason, *see* Valdimar Unnar Valdimarsson.

Halldór Halldórsson (1962), "Kring språkliga nybildningar i nutida isländska", *Scripta Islandica* XIII, 3-24.

Halldór Kiljan Laxness (1936), *Salka Valka*, transl. by F.H. Lyon, Houghton Mifflin, Boston.

—— (1945), *Independent People. An epic*, transl. from the Icelandic by J.A.

Thompson, George Allen & Unwin, London.

—— (1958), *The Happy Warriors*, transl. by Katherine John, Methuen, London.

—— (1961), *The Atom Station*, transl. by Magnus Magnusson, Methuen, London.

—— (1966), *The Fish Can Sing*, transl. by Magnus Magnusson, Methuen, London.

—— (1969), *World Light*, transl. by Magnus Magnusson, University of Wisconsin Press, Madison.

—— (1972), *Christianity at Glacier*, transl. by Magnus Magnusson, Helgafell, Reykjavík.

—— (1979), "Ræða um Snorra", *Snorri, átta alda minning* (Sögufélag, Reykjavík), 13-22.

Halldórsson, *see* Halldór Halldórsson, Jón Halldórsson, Ólafur Halldórsson.

Hallgrímsson, *see* Hallgrímur Hallgrímsson, Jónas Hallgrímsson.

Hallgrímur Guðmundsson (1979), *Uppruni Sjálfstæðisflokksins*, Félagsvísindadeild Háskóla Íslands, Reykjavík (*Íslensk þjóðfélagsfræði* VII).

Hallgrímur Hallgrímsson (1925), *Íslensk alþýðumentun á 18. öld*, repr. from *Tíminn*, Reykjavík.

Hallgrímur Pétursson (1966), *Hymns of the Passion: Mediations on the Passion of Christ*, transl. from the Icelandic by Arthur Charles Gook, Hallgríms Church, Reykjavík.

Hallgrímur Sveinsson (1996), *The National Hero of Iceland, Jón Sigurdsson: A concise biography*, transl. Hersteinn Pálsson, Vestfirska forlagið, Hrafnseyri.

Hallsdóttir, *see* Margrét Hallsdóttir.

Hannes Hólmsteinn Gissurarson (1989), *Sjálfstæðisflokkurinn í sextíu ár*, Sjálfstæðisflokkurinn, Reykjavík.

Hannes Jónsson (1982), *Friends in Conflict: The Anglo-Icelandic cod wars and the law of the sea*, Hurst, London.

Hannesson, *see* Guðmundur Hannesson, Helgi Hannesson.

Haraldur Matthíasson (1982), *Landið og Landnáma* I-II, Örn og Örlygur, Reykjavík.

Haraldur Ólafsson (1987), *Brimöldur. Frásögn Haralds Ólafssonar sjómanns*, recorded by Jón Guðnason, Mál og menning, Reykjavík.

Haraldur Sigurðsson (1972), "Skrá um verk Halldórs Laxness á íslenzku og erlendum málum", *Landsbókasafn Íslands. Árbók 1971*, 177-200.

—— (1976), "Fjögurra alda afmæli bókagerðar Guðbrands Þorlákssonar biskups 1575-1975", *Landsbókasafn Íslands. Árbók 1975*, 40-53.

Haraldur Sigurðsson (1991), "Kvikfénaðartalið 1703 og bústofnsbreytingar í upphafi 18. aldar", BA thesis in history, Háskóli Íslands.

Hardarson, Sólrún B. Jensdóttir, *see* Sólrún B. Jensdóttir.

Hart, Jeffrey A. (1976), *The Anglo-Icelandic Cod War of 1972-1973: A case study of fishery dispute*, Institute of International Studies, University of California, Berkeley.

Hastrup, Kirsten (1984), "Defining a Society: The Icelandic Free State Between two Worlds", *Scandinavian Studies* LVI, 235-55.

—— (1985), *Culture and History in Medieval Iceland: An anthropological analysis of structure and change*, Oxford University Press.

—— (1990), *Nature and Policy in Iceland 1400-1800: An anthropological analysis of history and mentality*, Oxford University Press.

Heimir Þorleifsson (1974), *Saga íslenzkrar togaraútgerðar fram til 1917*, Bókaútgáfa Menningarsjóðs, Reykjavík (*Sagnfræðirannsóknir* III) (summary, 202-6).

Helgadóttir, *see* Herdís Helgadóttir.

Helgason, *see* Þórkatla Óskarsdóttir.

Helgi P. Briem (1936), *Sjálfstæði Íslands 1809*, E. P. Briem, Reykjavík. (*Byltingin 1809* by the same author is the same book with one chapter omitted.)

Helgi Guðmundsson (1997), *Um haf innan. Vestrænir menn og íslenzk menning á miðöldum*, Háskólaútgáfan, Reykjavík.

Helgi Hannesson (1980), "Árásarhætta á Ísland vegna herstöðvarinnar", *Sex ritgerðir um herstöðvamál*, by students of history at the Faculty of Arts, University of Iceland (Sagnfræðistofnun Háskóla Íslands, Reyjavík, *Ritsafn Sagnfræðistofnunar* III), 17-29.

Helgi Skúli Kjartansson (1975), "Spáð í pýramíða um mannfjöldasögu Íslands á 17. öld", *Afmælisrit Björns Sigfússonar* (Sögufélag, Reykjavík), 120-34 (summary, 133-4).

—— (1977), "The Onset of Emigration from Iceland", *Nordic Population Mobility: Comparative Studies of Selected Parishes in the Nordic Countries 1850-1900*, ed. by Bo Kronborg *et al.*, Universitetsforlaget, Oslo (*American Studies in Scandinavia* IX:1-2), 87-93.

—— (1980), "Emigrant Fares and Emigration from Iceland to North America, 1874-1893", *Scandinavian Economic History Review* XXVIII:1, 53-71.

—— (1987), *Ágrip af sögu Alþýðuflokksins*, Alþýðuflokkurinn, Reykjavík.

—— (1989a), *Fjöldi goðorða samkvæmt Grágás*, lecture given at a conference held by the Sigurður Nordal Institute 24-26 July 1988, Félag áhugamanna um réttarsögu, Reykjavík (*Erindi og greinar* XXVI).

—— (1989b), "Ungbörn þjáð af þorsta. Stutt athugasemd um ungbarnadauða og viðurværi", *Sagnir* X, 98-100.

—— (1992), "Icelandic Emigration", *European Expansion and Migration. Essays on the Intercontinental Migration from Africa, Asia, and Europe*, ed. by P.C. Emmer and M. Mörner (Berg, New York), 105-19.

—— *see* Björn Þorsteinsson (1985).

—— *see* Íslenskur söguatlas.

Helgi Þorláksson (1982), "Rómarvald og kirkjugoðar", *Skírnir* CLVI, 51-67.

—— (1983), "Útflutningur íslenskra barna til Englands á miðöldum", *Sagnir* IV, 47-53.

—— (1987), "Að vita sann á sögunum. Hvaða vitneskju geta Íslendingasögurnar veitt um íslenskt þjóðfélag fyrir 1200?", *Ný Saga* I, 87-96 (summary, 100).

—— (1988), "Gráfeldr á gullöld og voðaverk kvenna", *Ný saga* II, 40-53 (summary, 120).

—— (1994), "Hvað er blóðhefnd?" *Sagnaþing helgað Jónasi Kristjánssyni sjötugum* I (Hið íslenska bókmenntafélag, Reykjavík), 389-414.

—— (1999), *Sjórán og siglingar. Ensk-íslensk samskipti 1580-1630*, Mál og menning, Reykjavík.

Herdís Helgadóttir (1996), *Vaknaðu kona! Barátta rauðsokka frá þeirra eigin sjónarhóli*, Skjaldborg, Reykjavík.

Hinriksson, *see* Þórður Hinriksson.

Hjalti Hugason (1983), *Bessastadaskolan. Ett försök till prästskola på Island 1805-1846*, Uppsala universitet (*Skrifter utgivna av Svenska Kyrkohistoriska föreningen* II. Ny följd XL) (German summary 124-32).

—— (1988), "Kristnir trúarhættir", *Íslensk þjóðmenning* V (Þjóðsaga, Reykjavík), 75-339 (summary, 406-14).

—— (1989), "Hverju breytti siðbreytingin? Tilraun til endurmats í tilefni af páfakomu", *Kirkjuritið* LV:1-2, 71-99.

Hjartarson, *see* Stefán F. Hjartarson.

Hjörtur Pálsson (1975), *Alaskaför Jóns Ólafssonar 1874*, Bókaútgáfa Menningarsjóðs, Reykjavík (*Sagnfræðirannsóknir* IV) (summary, 183-91).

Hogan, James Francis (1891), *The Convict King: Being the life and adventures of Jorgen Jorgenson, monarch of Iceland, naval captain, revolutionist, British diplomatic agent, author, dramatist, preacher, political prisoner, gambler, hospital dispenser, continental traveller, explorer, editor, expatriated exile, and colonial constable*, retold by James Francis Hogan, Ward & Downey, London.

Hood, John C.F. (1946), *Icelandic Church Saga*, SPCK, London.

Horrebow, Niels (1758), *The Natural History of Iceland, containing a particular and accurate account of the different soils, burning mountains, minerals, vegetables, metals, stones, beasts, birds, and fishes, together with the disposition, customs, and manner of living of the inhabitants. Interspersed with an account of the island by Mr. Andersson, late burgo-master of Hamburgh. To which is added a meteorological table, with remarks*, transl. from the Danish original, A. Linde, London.

Hrefna Róbertsdóttir (1990), *Reykjavíkurfélög. Félagshreyfing og menntastarf á ofanverðri 19. öld*, Sagnfræðistofnun, Reykjavík (*Ritsafn Sagnfræðistofnunar* XXVI).

Hugason, *see* Hjalti Hugason.

Hörður Ágústsson (1972), *Hér stóð bær. Líkan af þjóðveldisbæ*, Þjóðhátíðarnefnd 1974, Reykjavík.

—— (1987), "Íslenski torfbærinn", *Íslensk þjóðmenning* I (Þjóðsaga, Reykjavík), 227-344.

Höskuldsson, *see* Sveinn Skorri Höskuldsson.

Iceland: The Republic (1996), handbook ed. by Jóhannes Nordal and Valdimar Kristinsson, Central Bank of Iceland, Reykjavík.

Inga Dóra Björnsdóttir (1989), "Public View and Private Voices", *The Anthropology of Iceland*, ed. by E. Paul Durrenberger and Gísli Pálsson (University of Iowa Press, Iowa City), 98-118.

Inga Huld Hákonardóttir (1992), *Fjarri hlýju hjónasængur. Öðruvísi Íslandssaga*, Mál og menning, Reykjavík.

Ingi Sigurðsson (1972), "The Historical Works of Jón Espólín and his Contemporaries. Aspects of Icelandic Historiography", Ph.D. thesis, University of Edinburgh.

—— (1996), *Hugmyndaheimur Magnúsar Stephensens*, Hið íslenzka bókmenntafélag, Reykjavík (summary, 179-82).

Ingimundarson *see* Valur Ingimundarson.

Ingimundur Sigurpálsson (1976), "Herinn og hagkerfið. Efnahagsleg áhrif varnarliðsins", *Fjármálatíðindi* XXIII, 23-48.

Ingólfur XI (1913), Reykjavík.

Ingólfur V. Gíslason (1990), *Enter the Bourgeoisie: Aspects of the formation and organization of Icelandic employers 1894-1934*, University of Lund.

Ingstad, Anne Stine (1977), *The Discovery of a Norse Settlement in America: Excavations at L'Anse aux Meadows, Newfoundland 1961-1968*. Universitetsforlaget, Oslo. Republ. as *The Norse Discovery of America* I (1985).

Ingstad, Helge (1985), *The Norse Discovery of America*, II: *The Historical Background and the Evidence of the Norse Settlement Discovered in Newfoundland*, Universitetsforlaget, Oslo.

Ingvarsson, *see* Lúðvík Ingvarsson.

Ísberg, *see* Jón Ólafur Ísberg.

Islandske Annaler indtil 1578 (1888), published for the Norske Historiske Kildeskriftfond by Dr Gustav Storm, Christiania.

Ísleifsdóttir, *see* Vilborg Auður Ísleifsdóttir.

Íslensk bókmenntasaga II-III (1993-6), Mál og menning, Reykjavík.

Íslensk þjóðmenning I, V-VII (1987-90), Þjóðsaga, Reykjavík.

Íslenskur söguatlas I-III (1989-93), ed. by Árni Daníel Júlíusson, Jón Ólafur Ísberg, Helgi Skúli Kjartansson, Almenna bókafélagið/Iðunn, Reykjavík.

Íslenzk fornrit I (1968), *Íslendingabók. Landnámabók*, ed. by Jakob Benediktsson, Hið íslenzka fornritafélag, Reykjavík.

—— VII (1936), *Grettis saga Ásmundarsonar. Bandamanna saga*, ed. by Guðni Jónsson, Hið íslenzka fornritafélag, Reykjavík.

—— XXVII (1945), *Heimskringla* II, ed. by Bjarni Aðalbjarnarson, Hið íslenzka fornritafélag, Reykjavík.

—— XXXV (1982), *Danakonunga sögur*, ed. by Bjarni Guðnason, Hið íslenzka fornritafélag, Reykjavík.

Íslenzkt fornbréfasafn, see Diplomatarium Islandicum.

Jakob Benediktsson (1957), *Arngrímur Jónsson and his Works*, Ejnar Munksgaard, Copenhagen.

Jakobsson, *see* Sverrir Jakobsson.

Járnsíða (1847). *Hin forna lögbók Íslendínga sem nefnist Járnsida eðr Hákonarbók. Codex Juris Islandorum Antiqvus, qui nominatur Jarnsida seu Liber Haconis. Ex manuscripto pergameno (quod solum superest) Legati Arnæ-Magnæani editus. Cum interpretatione latina, lectionibus variis, indicibus vocum et rerum p.p.*

præmisso historico in hujus juris origines et fata tentamine, a Th. Sveinbjörnsson conscripto. Legat Arnamagnæani, Copenhagen.

Jensdóttir, *see* Sólrún B. Jensdóttir.

Jochens, Jenny (1995), *Women in Old Norse Society*, Cornell University Press, Ithaca, NY.

Jóhannesson, *see* Jón Jóhannesson, Kristinn Jóhannesson, Þorkell Jóhannesson.

Jón Hnefill Aðalsteinsson (1978), *Under the Cloak*, Almqvist & Wiksell, Uppsala (*Studia Ethnologica Upsaliensia* IV).

——(1988), "Hofgyðja á Héraði", *Saga og kirkja. Afmælisrit Magnúsar Más Lárussonar* (Sögufélag, Reykjavík), 59-68.

Jón Jónsson Aðils (1906), *Gullöld Íslendinga. Menning og lífshættir feðra vorra á söguöldinni. Alþýðufyrirlestrar með myndum*, Sigurður Kristjánsson, Reykjavík.

——(1911), *Skúli Magnússon landfógeti*, Sigurður Kristjánsson, Reykjavík.

——(1919), *Einokunarverzlun Dana á Íslandi 1602-1787*, Verzlunarráð Íslands, Reykjavík.

——(1926-7), *Den danske Monopolhandel på Island 1602-1787*, transl. by Friðrik Ásmundsson Brekkan, Dansk-islandsk Samfund, Copenhagen.

Jón Blöndal and Sverrir Kristjánsson (1954), *Alþingi og félagsmálin*, Alþingissögunefnd, Reykjavík (*Saga Alþingis* IV).

Jón Espólín (1821-55), *Íslands Árbækur í sögu-formi* I-XII. Eð Islendska Bókmentafélag, Copenhagen.

Jón Gunnar Grjetarsson (1988), *Síbería. Atvinnubótavinna á kreppuárunum, Sagnfræðistofnun*, Reykjavík (*Ritsafn Sagnfræðistofnunar* XXIV).

Jón Guðnason (1968-74), *Skúli Thoroddsen* I-II, Heimskringla, Reykjavík.

—— *see* Haraldur Ólafsson.

Jón Halldórsson (1903-15), *Biskupasögur Jóns prófasts Haldórssonar í Hítardal. Með viðbæti*, I-II, Sögufélag, Reykjavík.

Jón Ólafur Ísberg (1989), "Íslensk nýlendustefna", *Sagnir* X, 90-5.

—— *see Íslenskur söguatlas.*

Jón Jóhannesson (1956-8), *Íslendinga saga* I-II, Almenna bókafélagið, Reykjavík.

——(1974), *A History of the Old Icelandic Commonwealth. Íslendinga saga*, transl. by Haraldur Bessason, University of Manitoba Press, Winnipeg (*University of Manitoba Icelandic Studies* II).

Jón Jónsson (1988-90), *Hafrannsóknir við Ísland* I-II, Bókaútgáfa Menningarsjóðs, Reykjavík (summaries I, 293-311; II, 387-407).

——(1994), *Útgerð og aflabrögð við Ísland 1300-1900*, Hafrannsóknastofnun, Reykjavík (*Hafrannsóknir* XLVIII).

Jón Magnússon (1914), *Píslarsaga síra Jóns Magnússonar*, ed. by Sigfús Blöndal, Hið íslenska fræðafjelag, Copenhagen. Republ. 1967, ed. by Sigurður Nordal, Almenna bókafélagið, Reykjavík.

Jón Ólafsson (1923-32), *The Life of the Icelander Jón Ólafsson, Traveller to India, written by himself and completed about 1661 AD, with a continuation, by another hand, up to his death in 1679*, transl. from the Icelandic edition of Sigfús Blöndal by Bertha S. Phillpotts, I-II, Hakluyt Society, London.

Jón Sigurðsson (1974), "Verðbólga á Íslandi 1914-1974", *Fjármálatíðindi* XXI, 29-43.

Jón Viðar Sigurðsson (1984), *Keflavíkurflugvöllur 1947-1951*, Sagnfræðistofnun Háskóla Íslands, Reykjavík (*Ritsafn Sagnfræðistofnunar* XI).

—— (1989), *Frá goðorðum til ríkja. Þróun goðavalds á 12. og 13. öld*, Bókaútgáfa Menningarsjóðs, Reykjavík (*Sagnfræðirannsóknir* X) (summary, 138-42).

—— (1991), "Börn og gamalmenni á þjóðveldisöld", *Yfir Íslandsála. Afmælisrit til heiðurs Magnúsi Stefánssyni sextugum* (Sögufræðslusjóður, Reykjavík), 111-30.

—— (1999), *Chieftains and Power in the Icelandic Commonwealth*, transl. by Jean Lundskær-Nielsen, Odense University Press (*Viking Collection* XII).

Jón Steffensen (1954-8), "Líkamsvöxtur og lífsafkoma Íslendinga", *Saga* II, 280-308. Repr. and abridged in Jón Steffensen (1975), 426-33.

—— (1963), "Islands folkemængde gennem tiderne", *Medicinsk forum* XVI:5, 129-52.

—— (1974), "Plague in Iceland", *Nordisk medicinhistorisk årsbok* 1974, 40-55.

—— (1975), *Menning og meinsemdir. Ritgerðasafn um mótunarsögu íslenzkrar þjóðar og baráttu hennar við hungur og sóttir*, Sögufélag, Reykjavík.

Jón Steingrímsson (1913-16), *Æfisaga Jóns prófasts Steingrímssonar eptir sjálfan hann*, Sögufélag, Reykjavík. Republ. (1945), Skaftfellingafélagið/Helgafell, Reykjavík. Republ. (1973) as *Ævisagan og önnur rit*, ed. by Kristján Albertsson, Helgafell, Reykjavík.

—— (1998), *Fires of the Earth: The Laki Eruption 1783-1784*, with an introduction by Guðmundur E. Sigvaldason, transl. by Keneva Kunz, University of Iceland Press/Nordic Volcanological Institute, Reykjavík.

Jon Th. Thor, *see* Jón Þ. Þór.

Jón Thoroddsen (1887), *Sigrid: An Icelandic love story* by Jon Thordssön Thoroddsen, transl. from the Danish by C. Chrest, ed. by Thomas Tapper jr, Thomas Y. Crowell & Co., New York.

—— (1890), *Lad and Lass: A story of life in Iceland*, transl. from the Icelandic of Jón Þórðarson Thóroddsen by Arthur M. Reeves; Sampson Low, Marston, Searle & Rivington, London.

Jón Þ. Þór (1988), *Saga Ísafjarðar og Eyrarhrepps hins forna* III, Sögufélag Ísfirðinga, Ísafirði.

—— (1991), *Landhelgi Íslands 1901-1952*, Sagnfræðistofnun, Reykjavík (*Ritsafn Sagnfræðistofnunar* XXIX) (summary, 88-90).

—— (1992), *British Trawlers in Icelandic Waters: History of British steam trawling off Iceland 1889-1916 and the Anglo-Icelandic fisheries dispute 1896-1897*, transl. from the Icelandic by Hilmar Foss. Fjölvi, Reykjavík.

Jón Þorkelsson and Einar Arnórsson (1908), *Ríkisréttindi Íslands. Skjöl og skrif*, Sigurður Kristjánsson, Reykjavík.

Jónas Hallgrímsson (1996-7), *Selected Poetry and Prose*, ed. and transl. with notes and commentary by Dick Ringler, produced by University of Wisconsin-Madison General Library System. Internet: http://www.library.wisc.edu/etext/Jonas/html

382 *Bibliography*

Jónas Jónasson (1934), *Íslenzkir þjóðhættir*, ed. by Einar Ól. Sveinsson, Ísafoldarprentsmiðja, Reykjavík.

Jónas Kristjánsson (1988), *Eddas and Sagas: Iceland's Medieval Literature*, transl. by Peter Foote, Hið íslenska bókmenntafélag, Reykjavík.

Jónasson, *see* Jónas Jónasson, Kjartan Jónasson.

Jones, Gwyn (1986), *The Norse Atlantic Saga: Being the Norse Voyages of Discovery and Settlement to Iceland, Greenland, and North America*, new and enlarged edition, with contributions by Robert McGhee, Thomas H. McGovern and colleagues, and Birgitta Linderoth Wallace, Oxford University Press.

Jónsbók. Kong Magnus Hakonssons Lovbog for Island, vedtaget paa Altinget 1281, og Réttarbætr, de for Island givne Retterbøder af 1294, 1305 og 1314 (1904), ed. by Ólafur Halldórsson, S. Møllers Bogtrykkeri, Copenhagen.

Jónsson, *see* Agnar Kl. Jónsson, Bergsteinn Jónsson, Finnur Jónsson, Gísli Jónsson, Guðbrandur Jónsson, Guðmundur Jónsson, Hannes Jónsson, Jón Jónsson, Klemens Jónsson, Magnús Jónsson, Már Jónsson, Sigfús Jónsson, Steingrímur Jónsson.

Júlíusson, *see* Árni Daníel Júlíusson.

Júníus H. Kristinsson (1983), *Vesturfaraskrá 1870-1914: A Record of Emigrants from Iceland to America 1870-1914*, Sagnfræðistofnun, Reykjavík.

Karl Grönvold, Níels Óskarsson, Sigfús J. Johnsen, Henrik B. Clausen, Claus U. Hammer, Gerard Bond, Edouard Bard (1995), "Express Letter: Ash layers from Iceland in the Greenland GRIP ice core correlated with oceanic and land sediments", *Earth and Planetary Science Letters* CXXXV:1-4, 149-55.

Karlsdóttir, *see* Unnur B. Karlsdóttir.

Karlsson, *see* Gunnar Karlsson.

Kirkconnell, Watson (1930), *The North American Book of Icelandic Verse*, Louis Carrier and Alan Isles, New York and Montreal.

Kjartan Jónasson I (1986), *Kreppuárin á Íslandi 1930-1939* I, Örn og Örlygur, Reykjavík.

Kjartansson, *see* Helgi Skúli Kjartansson.

Klemens Jónsson (1929), *Saga Reykjavíkur* I-II, Steindór Gunnarsson, Reykjavík.

Kristinn E. Andrésson (1949), *Íslenzkar nútímabókmenntir 1918-1948*, Mál og menning, Reykjavík.

—— (1977), "Minnisblöð um leynifundi þingmanna um herstöðvamálið 1945", *Tímarit Máls og menningar* XXXVIII, 3-17.

Kristinn Jóhannesson (1968), "Þættir úr landvarnasögu Íslendinga", *Saga* VI, 122-38.

Kristinsson. See: Júníus H. Kristinsson.

Kristján Eldjárn (1956), *Kuml og haugfé úr heiðnum sið á Íslandi*, Norðri, Akureyri.

—— (1961), "Bær í Gjáskógum í Þjórsárdal", *Árbók Hins íslenzka fornleifafélags* 1961, 7-46 (summary, 44-6).

Kristjánsdóttir, *see* Ragnheiður Kristjánsdóttir.

Kristjanson, W. (1965), *The Icelandic People in Manitoba: A Manitoba saga*, Wallingford Press, Winnipeg.

Kristjánsson, *see* Aðalgeir Kristjánsson, Jónas Kristjánsson, Lúðvík Kristjánsson, Svanur Kristjánsson, Sverrir Kristjánsson.

Kristmundsdóttir, *see* Sigríður Dúna Kristmundsdóttir.

Kristnisaga. Þáttr Þorvalds ens víðförla. Þáttr Ísleifs biskups Gizurarsonar. Hungrvaka (1905), ed. by B. Kahle, Max Niemeyer, Halle (*Altnordische Saga-Bibliothek* XI).

Lagasafn. Íslensk lög 1. október 1999 (1999), Dóms– og kirkjumálaráðuneytið, Reykjavík.

Landshagir. Statistical Yearbook of Iceland 1997-8 (1997-8), Hagstofa Íslands, Reykjavík.

Landshagsskýrslur fyrir Ísland 1904, 1906, 1912 (1904-13), Reykjavík.

Lárusson, *see* Björn Lárusson, Ólafur Lárusson.

Laws of Early Iceland. Grágás. The Codex Regius of Grágás with material from other manuscripts I (1980), transl. by Andrew Dennis, Peter Foote, Richard Perkins, University of Manitoba Press, Winnipeg (*University of Manitoba Icelandic Studies* III).

Laxness, *see* Einar Laxness, Halldór Kiljan Laxness.

Lindal, Walter J. (1967), *The Icelanders in Canada*, National Publishers, Ottawa (*Canada Ethnica* II).

Líndal, *see* Sigurður Líndal.

Loftur Guttormsson (1981), "Island. Læsefærdighed og folkeuddannelse 1540-1800", *Ur nordisk kulturhistoria. Läskunnighet och folkbildning före folkskoleväsendet. XVIII nordiska historikermötet, Jyväskylä 1981. Mötesrapport* III, Jyväskylän Yliopisto, Jyväskylä (*Studia Historica Jyväkyläensia* XXII:3), 123-91.

——— (1983a), "Barnaeldi, ungbarnadauði og viðkoma á Íslandi 1750-1860", *Athöfn og orð. Amælisrit helgað Matthíasi Jónassyni áttræðum* (Mál og menning, Reykjavík), 137-69.

——— (1983b), *Bernska, ungdómur og uppeldi á einveldisöld. Tilraun til félagslegrar og lýðfræðilegrar greiningar*, Sagnfræðistofnun Háskóla Íslands, Reykjavík (*Ritsafn Sagnfræðistofnunar* X) (summary, 220-6).

——— (1989a), "Læsi", *Íslensk þjóðmenning* VI (Þjóðsaga, Reykjavík), 117-44 (summary, 442-3).

——— (1989b), "Staðfesti í flökkusamfélagi? Ábúðarhættir í Reykholtsprestakalli á 18. öld", *Skírnir* CLXIII, 9-40.

——— (1990), "The Development of Popular Religious Literacy in the Seventeenth and Eighteenth Centuries", *Scandinavian Journal of History* XV, 7-35.

——— (1992), "Farskólahald í sextíu ár (1890-1950): Nokkrir megindrættir", *Uppeldi og menntun* I:1, 207-22.

Lovsamling for Island, indeholdende Udvalg af de vigtigste ældre og nyere Love og Anordninger, Resolutioner, Instructioner og Reglementer, Althingsdomme og Vedtægter, Collegial-Breve, Fundatser og Gavebreve, samt andre Aktstykker, til Oplysning om Islands Retsforhold og Administration i ældre og nyere Tider I-XXI (1853-89), Andr. Fred. Höst/Andr. Fred. Höst & Sön, Copenhagen.

Lúðvík Ingvarsson (1986-7), *Goðorð og goðorðsmenn* I-III, publ. by the author, Egilsstöðum.

Lúðvík Kristjánsson (1980-6), *Íslenzkir sjávarhœttir* I-V, Bókaútgáfa Menningarsjóðs, Reykjavík (summaries).

Lýður Björnsson (1972-9), *Saga sveitarstjórnar á Íslandi* I-II, Almenna bókafélagið, Reykjavík.

——(1998), *Íslands hlutafélag. Rekstrarsaga Innréttinganna,* Hið íslenska bókmenntafélag, Reykjavík (*Safn til iðnsögu Íslendinga* XI).

Maanedsskrift for Litteratur, publ. by a Society VII (1832), Copenhagen.

Mackenzie, George Steuart (1811), *Travels in the Island of Iceland, During the Summer of the Year MDCCCX,* Archibald Constable, Edinburgh.

Magnús Guðmundsson (1988), *Ull verður gull. Ullariðnaður Íslendinga á síðari hluta 19. aldar og á 20. öld,* Hið íslenzka bókmenntafélag, Reykjavík (*Safn til Iðnsögu Íslendinga* II) (summary 327-37).

Magnús Jónsson (1947), *Hallgrímur Pétursson. Æfi hans og starf* I-II, Leiftur, Reykjavík.

—— (1952), *Alþingi og kirkjumálin 1845-1943,* Alþingissögunefnd, Reykjavík (*Saga Alþingis* V).

——(1957), *Sjálfstæðisflokkurinn fyrstu 15 árin,* Reykjavík.

Magnús S. Magnússon (1985), *Iceland in Transition: Labour and socio-economic change before 1940,* Ekonomisk-historiska föreningen, Lund (*Skrifter* XLV).

——(1993), "Efnahagsþróun á Íslandi 1880-1990", *Íslensk þjóðfélagsþróun 1880-1990* (Félagsvísindastofnun / Sagnfræðistofnun, Reykjavík), 112-214.

——, *see Hagskinna.*

Magnús Stefánsson (1978), "Frá goðakirkju til biskupskirkju, í íslenzkum búningi eftir Sigurð Líndal", *Saga Íslands* III (Hið íslenzka bókmenntafélag, Reykjavík), 109-257.

—— (1997a), "Isländisches Eigenkirchenwesen", *Proceedings of the Ninth International Congress of Medieval Canon Law,* Munich, 13-18 July 1992, 771-92.

—— (1997b), "Vínland eller Vinland?", *Festskrift til Historisk institutts 40-års jubileum 1997,* Geir Atle Ersland, Edgar Hovland and Ståle Dyrvik, eds (*Historisk institutt, Universitetet i Bergen. Skrifter* II), 13-28.

Magnúss, *see* Gunnar M. Magnúss.

Magnússon *see* Árni Magnússon, Jón Magnússon, Magnús S. Magnússon, Skúli Magnússon.

Manntal á Íslandi 1801. Suðuramt (1978), Ættfræðifélagið, Reykjavík.

Manntal á Íslandi árið 1703. Tekið að tilhlutun Árna Magnússonar og Páls Vídalín. Ásamt manntali 1729 í þrem sýslum (1924-47), Hagstofa Íslands, Reykjavík.

Manntalið 1703, see Hagskýrslur Íslands II:21.

Már Jónsson (1993), *Blóðskömm á Íslandi 1270-1870,* Háskólaútgáfan, Reykjavík.

—— (1998), *Árni Magnússon. Ævisaga,* Mál og menning, Reykjavík.

Margrét Guðmundsdóttir (1995a), *Aldarspor,* Skákprent, Reykjavík.

—— (1995b), "Pólitísk fatahönnun", *Ný saga* VII, 29-37 (summary, 104).

Margrét Hallsdóttir (1987), *Pollen Analytical Studies of Human Influence on*

Vegetation in Relation to the Landnám Tephra Layer in Southwest Iceland, Lund University, Department of Quaternary Geology, Lund (*Lundqua Thesis* XVIII.)

Margrét Hermanns-Auðardóttir, *see* Þorbjörn Á. Friðriksson and Margrét Hermanns-Auðardóttir.

Marx, Karl, and Frederick Engels (1969), *Selected Works in three volumes,* I, Progress Publishers, Moscow.

Matthíasson, *see* Haraldur Matthíasson.

McBride, Francis R. (1996), *Iceland,* revised edn Clio Press, Oxford (*World Bibliographical* Series XXXVII).

McKay, Derek (1973), "Great Britain and Iceland in 1809", *The Mariner's Mirror* LIX:1, 85-95.

McNeill, William H. (1979), *Plagues and Peoples,* Penguin, Harmondsworth (first publ. 1976).

Melsteð, *see* Bogi Th. Melsteð.

Miller, William Ian (1990), *Bloodtaking and Peacemaking: Feud, Law, and Society in Saga Iceland,* University of Chicago Press.

Monumenta Historica Norvegiæ. Latinske Kildeskrifter til Norges Historie i Middelalderen (1880), ed. by Gustav Storm, Kristiania.

Møller, Arne (1922), *Hallgrímur Péturssons Passionssalmer. En Studie over islandsk Salmedigtning fra det 16. og 17. Aarhundrede,* Gyldendalske Boghandel, Copenhagen.

Nanna Ólafsdóttir (1961), *Baldvin Einarsson og þjóðmálastarf hans,* Hið íslenzka bókmenntafélag, Reykjavík.

Nations and Nationalism II:3 (1996).

Nedkvitne, Arnved (1983), *Utenrikshandelen fra det vestafjelske Norge 1100-1600,* University of Bergen.

Nordal, *see* Sigurður Nordal.

Nuechterlein, Donald E. (1961), *Iceland, Reluctant Ally,* Greenwood Press, Westport, CT.

Oakley, Stewart (1969), *The Story of Sweden,* repr. Faber and Faber, London (1st edn 1966).

—— (1972), *The Story of Denmark,* Faber and Faber, London.

Ólafía Einarsdóttir (1964), *Studier i kronologisk metode i tidlig islandsk historieskrivning,* Natur och Kultur, Stockholm (*Bibliotheca Historica Lundensis* XIII).

—— (1994), "Om samtidssagaens kildeværdi, belyst ved Hákonar saga Hákonarsonar", *Samtíðarsögur. The Contemporary Sagas* II. *Forprent. Preprints,* Authors K-Ö (Ninth International Saga Conference, Akureyri), 638-53.

Ólafsdóttir, *see* Nanna Ólafsdóttir.

Ólafsson, *see* Eggert Ólafsson, Haraldur Ólafsson, Jón Ólafsson, Stefán Ólafsson.

Ólafur Ásgeirsson (1988), *Iðnbylting hugarfarsins. Átök um atvinnuþróun á Íslandi 1900-1940,* Bókaútgáfa Menningarsjóðs, Reykjavík (*Sagnfræðirannsóknir* IX) (summary, 148-52).

386   Bibliography

Ólafur Björnsson (1981), *Saga Íslandsbanka hf og Útvegsbanka Íslands 1904-1980*, Útvegsbanki Íslands, Reykjavík.

Ólafur Briem (1985), *Heiðinn siður á Íslandi*, 2nd edn revised and enlarged. Bókaútgáfa Menningarsjóðs, Reykjavík.

Ólafur Davíðsson (1940-3), *Galdur og galdramál á Íslandi*, Sögufélag, Reykjavík.

Ólafur Egilsson (1852), *Lítil saga um herhlaup Tyrkjans á Íslandi árið 1627*, ed. by Hallvarður Hængsson and Hrærekur Hrólfsson, Reykjavík. Repbl. (1969), as *Reisubók séra Ólafs Egilssonar*, ed. by Sverrir Kristjánsson, Almenna bókafélagið, Reykjavík.

Ólafur R. Einarsson (1969), "Upphaf íslenzkrar verkalýðshreyfingar 1887-1901", *Saga* VII, 1-127 (summary, 125-7).

―― (1974), "Bernska reykvískrar verkalýðshreyfingar", *Reykjavík í 1100 ár* (Sögufélag, Reykjavík), 204-25.

―― (1978), "Sendiförin og viðræðurnar 1918. Sendiför Ólafs Friðrikssonar til Kaupmannahafnar og þáttur jafnaðarmanna í fullveldisviðræðunum", *Saga* XVI, 37-74 (summary, 73-4).

―― (1979), "Fjárhagsaðstoð og stjórnmálaágreiningur. Áhrif erlendrar fjárhagsaðstoðar á stjórnmálaágreining innan Alþýðuflokksins 1919-1930", *Saga* XVII, 59-90.

―― and Einar Karl Haraldsson (1977), *Gúttóslagurinn 9. nóvember 1932, baráttuárið mikla í miðri heimskreppunni*, Örn og Örlygur, Reykjavík.

Ólafur R. Grímsson (1982), "Iceland: A Multilevel Coalition System", Eric C. Browne and John Dreijmanis, eds, *Government Coalitions in Western Democracies* (Longman, New York), 142-86.

Ólafur Halldórsson (1978), *Grænland í miðaldaritum*, ed. by Ólafur Halldórsson, Sögufélag, Reykjavík.

Ólafur Lárusson (1923), *Grágás og lögbækurnar*, fylgir *Árbók Háskóla Íslands* 1922 (yearbook), Reykjavík.

―― (1936), "Befolkning i Oldtiden 5. Island", *Nordisk kultur* I (J.H. Schultz, Copenhagen), 121-37.

Ólason, *see* Páll Eggert Ólason, Sigurður Ólason, Vésteinn Ólason.

Orri Vésteinsson (1996), "The Christianisation of Iceland: Priests, power and social change 1000-1300", Ph.D. thesis, University of London.

Óskar Guðmundsson (1987), *Alþýðubandalagið. Átakasaga*, Svart á hvítu, Reykjavík.

Óskarsdóttir, *see* Þórkatla Óskarsdóttir.

Páll Bergþórsson (1987), "Veðurfar á Íslandi", *Íslensk þjóðmenning* I (Þjóðsaga, Reykjavík), 195-225.

Páll Briem (1885), *Um frelsi og menntun kvenna. Sögulegur fyrirlestur*, Sigurður Kristjánsson, Reykjavík.

Páll Heiðar Jónsson, *see* Baldur Guðlaugsson and Páll Heiðar Jónsson.

Páll Eggert Ólason (1919-26), *Menn og menntir siðskiptaaldarinnar á Íslandi* I-IV, Bókaverzlun Guðm. Gamalíelssonar/Bókaverzlun Ársæls Árnasonar, Reykjavík.

―― (1929-33), *Jón Sigurðsson* I-V, Hið íslenzka þjóðvinafélag, Reykjavík.

Páll Vídalín, *see* Árni Magnússon and Páll Vídalín.

Pálsson, *see* Hjörtur Pálsson.

Pétur H. Ármannsson (1987), *Heimili og húsagerð 1967-1987*, Almenna bókafélagið, Reykjavík.

Pétur Pétursson (1983), *Church and Social Change: A study of the secularization process in Iceland, 1830-1930*, Plus Ultra, Lund (*Studies in Religious Experience and Behaviour* IV). 2nd edn (1990), Háskólaútgáfan, Reykjavík.

Pétursson, *see* Hallgrímur Pétursson, Pétur Pétursson, Skarphéðinn Pétursson.

Plomley, N.J.B. (1991), *Jorgen Jorgenson and the Aborigines of Van Diemen's Land, being a reconstruction of his 'lost' book on their customs and habits, and on his role in the Roving Parties and the Black Line*, ed. by N.J.B. Plomley, Blubber Head Press, Sandy Bay, Tasmania.

The Poetic Edda (1986), transl. with an Introduction and Explanatory Notes by Lee M. Hollander, 2nd edn, revised, University of Texas Press, Austin.

Popperwell, Ronald G. (1972), *Norway*, Ernest Benn, London.

Purchas' Haklvytus Posthumus, or Purchas his pilgrimes III (1625), ed. Samuel Purchas, London.

Rafnsson, *see* Sveinbjörn Rafnsson.

Ragnar Árnason, *see* Anna Agnarsdóttir and Ragnar Árnason.

Ragnheiður Kristjánsdóttir (1996), "Rætur íslenskrar þjóðernisstefnu", *Saga* XXXIV, 131-75 (summary, 175).

Reykjavík í 1100 ár (1974), ed. by Helgi Þorláksson, Sögufélag, Reykjavík (*Safn til sögu Reykjavíkur. Miscellanea Reyciavicensia*).

Reykjavík miðstöð þjóðlífs (1978), 2nd edn revised, ed. by Helgi Þorláksson, Sögufélag, Reykjavík (*Safn til sögu Reykjavíkur. Miscellanea Reyciavicensia*).

Róbertsdóttir, *see* Hrefna Róbertsdóttir.

Safn til sögu Íslands og íslenzkra bókmenta að fornu og nýju I, IV (1856, 1907-15), Hið íslenzka bókmentafélag, Copenhagen and Reykjavík.

Saga Íslands I-V (1974-90), written through the agency of Þjóðhátíðarnefnd 1974, ed. in chief Sigurður Líndal, Hið íslenzka bókmenntafélag, Reykjavík.

Saga Íslendinga IV-IX:2 (1942-58), Menntamálaráð/Þjóðvinafélag, Reykjavík.

Schier, Kurt (1975), "Iceland and the Rise of Literature in 'Terra Nova', Some comparative reflections", *Gripla* I, 168-81.

Sigfús Haukur Andrésson (1981), "Samtök gegn verzlunareinokun 1795", *Saga* XIX, 122-40 (summary, 139-40).

——(1988), *Verzlunarsaga Íslands 1774-1807. Upphaf fríhöndlunar og almenna bænarskráin* I-II, Verzlunarráð Íslands/Fjölsýn, Reykjavík.

Sigfús Jónsson (1980), "The Development of the Icelandic Fishing Industry, 1900-1940, and its Regional Implications", Ph.D. thesis, University of Newcastle upon Tyne.

——(1984), *Sjávarútvegur Íslendinga á 20. öld*, Hið íslenzka bókmenntafélag, Reykjavík.

Sigfússon, *see* Björn Sigfússon.

Sigríður Th. Erlendsdóttir (1993), *Veröld sem ég vil. Saga Kvenréttindafélags Íslands 1907-1992*, Kvenréttindafélag Íslands, Reykjavík.

Sigríður Dúna Kristmundsdóttir (1989), "Outside, Muted, and Different: Icelandic women's movements and their notions of authority and cultural separateness", *The Anthropology of Iceland*, ed. by E. Paul Durrenberger and Gísli Pálsson (University of Iowa Press, Iowa City), 80-97.

Sigríður Helga Sigurbjarnardóttir (1993), "Kvinnelisten in Iceland: A political experiment linking the grassroots level and the formal political power structures", *Politics: A Power Base for Women?* Report from a conference at the University of Örebro, Sweden, May 12-16, 1993 (*Örebro Women's Studies* III), 89-97.

Sigrún Davíðsdóttir (1999), *Håndskriftsagens saga i politisk belysning*, transl. by Kim Lembek, Odense Universitetsforlag (*Odense University Studies in History and Social Sciences* CCXVI).

Sigurbjarnardóttir, *see* Sigríður Helga Sigurbjarnardóttir.

Sigurðardóttir, *see* Arnheiður Sigurðardóttir.

Sigurðsson, *see* Gísli Sigurðsson, Haraldur Sigurðsson, Ingi Sigurðsson, Jón Sigurðsson, Jón Viðar Sigurðsson.

Sigurður Líndal (1959), "Stjórnbótarmál Íslendinga á Þingvallafundi 1973", *Nýtt Helgafell* IV, 199-213.

—— (1964), "Utanríkisstefna Íslendinga á 13. öld og aðdragandi sáttmálans 1262-64", *Úlfljótur* XVII, 5-36.

—— (1969), "Sendiför Úlfljóts. Ásamt nokkrum athugasemdum um landnám Ingólfs Arnarsonar", *Skírnir* CXLIII, 5-26.

—— (1974), "Upphaf kristni og kirkju", *Saga Íslands* I (Hið íslenzka bókmenntafélag, Reykjavík), 225-88.

—— *see Saga Íslands.*

Sigurður Nordal (1990), *Icelandic Culture*, transl. with notes by Vilhjálmur T. Bjarnar, Cornell University Library, Ithaca, NY (first publ. in Icelandic 1942).

Sigurður Ólason (1964), *Yfir alda haf. Greinar um söguleg og þjóðleg fræði*, Hildur, Reykjavík.

Sigurður Skúlason (1933), *Saga Hafnarfjarðar*, Bæjarsjóður Hafnarfjarðar, Hafnarfirði.

Sigurður Snævarr (1993), *Haglýsing Íslands*. Heimskringla, Reykjavík.

Sigurður Þórarinsson (1944), *Tefrokronologiska studier på Island. Þjórsárdalur och dess förödelse*, Ejnar Munksgaard, Copenhagen (summary, 204-15). Also in *Geografiska annaler* 1944: 1-2.

Sigurjónsson, *see* Arnór Sigurjónsson.

Sigurpálsson, *see* Ingimundur Sigurpálsson.

Skaftáreldar 1783-1784. Ritgerðir og heimildir (1984), Mál og menning, Reykjavík (summaries).

Skarphéðinn Pétursson (1959), "Um Jón Gerreksson", *Skírnir* CXXXIII, 43-80.

Skjöl um hylling Íslendinga 1649 við Friðrik konung þriðja með viðbæti um Kópavogssærin 1662 (1914), Sögufélag, Reykjavík.

Skúlason, *see* Sigurður Skúlason.

Skúli Magnússon (1944), *Forsøg til en kort Beskrivelse af Island (1786)*, ed. by Jón Helgason, Ejnar Munksgaard, Copenhagen (*Bibliotheca Arnamagnœana* V).

Skýrslur um landshagi á Íslandi I-V (1858-75), Hið íslenzka bókmentafélag, Kaupmannahöfn.

Smith, Anthony D. (1986), *The Ethnic Origins of Nations*, Basil Blackwell, Oxford.

Snorri Sturluson (1964), *Heimskringla: History of the Kings of Norway*, transl. with introduction and notes by Lee M. Hollander, University of Texas Press, Austin.

—— (1987), *Edda*, transl. from the Icelandic and introduced by Anthony Faulkes, Dent, London.

Snævarr, *see* Sigurður Snævarr.

Sólrún B. Jensdóttir (1974), "The 'Republic of Iceland' 1940-44: Anglo-American attitudes and influences", *Journal of Contemporary History* IX:4, 27-56.

—— (1986), *Anglo-Icelandic Relations during the First World War*, Garland, New York.

Statistisk tabelværk, Femte Række, Litra A, Nr. 4 (1904), *Folketællingen i Kongeriget Danmark den 1. Februar 1901*, part II: *Population du Royaume de Danemark le 1er février 1901*, part 2, Statens statistiske bureau, Copenhagen.

Stefán Einarsson (1957), *A History of Icelandic Literature*, Johns Hopkins University Press, Baltimore.

Stefán F. Hjartarson (1989), *Kampen om fackföreningsrörelsen. Ideologi och politisk aktivitet på Island 1920-1938*, Almqvist & Wiksell, Stockholm (*Studia Historica Upsaliensia* CLVIII) (summary, 249-63).

Stefán Ólafsson (1989), *The Making of the Icelandic Welfare State: A Scandinavian comparison*, Social Science Research Institute, University of Iceland, Reykjavík.

—— (1993), "Þróun velferðarríkisins", *Íslensk þjóðfélagsþróun 1880-1980* (Félagsvísindastofnun/Sagnfræðistofnun, Reykjavík), 399-430.

Stefánsson, *see* Magnús Stefánsson, Sæmundur Stefánsson.

Steffensen, *see* Jón Steffensen.

Steingrímsson, *see* Jón Steingrímsson.

Steingrímur Jónsson (1989), "Prentaðar bækur", *Íslensk þjóðmenning* VI (Þjóðsaga, Reykjavík), 91-115 (summary, 441-2).

Stenberger, Mårten, ed. (1943), *Forntida gårdar i Island. Meddelanden från den nordiska arkeologiska undersökningen i Island sommaren 1939*, Ejnar Munksgaard, Copenhagen (summary, 313-26).

Stjórnartíðindi fyrir Ísland. Árið 1903, 1925, 1929, 1938 (1925-38), A-deild, Reykjavík.

Strömbäck, Dag (1975), *The Conversion of Iceland: A survey*, transl. and annotated by Peter Foote, Viking Society for Northern Research, London.

Sturlunga saga (1946) I-II, ed. by Jón Jóhannesson, Magnús Finnbogason and Kristján Eldjárn, Sturlunguútgáfan, Reykjavík.

Sturlunga Saga I-II (1970-4), transl. from the Old Icelandic by Julia H. McGrew and R. George Thomas, Twayne Publishers, New York.

Sturluson, *see* Snorri Sturluson.

390   Bibliography

Styrkársdóttir, see Auður Styrkársdóttir.

Svanur Kristjánsson (1979), *Sjálfstæðisflokkurinn. Klassíska tímabilið 1929-1944*, transl. by Auður Styrkársdóttir, Félagsvísindadeild Háskóla Íslands, Reykjavík (*Íslensk þjóðfélagsfræði* V). A revised version in English has been publ. in *Scandinavian Political Studies* II:1 (1979), 31-52.

Sveinbjarnardóttir, see Guðrún Sveinbjarnardóttir.

Sveinbjörn Blöndal (1982), *Sauðasalan til Bretlands*, Sagnfræðistofnun Háskóla Íslands, Reykjavík (*Ritsafn Sagnfræðistofnunar* VIII).

Sveinbjörn Rafnsson (1977), "Sámsstaðir í Þjórsárdal", *Árbók Hins íslenzka fornleifafélags* 1976, 39-120 (summary, 117-20).

Sveinn Skorri Höskuldsson (1970), "Ófeigur í Skörðum og félagar. Drög að athugun á bókafélagi", *Skírnir* CXLIV, 34-110.

Sveinsson, see Einar Ól. Sveinsson, Hallgrímur Sveinsson.

Sverrir Jakobsson (1998), "Friðarviðleitni kirkjunnar á 13. öld", *Saga* XXXVI, 7-46 (summary, 46).

Sverrir Kristjánsson (1981), *Ritsafn* I, Mál og menning, Reykjavík.

―――― see Jón Blöndal and Sverrir Kristjánsson.

Sæmundur Stefánsson (1929), *Æfisaga og draumar*, Fjelagsprentsmiðjan, Reykjavík.

Thor, see Jón Þ. Þór.

Thor Whitehead, see Þór Whitehead.

Thorarensen, see Bjarni Thorarensen.

Thórkatla Óskarsdóttir Helgason, see Þórkatla Óskarsdóttir.

Thorleifur Fridriksson, see Þorleifur Friðriksson.

Thoroddsen, see Jón Thoroddsen, Þorvaldur Thoroddsen.

Tíðindi frá Alþingi Íslendínga, see Alþingistíðindi.

Tíðindi frá þjóðfundi Íslendínga árið 1851, see Alþingistíðindi.

Tobiasson, see Brynleifur Tobiasson.

Tryggvi Emilsson (1976), *Fátækt fólk. Æviminningar* I, Mál og menning, Reykjavík.

Tryggvi J. Oleson, see Þorsteinn Þ. Þorsteinsson and Tryggvi J. Oleson.

Tryggvi Þórhallsson (1989), *Gissur biskup Einarsson og siðaskiptin*, published by the children of the author, Reykjavík.

Tyrkjaránið á Íslandi 1627 (1906-09), Sögufélag, Reykjavík.

Unnar Ingvarsson, see Arnar Guðmundsson and Unnar Ingvarsson.

Unnur B. Karlsdóttir (1998), *Mannkynbætur. Hugmyndir um bætta kynstofna hérlendis og erlendis á 19. og 20. öld*, Sagnfræðistofnun Háskóla Íslands/ Háskólaútgáfan, Reykjavík (*Sagnfræðirannsóknir* XIV) (summary, 155-9).

Valdimar Jakobsson Líndal, see Lindal, Walter J.

Valdimar Unnar Valdimarsson (1997), *Saltfiskur í sögu þjóðar. Saga íslenskrar saltfiskframleiðslu og -verslunar frá 18. öld til okkar daga* I-II, completed and

Bibliography 391

ed. by Halldór Bjarnason, Hið íslenska bókmenntafélag, Reykjavík (summary II, 321-34).

Valdimarsson, *see* Valdimar Unnar Valdimarsson.

Valur Ingimundarson (1996), *Í eldlínu kalda stríðsins*. Samskipti Íslands og Bandaríkjanna 1945-1960, Vaka-Helgafell, Reykjavík.

Vésteinn Ólason (1998), *Dialogues with the Viking Age: Narration and Representation in the Sagas of the Icelanders*, transl. by Andrew Wawn, Mál og menning, Reykjavík.

Vésteinsson, *see* Orri Vésteinsson.

Vilborg Auður Ísleifsdóttir (1997), *Siðbreytingin á Íslandi 1537-1565. Byltingin að ofan*, Hið íslenska bókmenntafélag, Reykjavík (summary, 367-8).

Vilhjálmur Árnason (1991), "Mortality and Social Structure in the Icelandic Sagas", *Journal of English and Germanic Philology* XC, 157-74.

Vilhjálmur Finsen (1883), "Ordregister", *Grágás* [III] (Gyldendalske Boghandel, Copenhagen), 579-714.

Wallace, Birgitta Linderoth (1986), "The L'Anse aux Meadows Site", Gwyn Jones, *The North Atlantic Saga* (Oxford University Press), 285-304 (Appendix VII).

Walløe, Lars (1995), *Plague and Population: Norway 1350-1750*, Department of Physiology, Institute of Basic Medical Science, University of Oslo (*Det norske Videnskaps-Akademi*. I. Mat.-Naturv. Klasse. Avhandlinger, new series no. 17).

Whitehead, *see* Þór Whitehead.

Wilhelm Kristjánsson, *see* Kristjanson, W.

Þór, *see* Jón Þ. Þór.

Þór Whitehead (1973), "Stórveldin og lýðveldið 1941-1944", *Skírnir* CXLVII, 202-41.

—— (1976), "Lýðveldi og herstöðvar 1941-46", *Skírnir* CL, 126-72.

—— (1978), "Iceland in the Second World War 1939-1946", Ph.D. thesis, University of Oxford.

—— (1979), *Kommúnistahreyfingin á Íslandi 1921-1934*, Bókaútgáfa Menningarsjóðs, Reykjavík (*Sagnfræðirannsóknir* V).

—— (1980), *Ófriður í aðsigi*, Almenna bókafélagið, Reykjavík (*Ísland í síðari heimsstyrjöld*).

—— (1985), *Stríð fyrir ströndum*, Almenna bókafélagið, Reykjavík (*Ísland í síðari heimsstyrjöld*).

—— (1995), *Milli vonar og ótta*, Vaka-Helgafell, Reykjavík (*Ísland í síðari heimsstyrjöld*).

—— (1998), *The Ally Who Came in from the Cold: A survey of Icelandic foreign policy 1946-1956*, Centre for International Studies, Reykjavík.

—— (1999), *Bretarnir koma*, Vaka–Helgafell, Reykjavík (*Ísland í síðari heimsstyrjöld*).

Þórarinn Þórarinsson (1966-87), *Sókn og sigrar. Saga Framsóknarflokksins* I-III, Framsóknarflokkurinn, Reykjavík.

Þórarinsson, *see* Sigurður Þórarinsson, Þórarinn Þórarinsson.

Bibliography

Þorbjörn Á. Friðriksson and Margrét Hermanns-Auðardóttir (1991), "Ironmaking in Iceland", among papers from a seminar at Budalen, Norway, on *Bloomery Ironmaking during 2000 Years,* ed. by A. Espelund, Budalseminaret, Trondheim.

Þórðarson, *see* Björn Þórðarson, Gunnlaugur Þórðarson.

Þórður Eyjólfsson (1952), *Alþingi og héraðsstjórn,* Alþingissögunefnd, Reykjavík (*Saga Alþingis* V).

Þórður Hinriksson (1912), "Frá einokunartíðinni. Kæra Þórðar sýslumanns Hinrikssonar 1647 fyrir hönd Borgfirðinga yfir verzlaninni", *Andvari* XXXVII, 123-28.

Þórhallsson, *see* Tryggvi Þórhallsson.

Þórkatla Óskarsdóttir (1982), "Ideas of Nationality in Icelandic Poetry 1830-1874", Ph.D. thesis, University of Edinburgh.

Þorkell Jóhannesson (1958), "Brot úr verzlunarsögu II", *Andvari* LXXXIII, 37-67.

—— and Bergsteinn Jónsson (1965-90), *Tryggvi Gunnarsson* II, IV, Bókaútgáfa Menningarsjóðs, Reykjavík.

Þorkelsson, *see* Jón Þorkelsson.

Þorláksson, *see* Helgi Þorláksson.

Þorleifsson, *see* Heimir Þorleifsson.

Þorleifur Einarsson (1960-3), "Vitnisburður frjógreiningar um gróður, veðurfar og landnám á Íslandi", *Saga* III, 442-69 (summary, 468).

Þorleifur Friðriksson (1990), *Den gyldne flue. De skandinaviske socialdemokratiers relationer til den islandske arbejderbevægelse 1916-56. Internationalisme eller indblanding?,* SFAH, Copenhagen (summary, 283-95).

Þorsteinn Þ. Þorsteinsson and Tryggvi J. Oleson (1940-53), *Saga Íslendinga í Vesturheimi* I-V, Þjóðræknisfélag Íslendinga í Vesturheimi/Bókaútgáfa Menningarsjóðs, Reykjavík.

Þorsteinsson, *see* Björn Þorsteinsson, Þorsteinn Þ. Þorsteinsson.

Þorvaldsson, *see* Eysteinn Þorvaldsson.

Þorvaldur Thoroddsen (1908), *Æfisaga Pjeturs Pjeturssonar, dr. theol., biskups yfir Íslandi,* Sigurður Kristjánsson, Reykjavík.

—— (1916-17), *Árferði á Íslandi í þúsund ár,* Hið íslenska fræðafjelag, Copenhagen.

—— (1919), *Lýsing Íslands* III. *Landbúnaður á Íslandi. Sögulegt yfirlit* I. Hið íslenzka Bókmentafélag, Copenhagen.

Index